LITERATURE

AND FILM

IN COLD WAR

SOUTH KOREA

Theodore Hughes

LITERATURE AND FILM IN COLD WAR SOUTH KOREA

Freedom's Frontier

COLUMBIA
UNIVERSITY
PRESS

NEW YORK

COLUMBIA UNIVERSITY PRESS
Publishers Since 1893
NEW YORK   CHICHESTER, WEST SUSSEX
cup.columbia.edu

Copyright © 2012 Columbia University Press
Paperback edition, 2014
All rights reserved

Library of Congress Cataloging-in-Publication Data
Hughes, Theodore.
Literature and film in Cold War South Korea : freedom's frontier / Theodore Hughes.
p.   cm.
Includes bibliographical references and index.
ISBN 978-0-231-15748-3 (cloth)—ISBN 978-0-231-15749-0 (pbk.)—
ISBN 978-0-231-50071-5 (e-book)
1. Korean literature—20th century—History and criticism.   2. Politics in literature.
3. Nationalism and literature—Korea (South)   4. Motion pictures—Korea (South)—20th century—History and criticism.   5. Motion pictures—Political aspects—Korea (South)
6. Politics in motion pictures.   I. Title.
PL957.5.P64H64 2012
895.7'093581—dc23
2011030288

Cover image: Shin Hak-chul, Modern Korean History: Incantation of the Dead, *oil on canvas,*
224cm x 122cm, 1994, courtesy of the artist
Cover design: Chang Jae Lee

CONTENTS

LIST OF ILLUSTRATIONS   VII
ACKNOWLEDGMENTS   IX

Introduction
1

1. Visuality and the Colonial Modern:
The Technics of Proletarian Culture, Nativism,
Modernism, and Mobilization
19

2. Visible and Invisible States:
Liberation, Occupation, Division
61

3. Ambivalent Anticommunism:
The Politics of Despair and the Erotics of Language
91

4. Development as Devolution:
Overcoming Communism and the
"Land of Excrement" Incident
129

5. Return to the Colonial Present:
Translation, Collaboration, Pan-Asianism
165

Postscript
205

NOTES   211
SELECTED BIBLIOGRAPHY   245
INDEX   259

LIST OF ILLUSTRATIONS

Figure 1.1. *Tonga Ilbo* (1923; artist unknown)   26
Figure 1.2. Installment of *Wandering*, with illustration (1928)   30
Figure 1.3. Yi Sang-bŏm, *Early Winter* (1926)   35
Figure 1.4. Yi In-sŏng, *A Day in Fall* (1934)   37
Figure 1.5. Installment of *Wheel of Fire*, with still (1930)   40
Figure 1.6. Yi Sang's illustration of the coins in *Kubo* (1934)   47
Figure 1.7. Writing and Image: Yi Sang's illustration in *Kubo* (1934)   48
Figure 1.8. "O.K. Cut!" (*Springtime on the Peninsula*, 1941)   57
Figure 2.1. Yi Chung-sŏp, *White Bull 1* (1953)   79
Figure 3.1. The Hand of Fate (*The Hand of Fate*, 1954)   96
Figure 3.2. Ae-ran "returns" from the mountains (*P'iagol*, 1955)   108
Figure 3.3. The mambo scene (*Madame Freedom*, 1956)   123
Figure 3.4. Professor Chang teaches Korean grammar (*Madame Freedom*, 1956)   125
Figure 4.1. Sarkhan superimposed over American suburbs (*The Ugly American*, 1963)   134
Figure 4.2. "We young people should fight until we hang our flag on the top of Mt. Paektu" (*Female Executive*, 1959)   159
Figure 4.3. The Republic of Korea National Space Research Center (*Yongary, Monster from the Deep*, 1967)   162
Figure 5.1. Chang U-sŏng, *Atelier* (1943)   187
Figure 5.2. Empire to nation: transforming the Japanese flag into the Korean flag (*Hurrah for Freedom!*, 1946)   194
Figure P.1. Lim Ok Sang, *A Questionable Death* (1987)   208

ACKNOWLEDGMENTS

MORE PEOPLE THAN I can mention by name here have given me support and encouragement since my days in graduate school. without their kindness, generosity, and advice, I could not have written this book.

I would first like to express my sincere thanks to all of my teachers at UCLA. I am grateful most of all to John Duncan for his guidance and mentorship over the years. He opened up the richness and complexity of Korean history for me, and his critical engagement with my work has always motivated me to try to see things in new ways. Michael Bourdaghs and Seiji Lippit provided me with the tools to think about Korean culture and literature in a broader, comparative context. Ali Behdad, Robert Buswell, Katherine King, Gi-Wook Shin, and Samuel Weber all contributed to the directions my research took in graduate school and beyond.

My colleagues in the Department of East Asian Languages and Cultures and the Program in Comparative and World Literature at the University of Illinois at Urbana-Champaign made my years there truly rich and rewarding. Nancy Abelmann is one of the most inspiring people I have ever met. I am particularly thankful to her for reading a draft of the manuscript and offering insightful suggestions for its improvement. I would also like to thank Nancy Blake, the late David Goodman, Makoto Hayashi, Brian Ruppert, Simona Sawhney, and Ron Toby.

I am very grateful to all of my colleagues in the Department of East Asian Languages and Cultures and the Weatherhead East Asian Institute at Columbia for providing a wonderful community within which to learn, teach, and write. I would like to particularly thank Paul Anderer, Charles Armstrong, Carol Gluck, Robert Hymes, Dorothy Ko, David Lurie, Shang Wei, and Haruo Shirane for all of the advice and encouragement they have given me over the years. Whenever I turned to the late Ja Hyun Kim Haboush, she was always ready with kind words of counsel tempered with her quiet sense of humor. Lydia Liu and Tomi Suzuki read my manuscript and gave key comments at different stages of the revision process.

So many colleagues and friends in the growing community of Korean studies and others in Asian studies have given me much-needed advice and support. I owe a debt that cannot be repaid to Paek Sang-gi of Kyungnam University for introducing me to the world of modern Korean literature during my years as an English teacher in the early 1990s. Kwon Youngmin took me under his wing during my time at Seoul National University. His lectures provided me with an understanding of Korean literary history that continues to guide my research and teaching. Kyeong-Hee Choi generously read a portion of the manuscript and gave thoughtful comments and advice. I would also particularly like to thank Jinsoo An, Baek Moon Im, Ruth Barraclough, Hyaeweol Choi, Steve Chung, Henry Em, John Frankl, Tak Fujitani, Bruce Fulton, Han Man-su, Hwang Jongyon, Kelly Jeong, Jennifer Jung-Kim, Chong Bum Kim, Kim Chul, Kyu Hyun Kim, Kim Jaeyong, Jongmyung Kim, Michael Kim, Suk-Young Kim, Sun Joo Kim, Ross King, Kwon Boduerae, Lee Kyung Hoon, Namhee Lee, Lee Sang-kyung, Walter K. Lew, John Lie, Lim Jie-hyun, David McCann, Paik Won-Dam, Chan Park, Sunyoung Park, Pori Park, Janet Poole, Michael Robinson, Andre Schmid, Shin Hyung Ki, Jiwon Shin, Jesook Song, Clark Sorensen, Serk-Bae Suh, Vladimir Tikhonov, Atsuko Ueda, Naoki Watanabe, and Jun Yoo. I have also benefited immensely from interactions with undergraduate and graduate students at Illinois and Columbia over the years.

The dissertation research that led to this book was funded by the Korea Foundation, Fulbright IIE, and a UCLA Chancellor's Dissertation Grant. Further research and writing were made possible by a fellowship from the Academy of Korean Studies and a Columbia University Summer Research Grant. The Northeast Asia Council of the Association for Asian Studies and the Sunshik Min Endowment administered by Harvard University provided generous publication subventions.

I am deeply grateful to Jennifer Crewe, the editor at Columbia University Press, for her interest in this project and for her guidance and advice from start to finish. It was truly a pleasure to work with Asya Graf,

Chang Jae Lee, Michael Haskell, and Rob Fellman. I would like to thank two anonymous readers of the manuscript for their detailed and incisive comments.

My family has been a constant source of encouragement along the way. I would like to express my gratitude to my father, John Hughes; my partner, Jin-kyung Lee; my father-in-law, Myung-Jae Lee; my mother-in-law, Hwa-Suh Park; and my brothers, Terry, Tim, and Chris. Jin-kyung Lee read the manuscript at an important stage in the revision process and gave crucial advice. My mother, Sally Ann Quinby Hughes, did not live to see me accepted to graduate school, but she has always been with me in spirit.

LITERATURE

AND FILM

IN COLD WAR

SOUTH KOREA

INTRODUCTION

THE END OF the Greater East Asian and Pacific War in 1945 brought about a new geopolitics. In Asia, this meant that the formerly colonized or semicolonized states (China, Korea, Taiwan, Vietnam) would now have to address the emerging U.S./Soviet bifurcation. Relations with these new Cold War powers often took the form of simultaneous alignment and contestation coupled with different degrees of subordination. The post-1945 U.S. occupation of South Korea, along with that of Japan, can be thought of in terms of a closing off of borders. The U.S./Soviet enforcement of division was accompanied by the removal of Korea from its former semiperipheral location in the Japanese empire, which meant, among other things, the cutting off of South Koreans both from the Manchurian periphery and the former Japanese metropole (in the form both of travel restrictions and a ban on Japanese cultural products and language). In Japan and Korea, this reordering signaled less of a break than a shift: the beginnings of a move away from wartime mobilization in the name of pan-Asia toward the mobilization cultures of the Cold War nation-state, in Japan's case from the position of empire, in Korea's case from the position of colony.

Coloniality in Korea, however, did not end with the Japanese defeat in 1945. This book looks at the ways in which the new post-1945 South Korean culture was formed in relation both to representations of what now became thought of as the colonial past and to the 1945 Cold War division of the peninsula. The shifting boundaries of the South Korean cultural field were organized through the late 1980s around three central disavowals: the ban (until 1988) on colonial-period proletarian works, the institutionalized forgetting of the late-colonial-period mass culture of mobilization and imperialization, and the effacement of contemporary North Korean cultural production. These disavowals are structured by an acknowledgment, often appearing at the border or on the margins of texts, of what is not to be spoken or seen.

The relations among the triple disavowals occur within what Jacques Rancière calls the "distribution of the sensible": "a delimitation of spaces and times, of the visible and invisible, of speech and noise, that simultaneously determines the place and the stakes of politics as a form of experience."[1] Certainly, the Cold War distribution of the sensible in South Korea is informed at once by division (the effacement of the North, its cultural production, the people living there) and the production of a certain kind of colonial past (a disavowal of the history of leftist resistance and imperialization/mobilization). At the same time, at stake is not only the formation of the South Korean cultural field in relation to what is not to be spoken or seen but also the relation between the spoken and the seen, between words and images. For this reason, I begin this book by tracing the shifting relations between the verbal and the visual that accompanied the formation of major cultural and literary movements—including the proletarian culture movement, literary modernism, nativism, and wartime mobilization culture—in colonial Korea. I then show how these movements informed, on multiple levels, the ways in which post-1945 writers and filmmakers negotiate the statist reworking of the colonial past that took place as part of the deployment of the Cold War order in South Korea.

The relation between the verbal and visual was central to the formation of the notion of literature in the colonial period and to the colonial history of identifications. This is a history that includes the emergence of Enlightenment, proletarian, modernist, and imperialized subject positions that would take different forms in Cold War South Korea. Post-1945 cultural production in South Korea cannot be understood without looking at what was excised, alluded to, or appropriated in different ways—the literary, artistic, and filmic movements of the Japanese colonial period (1910–1945). I thus underscore the relation among colonial discursive, artistic, and filmic practices and what occupies the center of this book, the agreements and disagreements, the visibilities and invisibilities that have organized the postcolonial culture of division, authoritarianism, and developmentalism in South Korea from the mid-1940s through the early 1970s. With the division of the peninsula in 1945 under the Soviet and U.S. military occupations in North and South and the subsequent inauguration of separate, competing sovereign regimes in 1948, the organization of the colonial past and the excision of the North set in motion a multilayered, shifting politics of what could be seen or spoken. This book traces the ways in which South Korean writers, cultural critics, and filmmakers from the mid-1940s through the early 1970s negotiated the formation of separate South/North cultural fields, the proscription on leftist cultural work, the erasure of the late colonial mass culture of mobilization, and the emergence of the United States as the Cold War metropole. I place particular emphasis on unpacking how Cold War South Korean statism (itself a rearticulation of the colonial statism that preceded it) relied on a visual order increasingly bound up, in turn, with the biopolitics of "free world" developmentalism. The visual and the biopolitical were mutually constitutive, the production of the visible linked at once to the promotion of South Korean developmentalist life and its citizen-subjects and to the rendering invisible of the North signaled in the well-known slogan "eradicate communism" (*myŏlgong*). We will see, then, how post-1945 cultural forms address the display of "South Korea" as a postcolonial, developmentalist space at once opposing and mirroring its northern counterpart in the global Cold War.

LITERARY AND VISUAL CULTURE IN THE COLONIAL MODERN

The first chapter of this book details the ways in which the articulations of the verbal/visual relation in the colonial period allowed for new identifications; new ways of thinking about writing, painting, representation, space, time, and the body; and new contestations among class, ethnonational, and imperial belonging—all of which are central to post-1945 South Korea. Importantly, the advent of modern forms of subjectivity is marked by the invocation of an accompanying technological progress associated with Western material culture. But the relationship, as Friedrich Kittler has shown, is complicated from the beginning, with the technological threatening to subsume the very aesthetics of the liberatory, humanist subject (national, proletarian, or national-proletarian, as the case may be) invoked along with it.[2] Take, for instance, what is often considered Korea's first modern novel, one that has stood at the center of scholarship on modern Korean literature since its publication in 1917, Yi Kwang-su's *The Heartless* (*Mujŏng*). The "technologized visuality" that Rey Chow describes in her discussion of Lu Xun in *Primitive Passions* is negotiated in *The Heartless* less by the attempt to privilege writing as means to counter the shock of the technovisual (the gesture that Chow views Lu Xun as making) than by incorporation: the technology of the modern and its modes of representation are drawn inside, producing a technics of the Enlightenment/developmentalist subject of history.[3] While *The Heartless* has been perhaps the most studied of any modern Korean literary text, existing scholarship overlooks the ways in which the cinema inhabits the city in the text in the form of a gaze upon the self, one repeatedly described as "hwaldongsajin moyangŭro [like a motion picture]."[4]

Technologized visuality, that is, appears in *The Heartless* in the form of a movie camera inside the mind. Images of past events in characters' lives are frequently described in terms of the cinema. This visuality of memory is, in turn, linked to an imaging of a future that has already happened. As Chow points out, "The projectional effect of film—throwing images on the screen—means that the time of retrospection is now, paradoxically, also a futuristic casting-in-front."[5] It is in this way that pro-jection, the mechanical reproduction of images, becomes, in *The Heartless*, temporal. The visualized recollection that constitutes the protagonist Yi Hyŏng-sik as a modern, interiorized subject becomes, by the end of the text, a throwing into a collective Korean future. The future already exists. The incorporation of the mechanical device as gaze (the motion picture inside the mind) signals that the future is not simply beyond but inside, already present. In Korea's first modern novel, then, visuality naturalizes progress in time and the formation of a homogeneous, shared space. Incorporation of the technovisual would take different forms in the colonial period, as we will see in my discussion both of the proletarian culture movement of the 1920s and of the relations among modernism, nativism, and mobilization culture in the 1930s and early 1940s.

Beginning in the 1910s, words could be linked to what W. J. T. Mitchell calls "ekphrastic hope," "a 'sense' in which language can do what so many writers have wanted it to do: 'to make us see.'"[6] The formation of the disciplines of modern literature and modern art, which also took place in the late 1910s, was necessary in order for words to invoke a new kind of visual order. This visual order, in turn, is part and parcel of the Heideggerian "world-as-picture" that Timothy Mitchell links to the staging of colonial modernity:

The significance of this world-as-picture for understanding the colonial-modern lies in the fact that representation always makes a double claim. On the one hand, something set up as representation denies its own reality. The representational text, image, model, game, structure, or project, however realistic, always asserts that it is only a text, a mere picture, a copy.... On the other hand, in asserting its own lack, a representation claims that the world it replicates, projects, reorganizes, enacts, or endows with meaning and structure must be, by contrast, original ... in a word (what we imagine as) real. Colonial European modernity stages the endless set-up that pictures and promises us this complete, unmediated, self-present, immediate reality.[7]

The "world-as-picture" ties the "double claim" to the production of the modern as referent: "the effectiveness of this world-as-picture lies not simply in the process of serialization. It lies in the apparent contrast created between images, which are repeatable, serializable ... and the opposing effect of an original, of what appears to be the actual nation, the people itself, the real economy."[8] If, as Kwon Boduerae points out, the construction in the 1910s of a subjective or particularized appreciation of beauty and differentiated affect in colonial Korea relies on the exploration of a universal, it was also in this period that literature became the vehicle of an ekphrastic hope, the place where this divulging of "immediate reality" can proceed.[9]

For this reason, colonial modern texts such as *The Heartless* often verbally enact or stage modernity in a way that points to what we might call a painterly or cinematic text. In her discussion of Victorian fiction, Nancy Armstrong offers four propositions meant "to reconceptualize literary realism in relation to the new medium of photography":

Proposition 1: By the mid-1850s, fiction was already promising to put readers in touch with the world itself by supplying them with certain kinds of visual information.

Proposition 2: In so doing, fiction equated seeing with knowing and made visual information the basis for the intelligibility of a verbal narrative.

Proposition 3: In order to be realistic, literary realism referenced a world of objects that either had been or could be photographed.

Proposition 4: Photography in turn offered up portions of this world to be seen by the same group of people whom novelists imagined as their readership.[10]

As Armstrong points out, the order of these four propositions underscores "the process by which fiction and photography authorized each other."[11] A text such as *The Heartless* certainly allows us to see how the advent of modern Korean literature in the late 1910s occurs in relation to the pictorial turn that Armstrong details in Victorian fiction. While Armstrong locates the pictorial turn in relation to photography, as the motion picture had yet to appear in the mid-1850s, Yi Kwang-su's text shows how the history of intermediation that makes up modern Korean literature must account for a visuality that exceeds photography, one that also includes both the emergence in the late 1910s of the motion picture and modern (Western) art.

Elder Kim—the father of Sŏn-hyŏng, Hyŏng-sik's fiancée—stands in between the premodern and the modern. He advocates enlightenment but is not fully aware of its meaning. Elder Kim's taste for things Western is matched by his inability to understand the importance of modern art: "He had never seen Western portrait paintings, or western paintings of women and nudes, nor did he make an effort to see them. Even if he had seen them, he would not have recognized their worth. He did not know the word 'art,' and, moreover, did not see the need for such things as paintings."[12] Hyŏng-sik locates Elder Kim on the level of the imitative, following Western forms and adopting Christianity out of nothing more than a blind belief in the superiority of the West. Elder Kim's words do not exist in a proper relation to the modern because he has not learned how to see. It is up to the readers of Yi's text to learn to read "properly" by linking words to visual representations meant to be seen as "identical to real things" (like portraits and nudes).[13]

The call in *The Heartless* for a modern subject, for a new affective register that will constitute the relations among Koreans as a collective, occurs only when it makes "visual information the basis for the intelligibility of a verbal narrative." At the same time, the importance placed on Western painting in *The Heartless* shows us how the verbal invoking of the visual exceeds the consideration of one medium (photography) in relation to a literature written in one language (English). To be sure, modern Korean literature emerges in relation to the pictorial turn. However, this emergence involves a question not only of the intermediation of fiction, art, photography, and film but also of the ways in which reference involves what Lydia Liu calls "hypothetical equivalence," the assumption of commensurability between European and non-European languages.[14] If, as Armstrong points out, the referent in Victorian fiction is an image, a visual representation, the question of the referent in colonial Korean fiction must take into account both intermediation and translingual practice (Hyŏng-sik, after, all is a teacher of English). Timothy Mitchell's unpacking of the deployment of the European "original" in colonial sites should also be seen in terms of a translation regime. The staging of a global, colonial modernity involves a hypothetical equivalence that is at once verbal and visual. The portability of the modern is bound up with a visual order, a staging, and a translation regime, because this staging cannot proceed without a carrying across of representations from one language, the European "original," to another.

Colonial modern works variously associated with the proletarian culture movement, literary modernism, nativism, and wartime mobilization involve the relation between writing and image. This relation is structured by the deployment of visual information that is to be read as the real. These works address in various ways the imperial staging of the real in colonial Korea, what Timothy Mitchell calls the "endless set-up" of an immediate reality associated with the original. A gap emerges between writing and image, one informed by the ways in which "collective approval" in the colony is itself a site of potential disruption. The history of the intermediation of literature, art, and film that in many ways begins with *The Heartless* traverses the hierarchical relations between metropolitan Japan and colonial Korea as well as between European and non-European languages.

Although proletarian literature, art, and film were considered separate categories in the proletkult movement of the 1920s and 1930s (the Korea Artists Proletarian Federation or KAPF, 1925–1935), the form of the KAPF debates over the cultural practices best suited to Korea's colonial, capitalist modernity (and what was viewed as the feudal past that continued to inform this modernity) meant that these categories would blur even as they were announced, bound up as they were with a shared concern regarding the question of the representation of social reality. In chapter 1, I show how this was a question that involved multiple imagings, first of the "people" (what KAPF writers and critics called the *minjung* or, often, *taejung*), followed by the artistic practices that would lift the *minjung* into an emancipatory historical trajectory. My aim in this chapter, however, is neither to accomplish the impossible task of locating in one space the breadth of the diverse, multidisciplinary cultural production that made up KAPF, which saw itself as a broad-based proletkult movement, nor to focus solely on the relation among the different disciplines eventually assigned separate departments by KAPF leadership. Instead, I will show how figures such as

Kim Ki-jin, Im Hwa, and Yi Chong-myŏng address the verbal-visual relation in KAPF literature, criticism, art, film, and, particularly, the hybrid genre of the "film-novel" (*yŏnghwa sosŏl*). This negotiation—one that precedes and, indeed, informs the experimentation with the visual register in the literary modernism of the 1930s—played a central role in producing a new way of seeing, reading, and "coming to consciousness."

Taking the proletarian culture movement as its point of departure, chapter 1 traces the relations among nativism, modernism, and mobilization culture. As we will see in our discussion of Yi Hyo-sŏk's "When the Buckwheat Blooms" (1936), literary nativism can often be read as a verbal description of nativist or *hyangt'o* painting. For their part, modernist writers such as Yi Sang and Pak T'ae-wŏn experiment with filmic techniques in their attempt to portray the colonial modern cityscape. But both nativism and modernism are "urban" forms of painting/writing, produced for a city-dwelling audience and seeking to locate a space other than that produced by capitalist relations. Indeed, *hyangt'o* discourse and images structure Pak's modernist "A Day in the Life of Kubo the Novelist" (1934), and his well-known *Stream Scenes* (1936) can be read as a series of verbal descriptions of *hyangt'o* stills set in motion in the colonial urban space.

Literary and filmic texts of wartime mobilization do not represent a break from these earlier movements but appropriate their techniques and concerns. Rather than a simple assimilationism, these works, as we will see in our discussion of the films *The Volunteer* (1941), *Springtime on the Peninsula* (1941), and *Military Train* (1938), make use of the notion of the "local" found in nativist art and literature to produce a multilayered subject constituted by both an isomorphism of person and place (the Korean peninsula) and a universalist, imperializing order, the Greater East Asia Co-Prosperity Sphere. The late 1930s and early 1940s culture of imperialization attempts to manage the shock of the urbanscape and destruction of form that make up modernist texts by turning at once to stasis (the local) and disciplined movement (mobilization in an expanding imperial space).

Colonial/Postcolonial and the Formation of the Early Cold War Order

The end of Japanese rule in August 1945 meant, among other things, the beginning of competing narratives of the colonial past. These narratives were accompanied by a return to the cultural debates of the late 1920s and early 1930s. The reemergence of proletarian writers and artists—both those who had stopped working in the late colonial period and those who had actively participated to varying degrees in the mass culture of wartime mobilization and were now re-recanting—set the stage for a renewal of the proletarian-cultural nationalist debates that had ended in the mid-1930s with the Japanese Government-General crackdown on the left. The reappearance of the proletarian subject in post-1945 literary and visual culture was soon followed by its effacement, beginning particularly in 1946 and 1947, when the U.S. military occupation took a series of measures that led to the evacuation of proletarian writers to the North. In many ways, what would soon be called South Korean literature (*Han'guk munhak*) was framed at this historical moment. Erasure of the proletarian literature of the colonial past occurred in tandem with the distancing and othering of the North. The cultural field that emerged in the South under the U.S. occupation organized itself around this simultaneous effacement, one that amounted to the spatialization of proletarian literature, its identification with the North. It was in the period of 1945 through 1948, with its sifting through of the new colonial past and its negotiation of a rapidly bifurcating Cold War order, that the framing of the South/North cultural fields took place, setting the stage for the discursive practices of the 1950s and 1960s.

Division on the Korean peninsula cannot be understood without taking into consideration a visual politics. The North quickly became invisible and highly visible at the same time during the U.S. occupation, emptied out yet omnipresent as communist threat. Later, especially during and after the Korean War (1950–1953), the North would become visible in a slightly different way, as both threat and target. We can locate this rapid formation of the North/South politics of the visual as standing somewhere between mourning—as Dominick LaCapra notes, the recognition of the other as other—and melancholia, in LaCapra's words, "a specular relation that confuses the self with the other."[15] The figuring of geospatial division as national division and as loss should be linked to the ways in which North Korea and those living in the North rapidly become spectral, experienced in their absence by way of images. In this way, the new notion of North Korea becomes marked by a certain encounter with death. Journals of the mid-1940s such as *Ibuk t'ongsin* (*Communique from up North*) show this early process of the North becoming an image, one that marks an absence, in fact a death or, more precisely, a living death. The period of 1945 through 1948, what

South Korean scholars often call the "liberation space" (*haebang konggan*), thus begins the process of what we might consider a South Korean Cold War mourning-melancholia. The final four chapters of this book show how the negotiations of the verbal-visual relation I trace in chapter 1 are reworked after 1945, when the distribution of the visible/invisible, always linked to the division of the peninsula, became the privileged site for the enforcement, and questioning, of the Cold War order on the Korean peninsula.

The brief appearance of collaboration confessionals from 1945 through 1948 only served to highlight well-known individual histories, thus effacing the ways in which colonial Korea had become a mass culture of wartime mobilization in the late 1930s and early 1940s. The post-1948 South Korean state found itself relying on a mass culture of mobilization in its organization of anticommunist subjects and its linkage of the health of the nation to the health of the economy, what we might call ethnodevelopmentalism. Cold War developmentalism, that is, relied in many ways on late colonial mobilization culture, anchoring South Korean identity in a nativism now figured not as local but as ethnonational, anticolonial, and transhistorical, mediating the anxiety of "free world" developmentalist subjects increasingly enmeshed in the project of national capitalism. The erasure of the late-colonial-period mass culture of mobilization ends up allowing its post-1945 reappearance in mirroring form, legitimating the developmentalist South Korean state as properly postcolonial.

The simultaneous erasure and appropriation of colonial-period discourse that took place first under the U.S. military occupation would play a major role, particularly through the late 1980s, but even into the present, in the organizing of the South Korean cultural field. As we will see in the final four chapters of this book, both colonial-period works and post-1945 representations of the colonial period inform the deployment and contestation of ethnodevelopmentalism and its accompanying visual order, as well as an array of discourses central to the formation of the early Cold War subject in the 1950s and 1960s, including, among others, the debates on the national language, existentialism, gender relations, and race.

Chapter 2 considers the 1945 "liberation" (*haebang*) of Korea, the ensuing U.S. and Soviet military occupations, and the formation of separate sovereign states in the North and South in 1948 in terms of the distribution of the sensible that informs the emerging North/South aesthetic-political relation.[16] In this chapter, I map out the trajectories that emerged on the immediate post-1945 cultural scene. These trajectories rearticulated the earlier colonial debates I trace in chapter 1. They would now graft themselves onto notions of sovereign space and historical rupture (or lack of it) as they began to outline the frame of cultural fields associated with North and South Korea.

We can think of colonized space in a variety of ways, on one level as imperial and sovereign (legally) while simultaneously marked by private possession and the ethnonational claim (culturally/affectively); on another level, as global/local (proletarian) or, later, as Western versus Asian/local (wartime Pan-Asian). Such a simultaneity or in-betweenness informs immediate post-1945 cultural production in South Korea, where we find literary texts that work to negotiate a break from the colonial past even as they quickly become implicated in competing Cold War sovereignties and their associated ways of seeing.

The figuring of liberation also becomes an occasion for the staking out of positions in the cultural field, one that we should link to the territorializing of North and South.[17] The emergence of a "divided" literature or, more precisely, a literature that produces division must be understood in relation to these two intersecting spatialities, that of the cultural field (both in terms of contemporary cultural production and in terms of canon selection/excision, the former bearing close relation, in its position taking, to the latter) and the territorialization of geographic space as sovereign. The excision of colonial-period texts involved not only proletarian works but also the works of any writer who went to North Korea after 1945, as well as Japanese-language texts. The construction of *Han'guk munhak*, or "South Korean literature," takes place as a cultural and legal positioning, insofar as the selection of the historical canon begun in 1945 turns upon the 1948 excision of legally banned works and contemporary censorship (from the U.S. military occupation and, after 1948, the National Security Law). *Han'guk munhak* is imbricated in the statist deployment of a space and temporality linked to the early imagining of colonial-period history.

The formation of *Han'guk munhak*, the focus of chapter 2, is thus closely tied to the increasing excision of texts—as well as cultural producers located north of the thirty-eighth parallel. I pay particular attention to the ways that writers such as Ch'ae Man-sik, Yi Sŏn-hŭi, Pak Ch'an-mo, Yi T'ae-jun, and Yŏm Sang-sŏp participate in the formation of separate cultural fields in the northern and southern halves of the peninsula. I do not assume a colonial/postcolonial historical break. Instead, I look at the ways in which writers grappled with the notions of "historical rupture," "coloniality," and "liberation." My focus is on verbal representations of the visual. I demonstrate how a constellation of texts (many of them overlooked in existing scholarship) engaged with the U.S. military government implicitly or explicitly as they reworked ways of seeing enabled by the proletarian, nativist, modernist, and wartime pan-Asian movements of the 1920s, 1930s, and early 1940s detailed in the previous chapter. These post-1945 texts drew on the earlier movements as they put into play a distribution of the visible and invisible that would frame the Cold War bifurcation of South and North through the rest of the twentieth century and into the present. Writers, artists, and filmmakers working in the forty-year period that followed—until 1988, when the 1948 ban on North Korean writers and KAPF was lifted—would find themselves negotiating this visual order, one first deployed under U.S. military occupation.

IMAGINING NONALIGNMENT AND
DEVELOPMENT IN THE 1950S AND 1960S

A double displacement of peoples took place in the late colonial period and in the first decade of division. The first displacement took the form of a disciplining and homogenization effected by mobilization, the deployment of Koreans to locations throughout the late-colonial-period imaginary of Greater East Asia. The second displacement resulted from the formation of North and South Korea and the accompanying movement of Koreans, many of them coming to the South, within the peninsula. The setting in place in the late 1940s and 1950s of "South Korea" (*Han'guk*) and the subjects who would territorialize this new geopolitical space south of the DMZ is intimately linked to this double dislocation.

In the 1950s, the state promoted a dual affiliation—with South Korea and with the anticommunist, democratic free world—that reworked the late-colonial-period dual identification with Korea and a Japan-led Greater East Asia. In South Korea, the assertion of sovereignty set the stage for both the state's claim to legitimacy and the critique of the state as comprador and authoritarian. This critique rests on the delinking of ethnonation from state and the latter's failure to put the democratic ideals it aligned itself with into practice. While this debate would take different forms over the ensuing decades, it would remain central to the ordering of both statist and dissenting subjects.

The double dislocation, however, opened up the possibility of forming new kinds of nonstatist, nonethnonationalized positions. This fissure between person and place emerges from the gap opened up via dual affiliation with South Korea and the free world. Rather than belonging to both, such a subject belonged to neither. The gesture toward nonbelonging represents a continuation of the calls for neutrality made in the immediate post-1945 period, even as it is informed by the 1950s global movements for nonalignment (both Bandung by "third world" states and the existentialism of the "first world"). The Korean War is often seen as solidifying the Cold War order, firming up anticommunism and national division. However, representations of the war and its effects did not always coincide with the securing of the South Korean anticommunist subject. Violence even in "anticommunist" films and literary texts of the 1950s tended at key moments to cross borders. A generalized violence, often linked to sexuality, unsettled a variety of oppositions (North Korea/South Korea, free world/communist other, East/West).

In chapter 3, I take into account the summoning of postcolonial, territorialized "South Korean" subjects and the appearance, often at the margins of texts, of early attempts to question Cold War oppositions. First, I examine three major strands of 1950s intellectual discourse: the return, in very different form, of the colonial debate on national literature, one that stands at the center of the attempt to form a South Korean literary field in the 1950s; the reworking of colonial nativism as a Cold War traditionalism; and the deployment of existentialism in South Korea, which interrupts both the national narrative/traditionalism and the universalism of its "first world" counterpart. I show how the questioning of the person/place isomorphism called for by the South Korean state intersects with the attempts of the writer Son Chang-sŏp to construct a nonaligned subject, one that emerges via a negotiation between seeing and writing, art and literature. Finally, I look at the ways in which the 1956 filmic adaptation of Chŏng Pi-sŏk's popular 1954 novel *Madame Freedom* (*Chayu puin*) addresses the post-1945 discourse on Korean as the new "national language" (as opposed to Japanese), the commodity culture of the 1950s, a Cold War politics of the body, and the emergence of popular culture and film spectatorships.

By the early 1960s, it was becoming increasingly clear that South Korea would play a major role in the enforcement of free-world economic development. In South Korea, the elaboration of this narrative took place in major intellectual journals such as *World of Thought* (*Sasanggye*). For example,

W. W. Rostow's influential *The Stages of Economic Growth: A Non-Communist Manifesto* appeared in installments in *World of Thought* in 1960, the year of its publication in English. The compilation of the developmental narrative in ethnonational form appeared in two early 1960s texts meant to legitimate General Park Chung Hee's coup d'état (May 16, 1961) as the revolutionary point of departure for South Korea's rise in the world system: Park's *Our Nation's Path* (Uri minjok ŭi nagal kil, 1962) and *The State, the Revolution, and I* (Kukka wa hyŏngmyŏng kwa na, 1963).

Chapter 4 looks at the ways in which the staging of growth in the developmentalist discourse of the 1960s confers formal autonomy upon the nation-to-be-developed, replacing the visual display of colonial occupation with a coercion that seeks to remain unseen. For the writer Nam Chŏnghyŏn, however, the statist assertion of economic development in the name of the ethnonation becomes nothing more than hyperassimilationism; the evolutionary narrative of development necessarily privileges the West as normative. Nam's texts, perhaps more than the works of any other writer in the early 1960s, contest not only the U.S. presence but also domestic authoritarianisms. Nam's response to the summoning of the developmental subject (the subject in training, the subject that is not yet a subject) is to render visible the historicist production of primitivity. It is precisely for this reason that Nam's works question Park's assertion of the national health/modernization coincidence by displaying a series of male bodies that are disfigured, emasculated by the insertion of South Korea into the evolutionary, historicist logic of development. To figure development as devolution is to make visible the relation between Cold War productivism and the history of colonial racism that informs it. I trace, therefore, the discursive relations among Nam's works, Park Chung Hee's articulation of statist, ethnonational developmentalism—itself a continuation of and reaction against the colonial past—and U.S. metropolitan representations of its developmentalist mission in films such as George Englund's 1963 *The Ugly American*.

Return to the Colonial Present

Chapter 5 examines the works of Ch'oe In-hun, the first South Korean writer to offer an extended treatment of late-colonial-period imperialization and wartime mobilization. Beginning with *The Square* (Kwangjang, 1960) and continuing in *The Tempest* (*T'aep'ung*, 1973), Ch'oe In-hun engaged in a sustained attempt to unpack what he saw as a multilayered coloniality informing the Cold War Koreas: the intersection of statist authoritarianisms and U.S. neocolonial developmentalism with an earlier, pre-1945 colonial history of ethnonational, classed, and pan-Asian identifications. Ch'oe's well-known concern with North/South division (*The Square* is considered a founding text of "division literature") arises as part of this attempt to address a colonial modernity that extends itself beyond the period of Japanese rule (1910–1945) and into the post-1945 era. The shifts in Ch'oe's "novels of ideas" (*kwannyŏm sosŏl*) of the early 1960s (*The Square*, "Imprisoned" ["Su," 1961]) through the mid-1960s (*Voice of the Governor-General* [*Ch'ongdok ŭi sori*, 1967, 1968, 1976]) to two early 1970s works (*A Day in the Life of Kubo the Novelist* [*Sosŏlga Kubossi ŭi iril*, 1970–1972] and *The Tempest*) took place at critical moments in Park Chung Hee's enforcement of an anticommunist, developmental trajectory and the emergence of its leftist-nationalist opposition. If the task of the South Korean developmental state in the 1960s and 1970s was to legitimize its project via the productivist eradication of communism (*myŏlgong*) in the North, Ch'oe increasingly sought to overcome the division of the peninsula by questioning the ways in which a reactive ethnonationalism posited itself as anticolonial while promoting integration within the capitalist free-world order.

Departing from the collaboration confessionals that appeared immediately following the end of Japanese colonial rule, Ch'oe rejects the assumption of a preexisting ethnonational subject that renders the collaborative act as mere performance. Ch'oe's return to the colonial takes place as part of an interrogation of post-1945 universals, both liberal-democratic and statist. Such a questioning, in turn, leads him to reconsider the relation between the act of writing and the distribution of the visible and invisible that structures both the representation of North Korea and the remembering of Japanese imperialism. For this reason, Ch'oe would turn his attention to the relation between words and images and particularly to how this relation informs both the act of translation and the scene of interpellation.

Ch'oe's reworking of late colonial pan-Asianism entails an unpacking of a Cold War visual order linked to division (the effacement of the North) and coloniality (erasure of the history of imperialization/mobilization). Ch'oe returns to the colonial in an effort to resume the questioning of the modern begun in the late 1930s and early 1940s. At stake is an attempt to pick up the pieces of a project, the "overcoming of modernity," that allowed for a consideration of some new kind of being in the world but ultimately led to a further disciplining in the form of militarism and imperialization.

My focus is on the ways the South Korean cultural field was formed during the first three decades of the Cold War, and I conclude this book with a discussion of Ch'oe's work of the early 1970s, a moment that saw both increasing authoritarianism (in the form of Park Chung Hee's Yushin Constitution, which made him president for life) and the beginnings of the antiauthoritarian National Literature Movement (*minjok munhak undong*). As we see in one of its first articulations, Paik Nak-chung's "The Idea of a National Literature" (1974),[18] the National Literature Movement, which would dominate the literary scene through the late 1980s, returned to both the proletarian-cultural nationalist debates of the 1920s and early 1930s and their rearticulation in 1945 through 1948, particularly to the post-1945 linkage, made by leftist critics such as Im Hwa, between the proletarian cultural movement and the national situation. Paik, however, could only allude to these debates in this article, leaving it to his readers to conjure up what had been written but could no longer be cited. While I end with the early 1970s, I hope my discussion of the colonial modern, the occupation period, and the 1950s and 1960s contributes to an understanding of the shifts in the cultural field that occurred with the advent of the National Literature Movement and the subsequent People's Movement (*minjung undong*) of the 1970s and 1980s.[19]

A number of important books and dissertations on Korean literature and film have appeared over the past ten years.[20] In some ways, however, the decades-long lack of an English-language cultural history has led to broad generalizations about the 1950s and 1960s as a period marked by a draconian anticommunist culture. To be sure, this was the case. But it is important to remember that literature and literary criticism provided one of the primary sites for the questioning of overlapping U.S./South Korean Cold War statisms/developmentalisms. We can locate considerable dissent in the 1950s and 1960s, well before the student and labor movements of the 1970s and 1980s. Indeed, the latter often drew upon the former for inspiration and legitimacy, particularly on the culture of dissent surrounding the April 1960 movement (discussed in chapters 4 and 5), which led to the downfall of the Syngman Rhee regime.

It was only in the mid-1990s, and particularly in the early 2000s, that scholarship in South Korea moved toward an interrogation of the close relation between nationalism and imperialism. Many of the important works by scholars such as Kim Chul, Hwang Jongyon, Kim Ye-rim, Ch'a Sŭng-gi, and others have demonstrated this relation by opening up texts that had not been studied before, particularly those associated with the late 1930s and early 1940s period of mobilization. (It is no accident that the mobilization films I discuss in chapter 2 came out on DVD for the first time in 2006 by way of an archaeological trope, under the title "The Unearthed Past.") No study, however, has addressed in a sustained way the relation between word and image in literature, art, and film. There remains, moreover, a tendency in both English- and Korean-language scholarship to divide modern Korean literature into pre- and post-1945 periods. In this book, I situate historically the ongoing negotiation of the verbal and the visual, the ways in which texts across the 1945 divide are both literary and visual, "literary-visual," in different, shifting ways. As we will see in chapters 2 through 5, the formation of the cultural field in South Korea cannot be understood without taking into account the colonial cultural history that preceded it and that is rearticulated by it in different ways.

I hope this book places overlooked or marginalized colonial Korean texts, art, and film in dialogue with existing studies of Japanese imperialism and the scholarship on colonial Korean history. The majority of this book, however, addresses the ways in which the formation of post-1945 "South Korean" culture is part of a transnational, global, Cold War discourse. South Korea has always been thought of as one of the key sites along what Lord Halifax called in a 1952 article "the frontier of freedom," defined as "a vast curve, stretching from the Baltic eastward to the North Pacific."[21] Here, I would like to add a consideration of the culture of the Cold War periphery to existing American Cold War studies. My aim is to begin to unpack what has been elided in discussions of modern Asia and the Cold War—early articulations by Korean writers, filmmakers, and intellectuals who sought to dismantle the post-1945 order and the enforcement of division on the Korean peninsula, often at a heavy price to themselves. Taken as a whole, this book seeks to rethink the relationship between literary and visual culture as well as between colonial discursive, artistic, and filmic practices and the postcolonial culture of "national division" on the Korean peninsula, itself central to an understanding of the trajectory of the Cold War in Asia.

1
VISUALITY AND THE COLONIAL MODERN

The Technics of Proletarian Culture, Nativism, Modernism, and Mobilization

THE EVACUATION OF former Korea Artista Proleta Federatio (the original Esperanto title of what is commonly known as KAPF) writers, artists, and filmmakers to the north during the 1945–1948 U.S. military occupation of the southern half of the Korean peninsula was followed by the anticommunist South Korean state's 1948 censorship of all of their colonial-period works. Along with the ban on all contemporary North Korean cultural production, these moves formalized the boundaries of what would become the South Korean cultural field.[1] It was only following the 1988 lifting of the ban in South Korea on the works of cultural producers who went north in the aftermath of liberation from Japanese rule that a questioning of the canon and the literary history that accompanied it could take place in institutional settings. All of the disciplines, including literature, art, and film, followed a similar historical trajectory. The work of figures central to the colonial art and film scenes such as Kim Pok-chin, Yi K'wae-dae, Kim Yŏng-jun, and Im Hwa could only be exhibited, shown, and studied for the first time in 1988.[2] The ban on the work of any cultural producer who went to the North after 1945, moreover, meant that important literary figures associated with the modernism of the 1930s, such as Pak T'ae-wŏn and Yi T'ae-jun, could not be discussed. Nor was the post-1945 emergence of a narrative of nationalist anticolonial resistance prepared to address the late 1930s and early 1940s mass culture of mobilization, except in the form of a displacement, the highlighting and rehearsal of the acts of individual archetypal collaborators. The notion of a South Korean literature and culture—one that began to take shape under the U.S. military occupation and to assume a fuller Cold War form following the formation of the South Korean state in 1948—was, in many ways, produced by these erasures.

In this chapter, I discuss the multilayered relations among the proletarian culture movement of the 1920s, the nativism of the late 1920s and 1930s, the modernism of the 1930s, and the mass mobilization of the late 1930s and early 1940s. These colonial-period literary and cultural movements possess significance for the post-1945 era beyond that of their complete or partial erasure. They can all be linked to new modes of literary and visual representation bound up with a negotiation of the colonial and the modern. To be sure, the formation of separate cultural fields in North and South Korea occurred as part of the Cold War first-world/second-world bifurcation. But this is only part of the story. In this chapter, I show how the proletarian culture movement, nativism, modernism, and mass mobilization set in motion ways of seeing and writing that would inform the later distribution of the visible and invisible that make up the Cold War politics of division on the Korean peninsula.

KAPF stands at the center of the organization of the newly emerging cultural sphere in the 1920s, one marked at once by the so-called cultural policy of this decade and by the emergence of a modern art scene, a new film industry, and a colonial-modern cityscape. A succession of literary and aesthetic debates took place at this time, appearing in the journals and newspapers published in colonial Seoul following the Government-General's issuing of publication permits in the aftermath of the March First movement (1919). These debates would play a central role in the cultural scene well beyond the 1920s, through the 1930s and 1940s, into the U.S. and Soviet military occupations, and, in different ways, up to the present in the two Koreas. KAPF members played a central role in these debates, both in their disagreements among themselves and in their exchanges with their cultural nationalist critics. Below, I look at three important KAPF debates—on popular culture, proletarian art, and the form/content relation. I underscore the importance of KAPF both in framing the cultural field of the 1920s and in setting the stage for the ways in which the modernism and mobilization movements of the 1930s and early 1940s would negotiate the relation among technology, representation, and colonialized/imperialized subjectivity.

As we will see below, this relation cannot be understood without considering the ways in which literature, film, and art inform and authorize one another by way of colonial nativism. Korean literary histories usually note the importance of the turn toward portrayals of the rural space in the mid-1930s, one that accompanies the increasing repression of the colonial state and the shift away from KAPF. Overlooked in discussions of this literary turn, however, is the close relation between literary nativism and nativist art (*hyangt'o*). Indeed, literary nativism follows the emerging discourse on nativist art already begun in the late 1920s and engages in different ways with nativist images throughout the 1930s.

Literary nativism is organized around the verbal description of nativist images. Nativist texts are inextricably linked to the nativist art movement, which achieved increasing prominence through the institutionalization of nativist painting in the Government-General-sponsored annual Chosŏn Art Exhibition (*Sŏnjŏn*). Once we move the history of colonial nativism back to the late 1920s, moreover, we encounter its importance in the early defining of a proletarian subject in KAPF texts. In fact, these works attempt to produce a way of seeing the rural space that challenges the nativist isomorphism of people and place discussed in essays on art in intellectual journals and displayed in galleries both in the colonial capital and in the Japanese metropole.

It is easy to think of nativism as standing in opposition to the modernism of the 1930s and its representation of the fractured cityscape. However, both movements grapple, in their different ways, with the increasing incorporation of Korea into the global colonial modern of the 1930s. Both confront the settling in of commodity exchange and consumption, the advent of 1930s popular culture, the isolation and anomie of the urban experience, the continuing displacement and impoverishment of peoples in the countryside, and Japan's increasing militarism. For their part, modernist writers such as Yi Sang and Pak T'ae-wŏn differ from nativists in their experiments with the ways in which the visual register calls attention both to the literary and the commodity form. But both nativism and modernism are "urban" forms of painting/writing, produced for a city-dwelling audience and seeking to locate a space other than that produced by capitalist relations. As we will see, *hyangt'o* discourse structures Pak's modernist *A Day in the Life of Kubo the Novelist* (1934), and his well-known *Stream Scenes* (1936) can be read as a series of verbal descriptions of *hyangt'o* stills set in motion in the colonial urban space.

Wartime-mobilization literary and filmic texts of the late 1930s and early 1940s do not represent a break from these earlier movements but instead an appropriation of their techniques and a continuation of their concerns. The culture of mobilization of the wartime Japanese empire in the late 1930s and first half of the 1940s addresses the modern by offering to overcome it. It promises to overcome the colonial via the incorporation of the colonized as true imperial subjects. It also rejects capitalism and its attendant consumerism/commodification.

Rather than a simple assimilationism, the culture of colonial mobilization, as we will see in our discussion of the films *The Volunteer* (1941), *Springtime on the Peninsula* (1941), and *Military Train* (1938), makes use of the notion of the "local" found in *hyangt'o* art and literature to produce a multilayered subject inextricably linked both to an isomorphism of person and place (the Korean peninsula) and to a universalist, imperializing order, the Greater East Asia Co-Prosperity Sphere. The late 1930s and early 1940s culture of mobilization attempts to manage the disenchantment of the capitalist modern by turning at once to a primordialist stasis (the local) and an ec-stasis, the ecstasy of mass, disciplined movement (mobilization in an expanding imperial space).[3] In fact, as we will see in later chapters, the post-1945 forgetting of the culture of mobilization would allow for its rearticulation. This would take the form of a Cold War subject anchored by a traditionalism drawing on the colonial-period nativist aesthetic, all the while remaining mobile. Only now, that subject would take part in the "free world" developmentalist order and, moving into the 1960s and beyond, in the increasing expansion of export markets.

Imaging the Proletarian Subject

The 1925 formation of KAPF out of earlier leftist organizations (Yŏmgunsa and PASKYULA) that had emerged in the early 1920s represents an important moment in colonial Korean history. An internationalist colonial proletarian arts (*p'ŭro yesul*) movement that in many ways dominated the cultural scene from its 1925 founding to its disbanding under Government-General pressure in 1935, KAPF was formed along with other leftist organizations in East Asia in the 1920s following the Russian Revolution.[4] KAPF members worked particularly closely with their counterparts in NAPF, the Japanese proletarian literature and arts movement. The leftist movements in colonial Korea in the early and mid-1920s also must be understood in relation to the 1919 March First independence movement and the "liberalization" in Government-General policies that occurred in its aftermath.⁵ Younger intellectuals who had come of age during the immediate precolonial period and the 1910s were growing frustrated at what they considered minor changes in the colonial landscape in the early 1920s. The result was twofold: (1) a move to work within and negotiate the "cultural policy" deployed by the colonial state in response to the March First movement, and (2) a growing call to radicalize resistance, one that found different strands of leftist thought appealing, particularly communism and anarchism.

While KAPF can and should be linked to the earlier "civilization and enlightenment" discourse of the early 1900s and its emphasis on educating the masses, the call for a class-based revolutionary subject signals a break with the Korean enlightenment invocation to step into the version of "modern" history associated broadly with such notions as nation, sovereignty, and capitalist accumulation.⁶ At the same time, as we will see below, most KAPF works do follow earlier enlightenment discourse when they seek to render "life-worlds into history" by attempting to dispense with the enchanted, the premodern, in favor of a secular, linear temporality.⁷ What emerges in the mid-1920s is an opposition between modern universalisms, class and ethnonation (*minjok*). This is an opposition that at moments breaks down, only to be once again shored up in the ambivalent, multilayered representations of colonial modernity in KAPF texts themselves, as well as in works by writers such as Yi Kwang-su, Shim Hun, and Yŏm Sang-sŏp, who were all affiliated in one way or another with the 1920s cultural nationalist contestation of KAPF.⁸

While the scholarship on proletarian literature begun in South Korea in 1988 is rich in many respects, it has remained discipline bound, with literary scholars focusing on KAPF criticism and literary works. It is important to recall that although proletarian literature, art, and film were considered separate categories in KAPF, the ways in which KAPF debates over the cultural forms best suited to colonial Korea's capitalist modernity took place meant that these categories would blur even as they were announced, bound up as they were with a shared concern regarding the question of the representation of social reality. This was a question that involved multiple imagings, first of the "people" (what KAPF writers and critics called the *minjung* or, often, *taejung*) themselves, followed by the artistic practices that would lift the *minjung* into an emancipatory historical trajectory.

My aim in this chapter, however, is neither to accomplish the impossible task of locating in one space the breadth of the diverse, multidisciplinary cultural production that made up KAPF, which saw itself as a broad-based proletkult movement, nor to focus solely on the relation between the different disciplines eventually assigned separate departments by KAPF leadership. Instead, I will show how the overlooked negotiation of the verbal-visual relation in KAPF literature, criticism, art, and film—a negotiation that precedes and, indeed, informs the later experimentation with the visual register in the literary modernism of the 1930s—played a central role in producing a new way of seeing, reading, and thinking, one that participates in the making of the colonial modern itself.

Proletarian texts are informed by the technics of the colonial modern, particularly film and the staging of urban space in the mid- and late 1920s. As we will see in our discussion of the critic and writer Kim Ki-jin,[9] the attempt to produce a new way of seeing in these texts involves the relation between the technological and the repeated calls to "awaken" or "educate" the *minjung* to the reality (*hyŏnsil*) of the class struggle. The question of representation addressed in proletarian literary debates and texts in the 1920s becomes one of how a true way of seeing will emancipate proletarian, laboring bodies. Awakening, coming to consciousness, accompanies the production of history itself. This awakening takes place by way of the verbal invoking in proletarian texts of an authentic visual order. This linkage between authenticity and a way of seeing would be an important one for later cultural history. It would inform the visual register making up 1930s literary modernism, nativism, and the late-colonial-period structure of mobilization/imperialization and its postcolonial rearticulations.

KAPF was formed in the mid-1920s, when the colonial modern was making itself visible through new factory and office workspaces, rural impoverishment and its accompanying displacement/migration, and the refashioning of the colonial capital. The display of Government-General economic and political power in the architecture that housed the new institutions went hand in hand with the formation of a new urban cultural sphere and served to rework both the space and temporality of the city as stage of a modern future. The attempt to address the colonial, capitalist modern by KAPF intellectuals meant that they would grapple with the technics that made it modern in the first place. They would confront the new technology that altered the cityscape through the addition of transportation networks and modern architecture, exemplified in structures such as the Government-General Building, Kyŏngsŏng Station, and the Bank of Chosŏn, many of which were completed in the mid-1920s. They would also encounter other means through which the colonial state could legitimize its modernizing project, such as the rotary press, radio, telegraph, and cinema.

The Japanese colonial state increasingly made use of its resources to discipline its colonial subjects by attempting to frame, often via censorship, what would constitute the newly emerging cultural sphere. In the 1920s and 1930s, KAPF writers were the primary target of the Government-General's censorship apparatus. The marks of the censor on the pages of proletarian texts provide another layer of writing, a co-authorship that displays the limits or borders of the "cultural policy," the etching of what can and cannot appear as a typed word on a page becoming visual register of coloniality.[10] This productive effacement would intensify with the disbanding of KAPF in 1935 and the recantations that followed, leading up to the formation of "imperial subjects literature" (*kungmin munhak*) in the late 1930s. Unsurprisingly, intellectuals who took part in the formation of KAPF or joined the movement at later stages demonstrated an abiding concern with the technics of visual and print culture.[11]

KAPF was from its inception closely linked to visual culture, posters, cartoons, art, sculpture, and quickly with film and a genre that has been elided in existing scholarship on KAPF, the "film-novel" (*yŏnghwa sosŏl*). The emergence of KAPF, in fact, coincided both with the beginning of the colonial film industry and with the formation and organizing of the colonial art scene, one that centered in large part on the Government-General-sponsored annual Chosŏn Art Exhibition, first held in 1922.[12] If KAPF writers thought of themselves as producing a new kind of literature, one that dispensed with both the nation-centered enlightenment literature associated with Yi Kwang-su and the writers they located in the art-for-art's-sake camp, this was a literature that was from the first concerned, in its desire for the "true," with the technics of film. KAPF texts seek to make visible, to display colonial-capitalist relations, precisely in order to locate the coming to consciousness of the proletarian subject.

The emphasis that KAPF placed on art, posters, and film was clearly motivated by an attempt to reach the people (*taejung*) as widely and directly as possible. Cartoons by artists such as An Sŏk-chu were central to the leftist cultural movement in colonial Korea from its very beginning, offering a critique of capitalist relations that predates the formation of KAPF.[13] The KAPF appropriation of visual culture carried over into proletarian literature. In fact, the KAPF literary text and the proletarian subject that

FIGURE I.I *Tonga Ilbo* (1923)
Source: Artist unknown

emerges on its pages is made up of the intermediation between visual and print culture.

In KAPF literature, the production of immediacy, central to the assertion by KAPF writers that their works reflected reality (*hyŏnsil*), as opposed to the obfuscations and mystifications of the cultural nationalists, relies upon the verbal invocation of the visual. Here, we see that what Ernesto Laclau calls the "transparency dimension" of emancipatory narratives occurs by way of the transformation of word into image.[14] The formation of a working-class subject in these texts, one that involves the sacralization of labor, is an effect of the desire to make visible. KAPF texts summon the proletarian body-as-subject in order to move this subject beyond the text in which it makes its appearance. The verbal invocation of the visual makes the subject appear, a manifestation that is to then extend itself, as real, a visible form, beyond the written text and into historical reality. The immediacy of text and world emerges on this visual register. The desire to make words real that runs through colonial Korean proletarian literature shows us how the immediacy crucial to literary realism proceeds by an optics that sees through words to images. To read is to see, as if one were watching a film. The latter, it turns out, was an exhortation to readers made by KAPF film-novelists such as Kim Ki-jin.

The Popular Literature Debate and *Yŏnghwa Sosŏl*: Film as Novel, Novel as Film

The critic and writer Kim Ki-jin, a founding member of KAPF, played a central role in the debates over the direction of the proletarian culture movement. Kim is perhaps best known as the adversary of Im Hwa in the important KAPF debate on popular literature that took place in the late 1920s. The major KAPF debates brought together questions of representation, form/content, and mass culture in ways that would prove important both to the proletarian culture movement and to modernism and the culture of total mobilization in the 1930s and early 1940s.

Kim's 1923 works, "Promenade Sentimental," "Globalization of the Clarté Movement," and the "Enlightenment of the Dominant Class, Enlightenment of the Dominated Class," turn to Henri Barbusse and his writings on the Clarté movement in an effort to shift the newly formed post–March First movement colonial-modern public sphere toward the left. Barbusse was widely read in Japan, with numerous translations of his work appearing in the early 1920s. Indeed, the study and activity of colonial Korean proletarian writers and thinkers in the Japanese metropole played a central role in the ways in which they imagined themselves as part of an internationalist proletarian community of writers and artists. Kim's leftist writings date from 1923, and they were crucial to the eventual emergence of KAPF as an umbrella organization for the internationalist proletarian cultural movement in 1925.

As a broad-based arts movement, KAPF included among its founding members not only writers but also artists and filmmakers, all participating in a cultural and political scene informed at once by the Government-General issuance of publication permits, the institutionalization of modern art in the Chosŏn Art Exhibition system, and the emergence of the colonial Korean film industry. The publication of literary works and debates in journals and newspapers that formed the new colonial literary scene was accompanied by the appearance of the first colonial Korean films in the mid-1920s. Five KAPF films were made in the late 1920s and early 1930s. The first truly wide readership of literary texts thus emerges in tandem with the formation of a spectatorship of colonial Korean cinema.

As Kim Ki-jin and others were aware, low rates of literacy meant that the majority of those designated by the new discursive categories of "worker" (*nodongja*) and "farmer" (*nongmin*)[15] were being read to; they were accessing literature aurally and imaging its contents via the spoken word. "Readership" in the 1920s comprised this form of textual consumption. Kim Ki-jin's call for "popularization" (*taejunghwa*) in the late 1920s both acknowledges this aural readership and intervenes in the broader cultural field. The latter was witnessing the increasing importance of popular culture, certainly film and radio (the Chosŏn Broadcasting System's first broadcast was in 1927) but also, of course, popular newspaper novels. Yi Kwang-su's 1917 serialization of *The Heartless* was frequently cited as an early example of the success this form could achieve.

In a 1928 article, Kim Ki-jin calls for a "step back" to the popular novel, one necessitated by the increasing repressiveness of Government-General censorship and warranted by the fact that the majority of the contemporary readership in Korea enjoyed popular writing more than any other literary form.[16] The task at hand is to rework existing popular forms with a Marxist worldview. In his 1929 "On Popular Novels" ("Taejung sosŏllon"), Kim expands on these ideas, pointing out that while the term "popular novel" (*taejung sosŏl*) has not been used in Korea,[17] the genre has a long history, because it is to be defined as those works read and written for the people. The genre would thus include storybooks (*iyagi ch'aek*) such as the Chosŏn-dynasty *Nine Cloud Dream* and *Tale of Ch'unhyang*. Having linked text inextricably to readership ("*Taejung* fiction cannot exist apart from the *taejung*"), Kim proceeds to define *taejung* not as people or populace but as "workers and farmers."[18] The storybooks of the past, however, are "no longer necessary. Why? Because they cause our workers and farmers to resort to escapism, to intoxicate themselves with fantasies; they breed superstition, foster a slave mentality, encourage a spirit of subservience to superiors, promote fatalistic thought, and cause a step back to feudalism."[19] A new form of *taejung* fiction is called for, one that must appeal to the desires of the *taejung*, giving them pleasure while enabling them to break away from both past and present. The new fiction must enable them to recognize their current subjugation and the duty they must perform as the proper subjects of the "current stage of world history."[20]

The low educational level of the majority of the *taejung* necessitates a turn to the emotive and moral framework that undergirds the storybook form.[21] The fact that the storybooks continue to sell so well, dominating the publishing market and widely read by the *taejung*, indicates their power. The new *taejung* fiction must, therefore, appeal to the very desires and pleasures offered by the storybooks while moving away from the slavish mentality these pleasures produce.[22]

Kim organizes his article into two sections: "What Must Be Written?" and "How Must One Write?" The content must focus on what the *taejung* experience in their everyday lives, showing them the inequality of material life and the causes of this inequality. While *taejung* fiction must examine the clash between new and old worldviews, it must always conclude with the victory of the former over the latter. Other topics, such as love affairs, add interest to a work but should be relegated to the background, not take center stage. How must one write? Simply, shortly, with rhythm and repetition, since workers and farmers listen to texts read to them by others. Plot development and "dialectical realism" must be emphasized over character and psychological description.[23] The text that is at once popular and proletarian aims to transform emotion/feeling associated with the premodern into class consciousness. This move from feeling to consciousness can only occur by acknowledging the former, by locating the premodern narrative and its associated structure of feeling within the text in order to assure its popular appeal. The popular-proletarian text is to make use of the premodern register it aims to jettison by way of the dialectic.

The oft-noted privileging of time over space in proletarian texts[24] plays an important role in Kim Ki-jin's location of *taejung* fiction in relation to what he calls world history. At the same time, it is important to note the ways in which movement becomes central to the time/space relation and to the emotion that is to be appealed to and then channeled toward the socialist telos. To move rather than to remain static is to progress forward in time and to transform space. Popular-proletarian texts exhort movement, in physical space, in time, and affectively.

The popular-proletarian text must lift its readers or listeners into an emancipatory history by making visible that which appears in reality but has been misunderstood (because of superstition, which is a slavish, feudal mentality). The movement away from the past and forward in time, the catching up with the teleological movement of history that the farmer/worker readership/listenership is to accomplish, occurs via the learning of a new way of seeing. Temporality cannot be separated out from visuality, from this imaging. It is in this way that temporality, as motion, does not oppose space, as static. The series of images presented in the text is at once temporal, summoning the farmer/worker to move forward in time, and spatial, displaying itself before and to the farmer/worker to be "properly" seen.

The mixture of popular and proletarian that Kim's theory puts into play is one that many KAPF writers would turn to even after the popular-literature debate ended in Kim's defeat. It was Im Hwa who emerged as Kim's adversary, declaring that Kim's self-styled "step back" was nothing more than a retreat in the face of colonial censorship. Im Hwa maintained that Kim's theory amounted to a declaration of farewell to proletarian writing and Marxism at a time that more than ever called for "heroic struggle in the face of adversity."[25] Im Hwa was particularly critical of Kim's writing of romantic film-novels (*yŏnae yŏnghwa sosŏl*).[26]

Elided in post-1945 literary histories of the colonial period, the film-novel (*yŏnghwa sosŏl*) appeared in the mid-1920s along with the screening of the first Korean films.[27] While not written in great number, the explicit intermediation of film, illustration, and literature that makes up the genre allows us to consider the relationship between the appropriation of filmic technique in colonial-period literature and the negotiation of the written word in filmic adaptations of both literary texts and film-novels themselves. In the 1920s, screenplays (*sinario*) were also occasionally serialized in newspapers prior to the screening of the film in theaters. While the serialized screenplays contained camera directions, short verbal descriptions of scenes, dialogue, illustrations (and, often, stills, if the film was under production), the film-novel consisted of dialogue set off in boxes, meant to replicate the intertitles of silent films, occasional dialogue in the body of the text, longer descriptions of scenes, illustrations, and no camera directions.

The KAPF film-novel was ridiculed at the time by KAPF members such as Im Hwa and has not been seriously taken into account in studies of KAPF literature. I would, however, like to underscore its importance in 1920s and 1930s proletarian cultural production, both as a genre that intermediated film and literature and as a medium that addressed the

FIGURE 1.2 Installment of *Wandering*, with illustration (1928).

popular and the proletarian. As we see, for example, in Yi Chong-myŏng's 1928 *Wandering* (*Yurang*)—the first KAPF film-novel, made into a film by the well-known KAPF director and later member of the modernist Group of Nine (*kuinhoe*) Kim Yu-yŏng—the film-novel makes explicit the ways in which KAPF literary texts themselves are intermediated by the verbal/visual relation.[28]

Yi Chong-myŏng's preface to the first installment of *Wandering* (which appeared in filmic form in theaters in April 1928, shortly after its January 1928 serialization) indicates the intersection between readership and spectatorship in the film-novel:

> Reading a film-novel is like watching a movie. The only difference is that one watches it in one's imagination. Therefore, reading while critiquing the style and technique [*kigyo*] of this kind of writing, as if it were a novel, is unreasonable. Readers, if you read this novel and shine each scene on the "screen" in your mind, a film put together with love will appear before your eyes. This [story] is currently in production and will actually appear before you as a picture in the near future.[29]

The illustration of an audience watching a film in a movie theater at the beginning of each serialized installment of *Wandering* serves as the visual description of this verbal injunction. The film-novel entails an act of reading, one in which words are visually encountered on a page, but it is a reading that seeks to eliminate language, to have it drop away in favor of the "'screen' in your mind." This is a mode of readership that calls for the suture, the alignment of viewer with camera. One is to read as if one were already in a theater watching a film (like the illustration that precedes each installment) and as if one were shooting a film with reference to a screenplay, transforming words on a page into images and intertitle boxes to be viewed on a screen. The film-novel, then, allows us to consider the relation between silent films and serialized novels with illustrations.[30] If the silent film is at once image and text (a form to be viewed and read), the illustrated novel is made of text and image. Both forms call explicitly for an imaging in relation to the written word. In the case of the silent film, this involves an anticipation of text while watching the images on the screen, followed by an imagining of sound, actual speech, lifted from the intertitles, by the characters engaged in dialogue in the scene that has preceded the intertitle box.

If illustrations can be thought of as visual intertitles, the counterparts of intertitle boxes in silent films, we can consider the ways in which illustration/still, motion on the screen (of the mind or in a theater), and the written word intermediate not only silent film and the film-novel but also the serialized novel—a genre of considerable importance in the formation of modern Korean literature. We should think of the illustrations as part of the act of reading the serialized novel, not as separated-out visual aids or additions to the text. Text and illustration, regardless of the order of their production, appear in the same visual-textual space on the newspaper or journal page. Indeed, we can reverse the privileging of text over illustration (a privileging that forgets that the written word is encountered visually and is thus in itself a verbal-visual form) by considering the ways in which the written words making up an illustrated, serialized novel occur as lengthy captions, verbal descriptions surrounding the printed illustrations. Readers of illustrated novels, the most popular literary form in colonial Korea, were reader-spectators engaged in an act of setting images in motion (like a camera) by negotiating the movement between verbal descriptions of illustrations and illustrated descriptions of printed text. The later, post-1945 elision of illustrations in the anthologies and textbooks that make up the canon of South Korean literature effaces this act of readership-spectatorship.

Like a number of KAPF literary texts, *Wandering* presents us with a young male intellectual, Yŏng-jin (played by Im Hwa), who has left his hometown, been politicized through participation in the 1919 March First independence movement, and returned to find his village impoverished, exploited by a greedy landlord and his henchmen. Yŏng-jin sets about forming a night school and falls in love with Sun-i, the daughter of a destitute sharecropper. Sun-i is to stay at the landlord's house in preparation for her marriage to his "idiot son" Yun-gil, in exchange for financial help for her father. She decides, however, to flee and commit suicide but is rescued by Yŏng-jin before she can jump off a bridge. Yŏng-jin, Sun-i, and her father then set off from the village but are pursued by the landlord's henchman, with Yun-gil joining in the chase. The text concludes with Yun-gil unexpectedly turning on his father's henchman and rescuing the group.

As with other KAPF texts, *Wandering* remaps space, rejecting the imaging of the countryside as locus of the aesthetic—the kind of image Yŏng-jin encounters in the form of a waterwheel that is compared to a beautiful picture, one filled with "a sentiment [*chŏngjo*] impossible to describe."³¹ The waterwheel begins to move as the text offers a sequence of images associated with sadness and betrayal: Sun-i's deciding to marry the landlord, her appearing before Yŏng-jin in spectral form (*hwanyŏng*) begging for help, the disappearance of the specter. Here, in the film-novel, the still is put into motion, and this motion manifests itself on the screen of Yŏng-jin's mind, in the same way that readers are asked to "screen" the words they encounter in their own minds, assisted in this imaging by the series of illustrations that appear in the text. These are illustrations that can be linked together over time and across separate installments to form a film strip. This screening in the mind links emotion to image, changes in feeling to changes in visual experience. The movement from the kind of painting that was already in the late 1920s associated with colonial nativism (*hyangt'o*)³² to motion in the film-novel shifts the structure of feeling toward the modern. The movement from ahistory to what Kim Ki-jin above called world history takes place on the visual register.

Wandering serves as a point of transfer, routing affect (*chŏng*) away from the traditional to the modern, where *chŏng* will manifest itself among members of the exploited class. This is a movement away also from the enlightenment narrative of texts such as *The Heartless*, which nationalize affect, relocating *chŏng* as commonly felt by the Korean people. The break from both the traditional and the enlightenment-national occurs when Yŏng-jin declares that since the *chŏng* between father and daughter is not as powerful as that among members of the weak and exploited class, Sun-i's father will forgive her for not marrying the landlord's son. The transfer of affect accompanies the mobility/motion of the filmic form as well as the extraction of farmers from the ties of hometown.

This transformation of farmers into *minjung* is closely connected to the eyes, as we see in the unexpected alignment of Yun-gil, expected to assist in the capture of his runaway bride, with the departing group. Yong-gil's eyes "fill with angry emotion" as he looks upon the struggle between Yŏng-jin's group and his father's henchmen.³³ These eyes stand in for the silent group of reader-spectators imagining themselves in a theater at this final moment in the film-novel, coming to a spontaneous, unspoken awakening to reality (*hyŏnsil*) through seeing. The movement in the text from familial and romantic love to a class-based love is completed by this suture. *Wandering*, then, invokes the popular (*taejung*) motifs of hometown and romantic love in order to move a spectatorship away from the pleasure of the popular form to the pleasure of forming a class-based subject, precisely the gesture Kim Ki-jin calls for in his essays on popular-proletarian literature.

IMAGING HOME AND SOIL: NATIVIST ART AS TRANSVISUAL

While literary histories locate the nativist turn in the 1930s, one brought about by the waning of KAPF and the increasingly repressive Government-General cultural policies leading up to wartime mobilization and the organizing of imperial subjects literature, literary texts were already negotiating nativist discourse and images in the 1920s. The two ways of seeing that produce space in *Wandering*, one linked to a *hyangt'o*-like aesthetic image, the other to motion (and the motion picture), bear a close relation to contemporary debates on art. These debates already included calls to rework traditional landscape painting, now categorized as "oriental painting" (*tongyanghwa*), to picture real "Korean" landscapes, not landscapes that referred to mountains and streams (*sansu*) indistinguishable from what were now considered "Chinese." The critical discussions of "oriental painting" in the late 1920s, in fact, contributed to the emergence of *hyangt'o* discourse, the Hyangt'o Association forming in 1928, the year of *Wandering*'s serialization.

These 1920s discussions of art follow the earlier emergence of the new notion of "modern art" (*misul*) itself in the 1910s.[34] Karatani Kōjin and Kwon Boduerae have shown how a realism in the new modern art—appearing in the 1890s in Japan and the 1910s in Korea—is linked to perspective and the construction of interiority in modern Japanese and Korean literature. The emergence of the categories of Western painting (*yanghwa*) and oriental painting (*tongyanghwa*) in the 1920s certainly demonstrates that perspective/interiority set in place a new organization of the visual.[35] Western art and perspective, however, did not eliminate ways of seeing now associated with oriental art. *Yanghwa* and *tongyanghwa* were mutually constituted, but the story does not end there. Both continued to define the other. That many colonial painters worked in both genres shows not a jettisoning of oriental art into an objectified past but the ways in which both *tongyanghwa* and *yangwha* existed in an unstable relation.

As we see quite strikingly in Yi Sang-bŏm's work, the new category of oriental art refers to Western art in its supplementing of linear perspective to what is now a "traditional" form. The reference to Western art also

FIGURE 1.3 Yi Sang-bŏm, *Early Winter* (1926).
Source: Gallery Hyundai.

appears in the call to produce a coincidence of image and Korean space, a call that intersects with traditionalist imaginings in both art and literature in the 1920s.[36] For its part, Western art in colonial Korea always refers both to its discursive and pictorial relation to the West as a category (*yang*) and to the images—whether these are of a street in colonial Seoul or a village painted during a trip to France by a colonial painter such as Na Hye-sŏk—it displays artistically. The unstable dividing of art into two broad categories, oriental painting (*tongyanghwa*) and Western painting (*yanghwa*) takes place through artistic image and (verbal) discourse on art. That is, the categories *tongyanghwa* and *yanghwa* are themselves simultaneously visual and verbal. If the term *tongyanghwa* relativizes a mode of artistic representation formally associated with a universal cosmos, the term *yanghwa* also refers to a category, certainly one privileged as modern, but one always aware of itself as one mode of representation among other possibilities.

The same can be said for literary practice or what, more precisely, we can call literary-visual practice. Colonial Korean modern literature is visual and verbal, a textual practice that negotiates a continuously shifting, historical relation between different ways of seeing found both in literary texts and in other media, including not only art but also, as we have seen, film.[37]

The institutionalization of the modern art scene in the annual Chosŏn Art Exhibition was a colonial disciplining of the visual, an ordering of the cultural field. The selection of painters and their works by Japanese critics, the conferral of awards upon colonial painters, established the boundaries of what could be produced and displayed, how artistic representation was to function in the colonial cultural sphere. Metropolitan critical discourse, that is, combines with the paintings on display to constitute the Chosŏn Art Exhibition and its place in the larger cultural field. In the 1930s, nativist paintings by artists such as Yi In-sŏng and others took center stage at the exhibition. Their works were sanctioned by metropolitan critics as demonstrating an ineluctable Chosŏnness, a rustic simplicity displaying at once the emotional, geographical, and transhistorical landscape of the peninsula.[38] For their part, colonial Korean art critics varied in their appraisal of *hyangt'o*. Some critics praised nativist paintings as upholding Korean tradition in the midst of the colonial modern. Others, particularly critics associated with KAPF, critiqued nativist painting as catering to metropolitan desires.[39]

The metropolitan privileging of an isomorphism of feeling and place, a becoming homogeneous in space and timelessness, elides the look of the colonized artist as itself modern. The vast majority of colonial Korean painters participating in the exhibition were trained at the Tokyo School of Art. If there is, on one level, a colonized desire to "see" these paintings as "subjective Chosŏnness," it meets the metropolitan desire to gaze upon a particularlized, timeless landscape. Nativist paintings become a visual site of crossing essentialisms that mark the colonial modern production of subjects at once nationalized and colonized. But these desires cannot really be separated out, particularly if we recognize that the "native" painter may very well be locating him- or herself on a modern, or, more precisely, colonized-metropolitan register by painting nativist images. The imperative of the exhibition judges recalls what Rey Chow has called in another context "coercive mimeticism."[40] The colonized artists must act out their Chosŏnness. But this is a call for coincidence of painter and painted that cannot hold. Here is where the painting, displayed and framed at the exhibition, questions the very colonial institution that summons it. This questioning does not take place because the object in the painting becomes

FIGURE 1.4 Yi In-sŏng, *A Day in Fall* (1934).

subject. Instead, the painting itself puts on a display of the possibility of noncoincidence, certainly of the possible gap between painter and painted, but also of the gap between the ruralscape and its colonized urban viewers at the exhibition. The cultural field that emerges in and around the Chosŏn Art Exhibition in the 1930s is itself enabled by the multiple looks opening up and covering over this gap. As we will see below in our discussion of Yi In-sŏng, nativist painting, moreover, also reworks Western primitivisms, themselves drawing from "native" forms. Colonial nativism, even as it appeals to transhistorical authenticity, puts on display its own location in the global circulation and reworking of artistic images, what we might call, drawing on Lydia Liu's analysis of translingual practice, the transvisual.

Yi In-sŏng's nativism offers a reimaging of Gauguin as much as a portrayal of the colonial Korean ruralscape. Yi In-sŏng's work shows how nativism involves what W. J. T. Mitchell calls the metapicture or the hypericonic, a painting about a painting, at the same time as it paints "home and soil" (*hyangt'o*). Yi's work is at once a painting of Gauguin's painting and of Chosŏn, a carrying across or visual translation of Gauguin's work that, unlike translingual practice in Asia, does not rework meaning as it moves from one writing system to another, replacing, for example, the visible marks of the Roman alphabet both with Korean letters on the printed page. Instead, the transvisual displays movement, here from one painting to another. Gauguin's painting is there, visually, and not there at the same time, altered into a new form. Gauguin's "original" itself enters into a new signifying order and can now be seen differently. Its position shifts in the global cultural field. Yi In-sŏng's painting thus comments on Gauguin's work and its own reimaging of Gauguin itself. The transvisual is marked by this visual self-reflexivity, one that presents a multilayered spatiality. We encounter a landscape that is at once of a painting (Gauguin's portrayals of the South Seas) and of the colonial Korean rural space. The latter achieves nativist authenticity not by way of its uniqueness as Korean "home and soil" but by its intersection with global primitivisms. It is in this way that the colonial nativist Yi In-sŏng becomes a "modern" painter.

Literary Nativism: The Painterly Text

Literary nativism of the 1930s is part of the discursive field that includes the circulation of "home and soil" art and the commentary upon it. In fact, nativist literary texts are what we might call painterly, as we see, for example, in one of the works from the 1930s that has occupied a central place in South Korean literary histories and has been read by generations of South Korean students, Yi Hyo-sŏk's "When the Buckwheat Blooms."[41] It is no accident that the title of Yi's work reads as the title of a painting. "When the Buckwheat Blooms" is self-reflexive, hypericonic in a certain way. It is a literary text about painting, one that calls attention to the ways in which words invoke images. The text details the rural moonlit landscape in which it is set as if describing a *hyangt'o* painting, one brought to life in the form of a story of itinerant peddlers journeying from one market town to the next:

> They were traversing a hillside. It was probably after midnight by now, and it was so deathly still the moon seemed to come alive right there in front of you, its breath almost palpable. Awash in the moonlight, the bean plants and the drooping corn stalks were a shade greener. The hillside was covered with buckwheat coming into flower, and the sprinkling of white in the gentle moonlight was almost enough to take your breath away. The red stalks seemed delicate as a fragrance, and the donkeys appeared to have more life in their step.[42]

"Buckwheat" concludes with the youngest peddler, who earlier had quarreled with the oldest peddler in a tavern, helping his senior cross the stream.

By this time, we have been given enough clues to know that the youngest peddler is the son of the older peddler and the woman the latter has described encountering long ago. The two men are interfused at this closing moment with each other, the landscape, and the older peddler's anthropomorphized donkey.

Yi's painterly text celebrates the vitality and sexuality of the peddlers, traversing a landscape that, as in *hyangt'o* paintings, stands outside the colonial modern. The text eroticizes the relation among men, animals, and the landscape, producing a timelessness linked to the sexual desire of the peddlers (the earlier argument is over a woman working in a tavern) and the rutting donkey. Chosŏnness and the Chosŏnscape is at once sexualized and naturalized.[43] "Buckwheat" verbally presents a visual interpellation, a summoning of the reader to become a viewer of its images and identify with them as timelessly Korean.

"Buckwheat" demonstrates the ways in which mid-1930s recantation, the dispensing of the proletarian narrative, involves a reworking of the visual register. In "Buckwheat," the call is to become autochthonous. The verbal-visual summons aims for its own erasure, a move beyond both words and images to ecstatic bodily experience. A certain kind of sexuality emerges that is linked both to a becoming animal and a becoming landscape, if we think of becoming animal and landscape as a move to a register where words are no longer spoken and images seen can no longer be described—a register where to look is to identify and become the image itself.[44] The verbal invoking of the visual in "Buckwheat" sensualizes both the body and its labor as timeless landscape. It is in this way that Yi recants his earlier association with proletarian literature. "Life-worlds" are now to be written, and seen, outside of a linear history.

"Buckwheat," then, represents a reversal of the proletarian narrative found in earlier works such as *Wheel of Fire* (*Hwaryun*), a 1930 serialized screenplay co-authored by Yi Hyo-sŏk, An Sŏg-yŏng, Kim Yu-yŏng, and Sŏ Kwang-je.[45] The film, directed by Kim Yu-yŏng, script edited by Yi Hyo-sŏk and Sŏ Kwang-je, appeared in 1931. Featuring stills instead of illustrations and technical directions for camera movements, *Wheel of Fire*—like *Wandering* and well-known KAPF literary texts such as Cho Myŏng-hŭi's "Naktong River" (1927)—narrates a move away from the nationalism of the March First independence movement to an internationalist socialism. The screenplay begins with the appearance of a ring of fire that transforms into a ring of fists, followed by the appearance of an angry face that quickly

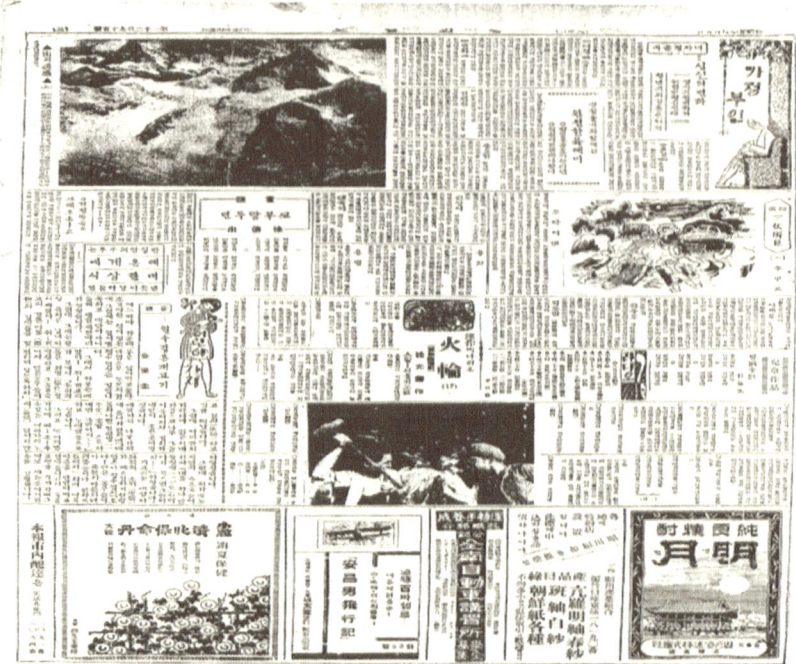

FIGURE 1.5 Installment of *Wheel of Fire*, with still (1930).

grows larger, approaching the camera and filling up the center of the ring. The close-up places emotion (anger) on a surface (the face) that is then transferred onto the resisting bodies (the fists) of the working class. The close-up, that is, produces a class affect and not psychologized emotion projected outward from the face.[46]

The screenplay then describes the release of its protagonist, Ch'ŏr-ho, from his ten-year incarceration. Ch'ŏr-ho, imprisoned immediately after the March First movement, has become a socialist in jail, now aligning himself with the international working class, as we see in the text's uniting of Chinese and Korean laborers in the mine where Ch'ŏr-ho lands a job. As in other proletarian texts, the melodramatic popular narrative of the family and its affectivity—the chance meeting of Ch'ŏr-ho and his son Pokkyu, the reunion of Ch'ŏr-ho and his wife (he saves her from suicide just as Yŏng-jin saves Sun-i from suicide in *Wandering*)—gives way to the proletarian narrative, the historical necessity of working-class struggle. It is, moreover, Ch'ŏr-ho's encounter, after a ten-year absence, with the radically transformed urban space that produces a contestation over the distribution of the sensible.

In *Wheel of Fire*, the colonial capital and the capitalist accumulation/exploitation that accompanies its refashioning is met by the resistance simultaneously mounted by male mine workers and women workers in a rubber factory. *Wheel of Fire* presents a series of crowd scenes, the fists in the opening sequence, the urban masses moving through the colonial-modern city (gathering as bystanders to watch any event out of the ordinary), workers engaged in struggle. It is the emergence of the latter as "workers of the world" (*man'guk nodongja*) that links the staging of the colonial modern to global capitalism. As serialized screenplay, *Wheel of Fire*, more explicitly than even the film-novel, places its readers in the position of both spectator and director. The reader is to take agency, actively eliding camera directions by transforming the screenplay into visual images "on the screen of the mind." This visual act of transformation and setting into motion links the reader-spectator-director to the growth and coming to awareness of workers in the diegesis of the screenplay itself.

We should recall that Yi Hyo-sŏk's move away from proletarian literature was toward modernism—a trajectory also followed by the filmmaker Kim Yu-yŏng, the co-author of "Wheel of Fire," and the KAPF film-novelist Yi Chong-myŏng. A founding member of the Group of Nine, the literary coterie most closely associated with 1930s modernism, Yi was very familiar with Western literatures and wrote a number of works portraying hybrid, cosmopolitan subjects circulating in urban spaces both within colonial Korea and outside its borders. The shift away from the proletarian narrative and toward the imagining of a timeless landscape in "Buckwheat" is one articulation among others of the experience of the change and flux of the urban modern in an expanding Japanese empire. That visual and popular culture, along with nativism, were central concerns of both KAPF and 1930s modernism points to the close relation between these two movements. This linkage will become clearer when we consider how 1930s modernism grappled with a common capitalist, colonial modernity and its attendant forms of commodification and desire.

Modernism and *Hyangt'o*: *A Day in the Life of Kubo the Novelist*

The modernist Group of Nine viewed itself explicitly as a departure from KAPF. From this point forward, the modernism/socialist-realism divide would inform literary histories and debates in colonial and divided Korea. The inclusion of Yi Hyo-sŏk, a former fellow traveler, in the original Group of Nine (the group would change its membership on several occasions but always kept the number to nine), as well as the film directors and former KAPF members Kim Yu-yŏng and Yi Chong-myŏng, shows how 1930s modernism bears a close relation to KAPF even as its central figures declare a newfound distance from the proletarian culture movement. Indeed, the well-known modernist calling attention to form represents a continuation of the earlier KAPF form-content debate that had ended with the victory of Im Hwa and Pak Yŏng-hŭi over Kim Ki-jin.

Unsurprisingly, the KAPF form/content debate of the late 1920s was organized along lines similar to those regarding popular culture. Kim Ki-jin argued for the importance of form, while Im Hwa and Pak Yŏng-hŭi dismissed such an emphasis as detracting from the central purpose of KAPF, which, according to them, was to provide an understanding of social reality that would politicize the masses and bring about revolution. Pak Yŏng-hŭi followed Im Hwa in dismissing the question of form as little more than an obfuscation of the proletarian content of a work. This rejection led Kim Ki-jin to remark that form should be thought of as a kind of architecture. Without it, as evidenced in Pak's literary works, one is left with only a roof. At stake, as we see in Kim's 1927 "Content and Expression: One Aspect of the Problems of Chosŏn Proletarian Literature," is the materiality of form.

In this article, Kim Ki-jin locates literature in relation to other arts such as music, dance, the fine arts, and film. All of these artistic practices, Kim writes, possess a medium. For literature, this medium is language. According to Kim, without the phenomena to be expressed and the spirit of the person expressing them, language stops at being nothing more than language. Therefore, rather than ask how one should express something, what must first be established are two things: (1) the "what" and (2) the mental activity that determines how to express the "what." Phenomena are at once the stuff of the novel and comprise a portion of its content. But it is the writer who determines how to express the phenomena. The writer's views, ideology, tastes, sensibility—all of these mental activities are mustered in a fictional work. And mental activity itself is content. Style, description, explanation are a mode of expression and at the same time an aspect of the content insofar as the mode of expression arises from the writer's mental activity, just as simple colors and an elegant style speak of an artist's tastes, perception, and ideology.[47]

Kim's linkage of content to form relies upon the connection made between the mind/spirit of the author and the phenomena to be expressed. Language, phenomena, and the author's mind come together to create a novel. But all are material, insofar as the content is associated with phenomena and in that the content precedes form. Mode of expression, moreover, is linked to content through the writer's mental activity. The "how" is not distinct from the "what," because mental activity is an element of the content. Mental activity (the writer's ideology, etc.) plays a critical role, along with the phenomena themselves, in determining the "what" first, with form following. The movement from phenomena to expression is thus at once material and objective. At the same time, language in and of itself is meaningless without phenomena and the writer. Phenomena and the writer thus exist outside language, approaching it and making it come alive, at once material, objective, and meaningful. We are left with a materialist expressivism.

Kim lays out his argument, as we saw above, by invoking a comparison among music, dance, and painting. He returns to painting at the close of this passage. It is the material appearance of colors that shows an artist's tastes, perception, and ideology. And it is this material appearance that is equated with the movement in literature from phenomena to expression. Kim's materialist expressivism turns upon painting as a figure, one that anchors expression as objective, real.

If the question of the image and the transformation of consciousness via a form that is also content emerges as a central concern in KAPF discourse, it is one that should be seen in relation to the reworking of the form and space of the cityscape in the mid- and late 1920s, the setting in place of the colonial urban stage. We should also note how the spatial trope and the concern with architecture in proletarian writing and criticism is important for the colonial literary scene in general, particularly for the modernism of the 1930s. The latter, with its calling attention to form, resumes the debate lost by Kim Ki-jin. For representative modernist writers such as Pak T'ae-wŏn and Yi Sang, the task becomes to put on display the conditions of a text's own production and circulation as literature.

Pak T'ae-wŏn's well-known novella *A Day in the Life of Kubo the Novelist* (1934) calls attention to form in different ways, one of which is accomplished by the dispersal of Yi Sang's illustrations in Pak's work.[48] It turns out that these illustrations, largely overlooked in the extensive existing scholarship on *Kubo*, are central to the ways the text offers a self-reflexive view of literature as a verbal-visual medium. The illustrations comment upon the serialized text's location on the printed page itself, on the ways the text stands in relation to a dispersal of the urban modern, including the location of the "literary" as one form of signifying work among others, for example, nonfiction essays on a variety of topics and the visual summons of the illustrated advertisement. The appropriation of the literary technique of stream of consciousness in Pak's text—Kubo, the modernist flaneur whose day-long wanderings through the colonial capital make up Pak's work, references Joyce—offers a series of associations linked to this dispersal.

Kubo's perambulations point to an imagining of modern urban space that moves across borders. Kubo, that is, experiences a city linked to a global circulation of images, commodities, and associations, just as the illustrated text *Kubo* enters into a global circulation of modernist texts. At stake in the text is the way in which its entrance into a global stream of consciousness maps the colonial modern, the modern as colonial. Jonathan Crary writes of William James's "stream of thought" that "the stream is James's figuration of an impossible harmony: that is, in which the unstable, kinetic, and fragmented character of modern subjective life is at once acknowledged but reconceived as fundamentally continuous and as that which endows subjectivity with an irreducible unity."[49]

In *Kubo*, however, the location of an impossible harmony through a stream of consciousness, the associations Kubo makes throughout the day, is not enough. The text begins and ends at home, a space bounded off from the modern city, associated with domesticity and Kubo's mother, whom he thinks of at critical moments throughout the entire day. The tension between flaneuring in the city streets and the attentiveness to home can be thought of as an oscillation between instability and the imagining of a space interrupting the modern. This oscillation is mapped spatially in terms of interior (home) and exterior (city streets). This mapping, however, also takes place in Kubo's associations. A simultaneous being at home and walking the city streets constitutes consciousness and its stream. It is a split subjectivity, one linked to the city, the other to the affectivity of home (and its rural associations, the image of the mother) that the associations making up Kubo's stream of consciousness unite. In *Kubo*, the stream brings together modernist fragmentation and *hyangt'o* imaginings. It is the negotiation itself, the dispersal brought together in a shifting relationship, not a dispensing of one in favor of the other, that constitutes the colonial modernist subject.

Here, we see how mid-1930s modernism shares with the later discourse of total mobilization/imperialization a confrontation with the unstable and the kinetic. As we will discuss below, the mobilized subject transforms fragment into function, allowing for separated-out capacities and affiliations to come together in the form of a simultaneous but larger attentiveness to empire and emperor.[50] The latter points to the visual experience associated in Walter Benjamin's work with the modern panorama, particularly the "harmonizing perspective" achieved by the "popularization of Darwin's theory as a 'panorama of evolution.'"[51] We should recall that the colonial remaking of the urban space underway in the 1920s and 1930s indeed operated by way of a visual regime tied to the "panorama of evolution," the material restructuring of the city itself as a panorama, a kind of permanent colonial exposition. The panorama unfolds from the perspective of Namsan and the Shinto Shrine constructed there in the mid-1920s, as we see detailed in works such as Yŏm Sang-sŏp's 1927 *Love and Crime*. In Pak's modernist text, however, the colonized's experience of the images encountered in the city fissures perspective itself.[52] The "stream" of consciousness can only partially shore up a sense of harmony. The fragmentation of the modern displayed in the colonial montage making up Kubo's associations disallows a reconciliation of experience of the city with the spatiotemporal coordinates of the panoramic perspective, the imperial picture viewed from on high.

Pak's frequent use of the comma in *Kubo*, moreover, forces an awareness of the fragmentation of the text. The text interrupts a reading that would see through writing. The continuous forcing of a pause between words highlights the materiality of the printed page, the blank spaces surrounding type. The comma, that is, does more than direct attention to literary form. It produces a stop or a jerk, forces a reflex that brings out the ways in which reading is a seeing.[53] The visual act of reading cannot provide a site where the modern is viewed by a reader somehow located outside of fragmentation, dispersal. Self-reflexivity involves a look at the comma, which stops the eye from proceeding along the line, or stream, of type. By calling attention to the printed page, the comma brings to the fore the imbrication of literature with the technics of the modern, the age of mechanical reproduction.

The pause called for by the comma organizes the stream and its associations and signals the ways in which the words surrounding it are to confer meaning. But it also produces a disruption, a signal that the flow of words on the page may disaggregate, become nonsensical. In *Kubo*, the comma is located at the interstices of meaning and nonsense, calling attention not only to language but to the machine, the pause or delay between strikes on a key, the movement the printing press makes in spacing words on the page. The visual pause of the comma bears relation to the cut or splice, the fleeting space between images in filmic montage, a technique Pak was aware of and attempted to deploy in his writing. It is in this way that the stream of associations that make up Kubo's dispersed yet continuous consciousness is filmic.

Picturing the Stream: Yi Sang's Illustrations

The excision of Yi Sang's illustrations from the anthologized versions of *Kubo* in which contemporary readers encounter the work allows us to reconsider the relation between the oft-noted turn to the psychological and the new awareness of literary form in 1930s colonial modernism. Psychoanalysis, as Friedrich Kittler points out, bears a close relation to film. While Otto Rank considered cinematography as reminiscent of the dream-work, Freud "stills the pictures that the bodies of his female patients produce" and proceeds to move to the "talking cure," away from "memories . . . in the form of pictures."[54] Discussions of Korean colonial modernism, even when they address the visual in modernist works, trace the steps of the "talking cure," eliding illustrations while focusing on the ways in which modernism is primarily attentive to language.

As an illustrated text produced by two artists, Pak T'ae-wŏn and Yi Sang, *Kubo* demonstrates the ways in which both the movement from the visual to the verbal and the verbal invoking of the visual involve the structure of the "talking cure." Yi Sang's illustrations introduce the possibility of a countermove from the verbal and the descriptive to the visual imagery of the dream-work. We encounter a reversal of the movement from visual to verbal involved in the talking cure. This reentry of the pathological in the form of an interruption of the movement from visual to verbal allows, moreover, for a questioning of coloniality. The illustrated text combines with the deployment of the cinematic technique of montage to set in motion a visual regime, a mode of seeing, that delinks Kubo from the assimilatory colonial modern, the spectacle of the colonial capital. The construction, as Kubo moves through urban colonial space, of an interiorized visuality, of interiorized images, effects not just an alienation but an interruption of the hailing, at once verbal and visual, of colonial subjects. Coloniality itself becomes the object of the text's gaze. The instability of montage, Kubo's gaze upon one thing only to image, or attempt to image, another, combines with self-reflexivity, the consciousness of form, to disrupt the Japanese imperium by putting on display its attempt to secure a univocal regime of meaning and visuality.

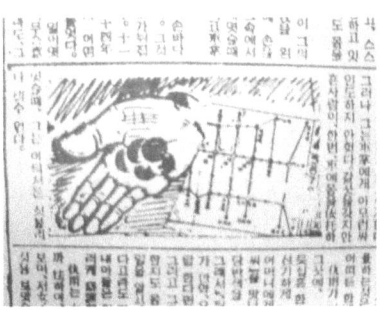

FIGURE 1.6 Yi Sang's illustration of the coins in *Kubo* (1934).

Consider, for example, a scene in Pak's text where Kubo looks at the reign years of five Taishō coins he holds in his hand while riding a streetcar. The reign years indicate the value of time in colonial Korea: a temporality equated with the exchange of commodities and a linear, forward-moving empire.[55] Kubo's gaze upon the register of imperial time, his attempt to produce meaning by adding the numbers up, ruptures the imperial narrative. It is no accident that Yi Sang chooses to illustrate this moment in the text. Here, the reintroduction of the visual (Yi Sang's illustration) supplements the modernist calling attention to form, revealing imperialism's own constructedness. The linearity of the reign dates on the Taishō coins become inscriptions that produce imperial form, not given expressions of a naturalized emperor system but a temporality that can be illustrated, imaged otherwise. It is the text's disjunctive verbal-visual relation that enables the rejection of an imperialized subjectivity, of an incorporation into colonial temporality, the time of money and the emperor.

Kubo's fixing of his eye on the coins, signs of value only insofar as they are in perpetual movement along the circuits of capitalist exchange while linked to temporality of the empire/emperor, overlaps with the stop in the visual act of reading, the pause that occurs as the eye moves from Pak T'aewŏn's words to Yi Sang's illustration and then back to the verbal text. This fixing of the eye and its subsequent remobilization back to the printed word refuses both the translation of the visual to the verbal and the verbal to the visual. Pak's and Yi's colonial illustrated text thus stands between the move toward the talking cure (the verbal) and the move back to rehystericization (the visual) as well as between the verbal-visual hailing (the call of the coins, at once image and inscription) of the capitalist imperial subject.[56]

FIGURE 1.7 Writing and Image: Yi Sang's illustration in *Kubo* (1934).

The illustrated text's experiment with stream of consciousness, one involving a dispersal of images and their coalescence, is less a turn to interiority and the psychological than a verbal-visual display that interrupts the movement from signifier (sound-image) to signified (concept). As in Saussure's *Course in General Linguistics*, itself an illustrated text with its famous diagrams and pictures of trees, illustrations take up the task of transforming the verbal invoking of the visual into the image itself. In both Saussure's *Course* and Pak's *Kubo*, the illustration produces an otherness, something that moves beyond words or the comfort of the signifier/signified dyad. In *Kubo*, we can consider this unspoken but illustrated site located at the interstices of signifier and signified an interrogating look at the space-time of empire, the potential mark of the censor, the modernizing of the colonial city (the staging of the fragmented colonial modern as panoramic).

The fragmentation of the modern involves, moreover, the dispersal of the body across handwritten manuscript and mechanized print. Yi Sang illustrates the act of writing itself in *Kubo* with his picture of a woman split into two, her head placed next to a hand holding a pen to manuscript paper. If this is an image of Kubo the Novelist imagining a woman, as he does throughout the text, the fragmentation of the woman's body accompanies the severing of the author's hand, associated with writing. The image thus offers a self-reflexive display at once of imaging while writing and of the handwritten manuscript (all literary texts were first written by hand in the colonial period) effaced by mass circulation of the text/print technology. That this traffic between verbal and visual, hand and technology is associated with bodily dispersal and the image of woman allows us to see how Yi Sang's illustration extends the pathological to the gendering of the visual-verbal relation. The illustration thus marks the "return of the visual" and speaking bodies as well as the dispersal of an author's authority to transform images to verbal descriptions.

Like the proletarian literature of the 1920s and 1930s and the imperial subjects literature (*kungmin munhak*) of the late 1930s and early 1940s, literary modernism addresses the modern as technological. The portrayal of the factory and the machine/body relation in numerous KAPF works shifts, in modernism, to a representation of sensory impressions and the accompanying thoughts/images that occur in tandem with the shock and fracturing of experience in the colonial, capitalist urban space. As we will see below, the late 1930s and early 1940s wartime culture of imperialization localizes Korean "home and soil" as timeless on two levels. It is what is to be moved beyond spatiality through the achievement of Co-Prosperity Sphere universalism. At the same time, it is what is to be kept as the locus of inevitable return. "Overcoming modernity" in late colonial Chosŏn bears this relation to what Ming-yan Lai points out is the flexibility of nativism to interrupt the national narrative by moving at once to the subnational and the supranational. Under wartime imperialization, timeless *hyangt'o* extends at once to the imagining of a pan-Asian communality and an immediacy that will dispense with capitalist exchange and commodification.[57] In the culture of imperialization, modernism and the *hyangt'o* traditionalism that accompanied it in the 1930s in writers such as Pak T'ae-wŏn find articulation in the form of a love of the machine as prosthetic (often a visual prosthetic) that enables and enhances *hyangt'o* affectivity. Imperial subjects literature, that is, shares with 1930s literary modernism a confrontation with capitalism, the shock of the city, and the technological.

Becoming Imperial Subject: Japan and Korea as One Body

The 1935 disbanding of KAPF was accompanied by the end of modernist experimentation and the first steps toward incorporation of the cultural sphere into what would become the regime of total mobilization (*ch'ongdongwŏn*) and imperialization (*hwangminhwa*). Mobilization culture can be thought of as a movement about movement or motion and thus represents less of a break than a rearticulation of many of the concerns shared by KAPF and modernist writers and artists—to name a few, the technological, sensation, interiority, self-reflexivity, and the fractures brought about by urban capitalist modernity.[58] The culture of mobilization that emerged in the late 1930s, moreover, would become central to the militarization of both postcolonial Koreas, particularly following the outbreak of the Korean War in 1950. As we will see in later chapters, the post-1945 transformation of mass colonial mobilization culture into individual acts of collaboration proceeds by simultaneously denouncing selected works of the late colonial period while eliding nearly all of them from the literary, artistic, and filmic canon. Such a transformation points to the close relation between colonial mobilization and Cold War developmentalism in South Korea. The two share an anticommunism, but, more than that, we will encounter a repetition of the form of empire in the name of nation.

Here, I look at the ways in which three films, An Sŏg-yŏng's 1940 *The Volunteer* (*Chiwŏnbyŏng*), Sŏ Kwang-je's 1938 *Military Train* (*Kunyongyŏlch'a*), and Yi Pyŏng-il's 1941 *Springtime on the Peninsula* (*Pando ŭi pom*) set in motion a multilayered subject, one that was at once local/Korean and imperialized/militarist, belonging to a broader, geospatial pan-Asia.[59] These films intersect in a number of ways, particularly in their invoking of *hyangt'o* nativism and in their representations of movement: the self-reflexive portrayal of the movement of cinema in *Springtime*; the negotiation of the body/technology relation by way of the scopic regime of camera and train in *Military Train*; and, in *The Volunteer*, the movement of soldiers' bodies in sync, mobilization. In *Springtime*, we encounter a form of hypericonicity. The film revolves around the making of a traditionalist film, *Ch'unhyang*, the act of filmmaking itself producing two sites, one modern, occupied by the filmmaker, and one traditional, the filmed *Ch'unhyang*, closely associated in the late 1930s with the status of colonial Korean culture as "lok'al k'alla" within the empire. We should recall that the "local" came to signal colonial Korea itself, which was increasingly referred to in the late 1930s not as Chosŏn but as "the peninsula" (*pando*). While *The Volunteer* does not offer a film within a film, it is composed of a montage of three spaces: local, rural space, the site of authenticity but also of a feudal pastness; Seoul, the path to the metropole and greater East Asia but also located with the colony and thus linked to the local; and an imagined horizon of Greater East Asia, the vanishing point toward which the film and the Volunteer move.

The trajectory of Japanese colonialism in Korea differed from its Euro-American counterparts in its emphasis on the incorporation of its Korean subjects and their economic development. The late-colonial-period assertion of *naisen ittai* (K.: *naesŏn ilch'e*; "Japan and Korea as One Body") and *nissen dōso* (K.: *ilsŏndongjo*, "Japan and Chosŏn Share a Common Ancestry") positioned Japan as a pan-Asian vanguard and demonstrated how the Japanese colonial project rejected, in a strict sense, a racialized colonizer/colonized bifurcation.[60] The formulation *naesŏn* signaled a leveling in the name of a common racial identification, linking colonizer and colonized to a shared developmentalist subjectivity vis-à-vis Western imperialism and capitalist modernity. The location, however, of Japan as "inside" (*nae*) reveals its ambivalent position as subject in relation to a colonial other (*sŏn*).⁶¹ *Sŏn* becomes a particularized, geographically marked supplement that enables a universalist inside (*nae*) even as the phrase equates *nae* and *sŏn* (as one body).

Naesŏn ilch'e works by a kind of proximity, an organicism that calls for the oneness of a body whose parts do not touch, kept separate like the characters on the space of a page or the side of a building, as we see in a key scene in *The Volunteer*, when the protagonist walks by the slogans—*naesŏn ilch'e* and *kungmin chŏngsin ch'ongdongwŏn* ("total spiritual mobilization of the people")—that summon him, verbally and visually, as Korean and imperial subject. The call to oneness by way of the *nae* in *naesŏnilch'e* or the *chŏngsin* (spirit) in *kungmin chŏngsin ch'ongdongwŏn* invokes a spiritual immediacy only to withdraw its possibility. *Nae* and *sŏn* are afforded a particular kind of intimacy located between universal inside/spirit and particularized locality, a spacing that allows for a movement, a becoming that will always involve proximity without coincidence. The separation and hierarchization of *nae* and *sŏn* rehearses the formation of the Korean imperial subject, at once local and pan-Asian imperial, attached to the one body and detached from the inside/spirit at the same time. It is in this spacing and the movement it allows between local and pan-Asian or *sŏn* and *nae* that we find the relation between mobilization (*tongwŏn*) and imperialization (*hwangminhwa*). The subject-to-become-imperialized is in perpetual motion. The slogans summon a subject-in-motion who can never truly be a *hwangmin* but who is always taking part in *hwangminhwa*, a becoming-*hwangmin* that moves toward what simultaneously approaches and recedes.

This spatiotemporal structure of *naesŏn ilch'e* allows us to see how the colonial state manages its subjects by way of what Giorgio Agamben, theorizing the state of exception, calls "a zone of indeterminacy in which the outside is nothing but the exclusion of an inside and the inside is in turn only the inclusion of an outside."⁶² *Nae* (the inside) includes and excludes *sŏn*. As Agamben points out in his discussion of the "anthropological machine," the exclusion, "which is also already a capturing," and the inclusion, "which is also already an exclusion," make up this zone of indeterminacy.⁶³ It is the invocation to mobilize, to become the subject-in-motion, that works to cover over the indeterminacy of the metropolitan/colonial relation. Early 1930s modernism and late 1930s and early 1940s wartime mobilization thus share the same relation of unity/disunity. In a manner resembling the aggregation of the "stream" to overcome the randomness of "free association," the indeterminacy of movement within a field delimited by *nae* and *sŏn* is replaced by the potentiality of becoming, *hwangminhwa*.

The perpetual movement toward that which offers and takes away is another name for the production of desire in the regime of imperialization/mobilization. If it is the profit motive and desire for the commodity of the capitalist modern that the culture of imperialization promises to "overcome" (and that enables the late colonial recantations of many proletarian writers and intellectuals), the very reproducibility of disciplined, militarized soldiers to be deployed throughout the empire mimes the homogeneous commodity form and its travel in expanding capitalist circuits of exchange. This rearticulating of a culture of consumption works in at least two ways. First, we have the exchange of the body standing in for the local/Korean and the emperor, the call for "the volunteer," the willing subject who, by offering himself up to die, declares both his exhaustibility and his serial reproducibility, as one disciplined soldier trained, to the greatest extent possible, to act and circulate as the equivalent of millions of other expendables.[64] Second, we encounter the verbal-visual consumption of slogans/propaganda, where the summoning of the slogan and that of the advertisement meet. The Volunteer, like Benjamin's flaneur or Pak's Kubo, walks the streets of the city and is hailed by advertising in the form of the verbal-visual slogan, which, here, calls upon the crowd of the urban modern to transform themselves into mobilized subjects.

The Subject as Cinematic: Visuality and the Kinetics of Imperialization

To remain inextricably attached to the local while moving beyond its borders is another way of naming the Korean colonial-imperial subject.[65] The Korean local is associated at once with *hyangt'o* nativism and the still, insofar as the latter, like the nativist image, stops time. The *hwangmin*, the subject both local/colonial and universal/imperial, is thus hybrid in a certain way, still and in motion, at once painting/photograph/poster and film. As Laura Mulvey points out in her reworking of Godard's definition of cinema as "death 24 times a second," the rapid repetition of stills that produces the illusion of motion in cinema conjures up life from death.⁶⁶ The verbal and visual hailing of the slogans above the Volunteer gives meaning to bodily movement, the steps of the Volunteer as he walks along. This bodily movement, in turn, brings words to life. It animates the slogans, a series of stills, by enacting precisely what is called for by one of the slogans on the building, *kungmin chŏngsin ch'ongdongwŏn* ("total spiritual mobilization of the people"). The slogan sequence in *The Volunteer* thus rehearses the defining characteristic of film, demonstrating the close relationship among motion picture, mobilization, life, and death. The summoning of subjects under the banner of "total mobilization," then, is a scopic bringing-to-life, a visual biopolitics of interpellation.

One imagines oneself as local while given the opportunity to partake in the universal by the act of volunteering. Here, we see the close relation between voluntarism and motion, will and movement. Volunteering becomes a visual act, a self-mobilizing that covers over the gap between stillness and motion, effecting the bringing to life of the subject who can picture himself in motion in the empire.⁶⁷ In *The Volunteer*, we watch the protagonist, the would-be volunteer, gaze at slogans. He moves through time but cannot truly become the embodiment of the slogans hung on banners over the wall of the building he passes by. The Government-General, at this point in the film, calls for total mobilization and the formation of Japan and Korea as one body but has yet to implement the Volunteer Army.⁶⁸ In this documentary-like mobilization film, the trajectory of the Volunteer becomes emblematic of cinematic narrative itself, which "gains credibility by weaving together a series of apparently obvious 'truths'—the truths of movement, instantaneity, heterosexuality, and visibility."⁶⁹ All four of these attributes inform late colonial mobilization films.

If truth is movement, it is also, as Nietzsche's oft-quoted phrase has it, "a mobile army of metaphors." At stake in the mobilization film is the identification of its spectatorship with the language of empire, slogans such as *naesŏn ilch'e* and *kungmin chŏngsin ch'ongdongwŏn*. The slogan made visible in the film shows us how the filmic suture, usually discussed as that between camera and spectator, informs the visual act of reading. To gaze upon the printed word and believe in it as truth is to join the movement of the reading eye with the printed word on a page. Here, reference can be thought of somewhat differently, not as an equation of signifier/signified with an "actual" object but as the suture of eye with print. The documentary, after all, recalls documentation/the document. This filmic genre invokes a spectatorship that *reads* the visual presentation of movement, instantaneity, heterosexuality, and visibility as referents. It is for this reason that the realization of the imperial promise occurs when the Volunteer, and the film's spectators, read the headlines printed in the newspaper announcing that the "volunteer system" will be put into effect. The newspaper, like the slogans on the walls, is presented on the screen as a document to be read as truth made manifest in the form of a visual image.

The Volunteer looks up at each of the slogans as he walks, but, of course, the point-of-view sequence involves, as is common in film, a series of cuts. The Volunteer glances up, next frame a slogan, a return to the Volunteer, then another slogan. It is the task of the spectator to connect the Volunteer's gaze to the slogan, to imagine both in the same frame. It is the visual act of covering over this gap, one that sutures the look of the Volunteer with that of a colonial Korean spectatorship, that produces the desire to imperialize. The desire to suture mobilizes, pulls movement inside by incorporating motion on the screen into the spectatorship. That desire and the act of seeing are linked to movement allows us to see how the negotiation among the three spaces in the film—rural, colonial cityscape, and imagined pan-Asia—does not end with the subsumption of the first two terms by the third. That is, the movement outward to a broader pan-Asian sphere that the Volunteer (and the film's spectatorship) can only imagine does not divest him of his association with the differing levels of rural and urban locality that make up the "peninsula." Instead, these images of the local remain as the visual marks of his perspective, the background from which he looks out, the site from which he sees into the vanishing point of Greater East Asia.[70] The visual summoning of the imperial subject in *The Volunteer* allows us to see the ways in which the technics of *hwangminhwa* is itself cine-matic, a setting into motion.

In the earlier *Military Train* (1938), such a setting in motion involves a suturing both with camera and with its scopic counterpart, weapon.[71] *Military Train* brings this figure together, the camera occasionally moving forward along with the train, itself a technology mobilized as a weapon moving north to support the war effort in China. The suture is among camera, train, and spectator. The spectator is mobilized and technologized, just as the train is anthropomorphized, made to see. The imperial subject is mobilized in a relation to the technological that neither subordinates anthropos to the machine nor figures the latter simply as prosthetic. Instead, the mobilized *hwangmin*, set in motion by the visual act of the suture, is neither human nor machine but both at the same time.[72]

Military Train enables us to see the close relation between the culture of mobilization and the ways in which, in its recording of movement, its indexicality, "Cinema comprises simultaneously the rationalization of time and an homage to contingency."[73] Like *The Volunteer* and *Springtime on the Peninsula*, *Military Train* offers multiple temporalities: the rationalized time of the train schedule and the machine and the affective, contingent temporality of love and attraction (the *kisaeng*-rescue love narrative in the film). In these films, a technointimacy brings the two temporalities together. The rational becomes immediate and intimate. It is, moreover, filmic montage, the temporal flow/connectedness and the disconnection/cut between scenes, that displays the rationalization/linearization of time and contingency simultaneously on the screen. As we have seen, this dual temporality informs literary texts such as Pak's *Kubo*, allowing Kubo to exist in two modalities: (1) in the streets encountering the contingent, moving mentally and physically through a montage of urban and mental spaces (with occasional overlaps), and (2) imaging his mother and home throughout the text, eventually coming back to home and mother in the end (the "safe return"). Both colonial Korean modernism and wartime mobilization films negotiate the shock of the modern by way of montage. In mobilization films, the becoming-*hwangmin* (*hwangminhwa*) attempts to counter the contingent with a linearity and continuity, a visual knitting together of time and space into the projected local/imperial subject of the future.

Mobilization, then, attempts to overcome contingency through its hyperrationalization of motion. We see this, for example, in the display of the synchronicity or mechanizing of bodily movements, the becoming one-form or uni-form. Still, the *hwangmin* in mobilization films is always threatened by its un-becoming, the overtaking of the rational by the contingent. In *Military Train*, this tension is brought to a point of no return when the conductor's friend-turned-spy for the Chinese cannot be brought back to the immediacy/intimacy of the homosocial and the machine. It is for this reason that he kills himself by throwing himself in front of the machine he has betrayed, the train. Couched in terms of redemption, his testament (displayed to the film's spectatorship in the final scene) demonstrates how the notion of sacrifice turns upon an erotics of absence, a move to the nonpresent and the unnamable. Death is where the rational meets the contingent; the two registers come together in a nonplace and nontime. The *hwangmin*, then, is a disarticulated subject, moving between *nae* and *sŏn*, in a further way. It is a subject that combines the rational and the contingent in one body.

The Imperial Close Up, or the Imperial as a Close-Up

In mobilization films, the chronotope—one that makes up the space and time of becoming *hwangmin*—takes the form of a simultaneous local/timelessness and pan-Asian future. This is a simultaneity of the small and the large. Martin Heidegger, Susan Stewart, and Mary Anne Doane have all discussed the ways in which the modern advent of "the world as picture" involves precisely this relation. Stewart asserts that preindustrial societies located the gigantic in nature, while industrial capitalism links the gigantic to an exchange economy and the commodity. As Doane points out, for Stewart, "The miniature can be held in the hand, possessed, and hence imparts an illusion of mastery, the imprimatur of the subject."[74] For Doane, it is the filmic close-up that reveals the ambivalence of this gigantic/miniature relation:

> As simultaneously microcosm and macrocosm, the miniature and the gigantic, the close-up acts as a nodal point linking the ideologies of intimacy and interiority to public space and the authority of the monumental. In the close-up, the cinema plays simultaneously with the desire for totalization and its impossibility. The cinematic spectator clings to the fragment of a partial reality—a fragment that mimics the effect of a self-sufficient totality.[75]

The close-up, in fact, must be thought of not only in terms of the fragment or partial reality presented as totality (in the form of the face, for example) but as the oscillation between small and large, large and small that occurs as the camera zooms in and out. To become *hwangmin* is at once to move beyond the local, become larger than oneself, and take up the space of the screen, as we see in the close-up shots of the Volunteer looking up at the slogans on the building. The movement of the camera rehearses the structure of mobilization/imperialization as an oscillation between the local and the pan-Asian. It is pan-Asia that replaces the gigantic of the exchange economy and commodity

VISUALITY AND THE COLONIAL MODERN   57

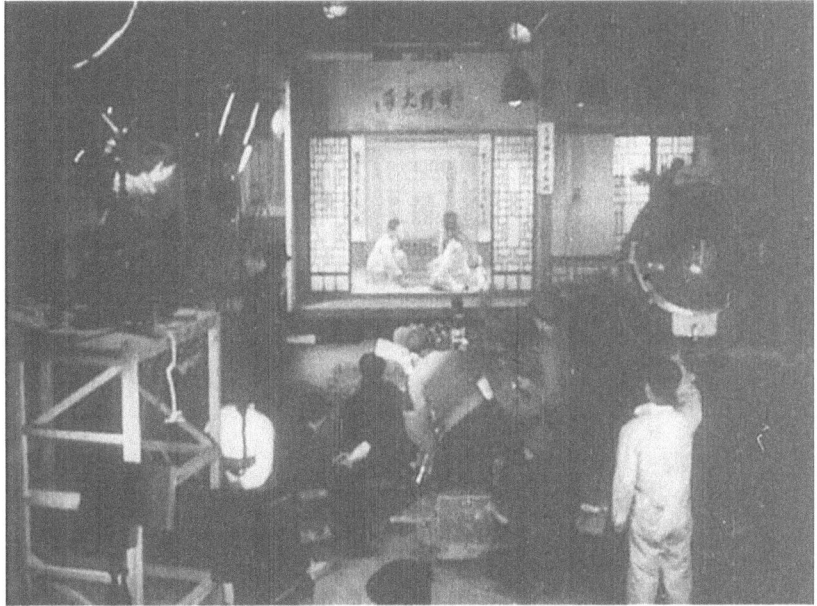

FIGURE 1.8 "O.K. Cut!" (*Springtime on the Peninsula*, 1941).

The local in *Springtime on the Peninsula* and *The Volunteer* (which contains several scenes portraying the everyday activities of women in a rural timespace) occurs as part of the 1930s constellation of nativist literary and artistic works. These works were themselves scenes within scenes, produced, framed, and put on display by the cultural institutions of the urban modern, the publishing industry, the movie theater, and the art gallery. *Springtime on the Peninsula* iterates this staging of a scene within a scene, linking camera movement to mobilization by way of its filming the making of a film, *Ch'unhyang*.

The film begins with *Ch'unhyang* as diegesis, only for the camera to move to a long shot, revealing that the film is hypericonic, a film about film.[76] *Ch'unhyang* moves, visually, from totality/gigantic to partiality/miniature, a movement that coincides with the filmic structure of diegesis within a diegesis and the positing of Chosŏn as local within a universalist Japan-led pan-Asia. The film thus organizes itself by way of a move back in time to the traditional/authentic (as miniature, the smaller diegesis, or the local) enabled by the technological present (the gigantic, the larger diegesis, or the empire). The latter, the time of empire and mobilization, bears a close relation with the ability to display temporal and spatial movement through filmmaking. It is for this reason that the film concludes with the filmmakers leaving on a train that will take them on the first leg of their journey to the metropole (*naeji*), where they will learn more advanced filmmaking techniques.

Late colonial mobilization films rehearse a summoning to imperialization that is accompanied by interruptions. In *The Volunteer*, even as a colonial spectatorship is called upon to perform the visual act of suturing the Volunteer with the slogans above him, his passing by disinterested people on the street offers the possibility of other forms of desire and belonging unrelated to the imperial project. In *Springtime on the Peninsula*, the mixed use of Japanese (tied to power and the public space) and Korean (linked to more intimate conversations and spaces) ends up producing an "inside" associated not with the *nae* of the metropole and the Japanese language but with the use of Korean. As Baek Moon Im points out, the enunciation of empathy with the imperializing trajectory by women at key moments in *The Volunteer* and other late colonial mobilization films such as *The Straits of Chosŏn* (dir., Pak Ki-ch'ae; 1943) is severed from their bodies. In *The Volunteer*, for example, the audience hears the Volunteer's mother tell him to "take care of himself" prior to the appearance of the mother gazing ambivalently toward the camera for a ten-second shot.[77] This disjunct between voice and women's bodies interrupts the sanctioning of the imperial summons and its promise of masculinization through militarization.[78] Such a disjunction is melancholic. But here the sense of loss represents an irruption that cannot be done away with by a jettisoning of the anxiety and uncertainty of life in the colony in favor of the universalism of the pan-Asian "oriental" (*tongyangin*).[79] Baek Moon Im demonstrates how a colonial melancholia remains in these films, one that gazes ambivalently toward the camera. A visual display of nonresponse reopens anxiety and interrupts the identification with pan-Asia by visually speaking of the possibility of some other desire.

Indeed, a sense of loss runs through these late-colonial-period films. Alan Tansman underscores the importance of a "pervasive melancholy" in Japanese aesthetic fascism: "In calling on its own traditions to form this aesthetic, Japan was no different from other nations, like Germany, filling fascist 'form' with native 'content.'"[80] The response to loss, in turn, becomes "a search for a new point of cultural origin, a place from which to create new myths as yet unencumbered by the weight of history."[81] Let us recall that Japanese aesthetic fascism is neither limited to the metropole proper nor to Japanese imaginings of a trajectory of conquest and colonization in Korea, Taiwan, and Manchuria. The call is for mobilization in the name of pan-Asia and the emperor in both metropole and colony. The circulation of late colonial Korean mobilization films in the metropole points to the ways in which the summoning of colonized imperials mediated the assimilation of metropolitan imperials.[82]

The metropolitan desire for beauty and authenticity is accompanied by the desire to assimilate the colonized as imperial, to gaze upon this summoning and its preferred response. Wartime mobilization calls for the production of a colonial desire to be imperial. Yet the fulfillment of this desire threatens the *nae/sŏn* relation. The metropolitan subject gazes upon this colonial desire with ambivalence. As Yi Yŏng-jae has shown in her analysis of the Government-General's sanctioning of Ch'oe In-gyu's *Homeless Angels* (*Chip ŭmnŭn chŏnsa*, 1941) and its subsequent censorship following its move to the metropole, the fact that colonials were seen as summoning themselves to the imperial cause in a bounded-off space threatened the role of the metropole as mediator of the summons.[83] This bounded-off space had come too close to mirroring the metropole itself. The colonized must bear the trace of the local while remaining desirous of becoming imperial. They must be on the move to a space that always approaches only to recede, the *nae*.

The multilayered discursive practices making up late colonial mobilization culture would play a crucial role in the historical trajectories of the post-1945 Koreas, appearing in different and shifting forms in the militarisms/developmentalisms that continue to face each other across the demilitarized zone. This has always been the case, even when the importance of the pre-1945 attempt to overcome the modern remained necessarily unacknowledged. In South Korea, the selective remembering and forgetting of imperialization/mobilization would inform both the formation of Cold War anticommunist subjects and the post-1945 history of opposition to the state.

The post-1945 attempt to "overcome coloniality" in what became South Korea turned upon the excision of *nae* from *naesŏn ilch'e*, or, more precisely, the collapse of *nae* into *sŏn* (located south of the DMZ). At the same time, a Korea/Japan opposition was put into place by figuring late colonial pan-Asian *hwangminhwa* discourse as collaborative act. Certainly, this excision also works on the linguistic register, the post-1945 repression of Japanese, but also by the maintaining in the 1950s of the *sŏyang/tongyang* (occident/orient) binary that had become central to the notion of the pan-Asian Greater East Asia Co-Prosperity Sphere. As we will see in later chapters, colonial-period nativism and the notion of *tongyang* played important roles in the formation of 1950s traditionalism in South Korea. Early South Korean statism relies upon a continuous slippage between *tongyang* and *Han'guk*, "oriental spirit" and "(South) Korean spirit." In the next chapter, we will examine the ways in which literary texts in the military-occupation period (1945–1948) negotiate this Cold War reordering of late colonial spatial imaginings.

The 1945–1948 U.S. and Soviet military-occupation period stands between the colonial and the postcolonial, offering the promise of movement to the latter while retaining many of the assumptions and hierarchies that made up the former. This is a period that witnessed the return of the proletarian subject and its subsequent erasure in the southern half of the peninsula. This return/erasure was accompanied by a reemergence of earlier proletarian-cultural nationalist debates. It was in the occupation period, then, that the first attempts were made to rework ways of seeing and writing associated with the different movements of the 1920s and 1930s discussed in this chapter. These colonial-period movements would take new form in the politics of visibility/invisibility that has structured the division of the Korean peninsula from 1945 into the present.

2

VISIBLE AND INVISIBLE STATES

Liberation, Occupation, Division

THE END OF Japanese rule in 1945 was immediately followed by U.S. and Soviet military occupations in the southern and northern halves of the Korean peninsula. The occupations set in motion the formation of rival polities that would soon enter into a state of war. Given the continuing division of the peninsula, it should come as no surprise that scholars find themselves returning to the period of occupation between the end of colonial rule and the inauguration of separate regimes in 1948 in an effort to sift through the welter of postcolonial possibilities opened up and denied. There is a way in which the contestations that make up the 1945–1948 period remain coeval with what follows, moving along in time with a post-1948 history of competing militarisms and mass mobilizations that continue into the present.

In English-language scholarship, the highlighting of this immediate postliberation period by historians is accompanied by a relative absence of work on cultural production. This has led to an elision of important shifts that took place with the sudden end of late colonial wartime mobilization and the move to the postcolonial Cold War order. For their part, prominent critics working in Korean such as Kim Yun-sik, Kwŏn Yŏng-min, and Shin Hyŏng-gi have detailed for us the complexity of the immediate postliberation scene: the trajectory of collaboration confessionals, the reemergence of proletarian writers soon opposed by the reassertion of literature as an autonomous sphere in the name of pure literature (*sunsu munhak*), and the rapid formation of rival literary organizations.[1] Much of this work was begun in 1988, the year of the lifting of the ban on the works of the "writers who went north" (*wŏlbuk chakka*). The year 1988 itself, then, marks an emancipation of sorts, a freedom given to texts censored for forty years.

The abrupt end of Japanese colonialism and the almost immediate deployment of the U.S. and Soviet military occupations meant that the very first attempts to represent colonial pasts and postcolonial futures were bound up with a continuing negotiation with "on the ground" foreign powers who, like the Japanese, assumed a legality of rule. The post-1945 cultural scene was centered in U.S.-occupied Seoul, and in this chapter I will pay particular attention to the ways in which the rapid formation of separate cultural fields was bound up with the United States Military Government in Korea (USAMGIK). Most of the prominent leftist writers who would leave Seoul for the North did not do so until 1947. The texts we will encounter help to open up a Cold War history marked by the emergence of the United States as a dominant power in East Asia. Insofar as many of these texts were written under formal U.S. rule, I locate them as part of an "American literature" that remains excised from its English-language canon—not forgotten, just ignored, and almost none of them translated.

I address a constellation of works in this chapter. My aim is to unpack the ways in which writers participated in the formation, under U.S. military occupation, of what would become separate cultural fields in the northern and southern halves of the peninsula. I do not assume a colonial/postcolonial historical break. Instead, I look at the ways in which writers grappled with the notions of "historical rupture," "coloniality," and "liberation." In this chapter, my focus is on verbal representations of the visual. My concern is less with USAMGIK policies and practices, which have been detailed elsewhere,[2] than to demonstrate how a constellation of texts (many of them overlooked in existing scholarship) engaged with USAMGIK implicitly or explicitly as they reworked ways of seeing enabled by the proletarian, nativist, modernist, and imperialization movements of the 1920s, 1930s, and early 1940s detailed in the previous chapter. These post-1945 texts drew on these earlier movements as they put into play a distribution of the visible and invisible that would frame the Cold War bifurcation of South and North through the rest of the twentieth century and into the present.

We can think of colonized space in a variety of ways: on one level, as simultaneously imperial sovereign (legally) while marked by private possession and the ethnonational claim (culturally/affectively); on another level, as global/local (KAPF proletarian internationalist) or, later, as Western versus Asian/local (wartime Pan-Asian). The early attempts to articulate a new postcolonial present and future entailed a "return" to the past and the colonial-period literary debates shut down by the Government-General in the mid-1930s. The writers working in the immediate post-1945 literary scene had all been active in the colonial period, and many of them had played major roles in the earlier debates among the proletarian, cultural nationalist, and modernist groups during the 1920s and 1930s. The attempt to negotiate a break from the colonial past could not occur without an engagement with the representations of space that informed earlier colonial-period debates and movements.

The years 1945 through 1948 comprised a postwar period. "Liberation," as we see time and again in 1945–1948 newspapers, journals, and literary works, was celebrated as a demobilization. In Yi Sŏn-hŭi's "Window" ("Ch'ang," 1946), for example, the end of the Greater East Asian and Pacific Wars means the end of conscription, something that "is more important to the villagers than independence."[3] At the same time, as we will see below, literary texts performing the historical break had to do so in relation to a consideration of a number of continuities, including the denial of sovereignty in the U.S. proposal to the Soviet Union that Korea be divided and occupied. In fact, a number of immediate post-1945 literary texts portray less of a "break" from the multilayered spatiality of the colonial period than its rearticulation, one that takes the form of a "neither this nor that"—often as a nonevent.

The figuring of liberation also becomes an occasion for the staking out of positions in the cultural field, one that we should link to the new notions of a North and a South.[4] The emergence of a "divided" literature or, more precisely, a literature that produces division must be understood in relation to these two intersecting spatialities, that of the cultural field (both in terms of contemporary cultural production and in terms of canon selection/excision, the former bearing close relation, in its position taking, to the latter) and the territorialization of geospace as sovereign. The construction of *Han'guk munhak* or "South Korean literature" involves a cultural and legal positioning as well the deployment of a visual regime. The selection of the historical canon would turn upon the excision of legally banned works (KAPF works and those of writers gone to the North) and the reality of contemporary censorship (that of the U.S. military occupation and, after 1948, the National Security Law). As we will see, literary works written under USAMGIK were already producing the invisibility of the new geospace, that is, North Korea. The literary works of the 1945–1948 period narrate this process, while the forty-year period stretching from 1948 to 1988 (when the ban on North Korean writers and KAPF was lifted) negotiates this excision in the form of a relation to a cultural field and space that cannot be named or seen.

In this way, 1945–1948 texts make up a literature of the event (liberation) and its appropriation by competing postcolonial states formed under the U.S. and Soviet occupations (and thus always linked to a broader first-world/second-world division). In both South and North, the postcolonial process of ordering colonial literary history—one that includes the visual excision of Japanese-language texts by Korean writers—overlaps with the erasure of contemporary cultural production in the newly othered spatial counterpart on the other side of the thirty-eighth parallel. The process of canonization that makes up *Han'guk munhak* must be understood in relation to this temporal, spatial, and visual ordering. As we will see in the following chapters, this process, one that occasions a reworking of time and space from Japanese colonialism/imperialism/pan-Asianism toward a U.S./Soviet Cold War bifurcation, is never quite complete. Instead, the cultural field organizes itself around the contestations that make up the shifting, unstable borders that often take the name of "national division." The latter is largely an effect of the post-1945 "break" calling for the dispensing of pan-Asianism in favor of the Cold War socialist bloc versus free-world liberalism.

Below, I trace the early trajectories of two postcolonial modernities, each increasingly associated with opposing sovereign spaces (the spatialization of competing modernities/ideologies that constitutes the Cold War). First, I look at the ways in which the return to the colonial-period proletarian art and literature movement was accompanied by the representation of "liberation" as a moment in a dialectical progression of an unfolding revolutionary history. The proletarian subject of such a history would usher in a modernity denied in the first half of the twentieth century by taking control of the means of production while dismantling the network of feudal family and social relationships associated with ascriptive status and maintained by colonial rule. The post-1945 proletarian writers I discuss in this chapter, such as Chi Ha-ryŏn, Pak Ch'an-mo, and Yi Sŏn-hŭi, all allowed for the emergence, in time, of such a class-based subject of history. However, it was the prominent former modernist Yi T'ae-jun, a member of the 1930s Group of Nine, who played a more central role in the formation of what would become North Korean literature. Yi turned to the left in 1945 and proceeded to rework an earlier inflection of colonial nativism into what I call below an aesthetic socialism. Yi was purged in the early 1950s, but his grafting of a nativist aesthetics onto the proletarian narrative brought space and time together in a way that allowed for the association of territorial sovereignty and autonomy with revolutionary history in North Korea. The internationalism of KAPF would now be jettisoned. It was Yi T'ae-jun, more than any other writer, who allowed for the imaging of an authentic national culture (the local/aesthetic) located in a space, North Korea, and in relation to time—a future represented by the socialist model he discovered in the Soviet Union.

The other trajectory points to the formation of South Korea and South Korean literature in texts that figure "liberation" as allowing, variously, for the recovery of the autonomy of art, the shoring up of a public/private relation (one involving notions of home and masculinity/domesticity), and the location of moral legitimacy in national capital and a developmental subject. Younger writers such as Kim Tong-ni and Hwang Sun-wŏn, both discussed below, are often considered central to the formation of South Korean literature. It was, however, a writer belonging to an older generation, Yŏm Sang-sŏp, who did the most to draw what would become South Korean literature's unstable, shifting borders. Known for charting a middle course in the 1920s and 1930s that was at once cultural nationalist and "sympathetic" to the left, Yŏm would now render the North invisible even as he grappled with the relation of the coloniality of the past to the new forms/effects of power brought to bear by USAMGIK. Yŏm's work allows us to see how the articulation of a postcolonial South Korean subject emerges in relation to the effacing of the left/North Korea and to a post-1945 Cold War developmentalism and the attendant hierarchies that would be deployed and contested in the U.S.-led "free world" East Asia for years to come.

"Liberation Space" and the Return of the Proletarian Subject in History

The 1945–1948 period brought back together in one space and time the movements traced in the introduction and chapter 1. The simultaneity of their reappearance and the possibilities they seemed to offer contributed to a later naming of this period by scholars in South Korea as a "liberation space" (*haebang konggan*). The use of this term began in the early 1980s as, more than anything else, an effort to question the state-sponsored narrative privileging the date of Japanese surrender, August 15, 1945, as emancipatory in and of itself. Instead, the term *haebang konggan* signals the formation of the division system—the rapid incorporation of the peninsula into the Cold War world order by way of the twin occupations, Soviet in the North and American in the South. In short, *haebang konggan* refers to an ongoing contestation over the meaning of "liberation." Thus we should locate the cultural production of the 1945–1948 period in the context of the forty-year regime of censorship that followed. As we have noted, it was only in 1988 that the ban on KAPF texts and colonial-period works by "writers gone to the North," or *wŏlbuk chakka*, was lifted.

The rapid formation of rival literary organizations by the left and right set the stage for the debates of the *haebang konggan*. During this period, the Korean literary field became divided, broadly, into two camps: "pure literature" and proletarian literature.[5] It was the left that first organized following the Japanese surrender. The Headquarters for the Construction of Chosŏn Literature (*Chosŏn munhak kŏnsŏl ponbu*) was formed on August 16, 1945, under the leadership of Im Hwa. The Chosŏn Proletarian Literature Alliance (*Chosŏn p'ŭroret'aria munhak tongmaeng*) was created on September 17, 1945, by Yi Ki-yŏng and others who were dissatisfied with what they considered the overly inclusive platform of the HCCL. The HCCL and the CPLA consolidated as the Chosŏn Literature Alliance (*Chosŏn munhak tongmaeng*) on December 13, 1945. The fact that the leadership of the HCCL controlled this new organization led many writers associated with the CPLA, including Yi Ki-yŏng, to make an early departure to the North. The name of the CLA was changed to the Chosŏn Writers' Alliance (*Chosŏn munhakka tongmaeng*) at the National Writers' Conference (*Chŏnguk munhakcha taehoe*) held on February 8–9, 1946. The CWA was subsumed by the Chosŏn Federation of Cultural Organizations (*Chosŏn munhwa tanch'e ch'ong yŏnmaeng*) on February 24, 1946.

Many of those on the right were hesitant or unable to participate actively in the literary scene because they had engaged in what were now considered "pro-Japanese" (*ch'inil*) activities during the colonial period. The Central Cultural Association (*Chung'ang munhwa hyŏphoe*) formed on September 18, 1945, but its activities were limited. The All Chosŏn Writers' Association

(*Chŏn Chosŏn munp'ilga hyŏphoe*) formed on March 13, 1946, in response to the organizing activities of the left in the previous month. The formation of the Writers' Youth Association (*Chŏngnyŏn munhakka hyŏphoe*) on April 4, 1946, represented the emergence of younger writers on the right, most notably Kim Tong-ni, Cho Yŏn-hyŏn, and Cho Chi-hun. It was these writers, Kim in particular, who engaged in debates with the left. Formed on February 12, 1947, the National Association of Cultural Organizations (*Chŏnguk munhwa tanch'e ch'ong yŏnhap*) unified the various rightist cultural associations.[6]

Importantly, the critique marking the term *haebang konggan* in the 1980s was itself central to the censored works of proletarian writers in the immediate postliberation period, who were quick to question the assertion of liberation, pointing instead to the suppression of the left under U.S. military rule, the refashioning of collaborators into anticommunists, and the formation of a rightist satellite state in the South. At the same time, the reemergence of former KAPF members and other writers newly sympathetic to the left—such as the former modernists Yi T'ae-jun and Pak T'ae-wŏn—was itself accompanied by the need to address late-colonial-period recantations.

Let us recall the history of shifting identifications that occurred in the mid-1930s. As noted in chapter 1, KAPF texts often turn upon a transformative narrative, the coming to consciousness by workers and farmers of their class position, the transformation of petty bourgeois intellectuals into leftists, and the move away from nation to class. Subsequent declarations of leftist recantation—portrayed, for example, in Kim Nam-ch'ŏn's "Management" (1940) and "Barley" (1941)—take the form of the confessional, an attempt to link authenticity to the inner truth of the expressive self. Occupation-period collaboration narratives such as Ch'ae Man-sik's "The National Sinner" (1948), a text discussed in chapter 5, likewise turn to the confessional, here a move inward to sift through emotions and memories in order to locate an authentic national subject.

For many proletarian writers, August 15, 1945, set in motion the reworking of earlier coming-to-consciousness KAPF narratives, a reworking that must grapple with the recantations of the mid- and late 1930s. What ensues is a series of what we might call counter-recantations. It is no accident, for example, that in Chi Ha-ryŏn's widely acclaimed "Journey" ("Tojŏng," 1946) the protagonist Sŏk-chae experiences August 15 as nonevent: the fellow Koreans he finds himself with in a train station at the moment of Japan's surrender are silent, passive, and described as "stupid."[7] "Journey" takes the surrender announced on the radio not as an end but as a point of departure. What must now occur is a movement—by way of introspection, self-critique, confession—toward becoming a properly liberated subject prepared to participate in the making of history. It is only at the close of the text when Sŏk-chae joins the Party and enters his class position on the Party register as "petty bourgeois" (the subtitle of Chi's work) that he feels a sense of emancipation. It is this transformation, one that serves as a counter-recantation, that produces the meaning of August 15 as prelude to the formation of a socialist state and secures a position for intellectuals within the Party.

Chi's work points to a question central to the immediate postliberation scene: how to locate August 15, the date marking the formal end of Japanese colonial rule, as history? The first sustained answer to this question appeared in Kim Nam-ch'ŏn's *August 15, 1945*, a text later censored and appearing in book form in South Korea for the first time only in 2007, nineteen years after the lifting of the ban on writers who went to the North. Illustrated by the 1930s nativist painter Yi In-sŏng, Kim's work follows the awakening/transformation narrative we find in many colonial proletarian texts. The text describes the struggle of the young, educated elite to understand the bodily plight of the worker and participate meaningfully as activists in the proletarian movement. In *August 15, 1945*, this movement is mediated—as it would be in one of the most important novels from this period, Yŏm Sang-sŏp's *Dawn Wind* (1948)—via love triangles: Mun-gyŏng is in love with Chi-wŏn, a young man imprisoned in the last years of the colonial period for writing a leaflet rejecting the mobilization of students in the name of the "volunteer system." Chi-wŏn may have interests in another woman, and Mun-gyŏng's brother, Mu-gyŏng, is having an affair with the mother of the boy he is tutoring. As the text unfolds, Mun-gyŏng and Mu-gyŏng find themselves increasingly at odds with each other. Mun-gyŏng becomes sympathetic to the immediate postliberation struggle of the working class and the communist Pak Hŏn-yŏng. For his part, Mu-gyŏng associates himself with comprador capitalists, former collaborators who now curry favor with USAMGIK in an attempt to take over the factories formerly owned and run by the Japanese.

In *August 15, 1945*, the first full-length novel serialized under USAMGIK, we thus encounter a history of collaboration and anticolonial struggle that extends itself into the post-1945 occupation. This is a history that calls for generational change. Mu-gyŏng's and Mun-gyŏng's father left them and

Korea during the colonial period to participate in the independence movement overseas; he is a hero, but he never returns in the text, and his ideological position is unclear. It is up to the postcolonial youth of Korea to transform themselves. Mun-gyŏng's coming to awareness of social reality takes place in two stages: first by reading and second by active participation. The transformation occurs, as in many other proletarian texts, via the attempt to reconcile writing/reading with action/material struggle. *August 15, 1945* itself takes the form of a manifesto, an attempt to materialize/make manifest the revolutionary subjects that emerge on its pages. In Kim's work, the date August 15, 1945, signals the end of a war and the beginning of a revolutionary struggle, not a liberation.

Like *August 15, 1945* (and two texts I will discuss below, Ch'ae' Man-sik's "Once Upon a Rice Paddy" and Yŏm Sang-sŏp's "Western Cookie Box"), Yi Sŏn-hŭi's "Window" addresses the issue of the post-1945 redistribution of property, in this case land reform in the North. "Window," as the title implies, concerns itself with the politics of the visual. Set in the North, this text, in fact, narrates the vanishing of the South. A primal scene in "Window" takes place when Sa-yŏn, the farmer protagonist, discovers his wife in the landlord Haksa's home. This moment involves two looks: (1) Sa-yŏn's gaze upon this scene and (2) that of Haksa taking a photograph of Sa-yŏn's wife. "Window" revolves around the critique and dismissal of the latter gaze, which becomes associated with the South.

Haksa's possession of land is combined with his separation from it as a "modern," college-educated elite, and this possession/separation is linked to a way of seeing, a mode of representation that organizes space. To Haksa, Sa-yŏn's wife, who is incapable of following his instructions for assuming a proper pose, is at once beautiful and wild/primitive (*yasaeng*). Sa-yŏn's wife's desire for the modern, educated Haksa, the image of Haksa as a modern gentleman, is matched by the text's portrayal of his desire to picture her. Haksa's imagining of the beautiful/wild feminine rural signals a continuation of colonial-period nativist art and literature. The text turns that theme on its head. Haksa's aestheticizing/feminizing of the rural space is itself transformed into object of observation. But the central concern of "Window" is the relation between laboring body and the land.

We have two poles in the text: Haksa as landlord and Sa-yŏn as farmer, grounded in the land. Mediating between them is Teacher Kim, Sa-yŏn's brother, sympathetic to the left, coming from the sharecropper class, and self-educated. After starting a cottage-industry reed-mat business, he has become a small landowner. Teacher Kim is not a comprador, has the proper class background, and is a leftist, and therefore he has nothing to fear from the emerging North Korean regime. He had been, in fact, a teacher who worked in a private academy that refused to adopt the Government-General's curriculum and was thus shut down several times. But with the realization that the new order truly has begun, he finds himself unable to overcome his fear of losing the land he worked so hard to purchase.

"Window" is sympathetic in its portrayal of this sympathizer, Teacher Kim. But his immersion in the leftist texts he has been reading during the colonial period cannot bring him back to the land as a laborer. He has become a discursive Marxist and real-life small landowner. Teacher Kim cannot make the transformation called for by land reform and the new order. The result is death: his suicide. For his part, Haksa disappears one day, leaving, the text guesses, for Seoul and the South. The former photographer/observer now marks an invisibility. The nativist aesthetic to be jettisoned is linked to a space (the South) that cannot enter this text and will no longer be seen.

It is Sa-yŏn who stands as the subject of the new order, reuniting knowledge and labor. At the text's close, Sa-yŏn, still filled with a sense of the efforts his older brother had made to resist colonial rule, walks past the old schoolhouse and sees a light glimmering through the window: "All else dark enough to make ghosts cry out in fear."[8] He peers intently into the schoolhouse through the window, thinking that perhaps it was the ghost of Teacher Kim who lit the light. But then he is overcome by a sense of calm, and he retraces his steps: "He felt that our future will be as bright as that light in the window, one lit by an unknown hand."[9] We move from the liminality of haunting and the ghost to an optics of presence linked both to temporality in the form of a becoming-in-the-future and to a visual order, light, which will connect body to looking. Here, space and the image are not rejected for time in a manner considered typical in proletarian texts. The text invokes a visuality that does not stand outside the object as gaze but emanates from it, is "in touch with it." The aestheticizing of rural space (Haksa and his camera) is contested in a way similar to Oksoe's awakening in Yi T'ae-jun's "Farmland" ("Nongt'o," 1948). The text rehearses an awakening first to the beauty of the countryside (the aesthetic moment) and then to a move beyond, to a coming to awareness of social and labor relations that make up the rural order.

Recall our discussion in chapter 1 of the ways in which immediacy, the transparency dimension in proletarian literature, proceeds by way of an optics that sees through words to images. Yi Sŏn-hŭi's text shows us, further, how the emancipatory gesture, linked by Laclau to the "elimination of power, the abolition of the subject/object distinction,"[10] becomes at key moments a question of light and emanation: in "Window," visuality, in the form of light, pulls space into a temporal order. This is a space now associated with the North and a temporality that signals the beginning of a proper modernity and history.

Labor for Art's Sake: Yi T'ae-jun's Aesthetic Socialism

As we have seen in Yi Sŏn-hŭi's "Window," the proletarian narrative increasingly located itself north of the thirty-eighth parallel. We also encounter this spatialization in other texts set in the North, such as Pak Ch'an-mo's "Village of Dreams" ("Kkum kkunŭn maŭl," 1947). "Village of Dreams" moves away from explicit concern with the position of the leftist intellectual, tracing instead the post-1945 coming to consciousness of the uneducated Pa-u, the keeper of his clan's ancestral shrine (*sadang*) in a village outside Wŏnsan.[11] Here the ancestral shrine stands as the organizing center of a feudal space (the village), itself juxtaposed to Wŏnsan, the site of colonial capitalism. The task of extracting Pa-u from the feudal and colonial relations marking these spaces is accomplished by way of his gradual understanding of his rich relatives' former alignment with the Japanese colonial state. He comes to see how blood ties, the naturalizing of social relations in the village, have worked to obscure exploitative class relations throughout the colonial period. The shift from the blood-based, familial identity of the village to an internationalist class consciousness reveals itself at the close of the text, when the narrator announces the "unfolding of a new history in Wŏnsan"—a movement forward in time brought about by the dramatic appearance of Soviet ships in Wŏnsan harbor.

Pak's work addresses what has become one of the central concerns of North Korean literature for the past sixty years, the imagining of the North as a geospace in relation both to the South and to the socialist world of which it is a part. Two early postliberation works by the former modernist

Yi T'ae-jun, *Travels in the Soviet Union* (*Soryŏn kihaeng*, 1947) and "Dust" ("Mŏnji," 1950)—the latter written two years after the formation of North Korea but set during the 1945–1948 period—set the stage in many ways for the approach that many North Korean literary texts would take in figuring the relation between the narrative of nation/sovereignty and global socialism.[12]

As was the case with writers such as Pak T'ae-wŏn and An Hoe-nam, it was only during the occupation period that Yi T'ae-jun moved to the left. We can, in fact, read *Travels in the Soviet Union* and "Dust"—like An Hoe-nam's "Fire" (1947) and "History of the Storm" (1948)—as confessionals addressing Yi T'ae-jun's dismissal of KAPF in the 1930s. At the same time, Yi's texts differ from those of other post-1945 proletarian writers in the anxious glance they cast toward the possibility of assimilation. Yi demonstrates an abiding concern with the preservation of ethnonational identity as he works to locate the northern half of the peninsula in the Soviet-led socialist world (in *Travels in the Soviet Union*) while rejecting what he considers the coloniality of the U.S. military occupation in the southern half of the peninsula (in "Dust").

The confessional and the travelogue resemble each other insofar as both seek to produce an authenticity linked to a gaze—the former gaze on an interior and the latter upon an exterior. Like Yŏm Sang-sŏp's "Thirty-Eighth Parallel," "Parting and Meeting," and its sequel, "Reunion," three texts we will discuss below, *Travels in the Soviet Union* and "Dust" are in the form of travelogues.[13] In their early post-1945 works, both Yi and Yŏm set themselves to the task of mapping the relation of subject as observer to a newly forming division, the two Koreas emerging on either side of the thirty-eighth parallel.[14]

Travels in the Soviet Union, it turns out, links a temporality (past, present, future) to space: China ("spiritual past"), Korea (present), and the Soviet Union (vanguard pointing to a proper socialist future). Above we noted how "Village of Dreams" carefully dismantles the feudal familial relations it finds in the colonial period but does not seek to replace them with any form of blood-based or ethnoculturalist affiliation. *Travels in the Soviet Union* offers a different form of internationalism than both "Village of Dreams" and earlier colonial-period proletarian texts. Yi T'ae-jun's celebration of the Soviet Union occurs precisely because of the Soviet Union's allowing of multilayered identities. Such a move resembles the pan-Asian multiculturalism of the late 1930s and early 1940s, which allowed for the emergence of the simultaneously local/imperial subject. The post-1945 "return" to proletarian writing could not simply erase the ten-year cultural history that preceded it. Instead, as we see in Yi T'ae-jun's work, the multiculturalism of wartime mobilization and its call for an identity at once local and imperial mediates the formation of the new proletarian subject of history on the Korean peninsula. The new proletarian subject reworks the local/imperial relation by reintroducing the economic register while retaining a dual affiliation. This new subject is at once ethnonational (local and spatial) and class based (global and temporal).

What the traveler-observer Yi T'ae-jun, a 1930s modernist turned proletarian, locates in his trip to the Soviet Union is a socialist multiculturalism, a separation of the economic (linked to progress/change) from the transhistorical ethnocultural. For this reason, the text rests upon the parallel description of socialist policies implemented in different regions, the ways in which these policies will produce an economic and political assimilation approaching the normative socialism existing in Russia. At the same time, it makes allowance for ethnocultural difference. *Travels in the Soviet Union* produces a temporal relation to Moscow as socialist future while invoking an essentialized national and cultural sovereignty in the space south of the Yalu and north of the thirty-eighth parallel.

Yi T'ae-jun, in fact, emerged on the cultural scene in the context of the extended debate (1927–1930) on proletarian art among the sculptor and critic Kim Pok-chin (a central, founding figure of KAPF and the older brother of Kim Ki-jin), the artist and critic Kim Yŏng-jun, and Im-Hwa. The debate, which revolved around the issue of how to contest "art for art's sake" with an "art for the people's sake" movement, would end with Kim Yŏng-jun's move to a *hyangt'o* traditionalism in the 1930s, a decade in which he published a number of influential studies on premodern art history. After 1945, Kim would return to his earlier proletarian leanings and become one of the leading scholars of art history in North Korea. Im Hwa, who would be purged and executed in North Korea in the 1950s, maintained a position in this debate similar to the one he held in his literary criticism: literature and art were to politicize the masses by emphasizing a goal-oriented content (*mokchŏk ron*) meant to transform consciousness. For his part, Kim Yŏng-jun attempted to link anarchism to the expressionist emphasis on the eyes and senses; for Kim, this anarchist-expressionism offered the true form of proletarian art.[15] In Im Hwa's view, however, Kim's anarchism-expressionism was little more than a version of the art-for-art's-sake retreat to subjectivity/creativity separated from social reality: if art was aimed at the eyes, its goal was to enable the masses to broaden their vision, incite their emotions, and catalyze revolutionary struggle.[16]

Yi T'ae-jun's post-1945 turn to the left rearticulates the colonial-period discourse on art and visuality that informed his works in the 1930s. Much of his colonial-period work turns upon verbal descriptions of a particular kind of visual experience: an attempt to arrest temporal flow associated with the words that make up narrative by invoking an image or scene that will manifest itself as timeless, transcending the language that conjures it up in the first place. To the extent that Yi attempts to confer agency upon an aesthetic sensibility in the fashioning of a proletarian subject, he follows the earlier position taken by Kim Yŏng-jun. What links Yi's earlier aesthetics of the 1930s to his post-1945 turn to the left is a continuing aversion to the commodification of objects. Baudrillard notes that "Marx shattered the fiction of *homo economicus*, the myth which sums up the whole process of the naturalization of the system of exchange value, the market, and surplus value and its forms. But he did so in the name of labor power in action, of man's own power to give rise to value (*pro-ducere*)."[17] For Yi T'ae-jun, it is socialism that allows for the product to be separated out from profit, but this does not rest upon the consideration of labor power as giving rise to value. Instead, this separation decommodifies the product into a work of art. In *Travels in the Soviet Union*, production occurs for art's sake: "I truly enjoyed getting the chance to see the production process at the Soviet tractor factory today. I was deeply impressed. A factory does not have to be a dark, sad place where poverty-stricken people are forced to sell their hard, back-breaking labor. Instead, it can be a cooperative 'atelier' bringing together the creative capacities of free people."[18] Labor and the body, for all intents and purposes, place themselves on display as they create objects to be used and seen in and of themselves, extricated from circuits of exchange. In this text, Yi offers an aesthetic socialism: all laborers are artists. The production process becomes a creative act giving rise to a use value that is at once an aesthetic value.[19]

The notion of "liberation" (*haebang*), in the so-called liberation space, turns in many ways on the representation of the commodity form. In "Dust," Yi T'ae-jun makes use of the figure of Han-moe, a collector of Chosŏn-dynasty books, to negotiate the relation between the investment of national authenticity in objects, a central concern of colonial nativism and Yi's colonial-period writings, and the production of a leftist subject. While Han-moe's fetish for these books served as a refuge under Japanese colonialism, the text considers the occupation period as calling for a new kind of subject. Such a subject can emerge only by investing new forms of meaning into objects.

For Han-moe, during the colonial period, possession of the books as objects allowed the nation to manifest itself through the transformation of the discursive register (the Chosŏn dynasty texts as writing) into the material (texts to be observed, held, owned, fetishized). What "Dust" must accomplish is the task of producing allegiance to the left by reworking the notion of "tradition." It does this not by jettisoning traditionalism but by indigenizing communism. The transformation of the apolitical collector Han-moe to leftist occurs after his friend, Mr. Sŏng, suggests that the famous Chosŏn-dynasty intellectual Pak Chi-wŏn himself would have been a communist had such a system of thought existed at the time.[20] Han-moe's overriding desire for Pak Chi-wŏn's text no longer rests upon "tradition" standing alone in its own authenticity. Instead, desire is lifted to the register of "becoming." The collectible assumes a new form of materiality, retaining its aura while entering the dialectic. It is in this way that dialectical materialism is ethnonationalized. The move to the left in the occupation period is naturalized and legitimized as a logical extension of the thought of Chosŏn-dynasty forbears embodied in unique, irreplaceable material objects. Yi's text, then, also signals a rethinking of his own earlier relation to objects. If in Yi's colonial-period works the gaze upon the object produced a nostalgia and longing for the past, the object can now be associated with a movement forward in time.[21]

This reworking of tradition—the production of an auratic, indigenized leftism or socialist aesthetic—occurs in the visual realm. It is both the imagined gaze of Chosŏn-dynasty forbears and the stares of workers and students in the street that effects Han-moe's transformation. It is, moreover, this turn to the visual that places the ability to shift identifications away from a reworking of the body as labor power. The text, of course, explicitly locates truth in the gaze, believing in seeing: "Han-moe believed in North Korea's political agenda. But he didn't trust the description of the situation in South Korea that he read in North Korean newspapers. Why? Because he hadn't seen it with his own eyes."[22] Indeed, it is Han-moe's postliberation journey to the South that enables the text to portray the spectacle of occupied Seoul, the defilement of nationalized sites such as Kyŏngbok Palace and Tŏksu Palace by the U.S. military occupation.

"Dust" understands the U.S. military occupation as neocolonial. Following his new recognition of U.S. power at an auction of Chosŏn-dynasty collectibles, Han-moe considers that "The Japanese bastards annexed us and ate us up; these bastards eat us up in a clever way, even as they tell us they're here to give us aid."[23] The outbidding of Han-moe by U.S. officials at this auction, the scene of the loss of the object, points to the potential loss of ethnonational aura.[24] Here, there is no developmentalist transformation of exchange value into nationalist use value, a gesture, as we will see below, that informs both Yŏm Sang-sŏp's occupation-period works and later South Korean developmentalism. Possession of Chosŏn-dynasty books by U.S. occupation officials places socialism and the national aesthetic under siege. In the end, it is the association of the South with the dollar and an assimilationist global capitalism that marks its lack of sovereignty.

We can think of Yi T'ae-jun's aesthetic socialism both as an attempt to reconcile his 1930s nativism with proletarian literary production and as part of a broader effort to mediate the leftist/art-for-art's-sake literary debates of the 1920s and early 1930s that writers and intellectuals were revisiting in the 1945–1948 period. South Korean anticommunism of the late 1940s and 1950s, of course, would demonize the North, decry "Soviet imperialism," and, importantly, delegitimize communism as disallowing the creative potential of the individual. We see such a figuring of communism as "foreign ideology" in Hwang Sun-wŏn's canonical *Descendants of Cain* (*K'ain ŭi huye*, 1954), a text narrating the 1945–1948 history of division by privileging the artistic over the repetition, imitation, and formulaism of the communism its protagonist leaves behind in the North. It was, in fact, this opposition that also plays a central role in one of the more well-known repudiations of the Soviet Union, Andre Gide's *Back from the U.S.S.R.*, a text Yi T'ae-jun refers to in *Travels in the Soviet Union*.

We should note that a summary of Gide's work appeared during the Korean War in the inaugural issue of the South Korean intellectual journal *Sasang* (the precursor to the most prominent journal of the 1950s, *Sasanggye*, or *World of Thought*) and that Gide's text informs one of the most well-known attempts to mediate the location of the Korean peninsula in the Cold War world order, Ch'oe In-hun's *The Square* (1960), a text we will return to in chapter 5. One need only recall the high hopes that Yi Myŏng-jun, the protagonist of *The Square*, holds for life in North Korea after he has rejected the corruption and state violence of the South in the late 1940s, his subsequent disillusionment, his rejection of the formulaism of party dictates, and his consideration of the truth of revolution as lying in the creative act. We can, then, locate Yi T'ae-jun's assertion in *Travels in the Soviet Union* of the autonomy of national culture within global socialism and his aestheticizing of the production process as part and parcel of a continuing negotiation of the relations among art, visuality, and ideology that would take place in both halves of the divided peninsula.

Rendering the North Invisible

The disbanding of KAPF in 1935 spelled, for all intents and purposes, the end of the left on the colonial Korean literary scene. As we saw in chapter 1, the late 1930s witnessed the emergence of a culture of mobilization, one that went hand in hand with the expanding Greater East Asia Co-Prosperity Sphere. Liberation in August 1945 allowed not only for the return of the left but also for the emergence of a younger generation of nationalist writers, untainted by what was now called collaboration, such as Kim Tong-ni and Hwang Sun-wŏn. This group soon began to organize themselves under the rubric of "pure literature" (sunsu munhak).

The pure-proletarian literary debate of the occupation period can be viewed, on one level, as a contestation over the body, a question of blood versus labor. In "Cave Dwellers," ("Hyŏlgŏbujok," 1947), Kim Tong-ni, the leading advocate of pure literature, figures the dispossessed—refugees returned to the Korean peninsula from the outer reaches of the Japanese empire who find temporary shelter in air-raid bunkers dug during the Greater East Asian War—as the locus of ethnonational authenticity. The return to the cave, the reworking of the wartime bunker as living space, a site of spontaneous mutual aid, signals an end to mobilization and empire. The primal caves, closely associated in the text with mothers, naturalize a transhistorical, national community. "Ideology" (sasang) becomes an artificial imposition from the outside, a form of colonization that emerges in the text by way of the attempted rape of a young mother by a cave dweller imbued with what the text describes as half-baked leftist ideas. The elemental home is only secured by his expulsion from the community (read: erasure of the North).[25]

While this rebirth in the cave signals the end of colonial rule, it does not dispense with the East/West opposition and the questioning of modernity that informed the late colonial wartime cultural scene. As Kim Ye-rim has shown, Kim Tong-ni had sought to counter the modern in the late 1930s by portraying figures endowed with agency and bodily vitality who actively engaged in their own destruction. An "energy" thus emerges that rejects modern productivism. This bodily energy, in turn, is accompanied by a strength of spirit that demonstrates the superiority of *tongyang* over *sŏyang*.²⁶ The rebirth in the cave points to the possibility that this colonial-period body/spirit can now harness its energy to create a communality rather than its own end. This body/spirit remains, however, associated with the *minjok* and *tongyang*, opposed to the left, capitalism, and the West.

Recall, moreover, that colonial-period *hyangt'o* literary texts often offer a memory image linked to blood-based communality. In Yi Hyo-sŏk's "When the Buckwheat Blooms," the older peddler's memory of his encounter with the woman is made flesh in the form of the appearance of his son. Yi's text thus moves away from the emphasis in numerous proletarian texts in the 1920s and 1930s, including those written by Yi Hyo-sŏk himself, on severing affect from the familial in favor of class-based alliance.²⁷ While writers such as Kim Tong-ni, Yi Hyo-sŏk (Yi did not live to see liberation), and Hwang Sun-wŏn would become central to the post-1948 production of a South Korean canon, it is important to note that the colonial nativism that informs their works does not always coincide with the state's summoning of anticommunist subjects. As Ming-yan Lai points out, "Insofar as the term 'native' evokes natural belonging to a particular place and the culture and tradition 'rooted' in that place, it has no necessary connection to the nation as a collective unit. The native place, in other words, can be village, town, region at the subnational level, or an entire continent at the supranational level."²⁸

The short stories of Hwang Sun-wŏn, one of the most prominent writers in South Korea in the 1950s and 1960s, demonstrate how *hyangt'o* nativism contests national division by locating "home" in a rural space that does not coincide with the political formations of either North or South Korea. Others in the 1950s, such as O Yŏng-su and Yi Ho-ch'ŏl, would also produce agrarian lifeworlds outside of the history of national division and ideological conflict. Post-1945 painting in South Korea is similarly informed by this earlier *hyangt'o* discourse, as we see in the works of Yi Chung-sŏp, one of the most revered artists in South Korea and a close friend of Hwang Sun-wŏn (Yi illustrated the cover of one of Hwang's early short-story collections). Like "Buckwheat," Yi Chung-sŏp's paintings, which frequently borrow from Koryŏ-dynasty rock-wall paintings, turn to the autochthonous in their refusal to separate out the human from the animal and their location of a sexuality and vitality in the rural space, away from the state.²⁹

VISIBLE AND INVISIBLE STATES 79

FIGURE 2.1 Yi Chung-sŏp, *White Bull 1* (1953).

It is in Yŏm Sang-sŏp's numerous 1945–1948 texts that the reworking of the colonial period as history and the securing of the South as home etches the outlines of what would become the South Korean national narrative. This narrative must be understood in relation to the crisis of legitimacy faced by national capital at the 1945 crossroads of the colonial as past and the Cold War as present, the moment when pre-1945 pan-Asian mobilization becomes recoded as assimilation and collaboration. Yŏm Sang-sŏp's occupation-period texts address the post-1945 work of proletarian writers by way of an extended treatment of the home not as transhistorical but as bourgeois nationalist space. This is a space folded out, eventually, onto the borders of the newly formed Republic of Korea as noncommunist refuge.[30]

Consider, for example, "Thirty-Eighth Parallel" ("Samp'alsŏn," 1948), a travelogue following the movement of a family moving through the North as they return to their home in the South from Manchuria after the end of Japanese rule. It is the gaze of the narrator, the movement of his family through the landscape, that casts the North "outside" even as the text, at its close, calls into question the imposition of abstract space demarcated by the thirty-eighth parallel. "Parting and Meeting" ("Ihap," 1948) and its sequel "Reunion" ("Chaehoe," 1948) follow suit in their dismantling of familial space in the North and subsequent reconsolidation of the public/private split in the South.[31]

In "Parting and Meeting," set in the North, the wife of the protagonist turns, in the name of equal rights for men and women, further and further to the left, a move accompanied by her increasing distance from the home and eventual abandonment of her husband and children. The husband's call for moderation and an equal sharing of familial responsibilities falls on deaf ears, and he departs for the South with his son. "Reunion" critiques the malaise south of the thirty-eighth parallel but figures the South as locus of reconsolidation of the family. The protagonist's wife joins him in the South, he forgives her, and the text concludes with the two wallpapering a room together.

Kim Tong-ch'un has noted the importance of familism in the South—the construction of a family-based identity, the home as naturalized refuge from the capitalist relations of South Korean society.[32] In "Parting" and "Reunion," the home emerges as marking the dividing line between North and South. These texts narrate a transfer of affective belonging to the South, a belonging closely associated with the coincidence between domesticity and nationalized space. It is not only the North but also Japan that is thrown to the outside. *Nae* or "inside" no longer signals the Japanese metropole, as it did in the colonial period. Nor does the local refer to the "peninsula," the popular term for Korea in the late 1930s and early 1940s. Instead, the inside and the local reappear as a new center, the home that is to be built in the South.

In these works, the move toward the South is chronotopical. The North recedes in time as it is othered spatially; the Japanese metropole fades into the distance as the diaspora returns home. Eventually, in post-1948 South Korea, the North would appear on maps as blank space. Already in the 1945–1948 period we encounter the transformation of the North into memory. Over the years, the North would increasingly take the form of an image or appearance that conjures up the recollection of affective belonging associated with a precommunist past. The North would become a personal, felt past linked to childhood or adolescent memory. Such would be the case even as the North would also be associated with a threatening present exemplified by images on newsreels and television screens of goose-stepping, mechanized bodies. The repetitiveness itself of these images appearing in heavily censored state-run media divests the North of any geographical proximity or temporal movement. History would now exist only in the South and the free world.

ETHNONATION UNDER OCCUPATION: THE STAGING OF COLD WAR DEVELOPMENTALISM

"Thirty-Eighth Parallel" closes with the family finally making its way home to the South, crossing the thirty-eighth parallel, only to meet with a U.S. soldier. While the North has become a foreign country, the South, ruled by a foreign power, confronts its own crisis of legitimacy. It is precisely this crisis that Yŏm Sang-sŏp's *Dawn Wind* (1948) addresses in a way that will resemble that taken by the state, particularly beginning in the 1960s under Park Chung-Hee (as we will see in chapter 4). *Dawn Wind*, in fact, rearticulates both the developmentalist mapping laid out much earlier in texts such as Yi Kwang-su's *The Heartless* (1917) and Yŏm's own attempt in the 1920s and early 1930s to mediate between proletarian and nationalist writers by constructing a bourgeois nationalist subject sympathetic to the left.[33]

It is a curious oversight that *Dawn Wind*, a full-length novel serialized during a crucial moment in Korean history by one of the most prominent writers of the twentieth century, has not been canonized along with Yŏm's other works. *Dawn Wind* offers a more extensive treatment of USAMGIK than any other literary work written under occupation. The text was serialized in 1948 at first under USAMGIK but continuing into November of that year, thus concluding under the newly formed Republic of Korea, established on August 15, 1948. The text was not published in book form until 1998, and only then due to the efforts of Kim Jae-yong, who, in effect, "discovered" the work.[34] The occupation-period cultural scene is marked by these forgettings, excisions, and later rememberings.

Dawn Wind follows Kim Nam-ch'ŏn's earlier *August 15, 1945* and other works such as An Hoe-nam's "History of the Storm," which detail the remaking of collaborators into anticommnunists and the reliance of this class upon the police apparatus and the authority of USAMGIK. Like these texts, *Dawn Wind* offers a critique of USAMGIK and the colonial comprador elite. The text sets itself to a task that resembles Yŏm's efforts in the 1920s and 1930s to locate an ethics of national capital as site of resistance to the colonial state. In *Dawn Wind*, this takes the form of the separating of the formerly colonial and now immediate postliberation bourgeoisie into two strands: amoral (associated with foreign capital) and moral (associated with "national capital"). As is often the case in Yŏm's work, moreover, such a differentiation is worked out via the distribution of affect associated with love triangles. The separating out in *Dawn Wind* of a bourgeois nationalist subject both from the proletarian revolutionary and the formerly pro-Japanese, now pro-U.S. collaborative bourgeoisie works by way of a set of triangulated relationships: Pyŏng-jik must choose between Hye-ran (the woman protagonist of the text) and Hwa-sun, a Marxist who eventually goes North; Hye-ran must choose between Pyŏng-jik and Baker, a young U.S. orientalist affiliated with USAMGIK.

Pyŏng-jik and Hye-ran represent a new postcolonial generation, a recovery of the possibilities Yŏm explored in the early 1930s in one of his most famous works, *Three Generations* (*Samdae*, 1931), and its lesser-known sequel, *Fig* (*Muhwagwa*, 1931–1932), but soon abandoned under the increasing repression of the colonial state following the Manchurian Incident. The eventual coupling of Pyŏng-jik and Hye-ran that closes the text eliminates a dual threat (the left and the neocolonial) and consolidates a family that is at once folded out onto the trajectory of South Korean national development.

Pyŏng-jik and Hye-ran reject study overseas in favor of educating themselves at home. Their goal is to engage in a national self-strengthening on their own terms. Pyŏng-jik and Hye-ran, in fact, must be further differentiated by their opposition to the preceding generation, associated with differing responses to what is now figured as collaboration and the late-colonial-period policy of assimilation. Both must reject their fathers: Pyŏng-jik his comprador father, the owner of a brewery formerly aligned with the Japanese and now wielding influence with USAMGIK; Hye-ran her morally upright but inflexible English-speaking father, self-confined to his room, incapable of action (a figure resembling the father in Yŏm's "The Western Cookie Box," a text we will examine below).

Dawn Wind, like *Fig*, locates a new woman at the center of the detective-novel form. The narrative of the new woman's self-development and emergence as independent actor occurs in tandem with the unfolding of her investigative powers, particularly her ability to understand the complex networks making up the underworld of rightist gangs and leftist youth movements clashing under the U.S. military occupation. Nancy Armstrong has shown how the eighteenth-century British novel's conferring of psychological depth and moral value onto the domestic woman worked as a middle-class challenge to the aristocracy and its privileging of birth, title, and ascriptive status. At the same time, according to Armstrong, in the mid-nineteenth century, "one can see the discourse of sexuality lose interest in its critique of the aristocracy as the newly organizing working classes become the more obvious target of moral reform."[35] Armstrong's work helps us to see the ways in which *Dawn Wind* allows for a somewhat different positioning, one that takes the form of a differentiation, by way of the new woman, of a moral, nationalist bourgeoisie from its amoral counterpart. The new woman must ward off the lecherous advances of Chin-sŏk, a comprador returnee from Hawaii. At the same time, the text must mark her difference from leftist thought (in the form of the sexualized modern girl, Hwa-sun) and the mindless laboring bodies of the working class. The new woman is thus a sign of education, enlightenment, and development.[36]

The formation of an ethiconational bourgeoisie as neutral center of a postcolonial state, this performative historiography, works to dissolve anxiety produced by what is now considered the just-ended Japanese regime of assimilation and U.S. occupation. Hye-ran must distinguish herself from her uncanny double—the Korean-speaking Japanese woman, Kaneko—and must reject the advances of the Japanese-speaking orientalist Baker. Cosmopolitan (Hye-ran speaks fluent English) but unassimilated, she resists both sexual/gender trouble and Japanization/Americanization.

Hye-ran, in fact, must differentiate herself from two doubles, one past, one future—from Kaneko (Japanese colonialist assimilation) and from Baker's attempt to manufacture her identity as "Helen." More than anything else, it is the latter gesture, figured as assimilatory incorporation into the Pax Americana, that Yŏm's text works to unpack. Baker's desire is both to produce Hye-ran as oriental, timeless artifact, representative of the exotic East, and to lift her onto the Western register, bring her to the United States to study, rename her Helen, modernize her. The project mirrors that of the U.S. occupations of both South Korea and Japan.

Baker's desire for the "traditional" while advocating modernization, it turns out, plays a pivotal role in the construction of a space that stands outside the "political," the "ideological," even as his fantastical gaze is rejected, cast to the outside as inauthentic, in favor of the "everyday" lived experience of Koreans. Baker is possessed by an overwhelming desire to take a sixteen-millimeter film of Hye-ran wearing Chosŏn-style clothes and hairdo, and he informs Hye-ran that Chosŏn makes him think of a primitive, unsullied (*wŏnsí*) state of nature, one opposed to the "machines of modern civilization."[37] A gap opens up between this desire and Hye-ran's position as the protagonist of *Dawn Wind*, representative of the new Korea. In many ways, *Dawn Wind* revolves around this gap between Baker's desire to view the ethnic and the text's observation of this gaze. In the end, it is Baker who becomes the object of investigation, framed, pictured, by Hye-ran, from a position that Baker cannot see, one that already considers itself cosmopolitan, at home in the modern, familiar with Western languages and texts.

Dawn Wind, then, demonstrates Yŏm's abiding concern with the relation among literature, visuality, and coloniality.[38] After poking fun at Baker's desire to view her as a "Chosŏn fairy" (*Chosŏn sŏnnyŏ*), Hye-ran responds to his offer to go to the United States with a pun that alludes to Baker's earlier remark: "I'll visit when Chosŏn is no longer a primitive [*wŏnsí*] country but a nuclear [*wŏnja*] power."[39] The text points to what Said has called the post-1945 inheritance of the orient by the United States,[40] the move from a Japanese-led Greater East Asia to an aestheticized, historyless site to be incorporated into the U.S.-sponsored developmentalist project.[41] It is the appearance of the orientalist Baker in Asia that signals this shift. The marriage of Hye-ran and Pyŏng-jik, however, amounts less to a complete rejection of Baker and his project than the voluntarist assumption of the task, the responsibilizing of a national subject within a developmental, free-world teleology.[42]

If Yi T'ae-jun rejects exchange value in favor of a linkage between production and artistic value, Yŏm Sang-sŏp's texts show how the developmentalist narrative invests the commodity form with national affect. For bourgeois nationalism, exchange value in global capitalism is supplemented by a purposefulness that exceeds the profit motive. The commodity does not appear miraculously, invested with a life of its own that denies the process of production and the investment of labor in it. Rather, the commodity occurs as a prosthetic, an extension of the national body that is thought of as preceding and producing it. The commodity is invested with a national life moving its way through capitalist time. It is the commodity form that manifests this national body, even as labor power is elided. Such an elision, in fact, is constitutive of the bourgeois national subject in Yŏm's texts. The nationalizing of the commodity form underpins the assertion of bourgeois national independence and sovereignty within circuits of global capitalism.

Let us consider the negotiation between commodity and essentialized national culture that emerges by way of the antique in *Dawn Wind*, one that contrasts with our earlier discussion of Yi T'ae-jun's "Dust." It is no accident that Hye-ran works in Chin-sŏk's antique shop, which caters to Americans affiliated with USAMGIK. While Hye-ran is explicitly associated with the antiques for sale in the shop, what marks her as subject is precisely her awareness of the ways in which she is put on display as object (an awareness of the ways in which she is being commodified) and, at the same time, her complete lack of knowledge of Korean antiques. What is rejected here is the Western longing for the non-Western object (Baker's desire for Korean antiques), exchange value in and of itself (the sale of Hye-ran and the objects), and an essentialized, traditionalist identity. Hye-ran's Koreanness is not equated with an affinity for or innate knowledge of all things Korean but with her position as a cosmopolitan agent working on behalf of Korea. Yŏm rejects traditionalism in favor of a nationalist pragmatism—a reworking of exchange value into nationalist use value.

Yŏm Sang-sŏp's occupation-period works speak to the 1948 formation of the Republic of Korea by linking a temporal narrative of national development to a specific space (south of the thirty-eighth parallel). This narrative proceeds by sifting through desires, locating the proper partner, and joining the domestic space to the boundaries of the new nation-state. Yi T'ae-jun's "Dust" intersects with Yŏm Sang-sŏp's occupation-period project in "Parting and Meeting," "Reunion," and "Thirty-Eighth Parallel" by its own mapping out of space. "Dust" traces Han-moe's journey from South to North in the colonial period, back to the South after liberation, followed by his failed attempt to return North. Han-moe is shot and killed recrossing the thirty-eighth parallel. The proper place of refuge is in the North, but border crossing has become dangerous.

Importantly, both Yŏm Sang-sŏp (particularly in *Dawn Wind*) and Yi T'ae-jun coincide in their view of the U.S. military occupation as a rearticulation of coloniality even as they legitimize sovereign, autonomous spaces opposing each other, divided by the thirty-eighth parallel. Yi T'ae-jun's postliberation works offer an aesthetic socialism that brings together the autonomy of art and the proletarian subject, one that begins to take form in a sovereign space south of the Yalu and north of the thirty-eighth parallel. The nationalist capitalism of Yŏm's post-1945 work, in turn, locates the developmental trajectory of earlier colonial-period texts in the South. Yŏm's attempt to shore up an autonomous subject by figuring the commodity as national prosthetic casts an anxious glance at the assimilatory powers of U.S.-led global capitalism. The tension we find in Yŏm's work between the two narratives, the national narrative and the developmentalist narrative, would structure the continuing crisis of legitimacy faced by the South Korean state from this point—its inception on August 15, 1948, during the serialization of *Dawn Wind*—forward.

U.S. Aid, or the Cold War Economy of the Gift

The distribution of vacated Japanese factories, properties, and homes (*chŏksan*) by USAMGIK emerged as one of the central issues of the occupation period. We encounter the issue of *chŏksan* as the lynchpin organizing the move from the colonial to the new Cold War order in a number of literary works, including Ch'ae Man-sik's "Once Upon a Rice Paddy" ("Non iyagi," 1946), Ch'ae's "Mister Pang" ("Misŭt'ŏ Pang," 1946), Kim Nam-ch'ŏn's *August 15, 1945*, and Yŏm Sang-sŏp's "The Western Cookie Box" ("Yanggwaja kap," 1947).

Well known for his late colonial satirical critiques of comprador Koreans and the colonial state in texts such as *Peace Under Heaven* (*T'aep'yŏngch'ŏnha*, 1938), Ch'ae Man-sik is one of the only writers whose works would cross the new post-1948 border, appearing in both North and South Korean literary histories and anthologies published in the 1950s.[43] Ch'ae was clearly sympathetic to the proletarian camp during the colonial period but never formally joined KAPF. He maintained a similar position following the end of colonial rule, making use of his satirical abilities to address the new forms that foreign power was taking in post-1945 Korea.

Ch'ae's "Once Upon a Rice Paddy," for example, offers a history of territorializing, possession, and legality, central concerns in an immediate post-1945 context calling for both land reform, which stands at the center of Hwang Sun-wŏn's portrayal of a young landlord's departure from the North in *Descendants of Cain*, and the equitable allocation of the *chŏksan*. Ch'ae's work follows the transformation in the notion of land ownership that accompanied the shift from the Chosŏn dynasty to modernity. In Ch'ae's text, "feeling" is linked to private possession and its legal history in modernity, not to the history of loss and regaining of an ethnonationalized territory. Yet the national/imperial register enters the picture in the protagonist's assertion that his lost land must now be returned because of the financial manipulation of the Japanese colonial state and the unfair transfer of his property to a Japanese settler. The nonreturn of his land in 1945 figures August 15 as nonevent. For Ch'ae, as for many other writers, that land reform was carried out in the North in 1946 while USAMGIK busied itself shoring up support by way of the questionable distribution of *chŏksan* eroded the meaning of "liberation" south of the thirty-eighth parallel.[44]

Yŏm Sang-sŏp's "The Western Cookie Box" similarly narrates the move from the colonial to occupation as the transfer of the power to distribute property.[45] How does Yŏm's "Cookie" address code switching or Cold War interpellation, a shift from wartime mobilization and the summoning of the emperor to incorporation in a temporal, spatial, and racial order organized in very concrete, material ways by the U.S. occupation and the beginnings of free world ideology? It is this shift from wartime mobilization to U.S. military occupation, a shift of militarisms, that many immediate post-1945 texts negotiate in different and overlapping ways. We have seen how this occurs via a remaking of identities enabled by the repatriation of those dislocated during the Greater East Asian and Pacific Wars (the *chŏnjaemin*). We have also encountered the separation of an ethical bourgeoisie from a comprador elite associated with active participation in wartime mobilization and the profits it garnered. We focused above on Yŏm Sang-sŏp's texts, but this issue was also important for proletarian writers, who found themselves under pressure to produce transformative counter-recantations. Kim Nam-ch'ŏn's portrayal of wartime munitions factories in *August 15, 1945*, for example, underscores the centrality of the *chŏksan* as means of production. The repossession of *chŏksan* by workers provides a material basis for a new history, a twin victory over colonialism and capitalism.

"Cookie" takes a different tack than proletarian works. The text considers the shift in power on several levels, one of them, like Yŏm Sang-sŏp's *Dawn Wind* and Ch'ae Man-sik's "Mister Pang," the figuring of colonial to postcolonial transfer (the movement from formal Japanese to U.S. sovereignty) on the level of language. USAMGIK has often been called a "government by translation." The movement from Japanese to English as the language of power manifests itself in the form of the interpreter/translator central to "Cookie" as well as to "Mister Pang." These two texts, in fact, inaugurate the ensuing sixty years of U.S. military camptown literature (*kijich'on munhak*) and films that continue to articulate the coloniality of the U.S./South Korea relation.

In "Cookie," the act of translation is linked to the interpellatory moment, the call to the new order. This call, moreover, is at once verbal, visual, and organized by the production of desire for the commodity. Yŏm's text stages a "primal" encounter that has been repeated in different ways in U.S. military camptown literature and film for the past sixty years in South Korea. Pobae and her parents are destitute refugees from the North who are renting a room in a Japanese-style *chŏksan* home. The landlord's daughter offers a box of Western cookies as a gesture of goodwill to Pobae, who has learned some English from her English-speaking father. Pobae has been translating letters from Richardson, who is interested in the landlord's daughter and has been furnishing the landlord's family with an array of goods from his base. The "gift" relies on the production of desire, the visual hailing of a would-be consumer subject by encounter with the Western object.

Such a visual hailing involves the display of the object and the potential commodification of language itself. The gift, the box, is, in fact, part of a circuit of exchange, one that can only work by acknowledging a metropolitan-peripheral hierarchy of languages. The hierarchizing of language, of course, was quite familiar to Koreans, who had just emerged from a regime in which Japanese was the "national language" (*kugŏ*). The linkage of language to exchange value is precisely what Yŏm rejected in his colonial-period works, particularly *Fig* (1931–1932), with its critique of the commercialization of the formerly "cultural national" press Yom had painstakingly worked to portray in his earlier "Rotary Press" (1926). Here, the cookies are to be put into the mouth, ingested; the English language is to emerge from the lips of the occupied Korean subjects. The gift of the box is predicated upon the entrance of the family into the new, bodily experienced reality of a Korean-English translation regime.

The stops or interruptions that occur in the moment of translating in texts such as "Cookie" and "Mister Pang" allow us to see the relation between language and power. In "Cookie," Yŏm details an iconology: a move from language and naming in the text itself to a conjuring up of the visual register, the attempt to display the box as symbol. At the same time, the text stands between the colonial and the postcolonial, at the crossroads of the transfer of power and translation. The father rejects the gift and the possibility of securing a position in the new order. The circulation of objects and languages comes to a stop. This stop is made visible by the box, which does not change hands.

Yŏm's text rethinks the transfer of one form of colonial rule to another. Yŏm offers us a doubling of coloniality, precisely in the way the colonial "past" makes itself present via its inscription in the space-memory of the *chŏksan* home. The text disallows the erasure of the colonial past, embodied in the *chŏksan* home in which the characters reside, by the postcolonial present. This is the home transferred to Koreans but occupied by the United States, one that, in the text, is to be made into a club catering to U.S. military occupation personnel. The text thus represents a stop or interruption both of the linear movement from colonial past to postcolonial present and the movement across languages. This stop questions the Cold War summoning associated with the gift, the U.S. offer of a circuit of capitalist and linguistic exchange, value, and desire that would define the USAID project in South Korea and other sites to be incorporated into the developmental order.

Yŏm Sang-sŏp's "Cookie," Ch'ae Man-sik's "Once Upon a Rice Paddy," Yi Sŏn-hŭi's "Window," Kim Tong-ni's "Cave Dwellers," and Yi T'ae-jun's "Liberation: Before and After" (a text I discuss in chapter 5) were all included in the 1948 *Selected Stories of Liberation Literature* (*Haebang munhak sŏnjip*). Published under occupation, this text would never appear in North Korea and was censored in South Korea until 1988 because of its inclusion of writers who went North, Yi T'ae-jun and Yi Sŏn-hŭi.[46] I view this chapter as a return to this first major post-1945 anthology and its possibilities. Considering these works, particularly those rendered invisible for half a century, in relation to others that appeared in this anthology allows us to recall the shifting canon formation that makes up the history of "South Korean literature" (*Han'guk munhak*). This history of canon formation continues after 1988, when formerly censored works again appear in anthologies, alongside a variety of other works. Yi Sŏn-hŭi's "Window," for example, would first appear as a work of *Han'guk munhak* only in 1996, in yet another reworking of the canon, *Representative Works of Modern Korean Literature* (*Han'guk hyŏndae taep'yo sosŏlsŏn*), published by Ch'angbi Press.

The appearance and disappearance of *Selected Stories of Liberation Literature* in 1948 signals how the colonial past, mediated, as we have seen, in different ways by the writers included in this anthology, was to be organized and postcolonial division was to be imagined. A return to the writers included in this anthology allows us see how immediate post-1945 literary texts produce the meaning of liberation by mapping out spaces informed by pre-1945 articulations of the modern, particularly different forms of class-based, nationalized, and pan-Asianized identities. At the same time, we should pay attention to the ways in which writers figured the spatial and temporal transformability of the subject as they confronted the rapidly bifurcating Cold War order. We can, moreover, now more fully consider the ways in which "North" and "South" Korean literature is not a divided national literature but an array of texts forming themselves in relation to the colonial past, competing statisms, and global Cold War cultural production.

The anticommunist policies of the U.S. military occupation, the subsequent establishment of separate regimes on the peninsula in 1948, and the Korean War (1950–1953) effected the removal of the left from the literary scene in South Korea, allowing the right to move to a position of dominance. The departure of a large number of writers and filmmakers to the North, the deaths of prominent figures as a result of the war, the impoverishment and destruction caused by the war—all of this left the South Korean cultural field considerably weakened following the armistice agreement in 1953.[47] It was the publication of a number of literary journals in the mid-1950s such as *Literary Arts* (*Munhak yesul*; 1955), *Modern Literature* (*Hyŏndae munhak*; 1955) and *Free Literature* (*Chayu munhak*; 1956) and the reemergence of the film industry that opened the door for a number of new writers and filmmakers to emerge on the cultural scene. As we will see in chapter 3, it was only beginning in the mid-1950s that writers, filmmakers, and critics—many of them belonging to this "new generation" that made its debut either immediately preceding the war or following the armistice agreement—were able to engage in steady cultural production.

The year 1948 marks the disappearance of colonial and postcolonial proletarian works in the South, but this only meant that the proletarian narrative would help to constitute, precisely by way of its excision, both statist anticommunism and its discontents. In the next chapter, I will trace the ways that early South Korean cultural production in the immediate aftermath of the Korean War is marked less by a totalizing anticommunism, as the story often has it, than by the emergence of a politics of nonalignment. This is a politics that retains traces of the censored proletarian narrative. It is one in which figures of the marginalized and dispossessed stand neither here nor there. We will find them in another place, between sanctioned narratives (the ethnonational) and illegal texts (those of the colonial and postcolonial left).

3
AMBIVALENT ANTICOMMUNISM
The Politics of Despair and the Erotics of Language

KOREANS WERE DEPLOYED as laborers and soldiers to locations throughout the imaginary of Greater East Asia during the late 1930s and the first half of the 1940s. The 1945–1948 Soviet and U.S. military occupations in the northern and southern halves of the peninsula set in motion a second displacement of peoples, this time within Korea itself. This movement from north to south and, in lesser numbers, south to north across the new internal border would last until the end of the Korean War in 1953. The post-1945 formation of a new state in the geopolitical space south of the thirty-eighth parallel and, after the Korean War, the DMZ is intimately linked to these late colonial and early postcolonial dislocations.

In the 1950s, a new statist identity emerged, one that reworked the late-colonial-period dual identification with the local (the Korean peninsula) and a Japan-led Greater East Asia. The new subject retained a dual identification. The local became South Korea, while the U.S.-led anticommunist, democratic free world took the place of the Japanese imperium. The South Korean state's assertion of membership in the free world meant that it would always have to address the charge that it was not putting in practice what it claimed in theory to be doing. Already in the 1950s, the oppositional critique of the state as comprador and authoritarian rested upon the state's failure to implement the democratic ideals it espoused. While this debate would take different forms over the ensuing decades, it would remain central to the ordering of both statist and dissenting, oppositional subjects.

The double dislocation, in fact, opened up the possibility of forming new kinds of nonstatist, nonethnonationalized positions. Rather than identifying at once with the South Korean state and the broader free world, a sense of dislocation made it easier to make the claim that one belonged to neither. This move toward nonbelonging represents a continuation of the calls for neutrality made in the 1945–1948 occupation period. The attempt to locate an alternative to the first/second-world bifurcation is also informed by the 1950s global movements for nonalignment, both the attempts to form coalitions by "third world" states and by the existentialism of the "first world" itself. While the Korean War is often seen as solidifying the Cold War order, firming up anticommunism and national division, representations of the war and its effects did not always coincide with the securing of a mobilized, statist citizenry. As we will see below, portrayals of violence even in "anticommunist" films and literary texts of the 1950s tended at key moments to question the drawing of lines in the sand. A generalized violence itself, often linked to sexuality, unsettled a variety of oppositions (North Korea/South Korea, Free World/Communist Other, East/West). It is time to do away with the notion that the 1950s was a decade of draconian anticommunism and nothing more in South Korea. Certainly the state was authoritarian and anticommunist. But this is only part of the picture.

In this chapter, I trace the movement between the statist summoning of postcolonial, territorialized "South Korean" subjects and the appearance, often at the margins of literary and filmic texts, of early forms of Cold War nonalignment. In chapter 1, we saw how the relation among literature, art, and film is central to the formation of colonial proletarian, modernist, and mobilized subjects. In chapter 2, we unpacked the ways in which a constellation of texts refashioned ways of seeing that emerged in the colonial period into a distribution of the visible and invisible that enabled the imagining of separate geospaces on either side of the thirty-eighth parallel. Here, I underscore the importance of the relation between the rapid increase in literary production in the mid-1950s and the beginning of what many have called the "golden age" of South Korean cinema in the 1950s.[1]

I situate my discussion by first outlining three strands of intellectual discourse central to the 1950s, all related in different ways to the colonial-period cultural scene. I detail the return of the earlier colonial debate on national literature, one that stands at the center of the attempt to form a

South Korean literary field in the 1950s. I then show how the traditionalism of that decade drew on colonial-period nativism to construct a postcolonial space outside of the Cold War order. Finally, I demonstrate how the emergence of existentialism in South Korea interrupts both statist anticommunism and "first world" universalism.

These three discourses frame the arguments—the agreements and disagreements—that combined to form the South Korean cultural field in the aftermath of the Korean War. Their mid-1950s emergence in intellectual and literary journals coincided both with the post–Korean War reorganizing of the literary scene and with the first post-1945 production of blockbuster films. The mid-1950s saw a boom in Korean-language publications, which had been suppressed during the wartime mobilization of the late 1930s and early 1940s and limited during the post-1945 occupation period and the Korean War. The new opportunities provided filmmakers during the colonial wartime mobilization, the hiring of directors by USIS and other U.S. entities during the Korean War, and the availability of capital for a rapidly growing film industry all set the stage for a younger generation of directors to make the first post-1945 commercially successful films.[2] In the mid-1950s, we encounter a co-emergence of the first postcolonial readership of Korean-language texts and mass spectatorship of Korean-language films.

In chapter 1, we saw how the formation of a modern literary field in the mid-1920s took place in relation to the nascent colonial Korean film industry. The mid-1950s resembles this earlier moment. The appearance of new major intellectual and literary journals in the aftermath of the Korean War provided the venue for the production of a South Korean literary field at the same time as a postcolonial film industry was beginning to establish itself. This was a moment that also saw the broader distribution of Hollywood films, which had enjoyed considerable success in the 1920s and 1930s, prior to the outbreak of war between the United States and Japan, and had been reintroduced during the 1945–1948 U.S. military occupation.[3] As we will see below, literary and filmic texts in the mid-1950s are embedded in this multilayered, global Cold War circulation of images.

What is the relation between the literary and the visual in the 1950s? We find the most complex, sustained engagement with the verbal-visual relation and the newly forming Cold War order in the work of the writer Son Ch'ang-sŏp. Son grew up in poverty in Manchuria, was a self-supporting student in Japan in his early teens, and returned to Korea following liberation in 1945. He would leave permanently for Japan in the early 1970s and eventually became a Japanese citizen.[4] New to the cultural scene reemerging in the aftermath of the Korean War, Son quickly became one of the most prominent writers in South Korea. Like others of his generation, Son was educated in Japanese and struggled to write in Korean. However, he refuses the code switch from a colonial, pan-Asianized identity to Cold War national subject or the movement from one *kugŏ* or "national language" (the colonial term for Japanese) to another *kugŏ* (the postcolonial term for Korean). Instead, he attempts to locate a position elsewhere. In Son's work we encounter a politics of nonalignment, one that emerges by placing the Cold War visual regime that circulates between center (the United States) and periphery (South Korea) on display.

I conclude this chapter by examining the ways in which the literary becomes filmic and the filmic becomes literary. I show how the 1956 filmic adaptation of Chŏng Pi-sŏk's 1954 popular novel *Madame Freedom* (*Chayu puin*) occurs as an inflection of the hypericonic, here as a film about writing and language, the visual invoking of the verbal. I examine the ways in which this visual/verbal relation, one central to the notion of filmic adaptation itself, allows us to unpack the multilayered relations opened up in Son Ch'ang-sŏp's work among the ethnonational/anticommunist summons, the commodity culture of the 1950s, a Cold War politics of the body and its desires, and a colonial/postcolonial modern erotics of language.

NATIONAL LITERATURE AS SOUTH KOREAN LITERATURE

We can locate the rapid post-1945 formation of the North/South divide discussed in the preceding chapter as standing somewhere between mourning—as Dominick LaCapra notes, the recognition of the other as other—and melancholia: in LaCapra's words, "a specular relation that confuses the self with the other."[5] There is a way in which North Korea and those living in the North become spectral, experienced in their absence by way of images. The new notion of North Korea becomes marked by a certain encounter with death or, more precisely, a living death. It was in the 1945–1948 occupation period that what we might call South Korean Cold War mourning-melancholia begins. The mourning-melancholia of division is accompanied, of course, by a further ambivalence: the possibility of fissure between the notion of the ethnonation that would include all Koreans, North and South, and the emergence of competing states on either side of the thirty-eighth parallel. Each state lays claim to coincidence with the Korean people as transhistorical subject.

These ambivalences carry over into the twin, mirroring biopolitics of the contestation between the two states, North and South, each managing the life of its citizenry at the expense of, or more precisely, in relation to the death of an other that bears the traces of (ethnonational) self.[6] As we will see in chapter 5, here we encounter the relation between the biopolitical—the management of life Foucault considers central to modernity—and the politics of the visual, the distribution of the visible and invisible that produces Cold War subjects in the division system. The early imagining of Cold War South and North Korea is, in this way, informed by a way of seeing organized by the relation between life and death. Life/South is associated with the visible/presence; death/North belongs to the realm of the invisible/absence.

As we have seen, the cultural field formed in the southern half of the peninsula under U.S. military occupation increasingly rendered its communist counterpart as blank space. The march up and down the peninsula by the opposing armies during the first year of the Korean War broke down the visual and spatial border imposed by the United States at the thirty-eighth parallel. In effect, the battles caused the northern half of the peninsula to come back into view, if only briefly. The 1953 armistice and establishment of the DMZ brought the return of erasure, but with a difference. It was at this point, in the aftermath of the direct confrontation of the Korean War, that the figure of the communist became increasingly imagined as an unseen but ubiquitous threat, present in the midst.

We find the best example of this shift in the popular 1954 film *Hand of Fate* (*Unmyŏng ŭi son*; dir., Han Hyŏng-mo). This film provides a mass spectatorship that has just experienced the Cold War gone hot with a code switch from combat and direct engagement to unseen enemy. This enemy exists not only in the North but everywhere. As in other free-world contexts, the figure of the communist is caught up in a regime of passing. He or she could be one's neighbor—"redness" is hard to spot.

If *Hand of Fate* is at once film noir and a Cold War detective film, it is also a figuring of the communist as separated out from an authentic body. As

FIGURE 3.1 The Hand of Fate (*The Hand of Fate*, 1954).

the film begins, we have the hand of the communist, whose face we do not see, guiding the woman protagonist Margaret, a café waitress and North Korean spy. The hand fades into Margaret's body early in the film: the communist does not possess its own body; it can only exist by inhabiting another. The communist as there and not there, ghostly and threatening, delinked from the materiality of the body, overlaps with Margaret's alienation within the Cold War order.

Margaret, the post-1945 rearticulation of the colonial-period modern girl as "Western princess" (*yanggongju*) is, in fact, at once possessed by the ghostly communist other and U.S. power. The latter manifests its reality in a scene cut from a newsreel that shows the disembarking of columns of U.S. soldiers on the docks where black-market transactions take place. These are the soldiers who will purchase and appropriate Margaret's body. Her collaboration with communism/the United States emerges as beyond her control even as it is linked to the loss of the body, the breakdown of the body's borders. The film proceeds to shore up a subject that will be at once anticommunist (in relation to the ghostly communist other) and ethnonationalized (in relation to U.S. invasive economic and military power).

Importantly, Yŏng-ch'ŏl, the male protagonist who works on the docks unloading U.S. goods flowing into South Korea, ruminates on the status of the term laborer (*nodongja*) in the film. Later, however, we discover that he is actually a South Korean counterespionage agent. This 1954 film screens the possibility of a class-based subject, the image of the dock workers associated with Yŏng-ch'ŏl's pondering over the term "laborer," only to transform it into the object of surveillance. The laboring body is dispensed with as agent in favor of the acumen of the undercover detective. The call is to see the invisible, the possibility of a communism that inhabits and co-opts bodies. We are left with a Cold War injunction to maintain a vigilance over oneself and others that remains in effect in South Korea today.

At the close of the film, Margaret dies at the hands of Yŏng-ch'ŏl, who shoots her, at her request, to put her out of her misery. She is dying a slow death after having been shot by a communist for refusing to kill Yŏng-ch'ŏl: "I don't want to die by an enemy bullet," she declares. Yŏng-ch'ŏl calls out to her, "Margaret, Margaret," and she responds, "Please call me Chŏng-ae," the first we hear of her Korean name. The corpse of "Margaret" becomes the site of anticommunist identification. The audience witnesses a turn away from the "enemy" and an ethnonational recovery. Chŏng-ae is reborn and quickly martyred, even as a certain agency emerges. Yŏng-ch'ŏl, and those who follow in his wake in South Korea, are, in this film, to take matters into their own hands as assimilated anticommunists located south of the DMZ.

Already in the occupation period, as we saw in the previous chapter, writers and literary critics had begun such an attempt to locate a national subject in relation both to the class-based proletarian narrative and to the United States, the new foreign power in South Korea. Kwŏn Yŏng-min distinguishes two trajectories in the debate among critics on national literature that took place in the 1945–1948 occupation period, "national literature as class literature" and "national literature as pure literature." The former, articulated most famously by the proletarian poet and critic Im Hwa, locates the nation in the liberatory impetus of the *inmin* (the Korean Marxist term for people). The latter, as elaborated by Kim Tong-ni, locates the "national spirit" in the "humanism of the national unit."[7] As Sin Hyŏng-gi has pointed out, Kim Tong-ni's theorization of pure literature rests upon the notion of a "third humanism" that sublates capitalism and Marxism in order to create a truly global modern literary spirit.[8] Needless to say, such a sublation continues the earlier attempt by wartime Kyoto School philosophers to "overcome modernity."

As we noted in chapter 1, the notion of national literature was first articulated in the mid- and late 1920s to counter the increasing dominance of the literary scene by KAPF. Im Hwa's post-1945 reworking of national literature as proletarian literature underscores how the promise of impending sovereignty as well as the threat of a lasting division of the peninsula set in motion what would become a move away from KAPF's earlier internationalism. The fact that running debates could not be carried on with leftist critics shifted literary discourse in mid-1950s South Korea. In lieu of discrediting "national literature as class literature," critics now focused on defining the relation of national literature with "tradition" and the "West." Discussions in the 1950s of national literature revolve around the question of how to draw the boundaries of the South Korean literary field in relation to other literatures, how to locate the particular (national literature, or *minjok munhak*) as universal (world literature, or *segye munhak*).⁹ In other words, the discourse on national literature continues to address the relations among the subject, the modern, and literature in ways that resemble the colonial wartime roundtable discussions of the particular/universal and imperial subjects literature.¹⁰

At stake in this discourse on national literature is the location of the referent, one closely linked to the debates on tradition, and the question of resistance (*rejisŭt'angsŭ*), a term invoked perhaps more than any other in intellectual and literary journals of the 1950s. Consider, for example, Paek Ch'ŏl's "National Literature as Agrarian Literature" (1956).¹¹ A former KAPF member who recanted and participated in the late colonial roundtable discussions on imperial subjects literature, Paek underwent a further transformation following liberation, becoming one of the most influential literary critics in South Korea in the 1950s. Paek notes that the question of national literature has been an issue since liberation in 1945 from the "Japanese imperialist mechanism." However, with the left evacuated from the scene in South Korea, Paek does not return to the 1945–1948 proletarian–pure literature debates. Instead, Paek critiques the abiding concern with the "abstruse" (*nanhae*) among South Korean poets. While they maintain that they confront the same urban angst and mechanistic civilization as that addressed by intellectuals such as T. S. Eliot, an examination of the actual South Korean condition reveals a reality very different from that facing Western intellectuals. For Paek, "Placing emphasis, therefore, on a poetry which adheres to the Western twentieth-century literary impulse to form a self-consciousness is not part of a necessary literary historical process—it is mere imitation."[12] The call to Greater East Asia and imperial subjects literature in the late colonial period was often made in the name of a sublation of East and West that was itself a creative act, an overcoming of a modernity that had been all too mimetic.[13] Paek now turns away from Asia and to the Korean countryside as the locus of national literature. This is where the future lies for South Korea, the locus of what stands in contrast to the imitative and the corruption of the city. The formerly local and imperial subject of the late colonial period is jettisoned in favor of a new particular (nation) and universal (human), the national human (*minjokchŏk in'gan*).[14]

While demonstrating a similar concern with the issue of the imitative, in a 1956 article the critic Ch'oe Il-su locates the national in a different site, in the relation between Korean literature and foreign literatures. For Ch'oe, the moment of contact is marked by resistance to imitation. Ch'oe's move is to locate "equality" and "resistance" as the defining lineage of national literature through the ages; further, this tradition of equality and resistance has as its telos the overcoming of national division insofar as it seeks the leveling of all people within the nation and resists assimilation by foreign literatures (first Chinese, then Japanese, and finally Western).[15] In "On National Literature—A Provisional Delineation of the Concept" (1956),[16] Chŏng T'ae-yong also links national literature to the issue of division, but he locates the national neither in geospace nor in the relation between literatures conceptualized, as in Ch'oe's case, as bounded-off totalities. For Chŏng, the nation is not a static entity but one undergoing a centripetal process of formation that grants upon different groupings of people a collective destiny. Given that the South Korean nation (*Han'guk minjok*, a term that appears frequently in 1950s South Korean intellectual discourse) is one of these collectives, Chŏng tells us, the question is what sort of national literature it should have.[17]

Chŏng rejects versions of national literature he considers "exclusionary," which he links to the Nazi "blood and soil" policy.[18] Instead, the task of writers is to portray an event, one that has both national and global significance. Examples are the Reformation, the industrial revolution, the formation of civil society, and the two world wars. Goethe, Balzac, Turgenev, Dante, Cervantes, Shakespeare—these great writers of the world treated themes of global importance.[19] The "direct bodily experience" of the particular historical situation that has global relevance is what should be the subject matter for writers of national literature, and in South Korea's case, this means North/South division and the Korean War.[20]

Finally, Kim Yang-su adds a subject of resistance to the three above positions in his "Literary Spirit of the New Age—The Task of Establishing National Literature" (1958). Here, Kim emphasizes the lack of autonomy (*chuch'esŏng*) in Korean modernity, one that is "distorted" in a double manner insofar as it suffered external pressure both from the material civilization of the West and Japanese imperialism.[21] The colonial period saw literature that "either deluded itself into thinking the mask of the other it was wearing was really its own face, or lived in the past." A literature that does not know its own true reality, imitates the life of the other uncritically, and ignores the present for the life of the past cannot be considered a literature of "living humans," those who renew their lives by engaging in acts of resistance to the historical situation in which they find themselves.[22]

Kim's version of national literature calls for the construction of a subject that is at once unique, nonimitative, non-nostalgic, and universal. In contrast to Paek Ch'ŏl and Chŏng T'ae-yong, who seek to link national literature to its proper referent (for Paek, the agrarian; for Chŏng, the national-global event), Kim underscores the importance of the formation of a critical consciousness, one also emphasized by Ch'oe Il-su. At the same time, we should note that Kim, unlike Ch'oe, views "resistance" precisely as what is lacking in the Korean tradition.

We should note the absence in these articles of a conceptualizing of the formation of a national literature in relation to cultural production in the North. This is a structuring absence. Chŏng's article, for example, negotiates an unspoken relation with the North Korean other, since the locus of the *minjok* becomes equated only with South Korea (*Han'guk minjok*). *Minjok munhak* becomes *Han'guk munhak*. We see, then, that *Han'guk munhak* was formed, in the 1950s, less in opposition to its counterpart in the north (*Chosŏn munhak*) than through its elision.[23] *Han'guk munhak* of the 1950s performs its limits by means of this erasure, one that includes the formation of a colonial-period canon excising both KAPF texts and those of the "writers gone north" (*wŏlbuk chakka*). It is in this sense, as an effect of this erasure, that *Han'guk munhak* should be considered a "division literature" (*pundan munhak*).

In many ways, moreover, the different positions above regarding national literature in the 1950s worked upon the expressivist model of language linked to what we can call an organicist phoneticism, the figuring of the nation as embodied in the vernacular, what was now called "han'gul." We will return to the issue of national script below, in our discussion of *Madame Freedom*. This policing of borders, the subordination of gender, sexuality, class, can only proceed by eliminating the difference and deferring that accompany the act of writing itself. It is for this reason that national literature, in its different articulations, always relies upon a logic of transparency and expressivist realism. At the same time, Paek, Ch'oe, Chŏng, and Kim all show a desire to counter both the colonial past (Japan) and the postcolonial present (the West). In their work, this desire is linked in different ways to the traditional. Indeed, the discourse on tradition occupied a central place in the 1950s, providing, as we will see in the next section, one of the ways to stand against the colonial past and the location of South Korea under the continuing hegemony of the "West," now manifesting itself in the form of the U.S. presence in South Korea and the Cold War order.

Reinventing Pan-Asianism: Cold War Traditionalism in South Korea

The affiliation of South Korea (*Han'guk*) with the free world was implicitly rejected by the traditionalists of the 1950s. The orient (*tongyang*), central to the mobilizing of imperial subjects in the late colonial period, returns. But now Japan has dropped out of the picture. Instead, we find a slippage between *Han'guk* and *tongyang*. The former refers to a spatial sovereignty, while the latter signals the temporality of a broader "tradition."[24] The extensive discourse on "tradition" and *tongyang* in the 1950s was often figured as both a recovery of space and time from the Japanese imperium and a resistance to the contemporary hegemony of the West. In this way, an inflection of the *tongyang* of late colonial wartime mobilization plays an important role in the 1950s. The postcolonial *tongyang* retains its oppositional stance to the West but now renders Japan invisible.[25]

At the same time, 1950s traditionalism rearticulated the premodern/modern temporal disjunction that emerged in the late nineteenth/early twentieth century. As noted in chapter 1, the "traditional," set off from the "modern," was precisely what was to be jettisoned for many late nineteenth- and early twentieth-century Korean enlightenment and proletarian writers and thinkers.[26] Such a rejection, of course, did not entail a dismissal of the new notion of "tradition" itself and its accompanying temporal register.

Rather, it called for the rejection of the past as feudal, outdated, thus setting the stage for a different opposition, the advocating of the traditional as a site of authenticity in relation to the advent of the modern and its colonial imposition.

The following central lines of argument made in the literary and intellectual discourse on tradition in the 1950s all have their enlightenment- and colonial-period precedents (and are thus linked to the broader, global process of the "invention of tradition"), even as they intersect with the 1950s discussion of national literature and participate in the making of space south of the DMZ into the Republic of Korea: the wholesale rejection of the past as feudal or irrelevant, the attempt to grapple with the modern via selective appropriation of elements from the past, and the biologizing/racializing of tradition.[27]

Let us turn first to an antitraditionalist. In his "The Korean Structure of the Modern" (1956),[28] Hong Sa-jung, in a manner similar to Maruyama Masao, calls for the "human subject of civil society," one that can resist both fascism and what he considers the asocial (*pisahoejŏgin*), unmediated self.[29] According to Hong, the modern has thus far disallowed Korea from overcoming its feudal absolutism and repressive family structure. Both were left intact by the Japanese colonial state. Moreover,

> From Yi Kwang-su to Yŏm Sang-sŏp, the "progressivism" and "national" consciousness of nationalist literature [*minjokchuŭi munhak*] was, in the final analysis, nothing more than that of a colonized society. Therefore, the fact that one strand of national literature actively developed at that time later became what is called "imperial subjects literature," utterly bereft of national consciousness, cannot solely be attributed to the destruction of a spirit of resistance in the 1930s by Japanese imperialism.[30]

While liberation in 1945 provided the opportunity to overcome tradition and colonialism by constructing the social self, Korean literature has done nothing more than reflect a confused reality: "It cannot be denied that even after the Korean War writers are once again resorting to anxiety and escapism."[31] Hong encapsulates a Korean tradition and history that has allowed two choices: a retreat to the "asocial" or submission to totalizing structures such as family, class, or empire. Hong's antitraditionalist position naturalizes a universalist, liberal, democratic, free-world subject even as it offers an implicit critique of the Syngman Rhee regime.

Such a rejection of the feudal past contrasts with the position taken by others who attempt to locate elements in the Korean tradition that could ground the selective appropriation of the West in order to modernize. Ch'oe Il-su writes in the article on national literature cited above, for example, that, above all else, the new generation of writers must be able to make use of a "creative consciousness" (*ch'angjo ŭisik*) that will sublate (*chiyang*) the anxiety, despair, and fragmentation that characterizes the West of the first half of the twentieth century into a new form of humanism. Ch'oe's exhortation clearly draws upon Kim Tong-ni's theory of "pure literature" as well as on late-colonial-period pan-Asianism.[32] Ch'oe's call is to form a modern national consciousness grounded in a subjectivity (*chuch'esŏng*) achieved by properly fusing "the continuity of tradition" with a critical adoption of the modern. The formation of this subject is necessary in order to overcome the reality of the divided nation.[33] The fundamental task is to achieve unification of the fractured self through a firm belief in the national tradition and the spirit of resistance flowing within "our literature."[34]

Ch'oe's position finds further articulation in a 1957 article[35] by Yi Ŭn-sang, in which the latter relies on a *tongyang/sŏyang* (orient/occident) binary to construct a genetics of the spirit that resists the modern. According to Yi, the core elements of geography and blood are no different now than they were in the past. Insofar as the cultural achievements in cells (*sep'o*) have not been destroyed, the fundamental life possessed by literature and the spirit (*hon*) it emanates have not changed. Here and elsewhere in the 1950s, the invocation of *tongyang* is accompanied by its elision, the continuous slippage between *tongyang* and Han'guk, "oriental spirit" and "Korean spirit." The *tongyang*/Han'guk slippage rearticulates late-colonial-period pan-Asian imaginings to accord with the manufacture of South Korea as sovereign space. On another level, however, it also produces a subject that extends beyond South Korea's borders to include not only the North but also, without naming them, Japan and China—to be sure, a timeless, culturalist space, but one that contests Cold War divisions.

Yi Ŭn-sang's racializing of the spirit certainly resembles the statist thought of the 1950s, the assertion, for example, by Yi Sang-baek that if individual life (*kaein saenghwal*) is a line or a dot and social life (*sahoe saenghwal*) a half circle, national life (*kungmin saenghwal*) is the full circle.[36] According to Yi Sang-baek, "culture and life" should be understood as "culture and national life." National life is not the sum total of the lives of individuals; it is the destined fusion into one entity brought about by the reality faced by the state. National life does not exist outside of the state. Life outside of the state is nothing more than the life of the people (*minjung saenghwal*): "In this manner, national life is, first, a life which finds its completion in a total life; second, it is a life defined by the reality of the state, one which must, therefore, respond to the requests of the state. At the same time as this is a fact, it is destiny, and it is the ideal."[37] This articulation of the coincidence of self with nation and state, the investment of meaning in the self only as the national and statist self, intersects with both colonial-period imperialization and the "One-People Principle" (*ilminjuŭi*), the founding ideology of Syngman Rhee's Liberal Party. Elaborated by An Ho-sang, Yi Pŏm-sŏk, and Yang U-jŏng, *ilminjuŭi* rejects both communism and capitalism, emphasizing the timeless homogeneity of the Korean people, the nation as family, organic whole.[38] The emergence of existentialism, its popularity among youth and intellectuals, must be understood in the context of this call for nation-state coincidence, its concomitant organizing of anticommunist subjects, and its unspoken relation to the colonial statism and pan-Asianism very much alive in the memories of the majority of Koreans in the mid-1950s.

Existentialism as Antistatism

"Existence over essence" (*siljon i ponjil poda ap'sŏnda*) was a phrase often cited in 1950s South Korean intellectual journals. The phrase signals the rejection of social and religious authority in favor of the freedom of choice held by the individual. While it unsettles traditionalist and statist claims, it also tends to rely upon a universalizing gesture, the positing of a global and more-or-less uniform post–World War II condition. While privileging a metaphysics of presence/existence, existentialism played an important role in the 1950s, questioning both the people-place isomorphism of postcolonial nationalism and the essentialisms associated with traditionalism. It also provided an implicit way, under the National Security Law, to offer a critique of Syngman Rhee's authoritarianism.

Scholars of the time frequently noted that existentialism had achieved a position of prominence in the South Korean intellectual world. Indeed, in "The Problem of Modern Korean Novels—A General Analysis" (1959),[39] Chŏng Pong-nae writes that the attempt to emphasize the value of human existence in the wake of the Korean War caused "existential consciousness" to become the representative philosophy of Korean society.[40] At the same time, Chŏng asserts that the discussion of tradition and continuity in the 1950s was a reaction to the sense of a "loss of subjectivity" brought about by precisely this immersion in existentialism.[41] In other words, the turn to the existential subject arose from a specific need tied to the Korean War as referent but was, in the end, inauthentic, not properly coupled to the nation, a referent grounded by tradition.

The existentialism of the 1950s and the notion of the individual accompanying it in South Korea should also be understood in relation to the antifascism of French existentialism. In other words, the recovery of the self from totalitarianism, the extrapolation of the notion of "existence over essence" from widely read French existentialist texts such as Sartre's *Nausea*, occur as part of Korea's own experience with Japanese imperialism and a continuing statism in the form of the authoritarian Rhee regime. It is within this multilayered context that we should understand the outlining of existentialist thought in articles such as Chŏng Ha-ŭn's "Before Literature—Centering on Sartre" (1956). Here, Chŏng delineates anxiety, loneliness, and despair as the three central aspects of existentialism. These arise because of the rejection by the self of the restrictions placed on its freedom by the state or, for that matter, any system/ideology. The absence of God, faith, and morality engenders anxiety and loneliness because the free subject has no authority in which to ground responsible action. Despair arises because the subject confronts the fact that its unlimited freedom does not effect change. The subject becomes skeptical, distrustful. Even if struggle brings about social change, it does not last—a new struggle must begin. In the Sartrean dialectic, despair becomes the driving force for action; Sartrean ethics, that is, are not based on the normative "do this, do that" but on action grounded in one's own freedom.[42]

Chŏng Hŭi-mo delineates the differences in the 1950s postwar literary world between the "older generation" of writers and critics (which includes Kim Tong-ni and Cho Yŏn-hyŏn) and the "new generation" (including Hong Sa-jung and Chŏng Ch'ang-bŏm). The former turned to tradition and the purity (*sunsusŏng*) of literature; the latter emphasized the modernity (*hyŏndaesŏng*) of literature, the need to import Western literary thought.[43] Influenced by the British "angry young men" and the American "lost generation," the new generation accepted the Western notion of the absurd (*pujori*) as the "modern." Rebelling against the values of the older generation, they privileged the coincidental and the irrational over the systematic and the objective. For them, existentialism was associated not with ontological inquiry but was considered a "philosophy of agony":

In other words, writers and critics in the 1950s equated the sense of crisis arising from the absence of trust in the older generation, the despair and anxiety regarding civilizational progress, as the fundamental experience of existentialism. The despairing, discouraged monad [kaech'eja], the rebel rejecting existing reality, the alienated, isolated figure opposing a mechanistic, materialist civilization and modernity in the works of Son Ch'ang-sŏp, Chang Yong-hak, Kim Sŏng-han, and O Sang-wŏn are all part of this [intellectual] environment.[44]

Existentialism, as an attitude or a stance, denationalized the body and affect. Existential thought also provided a critique of postcolonial ethnonationalism and its figuring of colonial-period resistance by delinking human sovereignty from territorial integrity. Consider, for example, Son U-Song's emphasis on the coalition forming around Dr. Rieux, the protagonist of Camus' *The Plague*, in his "The Absurd Human—The Point of Departure in Camus' Thought" (1958).[45] Son notes that the human world is always, to some extent, infected with the plague; all humans are fighting this horrible disease. Dr. Rieux and his friends in the text are at once individuals and members of a more general humanity. Certainly, they do all they can to protect themselves against the disease. However, even while running the risk of infection, they expend every possible effort to cure others. No one thinks of himself or herself as a patriot. Nor is anyone motivated by the abstract notion of philanthropy. They fight on behalf of humanity because they themselves are human.[46]

The dismissal of patriotism/the state by Son U-song calls into question, necessarily in an indirect manner, not only the Rhee regime's authoritarianism and anticommunism but also the notion of the free world as putting in place a normative ethics of "do this, do that." Existentialism was thus the vehicle for an antistatist subject to emerge in South Korea, one that rejected the interpellation of subjects embedded in a national narrative of anticolonial opposition. But, as we will see below, its humanism could not account for the new power relations making up the Cold War world.

Lingering Among the Dead: Necrophilia and Nonalignment

As of this writing, the Korean War has not ended formally. The cessation of hostilities in July 1953 occurred in the form of an armistice, not a peace treaty. In the 1950s, *Han'guk munhak* acknowledged the North/South border and the continuing call for vigilance and possible combat in a very material way. Literary texts ended with the same conclusion, an anticommunist inscription on the last page calling for advance on the North:

OUR VOWS

1. As Sons and Daughters of the Republic of Korea, we will fight to the death in defense of the nation.
2. We will join together in an iron-clad solidarity to smash the communist invaders.
3. We will bring about South/North reunification and plant the Republic of Korea flag on the summit of Mount Paektu.[47]

Such a marking of state power displays a certain anxiety directed toward the textual space that precedes it, as well as toward its readership. In fact, despite the polarizing Korean War, 1950s cultural production often questions, in a necessarily vague way, the incorporation of South Korea into a newly forming free-world anticommunist order. Take, for example, the 1955 film *P'iagol* (dir., Yi Kang-ch'ŏn), which, as Kim So-yŏn points out, offers a portrayal of partisans fighting in Chŏlla Province that can actually lead to a certain sympathy for the leftist cause.[48] Rather than functioning to demonize the communist other, the film can be viewed as an "allegory of human history dealing with the abstract themes of human desires and faults."[49] The censors attempted to close down this possibility by forcing the film's director, Yi Kang-ch'ŏn, to superimpose the Republic of Korea flag over the partisan Ae-ran's body as she wanders across a sandy waste in the last scene after all the other partisans have been killed. Such an ending, of course, rehearses the slogan placed on the last page of 1950s literary texts. The aim is to remove the ambivalence of the film toward anticommunism by nationalizing both Ae-ran and the landscape.

Without the superimposition of the flag, this long, two-shot sequence of Ae-ran's wandering would have her fleeing through an unmarked territory, perhaps away from the Korean peninsula altogether. The closing shot leaves us with an image that points to the contestations of the 1950s cultural scene. The attempt to consider a "way out" of a postcolonial modern marked by Cold War division confronts the state power that enforces the new borders. An ambivalence that troubles Cold War oppositions makes itself manifest in the form of a diaphanous layering, the placing of the

FIGURE 3.2 Ae-ran "returns" from the mountains (*P'iagol*, 1955).

see-through flag over a body that might move through it and to some other destination outside of the frame, were the film not to end.[50]

We can, moreover, locate *P'iagol* in the history of recantation and counter-recantation narratives that signal the ideological shifts and position takings of the 1930s and, later, the 1945–1948 occupation period. Neither the increasing skepticism of the young partisan intellectual Ch'ŏl-su nor even the superimposition of Ae-ran and the ROK flag at the close of the film produces a seamless statist identification. At the same time, the abiding concern of this film is with ideological cleansing (*sukchŏng*), the targeting of the self and its "true" identification. Thus the clash between partisans and the anticommunist paramilitary (*t'obŏldae*) sent to eliminate them takes on secondary importance. The struggle is among the partisans themselves. The series of suspicions, doubts, and murders among the partisans actually ends up displaying the ways in which a generalized logic of *sukch'ŏng* attempts to produce a disciplined, statist subject (communist or anticommunist). Instead of the portrayal of any clearly delineated position in the film, for example a "good anticommunist" or "bad communist," we have a series of deaths that leave us nothing but inert bodies.

P'iagol concerns itself centrally with necrophilia. We find this in the double rape of Soju's corpse by fellow partisans and in Yi Kang-ch'ŏn's remark that one of the alternative endings for the film was a necrophilic scene between Ae-ran and the dead Ch'ŏl-su. The representation of sexual relations with an inert, dead body has the effect of moving beyond any kind of human relation or identification characterized by a clearly defined object or subject. Instead, the portrayal of necrophilia exposes the relation between film and audience. In her discussion of the German filmmaker Harun Farocki's *Images of the World and the Inscription of War*, Kaja Silverman draws on work by Roland Barthes and Christian Metz to elaborate the relation between memory and death in photography and film. Silverman shows how the visual image—for example, of a bomb approaching a military target or a young Jewish prisoner at Auschwitz—signals at once memorialization and mortification in the form of the preservation of an image and the destruction of its referent. Silverman's concern is to show how the camera "confers identity upon the subject only at the expense of his or her 'being.'"[51] Photographed by an SS camera, the prisoner becomes a "Jewish woman," a category that produces an identity at the same time as it signals her death. Silverman makes the useful distinction between *memory*, associated with a "resistant look," which puts into play a "constantly shifting conglomeration of images and values," for example, the look back at the camera by the Jewish woman that resists the objectifying SS gaze by pointing to a time that falls outside of the camera's frame, and *memorialization*. The latter is atemporal, relying upon the acceptance of a fixed and "clearly delineated object."[52]

When watching a film, the viewer is engaging in a relation with death, with images that point to the absence of the bodies of the actors that were filmed on a set. The task of the spectator is to imagine these images as live bodies. The portrayal of the necrophilac act in *P'iagol*, however, allows for no thought of life standing behind death. The viewer of the film is brought to a confrontation with death itself, to a mortification that does not produce memorialization or a subject. Necrophilia thus plays a central role in *P'iagol*'s refusal to permit the suture of camera and eye and the construction of an anticommunist spectatorship at the expense of a clearly defined other.

Memorialization is refused via the sexual encounter with the dead body, the becoming-dead that this encounter signals. Indeed, necrophilia in *P'iagol* points to the ways in which the North becomes a memory image in the 1950s, located in the interstices between memory and memorialization (or between mourning and melancholia). The film's trajectory turns upon the gradual elimination of the partisans, their disappearance. The process of their erasure, one associated with the removal of the last remnants of "North Korea" at the end of the Korean War, signals a move toward objectification, but it is a move interrupted by a lingering attraction to the corpse. The film *P'iagol* displays the ways in which imaging of the North in South Korea comes to involve a relation with the living dead.

Necrophilia becomes a "resistant" look, a refusal to acknowledge death. The alternative ending mentioned by Yi Kang-ch'ŏn would have placed Ae-ran in an ambivalent, lingering relationship with Ch'ŏl-su and the "other" modernity of the partisans and North Korea. *P'iagol* was censored and its distribution delayed because none of the partisans, including Ae-ran and Ch'ŏl-su, recant. Recantation narratives are structured by the killing off of one's former self and a rebirth as someone else. Ae-ran and Ch'ŏl-su attempt to escape from the murderous infighting brought on by the sadistic, authoritarian leader of the partisan unit, but they do not embrace life in the free world. The attempt to cover Ae-ran, and the film itself, with the ROK flag represents a kind of killing off, a desire to lay ambivalence to rest. The image of the flag at the close of the film tries to speak, to offer a statist memorialization. The film, however, provides a memory of attraction to the left and possible movement to some other space outside of the frame of the bifurcated peninsula that "looks back" at the last-minute attempt to efface it.

The Politics of Despair

South/North division; the devastation of war; the corrupt, autocratic regime of Syngman Rhee; and the failure of import-substitution industrialization to jumpstart the economy went hand in hand with what John Lie calls a 1950s "culture of despair."[53] While land reform brought about the stability the United States deemed necessary to ward off the communist threat and cleared the way for later industrialization by removing the landlord class from its power base, what Lie calls the "triple alliance"—U.S. aid, the Rhee regime, and dependent capitalists—proved to be a powerful obstacle to economic development in 1950s South Korea.[54]

Powerlessness, hopelessness, impoverishment, and solitude are indeed terms frequently invoked to describe the 1950s South Korean cultural scene. While canonizing Son Ch'ang-sŏp as the quintessential writer of despair, critics have differed in their assessment of Son's work.⁵⁵ Does despair represent a retreat from the social, or does it reflect the reality of the contemporaneous postwar condition? The influential critic Kim Yun-sik, who considers Son "the representative writer of the 1950s," writes,

> Son's works, unlike the majority of contemporaneous novels, bear no relation to the preconceptions of a naïve humanism or blind anticommunism. However, his substituting in their place contempt, a distrust of the human also relies on a preconception. In the same manner as these other works, then, Son's texts, in the end, construct an abstract, atemporal world.⁵⁶

Discussing the dark, cramped, confined spaces that figure prominently in Son's work, Yi Ki-in states that "Son's gaze is not directed at the rooms destroyed by war, but at the powerless characters confined to these rooms. His interest is limited to human despair for its own sake; the social conditions of the 1950s serve merely as a vague background for this despair."⁵⁷ Other critics oppose this view of despair as "subjective." Pointing to the prevalence of the "abnormal" in Son's texts, Kwŏn Yŏng-min asserts that "This human deformation does not come from human deficiency itself; it emanates from the reality of the postwar condition."⁵⁸ Yi Chae-sŏn, defining Son's work as a literature of disease, malaise, and meaninglessness states that "This world was created as a result of the disgrace of the war experience."⁵⁹ Han Su-yŏng writes that "insofar as Son's works revolve around a series of conflictual situations, they reveal the essential contradictions of 1950s Korean society, demonstrating the characteristics of a realist novel."⁶⁰

These two strands of criticism depart upon separate paths at the crossroads of the referent: Where does despair locate its origins? I do not discount the importance of the impoverished postwar condition. Rather than seeking to pin down the referent, however, I would add two intertextual layers to the culture of despair. First, to write the world as "diseased" is to enter into a discursive relation with "twentieth-century Western literature," itself often described by Korean critics of the time as a literature of "despair" and "anxiety." Second, the representation of the despairing subject in the 1950s entails an unspoken return to the late 1930s literature of malaise penned by Tanch'ŭng Group writers such as Ch'oe Myŏng-ik. The despair of these texts, the aimlessness, and the gap that opens up between the verbal description of people and objects and a sense that one cannot place them in any kind of a temporal narrative provide a feeling of stasis or even entropy that we also find in Son Ch'ang-sŏp's short fictions.[61]

Ch'oe Myŏng-ik's works are important for the ways in which they address the advent of imperialization, the moment that the proletarian cultural movement was shut down once and for all and the possibilities opened up by modernism dismissed. I read them as a form of antirecantation, a refusal to transform oneself that ends up calling into question not only what one is to become but also that position one was to leave behind. It is as if writing attempts to produce a still or stop that questions the ceaseless movement associated with modernity. Such writing finds itself unwilling to buy into a project that promises to "overcome modernity" by way of imperialization and mass mobilization.

The statist anticommunism of the 1950s continues that of the late 1930s. Son's works are not atemporal. Instead, they point to the multiple temporalities that work their way across cultural production in the newly forming Republic of Korea. They return to the colonial, particularly to the moment of imperialization. Son does not concern himself with distinguishing between colonial and postcolonial states. His texts resemble the late colonial antirecantations in the way they attempt to question the statist ordering and mobilizing of subjects, one now taking place in the 1950s. We encounter, here, a resistance to the state that is best called antianticommunist.

Such an antianticommunism also rejects the postwar promise of a future in the free world. Let us consider, for example, Son's "Unresolved Chapter" ("Mihaegyŏl ŭi chang," 1955), a text that distances itself from an appropriation of existentialism simply to place the subject on the level of the "modern."[62] The protagonist Chi-sang's figuring of himself as "stranger"[63] enables a rejection, among other things, of the older generation, the corrupt political economy of 1950s South Korea, the mechanism of Cold War free-world ideology appropriated by the South Korean state to legitimate itself, the postwar fetishization of the "United States," and the imbrication of the colonial and the neocolonial. At stake here, as in discussions of tradition, the modern, and the relations between national literature and world literature, is the universal/particular relation. In what ways does Chi-sang's critique of his family's obsessive desire to study in the United States occlude his own act of translating the discourse of Western existentialism into the subject position of "stranger"?

Importantly, the text demonstrates an awareness of Chi-sang's despair as the effect of representation rather than emerging of its own accord out of the particular material conditions of impoverished 1950s South Korea. Chi-sang has a habit of gazing at children in an elementary school playground through the holes ripped in a concrete wall during the Korean War by gunfire. He does this often, he tells us, engaging in the same reverie each time: Chi-sang is a pathologist, gazing into a microscope. He has been entrusted with finding a cure to a skin disease from which the (anthropomorphized) globe suffers. He has determined that the disease is caused by a bacteria called "humans" but has been unable to discover how the bacteria is produced and spreads. He is, therefore, "even more in the dark as to the cure."[64]

Chi-sang's "microscope," of course, observes the traces of a specific historical event: the Korean War. The latter frames what Chi-sang can see, having produced the holes in the wall, but Chi-sang cannot contemplate the origins of the war. This lies outside his vision, beyond the limits of the text he is writing. He can only examine a generalized condition of global pathology. This inability informs much of Son's work. It also places on display the limits of the 1950s South Korean cultural field. The topic of the Korean War, in fact, was largely avoided in the literature of the 1950s.

In "Unresolved Chapter," the visual regime of anticommunism is thus extended beyond the unseen but ubiquitous communist threat that disciplines anticommunist subjects to the framing of speech and vision by state, the censor, and the National Security Law.[65] The subject is located in the "unresolved" relation, the ambivalent space between sets of terms frequently invoked in postwar intellectual discourse such as East and West, particular and universal, tradition and the modern.

How does a 1950s South Korean writer critique the state without crossing the line, violating the National Security Law? The repetition itself of the "sick world" points to its limits, to a figuring of this representation as a "confined, enclosed space." At the same time, the existentialist assertion of existence over essence dismantles the "free world"/"communist" ideological antinomy dividing the Korean peninsula. As is often the case in Son's texts, "Unresolved Chapter" figures its own boundaries and refers to its present inability to resolve the issue at hand.

For Chi-sang, participation in the corrupt political economy of 1950s South Korea requires that he attempt to enter the ranks of the comprador elite by completing his legal studies, pimping the bodies of available women, or submitting to occupying the lowest position in the dependent economy, joining his family in piecing together the leftovers of leftovers, discarded bits of fabric sent to South Korea as part of the U.S. aid package. Rejection, withdrawal, in this context necessitates confrontation with hunger and possible death. Submission to dependent capitalism would signal the dismantling of the subject as "stranger," predicated, as it is here, upon its critical distance from the prevailing social order.

"Unresolved Chapter" does not write itself out of this dilemma. In the end, Chi-sang's calling out for his girlfriend Kwang-sun, one that contrasts sharply with Mersault's feelings toward Marie in *The Stranger*, indicates a radical ambivalence. Estranged both from the discursive stranger, the figure of Mersault, and from the material, from participating in what the text represents as a corrupt, dependent capitalist order, this reconfigured stranger cannot locate a position for himself. He exists in the space and time of the "unresolved."

Looking Back at the Rear Window, or the Cold War Visual Order on Display

Written at the height of his career, Son's "Position of the Stairs" ("Ch'ŭnggye ŭi wich'i," 1956) addresses the relation among the discursive, the visual, and the material. In Son's work, this relation takes place in a Cold War world that now locates the discursive encounter with the West in the same space as the material encounter with U.S. power "on the ground." In "Position," the entrance of the narrator into the space of his own gaze figures interiority collapsing in on itself. The folding in of what the narrator calls his "inner world" when he enters this space is portrayed, in turn, as the movement that blocks the protagonist from seeing the social, the "internal structure" (*naebu kujo*) of the "building."

The portrayal of the cityscape in "Position" is very much linked to the reality of a city destroyed by war. We have the spectacle of the materiality of destruction and the appearance in South Korea of U.S. power. The narrator of "Position," a worker in a print shop, has rented a second-story room. His window looks out upon a three-story building severely damaged during the Korean War. The narrator has no money and can find nothing to occupy himself following his return from work. He tells us he has gazed disinterestedly through his rear window at the building for some time, but recently he began to discover some facts that cannot but draw his interest. The first floor contains two establishments, a restaurant and a store that sells a variety of items (leather shoes, pipes, hats, overcoats) to U.S. soldiers. The second floor has two rooms; the third floor has one (the second room having been, the narrator surmises, destroyed during the Korean War).[66] The narrator watches, through windows in the stairwell, a young woman, a sex worker servicing U.S. soldiers, climb the stairs to the third floor: "Watching her, I was amazed at the mystery that presented itself to me. It was not anything directly related to the woman herself, but to the internal structure of the building."[67] The narrator cannot understand how the stairs are configured in such a way that the woman's back is toward him when she climbs from the first floor to the second floor but, after she disappears from his sight for a moment, is also toward him as she climbs from the second floor to the third floor. The narrator becomes obsessed with the mystery of the "internal structure" of the building.

Let us consider the relation between the urban mystery confronting this narrator in the "periphery" and an urban mystery of the U.S. metropolis. In his discussion of Hitchcock's *Rear Window* (1954), Slavoj Žižek tells us that "the window through which James Stewart ... gazes continually is clearly a fantasy-window—his desire is fascinated by what he can see through the window."[68] Grace Kelly can only become the object of his desire

> by literally entering the frame of his fantasy; by crossing the courtyard and appearing "on the other side" where he can see her through the window. When Stewart sees her in the murderer's apartment his gaze is immediately fascinated, greedy, desirous of her: she has found her place in his fantasy-space. This would be Lacan's "male chauvinist" lesson: man can relate to woman only in so far as she enters the frame of his fantasy.[69]

Following Žižek's analysis, "woman" is constructed by man as "other" precisely when she becomes the object of desire by an imaging. It is, moreover, through this imaging, this manufacture of the other as object of desire in the fantasy-frame, that interiority is constructed.

"Position" revolves around the figuration of desire. Desire for the woman is hinted at by the narrator's co-workers' joke that his obsession is not with the architecture of the building but with the "beauty" of the sex workers.[70]

That the woman who lives on the third floor "resembles my sister"[71] complicates this desire. Does I's imaging of this sex worker as sister posit her as the incestuous object of desire in his fantasy-frame? Does I's imaging of this woman as sister allegorize her as the national body violated by the U.S. soldier, with I's focus on the "position of the stairs" enabling him to avoid as much as possible this unbearable sight? Eventually I makes his way to the building. Here, the ability of the text to represent the embrace of the woman and the U.S. soldier problematizes the allegorization of the sister/sex worker's body as nation: "I saw the bed and something upon it. A woman, almost nude, and a foreign soldier tightly embraced."[72] The text does not repress this scene but invites the reader to view the position of the "sister."

I tells us following his witnessing of this scene that he "completely forgot to investigate the staircase."[73] The representation of national rape works as a screen to hide the "architecture" of the structure. What is off limits, what cannot be understood, is the internal structure, the "position of the stairs." Narrating South Korea/U.S. relations as rape of the nation (the allegorical nationalizing of bodies) falls safely within the bounds of the South Korean cultural field, a displacement of domestic, "internal" tensions. This allegorization, moreover, produces a way of seeing that elides the possibility of alternative forms of communality by summoning a subject at once anticommunist, statist, *and* ethnonational. As we will see in chapter 4, the repetition of this trope in the decades of camptown literature that would follow points, in fact, to its sanctioning by the state.[74]

"Position," then, occurs as a deallegorization, a revealing of the ways in which the borders of the South Korean cultural field are taking form in the 1950s. "Position," moreover, demonstrates how the disfigurement of bodies we find in many of Son's works further disrupts the notion of an interior, even as these bodies, as well as the narration, are often confined to small, cramped spaces. In Son's texts, the third-person narrators' interiorized gaze on disfigurement and a generalized entropy points to a porosity, a puncturing of the surface. Those cast outside, the marginalized and dispossessed, enter the interior space as a form of confinement. We thus have an interior that is radically "exterior," or, more precisely, social.

The narrator closes "Position" with the following: "It's okay, I thought, if the secret of my life as one element of society, as an individual entity named 'I,' cut off from the outside [*oebu wa ch'adandoench'e*], lay here forever along with the secret of the internal structure of this three-story building."[75] But, of course, this is not okay. By pointing to the limits of its own representation, to a "secret" structure that cannot be revealed, the text figures not only the process of a retreat to the self, to the "individual entity named I," but to the Cold War distribution of the visible: what can be seen, the identitarian fantasy-frame that allegorizes the U.S./South Korean relation as rape, and what is to be rendered invisible, the formation of the nonstatist, nonethnonationalized alliances, intimacies, and communalities that Son pursues at the margins of other texts seldom discussed or anthologized.

Sexuality and the Narrative of Anticolonial Resistance

Son Ch'ang-sŏp's first response to the pressure literary critics placed upon him to move away from the hopelessness and despair of his early works and create "positive," active characters occurred in a largely ignored text, "Wide Plain" ("Kwangya," 1956). This text centers on the anxiety, violence, and greed of a dysfunctional family making its living selling opium in Manchuria during the colonial period. The hopeless older generation is eventually left behind, and a coalition of young people head off to Shanghai, presumably to join the anticolonial resistance. The leader of the coalition, the young intellectual Tong-o, embodies in all respects the "positive character" Son was urged to write—*except that he is Chinese*. Here, as elsewhere, Son dismisses the privileging of ethnonational resistance to colonial rule.

Son pursued the politics of nonalignment in his first full-length novel, *The Scribblers* (*Naksŏjok*, 1959). This text seeks to disrupt the organizing of post-1945 ethnonationalism as part and a parcel of a longer state-sponsored grand narrative of resistance to Japanese colonial rule.[76] Literary texts set in the Japanese colonial period were, in fact, few and far between in the 1950s and 1960s, with most writers choosing to avoid issues involving the late 1930s and early 1940s culture of mass mobilization. Son, however, did not hesitate to set his full-length novel in the Japan of the late 1930s. It is in the former metropole that Son sets up a conflict between the call to participate in national resistance, one that intersects with the 1950s call to form a national literature, and what he considers an unmediated, "natural" sexuality.

Unsurprisingly, *The Scribblers* did not fare well. Son's work was severely critiqued in the journal *Sasanggye* following its appearance. Kim U-jong noted that by portraying the protagonist To-hyŏn—a Korean student studying in Japan and the son of a prominent member of the anti-Japanese resistance—as an "idiot," Son did precisely the opposite of what Yi Kwang-su would have done with such a character.[77] Yu Chong-ho declared Son the archetypal antiromanticist: "Given the sight of a rose in a garbage heap, Son Ch'ang-sŏp would find satisfaction only by delving into the trash."[78] Paek Ch'ŏl, notably, considered the work as failing to meet the "conditions of a modern novel": it was disjointed, lacked character development, a proper telos, and an "organic connection between parts."[79] However, the text is not unified, "organic," precisely because of the struggle between the narratives of the spontaneous, sexual self and the nationalist subject. These narratives intersect in To-hyŏn's rapes of Noriko, the daughter of his landlord.

To-hyŏn reveres Sang-hŭi (the "angelic" fellow student studying in Tokyo who attempts to educate To-hyŏn's desire, to provide him with the opportunity to engage productively in the anti-Japanese resistance) for her erudition, purity, and nobleness of spirit. Upon hearing her earnest prayers for him and the nation, To-hyŏn is overwhelmed, declaring "I, I am determined to die for the sake of the fatherland!"[80] To-hyŏn's feelings toward Sang-hŭi are complicated, however, when he comes across her modeling in a sleeveless dress for her brother, a would-be painter: "To-hyŏn was overcome with the devil of sexual desire. He felt an erection."[81] He returns home and summons Noriko to his room: "To-hyŏn hesitated a bit. But then he came across a plausible excuse. He discovered within himself a certain desire for revenge. Revenge on the Japanese police, no, on all of Japan. Maybe it wasn't just an excuse. Even though it hadn't taken clear form before, the desire for revenge had been burning inside."[82]

Subsequent encounters with Noriko occur when To-hyŏn feels "physically attracted" to Sang-hŭi, his "holy ideal of woman." Feeling guilty, To-hyŏn rushes home to "pour out his human weakness onto Noriko's body." At the same time, when "having relations" with Noriko, To-hyŏn develops "the strange habit of drawing the image of Sang-hŭi."[83] The irruption of sexuality in this text is at once an irruption of the image. Here, ekphrastic hope cannot be separated out from either masculinist sexual desire or objectification. What the text portrays as an uncontrollable, visual objectification of Sang-hŭi questions the legitimacy of the narrative of anticolonial, ethnonational resistance. The image overtakes the discursive. The verbal summoning of the national subject and the national narrative itself become the work of scribblers (*minjok* becomes the product of the *naksŏjok*). The awakening to immediacy and "truth" takes place in the painterly moment in the text, when To-hyŏn is "overcome with the devil of sexual desire" associated with the visual register.

Later in the text, To-hyŏn repeatedly attempts to convince himself, Noriko, and his friends that his motive for the rapes is revenge. When informing his friends Kwang-uk and Pyŏng-ho of the rapes, the narrator tells us, "To-hyŏn, of course, did not forget to explain that the peculiar relationship was not begun simply to satisfy sexual desire but out of the explosion of the desire for national revenge."[84] The text portrays To-hyŏn's "discovery" of a desire for national revenge as screening the truth of his sexual desire. The narrative of the nation, associated throughout this text with writing/scribbling/exhortations, becomes a kind of "talking cure" that aims to discipline the unruliness of the image, manifestation of sexual desire.

Dancing Body as Unruly Signifier: Filmic Adaptation and the Erotics of Language

It is precisely the relation between sexual desire/the image and national narrative/writing that one of the most widely read literary texts and most watched films of the 1950s, Chŏng Pi-sŏk's popular novel *Madame Freedom* (*Chayu puin*, serialized in 1954) and Han Hyŏng-mo's 1956 hit filmic adaptation of the same title, invoke in their portrayal of commodity culture and the mid-1950s Seoul cityscape. Existing scholarship on the film *Madame Freedom* either neglects or does not seem to be aware of the popular literary text it is drawn from and thus ignores the film's status as adaptation. As we will see, the movement between literary text and filmic adaptation takes place both as a form of ekphrastic hope, the desire to move from the verbal to the visual, and as a "look back" at language itself. My concern below will be to trace the movement between literary and filmic text, paying particular attention to the ways in which the film's portrayal of desire, consumption, and gender/sexuality is closely related to the literary text's extensive treatment of the debates surrounding the new "national language," han'gŭl, in the 1950s.

Chŏng's novel was a sensation and triggered a contentious debate regarding both the portrayal of Professor Chang and his wife, O Sŏn-yŏng, and the text's scathing critique of corrupt businessmen and politicians in South Korea. One commentator, for example, wrote that *Madame Freedom* was an instance of "enemy propaganda," offering a view of South Korea "identical to that of the Northern puppet regime."[85] The novel centers on the story of Sŏn-yŏng, who moves from what she considers her boring, "feudal" life at home to the workplace, Paris Imports, a shop in downtown Seoul that sells high-end imported perfumes and accessories. The text follows her subsequent Madame Bovary–like fall into a world of temptation, sexual desire, and corruption. This trajectory also bears a certain resemblance to that of Margaret in *Hand of Fate*, which appeared in theaters the same year *Madame Freedom* was serialized.[86]

While both the literary text and the film address the relations among desire, body, and commodity, the literary text, much more than the film, links these relations to contemporary debates on the new national language, han'gŭl. In the novel, Sŏn-yŏng's affective history concludes with her recognizing that her view of her husband as weak, useless, and hopelessly boring was a mistake. She now understands her husband's purity and sacrifice as a linguist in the midst of a society marked by calculation and self-interest, the world of capitalist exchange.

Professor Chang advocates the simplification of Korean orthography, but not at the expense of distorting grammar and the ways in which actual speakers use the language. He compares the laws of grammar to a constitution that brings order to a set of potentially unruly relations. At the same time, Professor Chang maintains that language is an organism, with its own physiology and makeup that must be respected, although linguistic research can lead to suggestions for its improvement. Simplification of orthography that ignores these qualities amounts to an arbitrary severing of the body. Professor Chang further locates his work in a history beginning in the Chosŏn dynasty, when han'gŭl was degraded as *ŏnmun* (the "vulgar script") and Chinese privileged as *chinsŏ* (the "truth language"), the subsequent elevation of Japanese to the status of *kugŏ* (the "national language"), and the contemporary disregard for the study of Korean in favor of English.

In this way, *Madame Freedom* locates itself in a modern history of phoneticism that we can trace back to the enlightenment period. Let us briefly consider this history. In the case of the late nineteenth- and early twentieth-century reworking of *ŏnmun* into *kungmun* and, later, Han'gul,[87] the work of Karatani Kōjin and Kwon Boduerae allows us to see the importance of *ŏnmunilch'i* (*genbun itchi*) as a privileging of the phonetic that considers sound as "Korean" for the first time, even as it now figures *chinsŏ* as "Chinese." An ethnonationalized immediacy, however, is not produced solely by a pneumatism, the self-presence of the voice. Instead, it appears in the materiality of the phonetic script itself on the printed page. Even as a certain phonocentrism is endorsed as marker of the modern, the investment of the voice *in* the ethnonationalized script disallows the figuring of writing as degradation from pure (ethnonational) self-presence. The act itself of writing in han'gŭl, one that later stands at the center of Professor Chang's project, thus emerges as one kind of ethnonational performance.

The privileging of sound invested within the materiality of the han'gŭl script as authentic turns the "meaning" associated with *chinsŏ* on its head. Chinese characters can now recede into the past. They appear as etymological residual, subordinated to the self-presence of "Korean" sounds embodied in han'gŭl. The investment of the ethnonational body in the material signifier itself, moreover, points to an organicist relation between "language" and "bodies." Script is not separated from the body but is an actual appendage of the organicist whole. The embodiment of the ethnonation in script, then, represents a kind of phoneticist organicism.

Such a phoneticist organicism stands in contrast to the emphasis in colonial-period proletarian literature on the transparent, universalizing movement of expression. Certainly the desire for immediacy, an assimilatory self-presence, marks both the proletarian and the ethnonational emancipatory views of language. KAPF texts, however, turn upon the logic of transparency/absolute representability linked to a phonetic script subordinated to the self-presence of the international proletarian body. Colonial-period proletarian texts dismiss ethnonational investment in the phonetic Korean script, as we see, for example, in the Esperanto titling of the proletarian culture movement as Korea Artista Proletaria Federatio (KAPF).

The suppression of Korean in the late colonial period, most dramatically instanced in the early 1940s wartime jailing of linguists, underscores the ways in which Japanese was deployed in relation to pan-Asian identification. 1945 marks the end of Japanese-language public discourse, a move toward what Serk-Bae Suh has called a "monolingual society."[88] The change accompanying the assertion of political/territorial sovereignty in the occupation period, the possessive shift in "national language" from Japanese to Korean, certainly occurs as one of the critical junctures in the modern history of the ethnonationalizing of script. This is a shift, moreover, that plays a significant role in the transformation of Japanese-language pan-Asian texts into collaborative acts and in the ways in which *uri mal* (our language) became in post-1945 South Korea an example of the lifting of repression, allowing for a properly postcolonial Korean identity.[89]

We should also note the ways in which post-1945 *uri mal* is embedded in the location of anticommunist South Korea under U.S. Cold War hegemony. Not only Japanese but a continuing negotiation with Chinese (the postliberation debates regarding the use of Sino-Korean characters, for example) and a shift in the relation to English (begun, as we saw in chapter 2, under U.S. military occupation) takes place in the 1950s.

Madame Freedom follows earlier texts written under U.S. military occupation such as Yŏm Sang-sŏp's "Western Cookie Box" and *Dawn Wind* and Ch'ae Man-sik's "Mister Pang," which negotiate the transfer of hegemony from Japan to the United States in terms of a shift in linguistic power relations. As we have noted, the command of English in these texts secures social mobility and consequent economic and political power. "Mister Pang" represents the earliest postliberation equation of English with non-nationalized, self-interested desire. For Mister Pang, English is cultural capital to be sold for personal profit. In *Dawn Wind*, English emerges not so much to signal the subordination of the Korean language but as a necessary means to construct a cosmopolitan identity that will allow for a postcolonial developmentalist trajectory—knowledge of the United States/West on South Korea's terms.

It turns out that the folding of body into language enables *Madame Freedom* to eroticize the new national script. Professor Chang's concern that the oversimplification of orthography will break up the linguistic organism bears a close relation with the emergence of transgressive, unruly bodies, particularly in the famous mambo scenes that take place in both the literary text and the filmic adaptation. The loss of Professor Chang's authority is linked to post–Korean War decadence, corruption, and an exchange economy in which han'gŭl and its study have no value.

If, in the end, *Madame Freedom* narrates the recovery of han'gŭl's value precisely in its resistance to exchange, this occurs via a necessary detour. The text endeavors to redirect both the unruly sexuality produced in dance and Sŏn-yŏng's association with the desire/fetishizing of foreign commodities toward han'gŭl. The turning point in the literary text occurs when Sŏn-yŏng is brought to tears by Professor Chang's speech at a hearing on the national language at the National Assembly. The eroticism of dance and desire for commodities is not dispensed with but lifted to a new, different

FIGURE 3.3 The mambo scene (*Madame Freedom*, 1956).

level: Sŏn-yŏng's recovery of her love for her husband based on his attachment and devotion to the corporealized script, his language fetishism.[90]

The serialized novel *Madame Freedom*, then, can be located in the broader context of a twentieth-century linguistic modernity and the 1950s discussion of the relation between tradition and a properly modern subject. Certainly, the text shows us how the latter relies upon an unnamed gendered public/private split. *Madame Freedom*, moreover, intersects with the organicism of Yi Ŭn-sang in its provision of an ethnonational grammar that stands against both the destabilizing of reference by an earlier proletarian phoneticist internationalism and an exchange economy associated linguistically with English. Here we see the importance of the text's frequent comparing of Sŏn-yŏng's unruliness to the threat of communism. Like Margaret in *Hand of Fate*, Sŏn-yŏng is at once closely associated with the desire for foreign commodities and inhabited by the communist other. In the novel, the containment of Sŏn-yŏng, her recovery from the scene of unruly dancing bodies, becomes a warding off both of the lure of the consumer culture of the city and the banned proletarian narrative.

We learn in the novel (though not in the film) that Professor Chang's favorite student—and potential love interest—was a typist working for the Japanese in Singapore during the colonial period. In both novel and film, she works in an American office in Seoul. The typewriter and its mediating/depersonalizing of language is thus linked to pre-1945 linguistic coloniality and its post-1945 iteration.[91] The trope of recovery of the national language occurs in relation to the history of a colonial/postcolonial generation more comfortable with Japanese than Korean and now associated with technics and English. This recovery, linked to the recovery of the body—and language as extension of the body—rejects commodification, sexual promiscuity, and technologization.

The initial seduction of Sŏn-yŏng in both novel and film, moreover, takes place via the sounds of jazz from their young male neighbor's record player passing through the walls into the domestic and study space of the Chang family home. This call to the outside—one that Sŏn-yŏng follows, eventually becoming involved with the young neighbor—figures her wandering as a move away from what Kittler calls the "melody of the heart" associated at once with male authorship, the touch of the hand to the pen (Professor Chang writes his treatises by hand), and a female readership. Thus the importance in both novel and film of Professor Chang's teaching Korean grammar to a group of young women, typists working for the Americans in Seoul.

While the classroom scene is one carried over from novel to film, the latter finds itself unable to return to an age antedating the typewriter or its own medium, the cinema. Even more than the film's erasure of the critical moment at the National Assembly, it is the filmic medium itself, particularly as adaptation translating the verbal into the visual, that disallows the movement away from technics (the record player, the typewriter, the camera). Recall, moreover, the visual component of language, its appearance on a page to be seen and read at the same time, as well as the linguistic component of film, certainly in the form of dialogue but also the written screenplay that precedes filming. The latter allows us to consider how filmic production in general takes place as a form of "adaptation," entailing, to be sure, a movement from verbal to visual but also a look back at the verbal in different ways (often via the dialogue or, in the case of silent

FIGURE 3.4 Professor Chang teaches Korean grammar (*Madame Freedom*, 1956).

films, intertitles accompanying filmic images). In the film *Madame Freedom*, this look back takes the form of a decentering of the national language portrayed in and making up the textual space of the novel. In the end, the call is to abandon readership in favor of the visual pleasure of spectatorship. This shift is evident in the ambivalent last scene of the film, the movement toward but visual denial of a return to the domestic space that houses the readerly activities taking place in Professor Chang's study.

While in the literary text Sŏn-yŏng's unequivocal return to the home reconsolidates a societal grammar, the film moves elsewhere. Both the disruptive visual excess of the mambo and the ambivalent final scene—where, head bowed, Sŏn-yŏng moves toward the home but is not shown entering it—disallow the containment of desire to the space of the home and the work on the national script that is taking place there.[92] The filmic *Madame Freedom* presents a visual erotics, a spectacle of dancing bodies and commodity display that overwhelms the national-language fetishism of the novel. Professor Chang's study of Korean linguistics, in fact, is almost never shown and thus moves to the margins of the film text. The classroom scene is hardly remembered, but no one forgets the mambo.

It is the film *Madame Freedom*, then, that points to the trajectory we find in Yi Kang-ch'ŏn's *P'iagol* and in Son Ch'ang-sŏp's work. The film's ambivalent ending becomes another attempt to locate some kind of alternative space. Often appearing in the form of fleeting glances, hesitations, or brief interruptions, these attempts work their way from the beginnings of Cold War culture under U.S. military occupation through the late 1980s.

If the "communist threat" is displaced in *Madame Freedom*, equated, as it is, with the fall and subsequent disciplining of a would-be 1950s modern girl, her ambivalent return to the home that is not a return recalls ways in which the marginalized and dispossessed enter the interior space in Son Ch'ang-sŏp's texts as a form of confinement.[93] That is, the figure of the dispossessed cannot help but refer to—and place under erasure—the precluded alternative, the proletarian narrative. The latter inhabits these texts.

The publication of the recanted proletarian writer Pak Yŏng-hŭi's "Solitary Confinement" ("Tokbang"; written in the 1930s but precise date unknown) in the late 1950s further speaks to a certain relation among Son's work, the contemporary excision of proletarian texts, and coloniality. Pak was particularly well known for his recantation in the early 1930s, his statement that all KAPF had gained was ideology and what it had lost was art. "Solitary Confinement" narrates this conversion in the form of a prison diary. Clearly, the text was published in the late 1950s as an anticommunist gesture, yet, taking place as a prison diary, Pak's text narrates less the oppressiveness of Japanese colonialism than it does the ways in which the South Korean state and the National Security Law worked to organize the literary and cultural field. KAPF literary production and writers can only be made visible in the 1950s via a display of confinement. Such a display intersects both with the closed spaces of Son's works and the move toward the home in *Madame Freedom*.

As noted above, Son was educated in Japanese and struggled to write in Korean. Indeed, two linguistic modalities inform his work: the relatively simple sentences that comprise his texts and the oft-remarked-upon use of Chinese characters rather than the Korean alphabet for proper names. The simple sentences reveal the negotiation between colonial and postcolonial writing—the uneasy textual space marked by the unspoken memory of a now disallowed metropolitan language and the postcolonial injunction to write in Korean.[94] The use of Chinese characters contests this injunction. The characters disrupt the production of the self in the han'gŭl texts, moving beyond the text's borders visually, and connecting it with spaces outside the peninsula and 1950s linguistic nationalism (one strand of which, as we saw above in our discussion of language policies in *Madame Freedom*, called for the abolition of Sino-Korean).

Son's emphasis on the dispossessed culminates in many ways in his I-novel "Divine Comedy" ("Sin ŭi hŭijak," 1961), a text meant at once to sum up the previous fifteen years following the end of Japanese rule and to bid farewell to the South Korean literary establishment. "Divine Comedy" tells the story of the rebellious S—victim of incest, protestor against the attempt of English to make him its "slave"—and his eventual joining of the marginalized "liberation trash" (*haebang ttaraji*), those penniless and homeless who have returned to Korea from Japan and Manchuria following liberation, to create an organization called the "Self-Supporting Construction Corps" (*chahwal kŏnsŏltae*). S joins with other young people and their families to form a "communal life," sharing living quarters and the food they obtain through relief agencies and odd jobs, all the while being constantly forced by the police to abandon the buildings in which they find temporary shelter. This text, then, rejects both statist consolidation in the occupation period and the kind of identity produced in Kim Tong-ni's "Cave Dwellers" ("Hyŏlgŏpujok," 1948), where, as noted in chapter 2, returnees from the outskirts of empire gather in a primordial cave and emerge reborn in their common Koreanness. For Son, dislocation brought on by imperial expansion and, later, by the Korean War leads to the possibility of a nonstatist cooperative community, not to the restoration of tradition or the subsumption of individual and social life to the state as advocated by the One-People Principle.

South Korea, as we know, would occupy center stage in the Cold War reworking of the colonial world, the shift to the register of the global "underdeveloped," and the unfolding production of a "Free Asia." In the immediate aftermath of the Korean War and through the late 1950s, however, the nexus of political and economic corruption, closely linked to dependency on U.S. AID, disallowed the emergence of a productivist subject able to "recover" ethnonational particularity. While an attempt was made to set this trajectory in motion through the Syngman Rhee regime's ISI policy of the 1950s, the implementation of developmentalist policies, taking their cue from adjustments in U.S. management of the free-world periphery, would only truly begin under the Park Chung Hee regime in the 1960s.[95] In chapter 4, we will encounter a questioning of the Park regime's legitimacy that draws upon the 1950s discourse on national literature, tradition, and existentialism. We will also see how resistance to the early developmentalist state involves a renewed critique of the "modern."

4
DEVELOPMENT AS DEVOLUTION
Overcoming Communism and the "Land of Excrement" Incident

IN THE EARLY 1960s, South Korea emerged as one of the most important sites for the articulation of U.S. Cold War developmentalism. If postwar Japan became a non-Western junior partner, continuously cited as a success story and model for the "underdeveloped" free world to follow, South Korea was to follow in its wake as a junior-junior partner.[1] Arturo Escobar has detailed the ways in which post-1945 developmentalism relies upon the placing of peoples on an economistic register that produces a "politics of poverty," one that transforms "society by turning the poor into objects of knowledge and management." The economistic creation of an impoverished "Third World" that must be elevated to higher standards signals a break with colonialism: "In colonial times the concern with poverty was conditioned by the belief that even if the 'natives' could be somewhat enlightened by the presence of the colonizer, not much could be done about their poverty because their economic development was pointless."[2] Escobar further links the developmental apparatus to a visual regime in which the individual is first turned "into a spectacle whose 'aesthetic' value increases with its/her increasing helplessness."[3] For Escobar, the bifurcation between subject and object is appropriated by developmental discourse less to locate the other as timeless abject than to position "peasants, women, nature, and a variety of spectacularized Third World others" on the teleological path of "sustainable development."[4]

It is important to recall that the trajectory of Japanese colonialism in Korea differed from its Euro-American counterpart, particularly in its eventual emphasis on the incorporation of its Korean colonials as imperial subjects. Late-colonial-period mobilization included the increasing industrialization of the peninsula. Throughout the colonial period, and particularly amid an intensifying pan-Asianism beginning in the mid-1930s, the consensus was that *much* could be done about their "poverty."[5]

The 1945–1948 U.S. military occupation of the southern half of the Korean peninsula did not, then, trigger a shift from colonial stasis to global economism. Instead, USAMGIK, like its SCAP counterpart in Japan, attempted to lay the foundation for the incorporation of the existing developmentalism of the Greater East Asian Co-Prosperity Sphere into what would become a U.S. led "free world." Such a move could only proceed by dismantling the pan-Asian yellow/white opposition of the late 1930s and early 1940s. The elimination of this racial divide was to be accomplished by the redefinition of the globe in terms of the "three worlds." Ethnonationalism becomes a local "expression" that supplements a broader participation in the capitalist free-world order.[6] The postoccupation assertion of a *de jure* sovereignty by the South Korean state has always been accompanied by a responsibilization and incorporation of South Koreans as free-world subjects.

We should qualify the shift to economism that Escobar locates in the post–World War II world by noting that what Cold War "development" offers Japan, the former metropole, and its former colonies (Korea and Taiwan) is the *promise*, in the name of economic emancipation, of a dismantling of the "old" Euro-American colonialism recently contested by the Japanese empire during the Greater East Asian and Pacific wars. The door is thus opened for a flexible strategy of accommodating Asian development in the name of a specific kind of identity, at once ethnonational-local and unmarked free-world subject. As we saw in chapter 2, capital, figured as national, possesses a use value enabling the simultaneous recovery of the ethnonational local and the securing of one's universalist position in the global order.

The developmental narrative of the late 1950s and early 1960s elaborated by theorists such as W. W. Rostow, David Lerner, and Talcott Parsons was, as Catherine Scott points out, evolutionary and masculinist, relying on sets of Enlightenment binaries such as nature/culture, primitive/civilized, female/male, irrational/rational, nonproductive/productive.[7] At the same time, this staging of growth confers formal autonomy upon the nation-to-be-developed, replacing the visual display of colonial power we discussed in chapter 1 with a coercion that seeks to remain unseen.

In this chapter, I look at the relation between Cold War metropolitan and peripheral developmentalisms. I begin by examining the ways in which the metropolitan production of "spectacularized third-world others" is accompanied by the attempt to make them disappear within the free-world communication networks that call for the unimpeded, global flow of information. I then show how the peripheral free-world state, the Park Chung Hee regime of the 1960s, asserts a nation/state coincidence that ends up placing it in a continuing state of crisis. Here, I pay particular attention to the relation between Park's early formulation of South Korean ethnodevelopmentalism and the opposition to the state and the Cold War division system that came to the fore during and in the aftermath of one of the most important events in post-1945 South Korean history, the April 19 movement of 1960. Finally, I look at the ways in which the works of Nam Chŏng-hyŏn (b. 1933)—considered the representative "anti-American" writer of the 1960s and the first writer to be prosecuted by the Park regime—offer a sustained critique not only of the U.S. presence in South Korea but also of domestic authoritarianism and the broader Cold War order. Nam's response to the early 1960s summoning of the developmental subject (the subject-in-training, the subject that is not yet a subject) is to render visible the historicist production of primitivity. For this reason, Nam attempts to counter Park Chung Hee's assertion of the national health/modernization coincidence by displaying a series of male bodies that are at once targeted, disfigured, and emasculated by the insertion of South Korea into the evolutionary logic of development.[8] It is in Nam's works, more than those of any other writer in the 1960s, that we encounter the visual politics of statist development and its contestations.

DEVELOPMENT AS COMMUNICATION AND KNOW-HOW: *THE UGLY AMERICAN*

While the global circulation of W. W. Rostow's *The Stages of Economic Growth: A Non-Communist Manifesto* signals the importance of this text both in the U.S. metropole and in South Korea, where it appeared in translation in 1960, perhaps the most popular, widely read Cold War developmentalist manifesto and handbook was written in the form of a novel: William Lederer's and Eugene Burdick's *The Ugly American* (1958). The filmic adaptation of Lederer's and Burdick's work appeared in 1963, directed by George Englund and starring Marlon Brando. Set in 1954 and partly in Vietnam, *The Ugly American* returns at once to the French defeat at Dien Bien Phu and, implicitly, by way of its title, to Graham Greene's critique of the new forms of U.S. power in *The Quiet American*. Dien Bien Phu, the text tells us, follows the Chinese Communist Revolution in 1949 and the stalemate in Korea in 1953. Clearly, the struggle in Asia was calling for a new approach. The fight is with Mao and his methods, and the failure to take account of the enemy's success has led to defeat. The French, with their pageantry and dated tactics (Clausewitz) fail to understand the integrated guerilla warfare of the communists, the close connections they make among the economic, political, and military.[9] *The Ugly American* reveals the ways in which the emerging U.S. modernization theory of the late 1950s attempts to distance itself from pre-1945 European colonialisms. The call is for efficiency, the need, for example, of opening up communicative channels to include the appropriation of the enemy's tactics. *The Ugly American*, in fact, offers a productivist fantasy frame in the name of anticolonialism. The free exchange of know-how will spell the end of old colonial racisms by responsibilizing the "developing world."

Both literary text and film begin with the figure of rape, here the false accusation that Colvin, who has been working with the Sarkhanese (the inhabitants of the fictional Sarkhan, located in Southeast Asia), is an "American rapist" who planned to drug and violate Sarkhanese women.[10] Colvin is attacked and bloodied, his wounds casting him as white victim and calling not for revenge but for a setting straight of the record.[11] That the accusation is false at once legitimizes the U.S. project in Sarkhan (standing in for all of Asia) and indicates the need for better relations with the Sarkhanese.

Moral legitimacy secured, *The Ugly American* proceeds to portray a struggle between disinformation and information that takes place on multiple levels. The first-world developmentalist is to be marked neither by race nor gender but is to be the neutral bearer of productivist information and knowledge that must, however, take into account the local/particular (as we see in Father Finian's use of the Socratic technique in the responsibilizing of the Sarkhanese). Post-1945 developmentalist discourse, in fact, follows Norbert Wiener's cybernetic notions of "pure information" in its figuring of a circuit already in place. To function properly, the circuit requires only the removal of blockages or impediments, what we might call embodiments.[12] The informational circuit resembles the geospatial grid and its coordinates: a scientific, rational organizing of space. Differences found in the local occur as incidentals, surfaces, to be accounted for but not to be miscommunicated as material blockage. The grid recuperates such surface resistance, "noise," to strengthen its flows. Metropolitan developmentalist utopianism relies on the positing of a fictional place like Sarkhan, everywhere and nowhere. The metropolitan developmentalist fantasy imagines the "local" as a node in what must become a free-flowing circuit.

The Cold War becomes a struggle for "hearts and minds," one that distances itself from "old world" colonialism's inefficiency and rigid racial hierarchies.[13] Let us recall that the phrase "ugly American," widely misunderstood as negative, is uniformly *positive* in Burdick's and Lederer's text. The ugly American, the appellation for Homer Atkins in the novel, refers to an American who does not hesitate to associate with the local and locals, to understand difference, learn the language, and "get his hands dirty." As we see throughout the text, the relationship between Atkins (the "ugly American") and Jeepo (the "ugly Sarkanhese") develops by jettisoning the old colonialism and the white/native hierarchy. Color and boundaries disappear, for example, when Atkins and Jeepo become covered in grease as they work on a machine together.[14] This moment in the text, one that produces an intense homosocial intimacy, becomes a mutual transfer of "know-how," a "proper" developmentalist exchange in which the machine is adapted to local conditions.

If this is a move to a regime of efficiency, it is also, following Etienne Balibar, the post-1945 recoding of racism away from phenotype and toward aptitude.[15] This code switching, one that intersects with the assertion of circuits of "pure" information, retains the essentialism and evolutionism of racism even as it dispenses with the history of racialized markings of the surface (covering them with grease). We encounter a move from the outside to the inside, from the visible to the essentialism/racism of the unseen. We are left with a desire for purity in the form of a disembodied but productivist informational core.

Needless to say, such a staging of growth as the exchange of know-how and information must elide the profit motive, the commodity form, and labor itself. Labor is subsumed by know-how. The transfer of the latter occurs as a flow of information that has a material effect, growth. Growth, the product, thus becomes the manifestation of informational transfer, not

FIGURE 4.1 Sarkhan superimposed over American suburbs (*The Ugly American*, 1963).

labor. It is in this way that *The Ugly American* covers over the structural imbalance and antagonisms of global capitalism as it responds to the revolutionary potential made real in Asia in the late 1940s and 1950s.

As in the "factual" epilogue of the novel, the 1963 film version of *The Ugly American* portrays development as an extension of the American Revolution to the world, what Homer Atkins calls his "world business." The film displays an anxiety similar to that of the novel. While it is communism that threatens the global expansion of the American Revolution, both film and novel worry over the apathy and nonattentiveness they locate on the homefront. This concern appears dramatically in the film's final scene. As Marlon Brando, the ambassador to Sarkhan, gives a press conference in Sarkhan, we move through dissolve shots from Sarkhan to a busy freeway intersection and to an American suburb. We are then shown a man, back toward the camera, watching the press conference on TV. He flips through a television schedule and then turns off the television via remote control. This is the end of the film. Space collapses between Sarkhan and middle America in this sequence. The dangers of the periphery are brought home to the center.

Both literary text and film are a call to Cold War total mobilization, a constant vigilance in the face of continuous crisis brought on at once by old-world European colonialist methods no longer applicable in the post-1945 world, the mass appeal of communism, the recalcitrant and resistive former colonized, and the apathetic homefront U.S. citizenry. Nonattentiveness interrupts the information flow of the developmentalist circuit. The desire for pure information confronts the emergence of what Debord has called the "society of the spectacle." Debord's analysis, as Jonathan Crary points out, "is not primarily concerned with a *looking at* images but rather with the construction of conditions that individuate, immobilize, and separate subjects, even within a world in which mobility and circulation are ubiquitous."[16] The film, aware of its own visual medium, addresses an additional threat, that of pure information entering the circulation and exchange of commodified images. Recall that both literary text and film posit themselves as testimonial/documentary, real but taking place nowhere and in all of Asia at the same time. Here, "documentary" meets the impasse *The Ugly American* attempts to cover over by way of its emphasis on production, know-how, and frugality. The documentary is to be placed in a circuit of global consumption.

The film attempts to mobilize vigilant subjects by calling attention to consumption and the society of the spectacle. To do this, however, it must move them away from its own medium, away from the commercialized screen and out of the movie theaters. Both literary text and film emphasize starting with the small and moving to the big, an emphasis that resembles the attempt to privilege a pure particle of information as neutral, moving naturally and efficiently through an expanding network grid. The film traces this trajectory visually, moving from bits of information in selected shots to a full, encompassing knowledge of Sarkhan. In this manner, it follows the vignettes and character sketches/dossiers that make up the novel. The return to the small, to the pixel, at the film's close is thus an attempt to jump back to the circuit of pure information, away from the capitalist circulation of images, the distribution network of Hollywood commercial film.

Development as Revolution

By the early 1960s, it was becoming increasingly clear that South Korea would play a major role in the enforcement of free-world economic development. The elaboration of this narrative was already taking place in major intellectual journals such as *World of Thought* (*Sasanggye*). As noted above, W. W. Rostow's influential *The Stages of Economic Growth: A Non-Communist Manifesto*, for example, appeared in installments in *World of Thought* in 1960, the year of its publication in English. The compilation of the developmental narrative in ethnonational form, moreover, appeared in two texts of the early 1960s meant to legitimate General Park Chung Hee's May 16, 1961, coup d'état as the revolutionary point of departure for South Korea's rise in the world system: Park's *Our Nation's Path* (*Uri minjok ŭi nagal kil*, 1962) and *The State, the Revolution, and I* (*Kukka wa hyŏngmyŏng kwa na*, 1963).

Park's coup and his subsequent eschewing of what he called a "false" anticommunism (*pan'gong*) in favor of "overcoming communism" (*sŭnggong*) through state-led capitalist development allows us to view his military takeover as a critical moment in the history of statist developmentalism. Bruce Cumings writes that

> the meaning of "state building" in Northeast Asia's fused state/societies is that recourse to the state comes first, followed by conscious or unconscious attempts to create industry, big business (the Korean *chaebol*, for example, all have a state-blessed birthright), and then and only then "society," that is, groups requisite for and appropriate to contemporary imaginings of "modernity."[17]

For Park, South Korea was to be placed on a path that posited economic growth as the only means to achieve the autonomy of the ethnonation (*minjok*), each increase in per capita GNP contributing to this autonomy. Under Park's formulation, an antigrowth stance becomes not only antinationalist but antidemocratic, given that political freedom *follows* economic growth. Such a prioritizing of the economic over the political not only resembles the general movement of the colonial modernization carried out on the Korean peninsula under Japanese rule but also closely follows the stagism of U.S. modernization theory, particularly that formulated by Rostow in *A Non-Communist Manifesto*.

The State, the Revolution, and I announces itself in its title as allegorical. Park himself becomes the hygienic subject of an "eternal revolution," the embodiment of the healthy ethnonation. Those who oppose "the state, the revolution, and I," both within South Korea and from North Korea, are "germs."[18] Park deploys the notion of a pure, homogeneous nation (*sunsuhan tongp'o minjok*), which possesses a "purity of blood [*sunhyŏl*] rarely seen in the world," in order to posit a health always latent but never achieved in Korean history. As Giorgio Agamben puts it, "The obsession with development is as effective as it is in our time because it coincides with the biopolitical project to produce an undivided people."[19] For Park, the purity of the *minjok* contrasts sharply with what he considers a history of diseased states, five thousand years of failure marked by feudalism, colonialism, poverty, factionalism, and fratricidal strife.[20]

Park's *Our Nation's Path* and *The State, the Revolution, and I* articulate what Žižek calls the "corporatist temptation," the desire "to have *capitalism without the antagonism that causes its structural imbalance.*"[21] As Žižek shows us, such a structure transforms the "antagonism *inherent* in the social structure . . . into a relationship of *power*, a struggle for domination between *us* and *them.*"[22] For Park, the health of the national body depends upon its advancement within the world system. The acquisition of a competitive edge over its capitalist competitors occurs in tandem with the "extermination of communism" (*myŏlgong*). Park's statist anticommunism, in other words, resembles the national populism of early 1990s Eastern Europe. The latter, Žižek tells us, perceives "Communism's 'threat' from the perspective of *Gemeinschaft*, as a foreign body corroding the organic texture of the national community; this way, national populism actually imputes to Communism the crucial feature of capitalism itself."[23]

Park's rejection of democracy, in turn, relies upon this trope of an organicist national body/history: "At first we thought that everything would turn out all right if we imported directly the democracy of Western Europe, but the luscious tree, democracy, did not blossom in inhospitable Korean soil. We failed at grafting the new tree. Our eyes are finally opened to the need for the growth of a native and national tree."[24] We have a dual impropriety here. First, the bottom, the soil, is improper and unprepared. Second, the act of implanting from the top—the "forced grafting" of the tree—is an improper "reversal of the order," an imitative act. The "luscious" tree must grow from the bottom up; it must be properly native to be properly Western European. The "inhospitable soil" of Korea inevitably resists "direct" translation. The target language is inhospitable. Park must place South Korea on the register of the West while simultaneously rejecting an imitation of its forms. This is the aporetic nationalist gesture of equivalence/difference.

Park Chung Hee's early elaboration of the narrative of modernization in *Our Nation's Path* and *The State, the Revolution, and I* offers, as the original title of the former work implies, a "way out" of the predicament of the modern. Park offers the promise of promotion through the world system, from periphery to core power, as the one-way road to achieving national autonomy and reunification. One of Park's central concerns, of course, was the legitimacy of May 16 vis-à-vis April 19 (1960), the event that led to the removal of Syngman Rhee from power. According to Park, the failure of April 19 lay in its inability to wipe out the evil of the former ruler: "The goal of the May 16 Revolution was to reconstruct the state and the economy, but if we look at its true essence it was to ensure the restoration to all the people of a political and economic system that had become the plaything of a miniscule, privileged class."²⁵ It is for this reason that May 16, the continuation of April 19, is a populist, *"sŏminjŏk kungmin hyŏngmyŏng* [revolution of the common people]": "In other words, the special characteristics of this revolution can be expressed as 'the group of entrenched forces versus the consciousness of the people + the power of the military.' "²⁶ It is, therefore, necessary to engage in a campaign of "human reconstruction" in order to make the May 16 revolution bear fruit as a *"kungmin hyŏngmyŏng* [people's revolution]."²⁷ The May coup, then, stands in for the common people in a particular way: it reflects their consciousness even as it must enlighten them about this consciousness.

April 19 occupies a significant position in the narrative of a history of resistance to the state, particularly for literary critics associated with the national literature movement that emerged in the 1970s. In "The Historical and Contemporary Significance of April 19," the literary critic Paik Nak-chung designates the event an "incomplete revolution" because its aims (academic freedom, fair elections, democratic constitution) have yet to be achieved in the present (1980).²⁸ Paik describes the basic desire of the people (*minjung*) during the colonial period as the establishment of an independent nation-state free from Japanese imperialism. To accomplish this, the nation (*uri minjok*) worked to expel the Japanese and foster democracy. Neither the U.S. military government nor the Syngman Rhee regime advanced this movement. The U.S. military government bequeathed division to the Rhee regime; the existence of the latter was maintained by former Japanese collaborators.²⁹ The desire of the *minjok* now became to overcome division by establishing a unified nation-state and eliminating the vestiges of Japanese imperialism. The rejection of this desire by the Rhee regime caused it to lose legitimacy: "Viewed in this light, April 19 was an event borne of the revolutionary desire of the Korean people [*Han'guk minjung*] to rectify the anti-historical course of the Rhee regime."³⁰

In "The April Revolution in the Context of National History," Kang Man-gil, one of the leading leftist historians in South Korea, locates April 19 in a history of people's movements (*minjung undong*):

As a struggle simultaneously against feudalism and foreign powers, the Kabo Peasants' War attained the heights of the *minjung undong* of the enlightenment period; as both a pro-democratic and an anti-Japanese movement, the March First movement was the greatest *minjung undong* of the colonial period. In its development from a democratic movement to a national unification movement, the April 19 movement became a momentous point of departure for *minjung undong* in the division era.[31]

Kang, that is, distinguishes two stages in the April 19–May 16 historical moment: the first stage was a "democratic movement" leading up to the establishment of the Chang Myŏn government; the second stage was the transformation of this movement into one for national unification. These two movements are related, continuous, and part of the larger history of *minjung undong*.[32]

According to Kang, the Rhee regime, in an effort to legitimate itself, transformed the resistance movement opposing the Japanese (*hang'il undong*) in the colonial period into anti-Japanese sentiment (*panilchuŭi*):

> However, this dictatorship ... had no choice but to reveal its limits; April 19 was the result of these limits reaching their critical point. In this light, we can understand April 19 as a *minjung undong* that ... sought to regain the proper historical course. In accordance with the national-historical requirements of the postdivision period, the former colonial resistance to the Japanese was sublimated into a movement for national unification.[33]

We should note both that these narratives of emancipation construct a lineage of resistance and that they occur as contestations of the ways in which the Park regime promulgated an official history privileging the moment of May 16 as true locus of revolution (*hyŏngmyŏng*) while diminishing the significance of April 19 as an uprising (*ŭigŏ*).[34]

It is important to recall that South Korea became in the early 1970s—and remains as of this writing—a favored site for the display of successful development; it followed Japan's postwar lead as a model-minority case in the world system. The logic of this Cold War ideology—which remains the lynchpin of South Korea–U.S. relations—demands strict adherence to the policy of "development first, reunification later." Faithful to the dictates of this policy, the Chang Myŏn regime, the successor to Syngman Rhee's government, proved itself, in late 1960 and early 1961, increasingly ineffective in containing the student movement. As Kang Man-gil points out, the students called for an extension of the April 19 movement to include not only a struggle for democratic rights but also for "national sovereignty" and reunification. Indeed, the latter was viewed, particularly by students, as the condition necessary to achieve the former.[35] This call for reunification in the name of the *minjok* asserted that the Korean peninsula must extract itself from the Cold War ideological struggle and that a unified Korea must be established on the basis of nonalignment and neutrality. When the Chang Myŏn regime lost what little legitimacy it had as a post–April 19 government, the threat to what Paik Nak-chung calls the "division system" and, consequently, to U.S. hegemony in South Korea (with wider implications for the U.S. role as "leader of the free world") became apparent. It was precisely at this point that the May coup occurred.

Park's portrayal of the May coup as continuing the work begun by April 19 contests the increasing calls—particularly by students and re-emerging socialist parties in 1960—for reunification as the proper extension of April 19. Park believed that post–April 19 developments distorted the promise of April in two ways, both related to the revolutionary subject: (1) the students' inability to extend the revolution to the common people allowed the pre–April 19 privileged elite to maintain their power, and (2) the calls for reunification by the "reformist forces" (*hyŏksin seryŏk*) turned April 19 toward the North Korean line, that is, communist revolution. At the same time, May 16 signals the recovery of ethnonational subjectivity in the face of post–April 19 "social decadence":

> I was keenly interested in the increasing powerlessness and breakdown of the spirit of the people. In other words, *Our Things*, Korean Things, *Koreans' Things*, were gradually receding, disappearing. I could not suppress the depth of the anger I felt at the emergence, in their place, of American Things, Western European Things, Japanese Things. The Democratic Party regime might call this a flowering, the development of a modern civilization and society. But clearly this meant that Korea was being lost.[36]

Here, as Catherine Scott helps to explain, Park privileges tradition/Koreanness not simply as a rhetorical strategy aimed at discrediting his opponents but as a means of dispensing with "backward" modes of being, family relations that Park elsewhere calls "clan consciousness" or "familism."[37] "Tradition" is articulated as the autonomy of a unique national culture, which allows the developmental state to assert its ethnonationalism as guardian of "our things," even as it seeks to dismantle whatever existing "backward" family networks stand in the way of modernization. Modernization will enable the recovery of what is being lost—tradition, Korea—even as it engages in a historicist "human reconstruction" project that jettisons what is seen, selectively, as the "premodern."

Development as Devolution

While the arrest and prosecution of Nam Chŏng-hyŏn following the publication of his "Land of Excrement" ("Punji," 1965) in North Korea is generally considered a significant event in postdivision South Korean literary history, Nam's works themselves have received relatively little critical attention.[38] At the same time, Nam is often mentioned as a seminal, if problematic, figure in the narrative of increasing awareness of postdivision U.S. neoimperialism on the Korean peninsula. Kim Yun-sik, for example, writes that "Nam Chŏng-hyŏn's controversial 'Land of Excrement' demonstrates a new understanding of the United States, revealing with a powerful anger its essential character, that of the invader."[39] Im Chin-yŏng considers Nam's work the product of an era that was the "age of allegory, in other words, the age of authoritarian dictatorship."[40] Indeed, Nam's work in the early 1960s turns largely upon an allegorizing of the fall of the Syngman Rhee regime as an emancipatory moment that offered the promise of overcoming the neocolonial condition. Park Chung Hee's May coup, by contrast, signals the return both of the repressive anticommunist state and the economic exploitation of the comprador elite and their foreign (U.S. and, later, Japanese) sponsors.[41]

Although Nam's texts of the early 1960s are explicit and specific responses to April 19 and May 16, they should also be seen in relation to the existentialist-inspired calls for social engagement (*anggajyumang*), resistance (*rejisŭt'angsŭ*), and action (*haengdong*) that began in the mid-1950s (Nam made his literary debut in 1958). As in many of his later works, the critique of the South Korean condition in Nam's early "Inheritance Under the Chimney" (1959), for example, invokes the figure of the superfluous man—the impoverished, college-educated young male intellectual who is precluded from participating meaningfully in society.

Nam differs from other writers such as Son Ch'ang-sŏp, Yi Pŏm-sŏn, and Ch'oe In-hun who also deployed this figure in the late 1950s and early 1960s, however, in his close association of resistance with the body of the superfluous male protagonist standing in for the ethnonation. This biologizing of resistance should be located in the context of the relation between race and culture that occurred as part of the 1950s discourse on tradition (*chŏnt'ong*), itself, as we saw in the preceding chapter, a rearticulation of the late-colonial-period pan-Asian local/imperial subject standing against the "occident" (*sŏyang*).[42] Yi Ŭn-sang's immanentist equation of race with culture to construct a Korea and Korean literature resistant to the modern (noted in chapter 3) finds further inflection in Sin Tong-han's "Humanism and the Spirit of the Author" (1959). In this article, Sin biologizes Sartrean *anggajyumang*, associated with existentialism in the 1950s, by linking it to the resisting national body:

> Everyone knows that in Korea too there have been numerous historical instances of resistance. This tradition continues to flow as before in the blood vessels of the ethnonation [*minjok ŭi hyŏlmaek*]. This bodily movement [*momburim*] to secure autonomous human subjectivity [*ingan ŭi chuch'esŏng*] is, precisely, the spirit of humanism; it achieves expression through love of fatherland [*choguk ae*] and love of the ethnonation [*minjok ae*].[43]

This biologized resistance appears in Nam's texts in the form of male protagonists who find their bodies moving spontaneously, resisting in spite of themselves. In Nam's work, these bodies have no choice but to reject the "modern" (*hyŏndae*). For Nam, *hyŏndae* represents the deployment of the historicist logic of modernization by the authoritarian South Korean state and the U.S. hegemon. But, clearly, *hyŏndae* also stands in for *kŭndae*, the term used in the late-colonial-period phrase "overcome the modern" (*kŭndae kŭkbok*). *Hyŏndae* thus possesses two temporalities: a return, which must remain unspoken, to the late colonial discourse of overcoming the modern; and a reference to the "contemporary."

Nam's "Inheritance Under the Chimney" possesses similarities both to Son Ch'ang-sŏp's work and to Yi Pŏm-sŏn's "Stray Bullet" ("Obalt'an," 1959), which was made into one of South Korea's most well-known films (directed by Yu Hyŏn-mok in 1960). The following elements, *mutatis mutandis*, can be found in a number of other 1950s and 1960s South Korean texts: a powerless, despairing, poverty-stricken male protagonist who has received higher education but cannot find a job or is underpaid/underemployed (Sŏk-chu, the protagonist of "Inheritance," is a college student forced to drop out of school because he is unable to afford the tuition); an acquaintance of the protagonist, usually his sister or a woman the protagonist considers as a sister, who is forced to earn a living as a sex worker, sometimes, but not always, laboring for U.S. soldiers (Yŏng-ok); an act of desperation on the part of one of the characters leading to tragedy (Sŏk-chu's father burglarizes a house to obtain the money to pay Sŏk-chu's tuition—he is caught and jailed); a fantasizing of the United States and a fetishizing of U.S. commodities (Kap-cha's fantasy space is in a coffee shop with a picture of the New York skyline covering one of the walls); a memory of the North (Yŏng-ok's sole desire is to see her parents in the North once more before she dies); and a critique of comprador capitalism (the corrupt Triangle Company).

"Inheritance," however, differs from the work of other writers by offering an explicitly allegorical critique of comprador capitalism and South Korean–U.S. relations. The text offers the following description of Kap-cha's fantasy space in the coffee shop "Royal House" (*wangsil*):

> Above all, Kap-cha liked the stairs leading up to "The Royal House" on the second floor. She said it made her feel like she was going up the stairs to board an airplane with its nose pointed toward the Pacific Ocean. Kap-cha said it gave her such a warm, contented feeling when she opened the door to a picture of the New York skyline, with the Empire State Building in the center, covering the entire wall on the left. This was because she could embrace the illusion that she had flown right over the Pacific. . . . In Kap-cha's view, it was only befitting that a place with such a bedazzling ambience become her "drawing room" [*tŭroring rum*]. It was as if Kap-cha, in making this claim, became the owner of the "Royal House."[44]

This portrayal of the coffee shop immediately follows Kap-cha's description of the home in which she actually lives:

> She said it was a house that no one in his or her right mind would enter. What blocked her from going in was the fear that if she opened the door

the first thing she would see would be a group of primitives [wŏnsiin] with disheveled hair, tails not yet fully disappeared, scratching after nuts and berries. . . . Living in the age of nuclear power, how could one, with any sense of decency, find the courage to enter such a house with one's eyes open?[45]

Kap-cha's fantasy in the "Royal House" mimes what the comprador capitalists perform in the Aju Building. After Sŏk-chu makes the "mistake" of spontaneously attacking a company president when he sees him having "acrobatic-like" sex with Yŏng-ok, Yŏng-ok patches things up by telling the president that Sŏk-chu is her brother and that he was drunk and mistook the president for a gangster; she arranges for Sŏk-chu to come to the president's building to clear the air. Sŏk-chu arrives at the building:

> Finally he could see the elegant front of the Aju Building. Most of it was made out of see-through glass. Above all, the sight of the shiny, clear, broad front door sent him into raptures. It was such a clean, bright entranceway, Sŏk-chu thought, that people must want to pass through it at least ten times an hour. Also especially attractive to Sŏk-chu was the way in which the people going in and out stuck out their bulbous potbellies like they were passports.[46]

Sŏk-chu's childlike attraction to the spectacle opposes the venality of the comprador capitalists. The latter, like Kap-cha, have created their own space, a foreign country within South Korea—the Aju Building stands in for the Empire State Building. Their desire to position themselves at the apex of the narrative of development entails their removal from what this narrative figures as a South Korea standing on the lower end of the evolutionary scale. Their response is to step into the shoes of the human, that is, the Western.

It is Kap-cha's entering into a movie theater–like space, not so much the gaze at the New York skyline but the location of herself within the image, the skyline becoming her background, that produces a timeline. The historicist logic of modernization necessarily primitivizes Korea as it privileges the U.S. modern metropolis as telos. Kap-cha's departure into fantasy, her insertion into the free-world imaginary, jettisons the patriarchal authority that informs the degraded (ethnonational) home. She is lost to another phallic ordering, the fantasy frame presided over by the Ur-skyscraper, the Empire State Building.

Kap-cha's location in cinema space demonstrates the ways in which Nam's texts take part in the transnational circulation of images associated with Hollywood filmic production. As we noted in the previous chapter, Hollywood films reappeared in 1950s South Korea following their late colonial wartime ban and were immensely popular. Many 1950s South Korean films, moreover, appropriated both classical Hollywood filmic techniques and themes. "Inheritance" invokes the desire we find in many 1950s South Korean films to produces scenes with backgrounds and landscapes resembling those found in Hollywood film.[47] Both the Royal House and the Aju Building, associated with transnational movement beyond South Korea's borders, point to these filmic sequences. The location of South Korean actors in these spaces produces the future anterior of developmentalism, an imaging of South Korea as a site that will have become "advanced." The South Korean present of the 1950s, the space outside of the movie theater, becomes the past.

Kap-cha signals a 1950s spectatorship of Hollywood and South Korean "golden age" cinema. Her cinematic experience, the pleasure she feels in the cinema space, is translated into a way of being by the comprador elite, who no longer see the "real" South Korea. By contrast, Sŏk-chu, the son of an illiterate vegetable seller (he attends college only because it is his mother's dying wish), is located "under the chimney," outside the fantasy frame that organizes the space and time of the Cold War metropole/periphery. His only possession is the "proud, precious inheritance" of a smile from his father. This "peculiar smile," which appears to others less a smile than a "grimace," arises uncontrollably when confronted with an oppressive reality, as when Sŏk-chu imagines the absurd, such as the contrast between the wrinkled fingers of his father and a gold ring he is caught stealing. The inheritance under the chimney, this father-to-son transfer, is the expression of a genetic resistance, a patrimony that opposes itself to the Cold War modern. For Nam, it would be April 19, 1960, that provided the opportunity for this patrimony to manifest itself as the proper subject of history.[48]

Written after Syngman Rhee's fall from power and before Park's May 16 coup, Nam's 1961 novella *Who Do You Think You Are?* (*Nŏnŭn muŏ nya*)—instantly canonized when it received the prestigious Tong-in Literary Prize for that year—attempts to construct the meaning of April 19. For Nam,

April 19 signals not only the overthrow of the Rhee regime but a much more profound liberation. This liberation takes the form of the superfluous man's emergence from his confinement in the home—a recovery from the emasculating despair of the 1950s portrayed in "Inheritance Under the Chimney." As in nearly all of Nam's work, *Who Do You Think You Are?* reverses gender relations, portraying the tyranny of *hyŏndae* by allegorizing the relationship of the protagonist Kwan-su and his wife, Sin-ok, a 1960s iteration of the colonial "modern girl." The questioning of *hyŏndae* is, in the text, a questioning of Sin-ok. The counterinterrogation of *hyŏndae* ("who do you think you are?") reinserts Sin-ok—an executive secretary who throughout the text spends nearly all of her time outside the home, some of it with another man—into the domestic space. This trajectory resembles that taken by Sŏn-yŏng in *Madame Freedom* and protagonists in other 1950s films, such as the comedy *Female Executive* (*Yŏsajang*; dir. Han Hyŏng-mo, 1959).[49]

Kwan-su, a college-educated translator of "thick books," works at home, receiving practically nothing for his efforts. Kwan-su is powerless, utterly dominated by Sin-ok and her habitual invocation of the term *hyŏndae* as a "weapon" to silence him at every opportunity. Kwan-su's superfluous existence inside the closed space of his room, the contempt and scorn that Sin-ok, their maid, and their landlord's children hold for him, only increase his sense of despair. He concludes that he is no more than a "bacterium" that should be wiped off the face of the earth. Primitivization—Kwan-su's devolution to the subhuman—accompanies his emasculation.

Sin-ok voices the ineluctability of *hyŏndae*:

"I wish you'd stop taking such a futile, outmoded approach to everything. I mean stop talking about all of that abstract stuff like feeling, sympathy, compassion. The modern knows no stopping—it's organized in the most efficient manner possible under the rule that if you live I die, if I'm going to live you will have to die.... As long as there are people like you caught up everyday in useless premodern notions that say 'you shouldn't do that' or 'that's a pitiful sight' our country will never be more than a market for someone else."[50]

Sin-ok's articulation of the premodern/modern divide, what Chakrabarty calls "historicism as a transition narrative,"[51] leaves no choice for South Korea but submission to a teleology that calls for a jumpstart in time, a Rostovian "take-off." April 19 enters the text only at its close, when Kwan-su emerges from his confinement in the home to discover the April 19 demonstrators in the street chanting, "Treat us as humans!":

> "I am a person. I am a person too!" Kwan-su shouted, working his way into the crowd, feeling such a relief that his stomach nearly burst open. There was no sign of fear of what might come next in anyone's eyes. The clear, blazing eyes of all lit up the sky, shining with an emotion that seemed to say "From this point forward all of time will be mine."[52]

Nam's text locates April 19, then, less as a specifically "political" event resulting in the removal of the authoritarian Rhee regime from power than as an ontological release. The April 19 demonstrators take history, temporality, away from the primitivizing logic of modernization. Such a move bears close relation to the late colonial discourse on overcoming the modern, even as it does not, of course, name the latter. The subject is no longer imperial but masculinist-nationalist. The recovery of the "human" in this crowd scene represents the attempt to overcome an emasculating *hyŏndae*. April 19 catalyzes the reintegration of dispersed male bodies. National time and space are inscribed in a sovereignty of the eyes, beyond words, experienced through feeling that speaks without speaking.

State, Nation, Body: A "Blur of Colors"

Park Chung Hee himself writes in *The State, the Revolution, and I* that there are those who oppose May 16 as a military takeover: "But that sort of noise has no effect on our ears."[53] If, as Seungsook Moon has pointed out, Park's project is part and parcel of a "militarized modernity," it is also call for mass mobilization.[54] The "noise" Nam generated following the May coup differed from appeals to the liberal democratic subject in journals such as *Sasanggye* both in its abiding concern for the ethnonational body and its interruption of Park's claims to legitimacy by questioning the possibility of autonomous national subjectivity within the historicist trajectory of postcolonial global capitalism.

In "Letter to Father" ("Puju chŏn sangsŏ," 1964), Nam works precisely to unravel the structure of equivalence/difference that marks the trajectory of development carried out in the name of the *minjok*. The text resembles Nam's later "Land of Excrement" both in its epistolary form and in the dire straits in which the narrating I finds himself. Branded a "beast" after murdering his wife, Ch'ŏng-ja, Yong-dal is incarcerated in a cage in the Ch'anggyŏngwŏn Zoo, the result of a "conclusion reached to preserve me indefinitely not only for the sake of academic research on a monstrous beast who looks like a human but also to earn foreign currency by turning me into a tourist attraction."[55] The location of Yong-dal's body in the zoo signals the degradation of the male body. The developmental state has placed this body (object of consumption and research) within the primitivizing grasp of the grand scientistic, classificatory schemes of nineteenth-century imperial knowledge and power.[56]

Yong-dal and Ch'ŏng-ja had one son, but Yong-dal wanted more. Upon discovering that Ch'ŏng-ja, in the name of state-sponsored "family planning," was using a diaphragm, he found himself unable to control his anger at the state for killing its own people. Yong-dal demanded that Ch'ŏng-ja remove the diaphragm, but she refused:

> Father, the poisonous power of rage can be tremendous. I lost my self-control. Truly, I wasn't in my right mind. After telling her that if she wouldn't take it out, I would, I threw her on the ground without hesitation. I shoved my hand deep into her vagina; my hand got a hold of something, and I ripped it out with a jerk. Unfortunately, though, it wasn't the diaphragm but a muscle. It all happened in an instant. Ch'ŏng-ja was finished off without even being able to scream. Blood flowing down over her lower body. But for some reason I didn't see it as blood. It was pus. Ch'ŏng-ja's, mine, no, the government's, the fatherland's—well, at any rate, it was a river of yellow pus rushing out of a festering boil that had burst. Why was it so pleasurable? It was refreshing.[57]

Yong-dal's satisfaction stems neither from his removal of the diaphragm from Ch'ŏng-ja's body (he fails in this task) nor from the murder itself. It is the movement of signifiers—blood to pus, the succession of possessives ("Ch'ŏng-ja's, mine, no, the government's, the fatherland's")—that produces pleasure. Yong-dal's own allegorizing of the event, his search for the proper trope, at once arrogates the reproductive function from Ch'ŏng-ja and mobilizes a series of words to produce the image it desires. The location of the proper signifier ("the fatherland's") becomes the proper way of seeing blood. We see how Yong-dal's allegorizing attempts to sever the ethnonational body from the biopolitcal state. In the end, the text's production of a masculinist subjectivity seeks to counter—in its mobilizing of an ascending hierarchy of terms, "Ch'ŏng-ja's, mine, no, the government's, the fatherland's"—Park's equation of the ethnonation with the "revolution, the state, and I."

"Letter to Father," in fact, tells us a story of competing masculinisms and nationalisms that centers on the elimination of anxiety over the frequently invoked term *tongp'o* (literally, "same womb"), sign of ethnonational homogeneity (and, as we saw above, used by Park Chung Hee at key moments in his work). It is the womb (*p'o*) that produces sameness (*tong*). Production of sameness marks woman as (m)other; the nonproducing woman becomes other.[58] As (m)other, the figure of woman produces homogeneity from difference. In "Letter to Father," Yong-dal's image of woman is "shattered" when he encounters Ch'ŏng-ja's use of a "diaper," a sign of menstruation. It is the menstrual flow that "others" Ch'ŏng-ja, a nonproducer of sons. *Blood becomes the site of difference rather than homogeneity.* The murder of Ch'ŏng-ja (accompanied by the figure of blood as ethnonational) signals a radical attempt to erase the alterity that inhabits the homogeneous, the nonequivalence of *tong* and *p'o*.

Tongp'o, of course, was and is frequently invoked as a nonideological site for overcoming national division. In the immediate aftermath of April 19, for example, Kim Kyŏng-t'ak wrote:

> We modern Korean intellectuals, compatriots of South and North [*nambuk tongp'o*], must not forget for an instant that we confront a historical reality in which democracy produces the side effect of capitalism and communism gives rise to the side effect of dictatorship. We cannot allow the national life force [*minjok saengmyŏng*] to be lost due to the side effect of capitalism that accompanies the process of democratizing Korea; likewise, we must not permit the national life force to be diminished as a result of the side effect of dictatorship brought on by the communization of Korea.
>
> We modern intellectuals, *nambuk tongp'o*, possessing personality [*kaesŏng*] that inheres the national character [*minjoksŏng*], will always work in accord with the national life regardless of field—political, economic, cultural.[59]

Kim's organicist deployment of *tongp'o*—the equation of national character and vitalist life force as ground for reunification of the divided nation—opposes the nonideological, undifferentiated national body to the ideological (capitalism, communism, democracy, dictatorship) by separating the inevitability of ethnonational belonging from the contingency of the political. Kim's biopolitics, his opposing of *tongp'o* and the national life force to "ideology" (which fractures the ethnonation), his uniting of North and South by way of *tongp'o* as supplement (*nambuk tongp'o*), intersects with Yong-dal's assertion that reunification is impossible, given the anticommunist education that fails to teach the distinction between the communist party and a "deep love for the *tongp'o*."

Nam seeks to show how South Korean anticommunism relies on the normalizing function of an evolutionary economics, one that entails a visual marking, the racializing/primitivizing both of the communist other and the resistances it encounters in the "developing world." Yong-dal tells his father that a young student comes every morning and spends all day observing him:

> Even if he says he is studying me in order to build up the knowledge to become a great zoologist, he's probably thinking that the race [*injong*] that lives in the North resembles this type of beast. That's right, Father. These days, for some reason, young people think that only the communist party lives in the North; they don't acknowledge the fact that people live there. If we told them that parents, wives, and children, siblings whom we love live there, would they believe it? It would just be cause for laughter. At any rate, the only thing young boys and girls know is that a bunch of evil monsters that deserve to be killed live in the North.[60]

The would-be zoologist's observation of the disfigured, beastlike Yong-dal (standing in for those who live in the North) is nothing more than a gaze in the mirror. It is by examining, categorizing his ethnonational body (the homogeneous body of the *tongp'o*) as primitivized other that the zoologist locates himself on the trajectory of the developed, modern, free-world subject.

Yong-dal informs his father that a foreign delegation is coming to observe him, that his face must be cosmetically altered because it is still considered too "humanlike." The foreign (white) gaze, however, will rest less upon the abject body of Yong-dal than on the South Korean production of a visual, carceral regime, the display of its ability to self-regulate, cage, and degrade Korean bodies, to produce Escobar's "spectacularized Third World others."[61] It is through the spectacle of the disfigured Yong-dal that the text reveals what it considers the obscured visual politics of the trope of development. Rather than exchange of know-how, relations between core and periphery turn upon a selective racializing/primitivizing. The face-altering "operation" Yong-dal must undergo before the arrival of the foreigners reintroduces the surface eschewed by the pure information model of *The Ugly American*.[62] Here, the shift from phenotype to aptitude is not seamless. Resistances to the system are to retain a racial surface, even if this surface must be manufactured. The production of the beast Yong-dal and its display to foreigners, moreover, earns currency in the same manner as the continued production of the North as "evil monster" ensures the inflow of U.S. economic "aid." "Letter to Father" portrays the South Korean state as locating itself on the other side of the bars, aligning itself with the metropolitan gaze, coauthoring the production of the North as radical other in order to place itself on the unmarked register of the "human," the zoologist.

Such an incarceration is at once a self-surveillance—the kind of watching over oneself and others that structures anticommunist statism. Nam explores this visual regime further in "Chaos" ("Ch'ŏnjihyŏnhwang," 1965), a text written in the turbulent year of protests against the normalization of diplomatic relations with Japan and one that again appeals to the genetic relation between father and son (*pujŏnjajŏn*) in an effort to recover the ethnonational body from the state.[63] Tŏk-su's father, a carpenter (Tŏk-su notes this is the job of the biblical Joseph), presents a table he has made to a high-ranking official in the hopes of securing his son a job. Heavily laden with food, the legs of the table collapse while the official entertains senior management from a Japanese conglomerate. Immediately branded a communist, Tŏk-su's father is sent to prison, where he dies. Prior to his death, Tŏk-su's father orders his son not to become a carpenter lest a similar fate befall him. Tŏk-su, however, finds his hands moving of their own accord, picking up tools to repair the house in which he lives. Unable to control his hands, Tŏk-su considers turning them in:

> If one goes against one's duty as a citizen, I mean if one goes against the orders of the state, then one gets punished. No matter how close I am to someone, no matter how much I empathize with a person's circumstances, I can't harbor a subversive element right under my nose. I mean as long as I don't have what it takes to make it in prison. Suddenly the satisfying feeling came over me that I was a patriot, and my shoulders straightened up.[64]

Although turning in his hands (the "subversive element") will make Tŏk-su an anticommunist patriot and a statist subject, it will render him unable to fix the house in which he rents a room. This is a house he initially found attractive for its modern, Western exterior, but one he later discovered to have an "internal structure" in which everything, literally, was askew, "twisted," including the physical appearance of the landlord and his family. Scene of *hyŏndae*, development, this home becomes the site of internal exile, disfigurement. Here, the modern and the West are associated with attraction to a surface, the exterior of the house. Tŏk-su's inability to control his hands produces a geneticized, spontaneous resistance that wells up from the inside. It is a bodily resistance, but it is not visible in and of itself; it only manifests itself in its actions. This is a resistance that contests the naturalizing of the developmental trajectory as unmarked, transcendent.

Who will possess Tŏk-su's body? Only by alienating himself from his own body can Tŏk-su become a proper subject of the ROK. Tŏk-su's body becomes the site of a struggle between nation and state:

> How is that my hand is similar to Father's, I mean to a subversive's.... Whose hand is it really? Unfilially enough, I fell into a predicament where I could not distinguish my hand from my father's. Fuzzy. But my hand was not the only hazy thing. The whole world was rolling up into a blur of colors. The shapes and colors of everything I could see became bleary, fragmented like in an abstract painting. Collapsing lines and colors. Suddenly even my body seemed misty, breaking apart, slowly blending into an indistinct mass of colors; when it occurred to me that its outlines were being erased, I broke out in a heavy sweat, and, as if announcing a crisis, I wildly shouted out my own name, "Tŏk-su, Tŏk-su."[65]

The state's rejection of this genetics of resistance, its attempt to extract the body of Tŏk-su from this patrilineage, becomes the imposition of an artificiality (ideology) upon the natural (body)—"Father" becomes "subversive." Nam's text opposes *minjok* to the *kukka* (state) that would appropriate the ethnonational body as its own, naturalize itself by way of its coincidence with this body. The state is equated with the modern, not the nation.

Alienated, superfluous Tŏk-su shouts out his own name in an effort to call himself back into an authentic ethnonational narrative, to reject the summoning of the anticommunist, comprador state. There is no argument about the existence of the ethnonational body itself, only about its location and the authenticity of the subject who will possess it. It is a question of ownership. Here, by way of a possessive nationalism, is where Nam's antistatism reveals the ways in which it overlaps with the statism it opposes.

Tŏk-su experiences this crisis over ownership of the ethnonational body as a chaotic blurring of interpellations. We thus encounter another struggle: the clash between Tŏk-su's verbal self-summoning and the "blur of colors" associated with the fragmentation of abstract art. At stake is the relation between body and seeing. The verbal summons attempts to organize the image, to pull the body back together. Its self-summoning—its call to the self to identify with the self—involves, first, an imagining of the body as whole/organicist, followed by an anxious watching of its disintegration. It then moves to an attempt to erase imaging altogether, since imaging threatens to get out of hand, to collapse distinctions or "lines and colors." The text reveals a desire to have words call out and name themselves, without the mediation of a potentially unruly imaging. The latter threatens to devolve into unintended meanings or, as in abstract art, to question the ways in which meaning is produced in the first place.

We can also see how this self-summoning versus statist-summoning opposition recalls late-colonial-period imperialization. In fact, anticolonial nationalism throughout the colonial period occurred as a form of discursive self-summoning, one taking place in the absence of a Korean sovereign state. In this way, Nam's antistatism represents the post-1945 iteration of an earlier anticolonial nationalism. At the same time, his rejection of the "modern" draws upon but cannot name the critique of the West and the United States that informed late colonial statist imperialization.

Border Crossing: The "Land of Excrement" Incident

Nam's ongoing critique of the Park regime was halted on July 9, 1965, when he was arrested on charges that "Land of Excrement" ("Punji," published in March 1965) violated the National Security Law.[66] The fact that Nam's arrest followed the reprinting of portions of "Land of Excrement" in North Korea certainly played a central role in the text's effacement in the South.[67] "Land of Excrement," that is, becomes a text at once "South Korean" and "North Korean," a troubling of the visible/invisible distribution that enforces the division system.

The following is an excerpt of testimony given at Nam's trial by Ch'oe Nam-sŏp, a convicted North Korean spy (as he was then serving a prison sentence, he appeared in court handcuffed):

PROSECUTION: What are your feelings after reading "Land of Excrement"?
CH'OE: The contents serve as malicious propaganda for the northern puppet regime.
DEFENSE: Did you feel that the Republic of Korea was free after reading the story? Were you outraged that the novel was anti-American?
CH'OE: I thought that it [the Republic of Korea] was free if this kind of story was permitted. It's something that can't be imagined in the North.
DEFENSE: When a writer's imagination inadvertently coincides with North Korean Communist propaganda, does he become a sympathizer?
CH'OE: The contents of this work are identical with the propaganda of the northern puppet regime.[68]

Ch'oe, inadvertently perhaps, demonstrates that the Republic of Korea is in the process of disabling a claim to be the locus of "freedom." Nam's lawyers contended that South Korea's place in the "free world" was threatened by the state's attempt to suppress free speech. South Korea should follow the lead of the pillar of the free world, the United States, whose ally it was and whose cause it championed, standing at the front line of freedom. The United States, the defense claimed, did not hesitate to allow self-critique. Steinbeck's work, for example, had been appropriated by the Nazis as anti-U.S. propaganda, but he was lionized in his home country.[69] The defense also cited an article in the U.S. weekly *Time*, in which Nam had been called a "patriot," as evidence that Nam's work "was utterly unconnected with the formation of anti-American sentiment." And Nam could not be sympathetic to the North, because he was a writer whose work had been "disseminated to the entire free world," appearing in the UNESCO-sponsored *Korea Journal*.[70]

The written decision handed down by the court, which rested on an interpretation of the meaning of the word "sympathize" (*tongjo*), relied heavily on the National Security Law in determining Nam's guilt. Following the defense's argument, the court stated that "the work is the expression of the author's earnest desire for the establishment of our nation's autonomy [*minjokchŏk chuch'esŏng*]."⁷¹ Nevertheless, the court concluded that, regardless of intent, if the contents of a writer's work were determined to coincide with the assertions of an anti-ROK organization, the author was a "sympathizer" in violation of the law. The court itself, it seems, wished to demonstrate sympathy for what it considered to be Nam's nationalist inclinations.

After offering South Korea up as a good model for South Vietnam to follow, "Hope in the Hermit Kingdom," the brief article in *Time* cited by Nam's lawyers, provides the following citation: "'When we hammered in the spikes for a new railroad recently,' said Deputy Prime Minister Key Young Chang last week, 'I was reminded of American cowboy movies and the winning of the West.'"⁷² As the title implies, hope (in the form of the promise of development) exists for South Korea to emerge from its inward-looking, premodern past. Chang's reiteration of the pioneer spirit aligns South Korea with the United States' historical trajectory and provides comforting evidence for a readership nervous about the rapidly escalating war in Vietnam that Asians can be assimilated as proper subjects of modernization. What has happened is that the U.S. national narrative, the production of "America," has traveled further west, accompanying the slippage of "America" into "free world." This is the kind of movement that enables Homer Atkins to go about what is called his "world business" in *The Ugly American*. In the *Time* article, this narrative of the free world recognizes subjects who will occupy the celebrated trajectory of "American" history in the form of identification with the white imaginary of the cowboy in Hollywood films.⁷³ We thus have a visual summoning to become part of what Tom Engelhardt has called U.S. "victory culture."⁷⁴

"Land of Excrement" is a testament addressed by Man-su, the tenth-generation descendant of Hong Kil-tong (who led a band of righteous bandits opposing corrupt officials in the Chosŏn dynasty), to his deceased mother. Man-su is hiding on Mount Hyangmi, surrounded by crack U.S. troops and "as many as ten thousand missiles and artillery pieces." A broadcast from the Pentagon interrupts his confession to declare that Man-su, "a pollutant vomited up by the devil," has twenty minutes to live. Man-su informs his mother that "shortly I will receive the full-force attack of a nuclear weapon and my body will explode and burst up in flames."⁷⁵

Man-su's father, a resistance fighter, left the family to fight the Japanese in the colonial period, never to return. Following liberation from

Japanese rule, Man-su's mother, carrying the Korean and American flags, went to a welcoming celebration for U.S. troops only to be raped by a U.S. soldier. Unable to find a job following the Korean War, Man-su earns a living black marketing the American goods his sister Pun-i obtains from the U.S. soldier she lives with, Sergeant Speed. The latter, however, beats and reviles Pun-i on a nightly basis, finding fault with the "lower half of her body," which compares unfavorably with that of Mrs. Speed. Man-su resents Sergeant Speed's abuse of his sister and declares he would like to see Mrs. Speed for himself. Unexpectedly, Mrs. Speed arrives from the United States to visit her husband, and Man-su, under the pretext of showing her the scenery of Korea, takes her to a mountain and rapes her: "I was drunk to the point of losing consciousness as I buried my face in her plump, blooming breasts, which were giving off a variety of fragrances—butter, jam, and chocolate."[76]

Man-su gives up on appealing to the member of the National Assembly from his district because he has heard that this politician has already prostrated himself and apologized profusely to Sergeant Speed's superior. With time running out, Man-su invokes the magical powers of his ancestor and closes the text with the following:

> Only ten seconds left. That's right. Now I will take off this running shirt emblazoned with the yin-yang symbol and make it into a glorious flag. I'll catch a ride on the clouds and cross the ocean. With all my heart, I'll drive this magnificent flag into the women sprawled across that great continent, into their glistening belly buttons, into the milk-colored skin I've tasted before. Please believe me. I am not lying, Mother. But your body is trembling, you cannot believe me. It's a shame to see you like that. Please look at me. At these eyes of mine bulging in their sockets. Does it look like this guy is going to die so easily? Hahaha.[77]

The epistolary form, the unpacking of the process of projecting the entirety of evil onto the criminalized other in order to produce the law of the ethical subject, the concern with a patrilineage of resistance (here extending ten generations)—all of this resembles Nam's earlier "Letter to Father." Man-su, like Yong-dal in "Letter to Father"—as well as Sŏk-chu in "Inheritance Under the Chimney" and Tŏk-su in "Chaos"—does not own his own body. It stands in for the ten generations that have preceded him. Like the other male protagonists who populate Nam's texts, his resistance is not voluntarist but spontaneous, occurring in spite of itself.

"Land of Excrement" interrogates the U.S. patriarchal/developmental injunction to a behavioral conformity—the summoning of the cowboy, masculinist protagonist of the hegemonic U.S. national narrative, hammering in the spikes of progress. At the same time, the text, as Judith Butler warns may happen to the parodic gesture, runs the risk of serving simply as "vehicle for a reconsolidation of hegemonic norms."[78] The United States, represented in the text by the Pentagon broadcast, condemns Man-su: "Cursed rapist! Treacherous criminal spattering shit over the honor of the American people, the people of the free world! Prepare to receive your punishment." Man-su responds: "Unbelievable. Now they're calling me a rapist. . . . But even if it were true that, due to unfortunate circumstances, I committed rape, why should I be punished? I mean it might be different if a certain long-nosed guy who raped you [Man-su's mother] and sent you to the Other World was also punished."[79]

The Pentagon broadcast, the law, can only register criminality in the other. Man-su's counter-rape rearticulates the performance of universalism, occurring, here, in the form of a slippage between "American people" and "people of the free world." "Land of Excrement" makes visible the site where unequal power relations are most evident: extraterritorial privilege. U.S. military personnel were not subject to Korean law in any form until the first Status of Forces Agreement, better known as SOFA, was implemented in 1967. Nam's "talking back," which was to be censored, violates the rules of core-periphery relations by testing the free-world truth claim, questioning the universalism of a law that fails to make good on its own insistence of uniformity. This is a law that does not afford equal treatment to the totality of free-world subjects it summons.

The pleasure Man-su experiences following his rape of Mrs. Speed occurs not because he has stepped into the shoes of Sergeant Speed but because of his own eventual consideration of Mrs. Speed's rape in terms of the nation (a movement similar to Yong-dal's representation of the murder of Ch'ŏng-ja). Man-su's intoxication arises from smelling butter, jam, and chocolate from Mrs. Speed's breasts. The figuring of Mrs. Speed's body as "America" begins with its association with commodities available on U.S. military bases and circulated in South Korea through the black market. The fleeing Mrs. Speed then appears to Man-su "exactly" like his mother, driven insane following her rape by the U.S. soldier. This image frightens Man-su: "But my worrying was only momentary—My heart was shaking, I was overwhelmed at the thought that I had held America, heaven on earth [*in'gan ŭi chŏn'guk*], in the space of my arms."[80]

The allegorical gesture demonstrates how women are "symbolically reduced, in male eyes, to the space on which male contests are waged."[81] Man-su can imagine woman only as outside history, as mother—eternalized, abstract, domesticated—or as nation. Who is Man-su's mother? We have, at this moment in the text, an instability, a potential disordering of what Anne McClintock calls "woman as boundary marker." It is at this moment that the figure of woman as mother threatens to subsume the figure of woman as nation. But the text quickly adjusts these registers: Mrs. Speed cannot be mother but must be other, America. This momentary blurring, then, is followed by a reordering accomplished by invoking national identity, drawing national borders. Man-su's separation of Mrs. Speed's body from his mother's body becomes the moment of his birthing as masculine, ethnonational subject.

More than anything else, Man-su's rape of Mrs. Speed stands somewhere between a parodic throwing back of neocolonial violence upon itself and the reconsolidation of a hegemonic masculinism. We can consider the text, in its very gesture of opposition to the United States and the South Korean state, to be acting out the violence underpinning the enforcement of Cold War "development in the name of the nation." It is precisely such a countermasculinism that appears at the close of the text, when Man-su declares his intention to drive his magnificent flag into the white women sprawled across North America.

We also find this countermasculinism in films such as *Madame Freedom* and *Female Executive*, which portray a threat to the patriarchal family in the aftermath of the Korean War. Popular culture of the 1950s and 1960s is marked by an abiding interest in gender reversals, all of which are followed by reconsolidations of the patriarchal order.[82] Such a concern with gender relations also informed U.S. popular culture in the 1950s. The containment of Rosie the Riveter was accomplished by the deployment of the sexualized glamour girl on the one hand and the cult of domesticity associated with housewives such as June Cleaver on the other.

Indeed, the laughter and parody that so many critics have associated with Nam's work point to a relation with comedy films such as *Female Executive*.[83] As in the filmic version of *Madame Freedom*, the domestication of

DEVELOPMENT AS DEVOLUTION 159

the subversive female executive (the president of a magazine company entitled New Woman, Inc.) happens all too quickly. Her relocation to the home cannot replace the visual pleasure produced by the gender reversal that constitutes most of the film. The very quickness of the refeminization leaves the impression that it is less a "natural" return than one performance among others.

Female Executive goes so far as to parody anticommunism and nationalism during a scene in which male job seekers to New Woman, Inc., are brought before women interviewers and rejected for different reasons. One of them stumbles and attempts to pull himself together by coming to attention and parroting anticommunist, nationalist slogans. He is met with nothing but laughter. Nam appropriates this laughter in his critique of the Cold War order while leaving its questioning of masculinist nationalism behind.

Earlier in "Land of Excrement," Man-su expresses, parodically, his respect for the U.S. national/developmental story, the "superhuman" efforts by which "Americans" created "heaven on earth," clearing the wilderness, which, he notes, was formerly the sacred land (*pokchi*) of the "Indians." Man-su's feminizing of the North American continent, his intention to cross the ocean and (re)nationalize this territory, is at once a counterfeminization of the occident (a response to the feminizing of the oriental other) and an oppositional miming of the trajectory of ethnonational developmentalism. It is also a violent inhabiting of the U.S. national narrative, a reiteration of the

FIGURE 4.2 "We young people should fight until we hang our flag on the top of Mt. Paektu" (*Female Executive*, 1959).

European crossing itself, the sort of white celebratory conquest of "virgin territory" found in shows such as "Buffalo Bill's Wild West," in which "Beginning with the Primeval Forest, peopled by the Indian and Wild Beasts only, the story of the gradual civilization of a vast continent is depicted."[84]

Here, we can link the elimination of Man-su to the state's censoring of Nam's text. Both serve less to efface an oppositional discourse than to attempt to cover over the ways in which Nam Chŏng-hyŏn renders visible the violence of competing Cold War metropolitan and peripheral masculinisms/countermasculinisms. Although the obliteration of Man-su, the dispersal of his ethnonationalized body (and the reduction of South Korea to bodily waste), occurs, in the text, as the Pentagon's (over)compensatory, remasculinizing response (a first-world punishment),[85] there is a way in which Nam's parodic gesture questions the countermasculinism that structures his text.

Finally, we should recall that Man-su is targeted by "as many as ten thousand missiles and artillery pieces," and in twenty minutes he "will receive the full-force attack of a nuclear weapon." Man-su occupies a similar position to that of North Korea in the Cold War order. He becomes a target that structures the scopic regime of an array of surveillance systems, weaponry, and bases that stretches from the DMZ through Japan, Guam, Hawai'i, and back to networks in the continental United States. Man-su, like North Korea, is rendered highly visible but only in a certain way, as target. Along with the publication of portions of "Land of Excrement" in the North, the unpacking of this scopic regime in a South Korean literary text troubles the division system. "Land of Excrement" thus enacts a border crossing that must be declared illicit.

For the past ten years, South Korea has been invoked as a privileged example of developmental success, a model-become-reality for Iraq, Afghanistan, and, eventually, other sites in the Middle East. A multilayered forgetting enables this instance of exemplarity. Recall that for Timothy Mitchell the "world-as-picture" stages a colonial European modernity marked by a "double claim": that the model or project is always a mere copy, that the world it replicates "must be, by contrast, original . . . in a word (what we imagine as) real." For Mitchell, as we saw earlier, "the effectiveness of this world-as-picture lies not simply in the process of serialization. It lies in the apparent contrast created between images, which are repeatable, serializable . . . and the opposing effect of an original, of what appears to be the actual nation, the people itself, the real economy."[86] Here, the site of the "original," which Mitchell proceeds to deconstruct, is Europe. The Cold War extends colonial European modernity, but with a modification of the picture linked to responsibilization and *de jure* sovereignty. Replacing Europe, or what we might more accurately call the Euro-American core, as the "actual" is a more flexible hierarchization that allows for the advance of postcolonial nation-state units in the evolutionist world system—for example, by possible inclusion in the OECD, the expanding G-series, etc.

Serialization now enters the picture in a different way. We encounter a serialized modularity that continuously transforms "copy" into "original," "model" into referent for the next project. In the end, we may witness the elimination of this transfer of model to referent altogether (a transfer, or its promise, that is itself currently the enactment of the global regime of responsibilization). This staging would involve what Baudrillard long ago designated as the "hyperreal" or, put somewhat differently, the seamless circulation of Wiener's "pure information." We live in the interstices, in a globalization marked by desires both for the imagining of transferable reference and for the cybertechnological doing away of reference altogether. The former, like the nation-state, is still with us, if, in no other place, at least in exemplarity or the imagining of the example.

Nam's works attempt to contest Park Chung Hee's articulation of statist, ethnonational developmentalism, which is itself a continuation of and reaction against the colonial past and U.S. metropolitan representations of its free-world developmentalist mission. To figure development as devolution is to make visible the relation between Cold War developmentalism and the history of Euro-American colonial racism that informs it. Both developmentalism and colonial racism rely upon an evolutionary narrative. Nam's attempt to interrupt the developmentalist imagination involves a location of the "original" in the immediacy of the ethnonationalized body, away from the exemplarity of Euro-America.

The interrogation of the developmentalist fantasy frame and its visual hailing of free-world subjects in Nam's work underscores the importance of appropriations of Hollywood-style backdrops, the imagining of the South Korean present landscape as having developed into a U.S. background populated by South Korean protagonists. As noted above, such imaginings are easily found in 1950s and 1960s popular culture. Kim Ki-dŏk's *Yongary, Monster from the Deep* (*Taegwoesu yonggari*, 1967), for example, provides us with a remake of *Godzilla* that turns upon the spectacle of an already developed

162 DEVELOPMENT AS DEVOLUTION

FIGURE 4.3 The Republic of Korea National Space Research Center (*Yongary, Monster from the Deep*, 1967).

Korea in full possession of a space program—we are presented with cars, roads, clothes, homes, and suburban spaces that seem very much in line with what we might expect in 1960s Pasadena or Cape Canaveral. The film and its 1967 audience enter into the space, in the movie theater, of the future perfect of development—development as an already accomplished fact and as yet to be achieved. *Yongary*, in fact, follows statist anticommunism in its portrayal of the monster as something more than degraded other. In a pivotal scene and in the midst of Yongary's rampage through Seoul, the child protagonist dances with the monster to the tune of a jazzed-up version of "Arirang." Indeed, Yongary and the boy have a special relationship, informed by the trope of the organicist nation—body (North Korea) has become separated from head, the boy genius, product and future vanguard of the developmental South Korean state. Body and mind, North and South Korea, unite momentarily and spontaneously, to the rhythm of "Arirang," jazzified, modernized, yet ethnonational.

I noted above the ways in which the resistance Nam mounts to the Cold War order rearticulates the questioning of Western exemplarity in the late

1930s and early 1940s. Certainly, Nam's nationalism coincides, on multiple levels, with the masculinisms and essentialisms informing both the Japanese imperialism of the past and the U.S. neocolonialism of the present. What is the relation between the call to overcome modernity by the pre-1945 pan-Asian imperial subject and the call to do the same by the post-1945 South Korean ethnonational subject? In Nam's texts, as in South Korean postcolonial statist-nationalism, this relation makes itself visible in a certain way: as what is to remain unseen and unspoken.

In the next chapter, we will look at the ways in which the writer Ch'oe In-hun seeks to move beyond oppositions such as colonial/anticolonial, nation/empire, East/West, and first world/second world, which played such a central role in organizing and disciplining Cold War subjects in South Korea. The search for an alternative begins with the flight to a "neutral country" in Ch'oe's 1960 *The Square* (published during the April 19–May 16 period) and comes to a certain end in his 1973 *The Tempest*, a much less well-known text that, like *The Ugly American*, locates a noncapitalist fantasy frame in a fictional country in Southeast Asia. As we will see, it was Ch'oe In-hun who first addressed the ways in which the contemporary division system was bound up both with the selective remembering of the colonial past in South Korea and the visual regime making up the broader Cold War order.

5
RETURN TO THE COLONIAL PRESENT
Translation, Collaboration, Pan-Asianism

BEGINNING WITH *THE Square* (*Kwangjang*, 1960) and moving through *The Tempest* (*T'aep'ung*, 1973), Ch'oe In-hun engaged in a series of attempts to write a performative history that would unpack what he saw as a multilayered coloniality informing the Cold War Koreas: the intersection of statist authoritarianisms and free-world developmentalism with an earlier, pre-1945 colonial history of ethnonational, classed, and pan-Asian identifications.[1] Ch'oe's well-known concern with North/South division (*The Square* is considered a founding text of "division literature") occurs as part of this attempt to address a colonial modernity that extends itself beyond the period of Japanese rule (1910–1945) and into the post-1945 era. The shifts in Ch'oe's "novels of ideas" (*kwannyŏm sosŏl*) of the early 1960s (*The Square* and "Imprisoned" ["Su," 1961]) through the mid-1960s (*Voice of the Governor-General* [*Ch'ongdok ŭi sori*, 1967, 1968, 1976]) to two early 1970s works (*A Day in the Life of Kubo the Novelist* [*Sosŏlga Kubossi ŭi iril*, 1970–1972] and *The Tempest*) took place at critical moments in Park Chung Hee's enforcement of an anticommunist developmental trajectory and the emergence of its leftist-nationalist opposition. If, as we saw in chapter 4, the task of the South Korean developmental state in the 1960s and 1970s was to legitimize its project via the productivist eradication of communism (*myŏlgong*) in the North, Ch'oe's work increasingly sought to overcome the division of the peninsula by questioning the ways in which post-1945 ethnonationalisms posited themselves as anticolonial either by promoting integration and advancement within the free-world order (Park

Chung Hee) or by fissuring ethnonation from the comprador state (Nam Chŏng-hyŏn).

Ch'oe's return to the colonial is preceded by a return, in *The Square*, to the five years that followed the formation of the Republic of Korea in 1948. In this first of his major works, Ch'oe attempts to recall the setting in place of the division system. The return to this history counters the naturalizing of a North/South border that had taken place in the aftermath of the Korean War. In the mid-1960s, however, Ch'oe begins to address a broader modernity. It becomes increasingly clear that the formation of the South Korean state and the production of its Cold War subjects cannot be understood without working through the relation between the post-1945 cultural field and the colonial modernity of 1910–1945.

Ch'oe was the first South Korean writer to address the post-1945 forgetting of the late colonial mass culture of mobilization discussed in chapter 1 and the importance of this erasure in the formation of South Korea and its historical trajectory. Departing from the collaboration confessionals that appeared briefly during the U.S. military occupation, Ch'oe rejects the assumption of a preexisting ethnonational subject that renders the collaborative act as mere performance. Ch'oe's return to the colonial takes place as part of an interrogation of post-1945 universals, both liberal-democratic and statist. Such a questioning, in turn, leads him to reconsider the relation between the act of writing and the distribution of the visible and invisible that plays a central role both in the representation of North Korea and in the remembering of Japanese imperialism. For this reason, Ch'oe would turn his attention to the relation between words and images and particularly to how this relation informs both the act of translation and the scene of interpellation.

Ch'oe's search for a "nonaligned" position from which to critique the division system represents a continuation of the antianticommunist discourse we traced in chapter 3. His reworking of late colonial pan-Asianism in the form of a nonaligned subject entails unpacking a Cold War visual order linked to division (the effacement of the North), coloniality (erasure of the history of imperialization/mobilization), and what Foucault calls "biological modernity." The last signals, as Giorgio Agamben tells us, "the point at which the species and the individual as a simple living body become what is at stake in a society's political strategies."[2] Ch'oe's works, that is, represent the most sustained, wide-ranging engagement by a post-1945 writer with the relation between the colonial modern and the Cold War division system as well as with the history of the attempts to overcome both.

Ch'oe returns to the colonial in an effort to resume the questioning of the modern begun in the late 1930s and early 1940s. At stake is an attempt to pick up the pieces of a project, the "overcoming of modernity," that allowed for a consideration of some new kind of being in the world but ultimately led to a further disciplining in the form of militarism and imperialization. Ch'oe refuses to view the colonial as past not only because the authoritarian Park regime repeats its imperial content in nationalist form but because the late colonial period also contained, at its close, an attempt to rethink the modern.

THE SQUARE AND THE EGO

Set during 1948–1953, the period of the formation of separate regimes in North and South and the subsequent Korean War, *The Square* produces a universalist subject informed by the call made in the late 1950s by many South Korean intellectuals and literary critics for "engagement" (*anggajyumang* in transliterated Korean, from the French)—a subject of action.[3] It does this by constructing an interiorized site, which the text names as both its protagonist, Yi Myŏng-jun, and, in the Roman alphabet, the "Ego." The tracing of this Ego's trajectory from 1948 through the end of the Korean War in 1953 rewrites the early histories of the ROK and the DPRK as the development of Cold War political formations disallowing the Ego's proper emergence.[4]

The Square tells the story of Myŏng-jun's recollection of the events that have brought him on board the *Tagore*, an Indian ship taking a group of POWs to a neutral country. Myŏng-jun returns to Seoul from China with his father and mother following liberation. His father, an associate of the prominent communist Pak Hŏn-yŏng, shortly leaves for the North. Myŏng-jun's mother dies, and Myŏng-jun is taken in by his father's friend, a bank manager, who provides room, board, and pays his college tuition. Myŏng-jun begins a relationship with Yun-ae, whom he meets at a dance party given by Yŏng-mi, the happy-go-lucky daughter of his benefactor. Because of the activities of his father in the North, however, Myŏng-jun is summoned by the police, interrogated, and beaten. This event, coupled with what Myŏng-jun considers Yun-ae's refusal to open herself completely to him, causes Myŏng-jun to arrange for secret passage to the North. In the DPRK, Myŏng-jun is disappointed both by the "nauseating" bourgeois life his father leads and the demands of his superiors that he submit without question to the party line. He enters into a relationship with Ŭn-hye, a dancer, but is further disappointed when she leaves him to perform for several months in Moscow. Myŏng-jun participates in the Korean War as an officer in the DPRK army, encountering Yun-ae (who has married T'ae-sik, Yŏng-mi's saxophone-playing brother) in Seoul and later reuniting with Ŭn-hye, now a nurse, at the Naktong River battlefront. Ŭn-hye is killed and Myŏng-jun taken prisoner. Following the armistice agreement, he chooses the option of passage to a neutral country rather than life in either the DPRK or the ROK. Aboard the *Tagore*, Myŏng-jun takes a final glance at two seagulls that have been following the ship since its departure from port and throws himself into the "blue square" of the South China Sea.

The movement of the Ego respatializes division, effecting a unification of the ROK and the DPRK. Both formations are united in their opposition to the development of the Ego, dividing the Ego from a meaningful, autonomous engagement with the social. Let us consider the relation between the Ego and the notion of private space in the text. The narrator informs us that

> The term called the Ego did not inhere in food, shoes, socks, clothes, blankets, beds, school fees, cigarettes, umbrellas. The Ego, rather, was what was remaining after all those things were removed. That final thing which, solitary, incontrovertible, remained after everything else had been put in doubt. For Yi Myŏng-jun, student of philosophy, that was the Ego that he could trust, which was meaningful. His father could not be part of this Ego. His mother had no role to play regarding this Ego. Myŏng-jun was the sole inhabitant of the Ego's room. The Ego was not the square. It was a room. Only one person was allowed in this room; like a prisoner's cell it was not for anyone else. . . . The road to the square where he could meet his father was blocked. The square in which his father made his appearance was located in another region. Machine guns were placed on its borders. He was, from the first, not to think of going there; indeed, he had never thought he would like to go. This was because he had no faith in the square. The only precious, valuable thing was the Ego's room [Ego *ŭi pang*].[5]

Regarding the political, economic, cultural "squares," Myŏng-jun tells his friend Mr. Chŏng that

> The only feeling people have about these kinds of squares is one of loss of faith. The most precious thing to them is their own room, just their own secret room [*milsil*].... This is because it is the last hole in which they can hide.... There is only the individual [*kaein*], no people [*kungmin*]. Only secret rooms abound, the square is dead. Each secret room is stocked in proportion to its owner's status.... No one stays in the square. When the plunder and deceit end, the square is completely empty. A dead square. Isn't this South Korea? The square is empty.[6]

Both *pang* (space of the doubting Ego stripped of all worldly possessions) and *milsil* (space of the materialistic, acquisitive *kaein*) stand in opposition to *kwangjang*. Both represent a retreat (the *pang* is a "prisoner's cell," the *milsil* a "hole") from the public space occasioned by a "loss of faith" and political repression. Indeed, Myŏng-jun considers that the "political" is little more than a dividing up of metropolitan leavings: "Politics? Is there any difference between Korean politics today and the disposal of refuse from the mess-halls of American army camps?"[7]

The inauthenticity of the room of the Ego is revealed by the ease with which the anticommunist state intrudes upon its space. Myŏng-jun is badly beaten during his interrogation at the police station. Ignoring Myŏng-jun for a moment, one of the detectives digresses into a nostalgic reminiscence of his "heyday" during the colonial period as a member of the secret police detailed to repress leftist activities: "Listening to his tale, Myŏng-jun was overcome by a sense that he was sitting in the office of the Japanese secret police. That was the extent to which the detective was conflating past and present. It was quite clear that as far as capturing Reds was concerned, the detective considered the present to be no different than the period under the Japanese bastards."[8]

This linkage of postcolonial anticommunism to the enforcement of colonialist regimes of power turns the interrogation of Myŏng-jun into a questioning of the legitimacy of the South Korean state. This scene of interrogation at the police station, the summoning of the anticommunist subject, becomes a colonialist gesture. At the same time, the summoning of this subject violates the rights of the juridical subject of liberal democracy: following the beating, Myŏng-jun asks himself, "Am I outside the law?" and then considers that "There is a law. The right to life of a citizen cannot be treated like that. Suddenly a thought arose in his head. I'll prosecute the detective for his assault. But immediately he shook his head."[9] The state does not recognize its laws; the anticommunist subject is not a citizen. Myŏng-jun now considers that the "precious" space of the Ego's room was a phantasm: "All the things I have relied on up to this point, all the things I believed in weren't to be trusted. At least it seems that the lock to the Ego's room was a toy lock."[10] The Ego cannot exist in South Korea. The anticommunist state disallows its activity in the public space (the square is empty) and intrudes at will into the private space in which it takes refuge (withdrawal to the Ego's room provides no guarantee of safety).

Myŏng-jun moves with high hopes from the solipsistic room of the Ego in the South toward the square in the North, dreaming on the boat of a scene in which "Clear fountains were painting a rainbow in the square. Fresh flowers ... were laughing to the sound of honeybees buzzing. The pavement was clean and solid."[11] But he soon comes to the conclusion that the DPRK has utterly failed to realize its ideals. As a reporter for the *Labor Daily*, Myŏng-jun is dispatched to a collective farm he considers emblematic of a society in which "Vigorous originality [*ch'angŭi*] was not to be seen, it was all just a forced carrying out of allotted work.... Individual desires were taboo [*t'abu*], and in the square there were only marionettes, no people."[12]

Myŏng-jun's reporting of conditions at the collective farm leads his editor to summon him for a self-criticism session to address his "outmoded petit bourgeois judgment." Myŏng-jun defends his article, claiming that "realism is reporting the facts as they are."[13] The editor responds with an outline of the mission of a socialist newspaper: "That is your dangerous, reactionary thought. Socialist realism must always strive to move in a direction that promotes class antagonism [*chŏkkaesim*] and fuels the desire to work among the people."[14] Confronted with the hostile, "sadistic" expressions on the faces of the party members present at the session, Myŏng-jun considers that protest is useless, that he has no choice but to follow the party line "with a serious expression and long-winded quotations."[15] Myŏng-jun's capitulation is "successful," reassuring the party members. It is also the moment that he rejects the DPRK.

In Ch'oe's text, South Korea is nothing more than a kleptocratic U.S. satellite state with no genuine democratic public sphere; North Korea offers only a false public, the rigid formulaism of communist party edicts. Myŏng-jun's rejection not only of the ROK and the DPRK but also, by way of his suicide, of life in a neutral foreign country, figures the April 19 movement of 1960 as enabling the possibility for this subject to overcome the inauthentic modernities of the two Koreas, to reemerge in the post–April 19 space and participate meaningfully in the building of a unified, nonaligned, liberal-democratic state. Ch'oe's work thus joins in the post–April 19 calls by the younger generation to recover historical possibilities considered lost during the 1945–1948 occupation period. In *The Square*, at least in the 1960 version, it is the nontransliterated English Ego, not the ethnonation, that serves as transhistorical subject, as neutral, universalist site that will perform the overcoming of the Cold War division of the peninsula.

Neutrality in Ch'oe's text, however, becomes something more than a repetition of the immediate post-1945 calls for political nonalignment as the only possible way to overcome North/South division. Laclau notes the ways in which the notion of incarnation inaugurates a history of the "*privileged agent of history*, the agent whose particular body was the expression of a universality transcending it. The various forms of Eurocentrism are nothing but the historical effects of the logic of incarnation."[16] The logic of incarnation is later reworked when Europe universalizes its own particularism, representing itself as the incarnation of universal human interests. Resistance from other cultures then becomes a struggle between universalism and "peoples without history expressing precisely their incapacity to represent the universal."[17] *The Square*, via its deployment of the universal on the Korean peninsula in the form of the nontransliterated, English Ego, thus invokes the possibility of active participation in the making of Eurocentric history itself.

Ch'oe tells another story of the Ego in his subsequent 1960s and 1970s revisions of *The Square*. While all but two appearances of the term "Ego" appear in English in the 1960 version, "Ego" is transliterated in the 1961 and 1968 versions. In 1976, following his three-year stay in the United States, Ch'oe removed the transliterations in favor of the Korean terms *na* and *chagi*.[18] The movement from the English "Ego" to the transliterated *ego* and, later, to *na* points to a continuing struggle to write the text out of its original positing of the English signifier as universal—the privilege conferred upon the metropolitan signifier by way of its nontranslation. However, precisely by securing a commensurability, the translation produces what Lydia Liu has shown to be the universalism of "hypothetical equivalence."[19] *Na* stands in for "Ego," the local incarnation/translation of a purportedly universal subject. *The Square* (and its revisions) can be read as a point of departure for Ch'oe's other works of the 1960s and early 1970s, which contest the knowledge/identities put into play by this imperial regime of equivalence.

For Ch'oe, as for Nam Chŏng-hyŏn and many other writers and intellectuals, Park Chung Hee's May 1961 military takeover and subsequent consolidation of power brought a crashing end to the possibilities opened up by April 19. If the freedoms granted from April 1960 to May 1961 allowed for the publication of *The Square*, for questions of neutrality, reunification, ideology to be raised in a much more open-ended manner than under the Syngman Rhee regime, Park's coup signaled a return to the political repression of the 1950s. Ch'oe explores the effects of the coup in his 1961 short story "Imprisoned" ("Su"), a text published two months after Park's assumption of power.

In "Imprisoned," the first-person narrator is confined to a psychiatric ward and subjected to the daily interrogations of a state psychiatrist. The space allotted to the narrator is a reconfigured square, not the liberal democratic public sphere but the four walls of a cell. This is a space also presented to us by way of the text's title, the sino-Korean character *su* (囚; the character for "person" placed inside a square box). Under the Park regime, Ch'oe's text warns, the proper subject of democracy has already become deviant, resistant to a normalizing function that seeks to produce statist, developmental subjects.

"Imprisoned" (囚) inaugurates a questioning of authoritarianism and its disciplining that demonstrates how the verbal/visual relation is involved in the representation of the subject in writing. 囚 becomes something more than a transformation of square to prison, the placing of the "Ego" in a box. 囚 translates "Ego"—a movement from English to sino-Korean that is at once verbal and visual. This movement bears close relation with the history of nontranslation, transliteration, and translation that takes place in the revisions of *The Square*. Locating 囚 within this trajectory allows us to see the ways in which the appearance of the English "Ego" in the first version of *The Square* universalizes the hailing of this English signifier. This is a universalism that proceeds by not seeing, by not considering the appearance of the "Ego" in the Roman alphabet as sign of difference.

Tracing the slow-motion process of translation of the Ego (1960–1976), then, allows us to see the importance of its visual transformation. Here, we should recall that Saussure's interruption of the correspondence between words and things occurs as both a linguistic and pictorial turn. Saussure tells us that

> Linguistic signs, though basically psychological, are not abstractions; associations which bear the stamp of collective approval—and which together constitute language—are realities that have their seat in the brain. Besides, linguistic signs are tangible; it is possible to reduce them to conventional written symbols, whereas it would be impossible to provide detailed photographs of acts of speaking [*actes de parole*]; the pronunciation of even the smallest word represents an infinite number of muscular movements that could be identified and put into graphic form only with great difficulty. In language, on the contrary, there is only the sound-image, and the latter can be translated into a fixed, visual image.[20]

I would like to underscore the importance in the above passage of the photograph for Saussure, his desire to translate sound-image to "fixed, visual image." If the Saussurean sign "unites not a thing and a name, but a concept and a sound-image," the act of translation is bound up with the visual. It is, of course, the sound-image that Saussure names the signifier, while the concept—that which replaces things—becomes the signified. For Saussure, the signifier "is not ... a purely physical thing, but the psychological imprint of the sound, the impression it makes on our senses."[21] As "sound-*image*," this impression involves the visual register. In his discussion of the signified, Saussure writes that concepts "become linguistic entities only when associated with sound-images; in language, a concept is a quality of its phonic substance just as a particular slice of sound is a quality of the concept."[22] The concept is part and parcel of the imaging that informs the signifier.

Saussure's delinking of names from things turns upon the ways in which the relation of concept to sound-image is at once verbal and visual. The thing becomes a concept, which, in turn, Saussure finds himself defining by way of a word and a picture. The two famous diagrams in the *Course in General Linguistics* are located side by side. The first places the word "tree" in quotation marks (the concept) on top of the word "arbor" (the sound-image). The second is identical to the first, except "tree" has been replaced by an illustration of a tree.[23] The thing has been replaced by an illustration—the referent has become an image. The reader of the *Course* experiences this shift visually, "translating" illustration to word in quotation marks, "tree," and then to word, arbor. Here, "tree," while located in the first diagram as signified, actually occupies the hybrid position of "sound-image," equated with the illustration on its right, while pointing to a movement to the word "arbor" placed below it. The task of these two diagrams is to equate "tree" and illustration while moving from the visual, the illustration, to a combination of visuality and sound, first to "tree," and then to "arbor," the "sound-image" that already "translates" itself into the "tangible form" of a "fixed, visual image" written on the page of Saussure's text.

We should, that is, note the ways in which the renaming of concept/sound-image as signified/signifier is accomplished by the appearance of a set of diagrams. An act of visual translation produces the notion of the sign. Let us move from the consideration of the ways in which the verbal-visual relation informs translation within a given language to the implications for a translation that moves from one writing system to another. If it is the concept that attempts to extricate itself from the sound-image in an effort to locate itself as transcendental, its association with the latter as an imaging brings us back to a material process. Translation takes place by way of the visual transformation of written marks on a page.

As a quality of its phonic substance, the concept is itself implicated in a sound-imaging that can change across writing systems. The material transformation that takes place in a move from one writing system to another is also a visual one, a change in form in the writing on a page. A gap thus opens between the act of transforming English to Korean visually and the positing of universality on the level of the concept. It is in this way that a reading of Ch'oe's revisions reveals the aporia of the sixteen-year translation project we can designate as *The Square*. At stake is the attempt to dismantle a metropolitan signified that has been imagined, fetishized as unchanging, universal. Ch'oe's move from nontranslation to transliteration represents the first step in writing a way out of the universalism of the Ego. This visual transformation of the written mark proves inadequate. The sound of the transliterated signifier allows the metropolitan signified to retain its universalist image. The next move is to translation, to a change that is both visual and aural: *na* and *chagi*. But these signifiers cannot extricate themselves from the published history of nontranslation and transliteration that precedes their appearance. The concept retains a trace of the universal. For this reason, Ch'oe would move to other texts to pursue this project, but in a much more explicit relation to the Cold War rearticulation of categories associated with colonial modernity.

A (Post)colonial Haunting:
In the Interstices of Empire and Nation

The mid-1960s saw the settling in place of what Bruce Cumings calls a "Bureaucratic-Authoritarian Industrializing Regime" (BAIR), a state similar to the "prewar Japanese model," one "ubiquitous in economy and society: penetrating, comprehensive, highly articulated, and relatively autonomous of particular groups and classes."[24] The 1965 ROK-Japan Normalization Treaty, coupled with the entrance of South Korea into the U.S. war against Vietnam in the same year, located South Korea on a statist trajectory that eschewed the question of democracy and asserted the primacy of economic modernization.[25] In his discussion of the mid-1960s debate on economic growth between the government and the opposition party, Kim Tong-ch'un points out that

> Modernization was now discussed only in terms of capitalization. . . . The debate on modernization and nationalism could only be carried on with restrictions. Therefore, rather than centering on a debate of what were called the irrefutable concepts of modernization and nationalism themselves, the debate centered on the problem of what [these concepts] meant in practice, on what relationship governmental policies had with these concepts in practice, on who, in practice, would benefit and who would be left out as these policies were pursued.[26]

The call for modernization, in turn, relied upon on the assumption of a nation/empire opposition to legitimate both the postcolonial regime and the normalization of relations with Japan.

Published in four installments, one in 1967, two in 1968, and one much later in 1976, Ch'oe In-hun's *Voice of the Governor-General*, as Kwŏn Yŏng-min has shown, can be considered a *yŏnjak sosŏl* (a series of interconnected stories published separately).[27] Each segment consists of a transcript of the underground radio broadcast of the Governor-General who, encouraged by the "polite farewell" given Japanese residents of the colony following defeat at the hands of the *"kwich'uk miyŏng* [Anglo-American devils]," decided to remain on the peninsula, awaiting the day when the empire would make a glorious return.[28] Directed at an audience of "loyal imperial subjects," the four broadcasts begin as commentaries on current events and evolve into explications of the Governor-General's views on a variety of political, ideological, and cultural issues. "Voice of the Governor-General I" (1967) occurs on the occasion of the 1967 presidential and National Assembly elections[29] and includes, among other things, a discussion of the nation as the subject of history, the comprador nature of the Korean ruling class, the "slavish mentality" of Koreans, the importance of the Korean peninsula to the Japanese empire, democracy, communism, and literary realism. "Voice of the Governor-General II" (1968) offers a response to the January 1968 North Korean commando attack on the presidential mansion and the *Pueblo* incident, noting with pleasure the ways in which national division prevents the emergence of a powerful nation on the Korean peninsula and how both the DPRK and ROK faithfully carry out the imperial mandate, the North representing the continuance of the imperial system with Kim Il Sung serving as proxy emperor, the South eschewing democracy in favor of an adherence to the time-honored imperial policy of anticommunism. "Voice of the Governor-General III" (1968), a celebratory response to Kawabata Yasunari's receiving the Nobel Prize for literature, presents an analysis of Japanese modernity that underscores the importance of preserving the national body (*kukch'e*; J.: *kokutai*) as a means to ward off Anglo-American and Soviet imperialisms. Finally, "Voice of the Governor-General IV" (1976) issues an official statement regarding U.S.-Soviet détente, followed by a discussion of the relation between post–World War II U.S.-Soviet global hegemonies and the division of the Korean peninsula.

In the four installments, the return of the former colonial ruler comes less from the outside, in the form of the influx of Japanese capital following normalization, than from within. Japanese imperialist ideology assumes the form of the Park regime's statist enforcement of modernization, one that enables the legitimizing of the deployment of South Korean troops to Vietnam as nothing more than a means to an end.

"Voice of the Governor-General I" dismantles the opposition between imperialism and statist ethnonationalism. One listening to this radio broadcast, after all, could very well be listening to the voice of Park Chung Hee making his official pronouncements while hearing the voice of the Japanese Governor-General. The voice of the latter inhabits, haunts the voice of the former. "Voice of the Governor-General I," in fact, signals the elimination of a "protagonist," the subject of action called for in a necessarily vague manner under the Syngman Rhee regime in the late 1950s and in more concrete terms in the immediate aftermath of April 19. The passive listener becomes something more (or less) than the protagonist of "Imprisoned," one not only confined to the darkness of his room, cut off from the square, but also denied a narrative, a voice, reduced to an inarticulate scream of excruciating pain, "Aguguaguguguaguguguu."[30]

If the Governor-General becomes a "presence," a ghostly inhabiting of the official word of South Korean authority, there is a way in which this text invokes the spirit of the Governor-General, summons it, fleshes it out, in order to exorcise it. More precisely, what is at stake in the text is how to reject authoritarianism without miming its logic—without, for example, sliding from "empire" to "nation." Let us turn, first, to Bakhtin's distinction between "authoritative discourse" and "internally persuasive discourse." Linking the former to recitation, Bakhtin tells us that

> it is not a free appropriation and assimilation of the word itself that authoritative discourse seeks to elicit from us; rather, it demands our unconditional allegiance . . . one must either totally affirm it, or totally reject it. It is indissolubly fused with its authority—with political power, an institution, a person—and it stands and falls together with that authority. One cannot divide it up—agree with one part, accept but not completely another part, reject utterly a third part.[31]

"Internally persuasive discourse," on the other hand, can be understood as the act of "retelling in one's own words."[32] Bakhtin states the following: "In the everyday rounds of our consciousness, the internally persuasive word is half-ours and half-someone else's. Its creativity and productiveness consist precisely in the fact that such a word awakens new and independent words, that it organizes masses of our words from within, and does not remain in an isolated and static condition."[33] For Bakhtin, "The struggle and dialogic interrelationship of these categories of ideological discourse are what usually determines the history of an individual ideological consciousness."[34] It is this struggle with which *Voice of the Governor-General* concerns itself.

Importantly, in the process of ideological becoming, "what first occurs is a separation between internally persuasive discourse and authoritarian enforced discourse."[35] The movement of ideological becoming is the liberatory process of selectivity, a movement from recitation to retelling, from the other's word to one that is increasingly one's own.[36] The problem is how to think through the relation between authoritarian discourse and internally persuasive discourse, insofar as it is only the latter, by definition, that can increasingly be made into one's own: authoritarian discourse "is by its very nature incapable of being double-voiced."[37] It is almost as if Bakhtin invites us to oppose authoritarian discourse to internally persuasive discourse. Ideological becoming is a process, but one that requires a leap between distinct categories, from authoritative discourse to internally persuasive discourse.[38] But what about those occasions, allowed by Bakhtin, when recitation and retelling are simultaneously present?

Bakhtin's emphasis is on the movement from the authoritative to the internally persuasive (a jump from one category to another) followed by a movement from other to self that is internal to internally persuasive discourse. It is by making a sharp distinction between authoritative discourse and internally persuasive discourse (even while allowing for the "rare" instance of simultaneity) that Bakhtin attempts to channel a movement *from* authoritative discourse *to* internally persuasive discourse, a movement that is prevented from moving back the other way. Once the jump has been made to internally persuasive discourse, the "other" one is dealing with—the retold, dialogized other—is a different category of "other" than the totalizing "other" of authoritative discourse.

Ch'oe's text attempts to unravel the process through which authoritarianism comes to view itself as pure liberation. As authoritative discourse, this sacred voice, verbal incarnation of the emperor, demands absolute obeisance. The acceptance of its "official line" produces the *sinmin* (imperial subject). We might locate *Voice of the Governor-General* in the "sharp gap," in the moment itself of "separation between internally persuasive discourse and authoritarian enforced discourse."[39] The text occupies this gap insofar as it forces an awareness, through its representation of the official transmission of the Governor-General's voice (of the authoritarian word), of the making of authoritarian discourse.

How to distinguish between representation of transmission and transmission as such? Is the reader listening in on a radio broadcast that is addressed to the *sinmin*, the faithful subjects of the emperor who have remained in Korea following the surrender, waiting for the reemergence of Japanese rule in Korea? Or does this radio broadcast address the reader him- or herself as *sinmin*? The burden is placed on the reader to accomplish what "first occurs" in ideological becoming, to engage in the "separation between internally persuasive discourse and authoritarian enforced discourse." The reader, that is, is confronted with the necessity of constituting himself or herself as subject other than *sinmin*.

Even if one agrees, selectively, with the voice, this partial agreement is always an uneasy one, conditioned by the reminder that, after all, this is the voice of the Governor-General. *The moment of forgetting is the moment of recolonization*, the moment of a jump back to authoritative discourse. The text thus prevents itself from slipping into an oppositional exhortation (which would run the danger itself of becoming authoritarian in its very opposition). The text does this by constructing a "contradictory" space for the reader in terms of selectivity: (1) summoning the reader to reject/accept its utterances *in toto* while (2) simultaneously engaging the reader in the necessity of sifting through its statements in an effort to locate the "truth." It is this contradictory space that confronts the reader with the necessity of considering the ways in which he or she is summoned as anticolonial subject by the authoritarian state. The text effects a decolonizing by locating the reader at a critical moment of ideological struggle, the point of "separation" between authoritative discourse and internally persuasive discourse.

Voice of the Governor-General allows us to consider authoritative discourse not as a category distinct from internally persuasive discourse but as an instance of internally persuasive discourse that has achieved the forgetting of its own process of selectivity, demanding that "one must either totally affirm it, or totally reject it."[40] If authoritative discourse is defined as distinct from internally persuasive discourse because it permits no selection, Ch'oe's text shows how this disallowance is itself a selection, even if it masks this by selecting itself and nothing else.

The *Kokutai* Cannot Die, or "Race Is Eternal"

The voice tells us of the satisfaction it felt at the "polite farewell" given the Japanese by Koreans following the Japanese surrender to the "Anglo-American devils."[41] After comparing this polite farewell after "forty years" of colonial rule to the attacks of the French against the Germans during their withdrawal after only two years of occupation, the Governor-General declares the following:

> It occurred to me that there was hope here. I decided to remain in Korea together with my subordinates and a loyal-to-the-death band of

civilians. You might say that this was more than to be expected, given the heteronomy [*t'ayulsŏng*] of Korean history, one that has been demonstrated by Japanese scholars. The successive regimes on the Korean peninsula have been, essentially, comprador: none of them could be said to have qualified as the leading stratum of the organic, independent national body. Instead, they preserved their position by serving as a proxy for the rule of foreign powers over Korea.[42]

Above all, the voice rejoices in the "deeply rooted slavishness" of Koreans.[43] According to the voice, this "slavishness" has manifested itself yet again in the rampant corruption of the recent presidential and National Assembly elections:

> It is pathetic beyond measure to expect that when Koreans participate in the ritual known as an election they will demonstrate a moral character they have never once given any hint of possessing. Koreans are now writhing under the heavy yoke of a freedom that they did not obtain by their own hands. They are crying out. They are calling me. The seeds sown during forty years of rule are growing by leaps and bounds—flowers of hope buried deep within the breasts of Koreans, loyal as they are in their adoration of the moral virtue of the emperor. This is their secret. The dream of an emancipated slave is to return to slavery.[44]

The Governor-General, further, informs his listeners of the following: "The nation [*minjok*] is the subject of history. The central issue is not whether it is right or wrong that the nation is the subject of history, but that, in reality, this is the case. That the world will, in the future, become one of mixed blood is not the issue; the issue is that until this happens the nation remains the subject. This is the human condition."[45]

In "Voice of the Governor-General III" (1968), the Governor-General links race and organicism to the question of coincidence/noncoincidence between language and reality, theory and practice. According to the Governor-General, both the Soviets and the Anglo-Americans demonstrate a hypocrisy in their treatment of different races (*chongjok*). The former professes an internationalism, an antiethnocentrism contradicted by the treatment it affords the races of its satellite states. The latter invokes its status as a nation of immigrants to provide evidence of racial tolerance contradicted by its treatment of African Americans (*hŭgin*).[46] The voice tells us that "This is due none other than to the fact that ... ideology is short; race is eternal."⁴⁷ Both Soviet and Anglo-American ideologies appeal to the notion of the "human" to legitimate themselves, but both are grounded in the noncoincidence of theory and practice, in a use of language that hides the reality of political authority:

> In the case of the [Japanese] Empire, however, the real and ideal are incarnated in the emperor. In other words, the fact that the emperor is of divine descent means that the real coincides with the ideal. Authority is not human, but divine.... The Empire stands alone in the world today, the sole entity preserving this religious principle by means of its national body [*kukch'e*; J.: *kokutai*].⁴⁸

Language is embodied in the nation via the emperor; it is bounded, made real, by the contours of this divine, eternal body. For the voice, race is eternal precisely because it stands in opposition to ideology. As the site of the coincidence between race (reality) and language (ideality), the national body is the nonideological site of immediacy—language made "true."

To accept the Governor-General's assertion that the nation is the subject of history may not have been difficult for many in mid-1960s South Korea. If the Governor-General's word is authoritative, however, one must also acknowledge the *kukch'e* as religious principle and revere the emperor as incarnation of the real and ideal. The notion of the *kukch'e* was a familiar one to Koreans who lived through the wartime mobilization of the late 1930s and early 1940s. Associated with the emperor system, it was a concept not to be discussed in South Korea. The Governor-General invokes both *kukch'e* and *minjok*. A listener of this broadcast cannot accept one as truth without accepting the other. Ch'oe's text reveals the ways in which the post-1945 truth claim of the *minjok* is haunted by that which is no longer to be named, the *kukch'e*.

The other haunting of this pirate broadcast (*yuryŏng pangsong*; literally, "ghost broadcast") takes place by way of its medium. In his discussion of the modern shift in memory systems from book to new media (gramophone, telephone, and radio), Friedrich Kittler writes that "psychoanalytic texts are haunted by the absolute faithfulness of phonography. Thus Freud's method of detecting unconscious signifiers in oral discourse and then interpreting these signifiers as letters of a grand rebus or syllable puzzle appears as the final attempt to establish writing under media conditions."⁴⁹

In its eliciting of the Governor-General's voice, Ch'oe's text attempts something of a "talking cure" (recall our discussion in chapter 1) insofar as it is a transcript of what it considers the colonial unconscious, the disavowed voice that inhabits the postcolonial nationalist project. The voicing of imperial desire, however, cannot be separated out from its medium. *Voice of the Governor-General* links media technology to imperialization through the textual representation of the radio broadcast.

Colonial memory is stored and reappears via a technics that drains the "humanity" of the listener, who can only mumble inarticulate groans. To be sure, Ch'oe's work unpacks the logic of the *kukch'e* and its postcolonial return, but it also reveals an anxiety regarding the technological that does not stop comfortably at the dismissal of state-controlled propaganda networks. Certainly, the voice's turn to the equation of language and body offers a hopeless opposition of organicist immediacy to its own medium (a radio frequency, the only place the Governor-General "exists").[50] At the same time, the text's giving the disembodied broadcast material form via the act of transcribing anxiously seeks to recover the human and shore up an agency for literature itself as emancipatory medium.

The Colonial/Postcolonial Double:
Two Days in the Life of Kubo the Novelist

In the early 1970s, South Korea was in the midst of its Vietnam deployment. This period saw the rise of the statist modernization narrative, the increasing authoritarianism of the Park Chung Hee regime, and the emergence of working-class protest. The colonial period was also receding into the past. A younger generation of South Koreans, those under the age of forty, either had not experienced Japanese colonial rule at all or had only a childhood memory of its final decade. This was also a generation that had come of age in the era of division and had no experience of life north of the DMZ. Ch'oe's work in the early 1970s increasingly turns to an unpacking of the relations among pre-1945 coloniality, the statist enforcing of division, and the deployment of Cold War developmentalism. We encounter this concern in the form of a familiar title, *A Day in the Life of Kubo the Novelist* (serialized from 1970–1972), Ch'oe's rewriting of the well-known 1934 modernist novella discussed in chapter 1. As we will see, the reappearance itself of Kubo—Pak T'ae-wŏn's modernist flaneur who roams the streets of the mid-1930s colonial capital—in contemporary Seoul questions developmental assumptions of progress and the colonial/postcolonial break.

Because Pak T'ae-wŏn was a *wŏlbuk chakka* ("writer who went to the North"), his 1934 text was banned in the South when Ch'oe wrote his *Kubo*. Like many other *wŏlbuk chakka*, Pak T'ae-wŏn, whose penname was Kubo, was purged in the 1950s. Unlike others, however, Pak reemerged on the North Korean literary scene in the early 1960s and was a prominent writer in Pyongyang in the early 1970s. Ch'oe's *Kubo* simultaneously names another place and time, the mid-1930s colonial capital of Pak T'ae-wŏn's *Kubo*, and the unnamable place and time of Pak himself in Pyongyang. In this way, the text contests the visual regime of the developmental state, its censoring/ordering of the colonial past and its contemporary effacement of the North. The irruption of the proper name Kubo in Ch'oe's text reinscribes a certain kind of colonial memory into the Seoul cityscape, privileged by Park Chung Hee as sign of South Korea's prosperous, modern future. At the same time, it invokes the censored North Korean other. The appearance of Kubo in Seoul represents both a return of the colonial and a surreptitious border crossing of North into South.

As we saw in chapter 1, Pak T'ae-wŏn's mid-1930s *Kubo* is a modernist, self-reflexive text highly aware of form and its own use of language, one that appropriates the Joycean stream of consciousness and Pudovkin's cinematic technique of montage to construct a psychological subject. Writer and modernologist, Kubo wanders through the markers of urban, colonial modernity: streetcars, tea rooms, the Hwashin department store, Seoul Station. Throughout the day, Kubo encounters a depoliticized white-collar Korean middle class that has become oblivious of the coloniality of the urban space and assimilated into a colonial capitalist order that allows them some access to the economic sphere while subordinating them to the emperor.

Consider also the ways in which Pak's *Stream Scenes* (*Chŏnbyŏn p'unggyŏng*, 1936) follows "Kubo" in its interruption of the colonial panorama we discussed in chapter 1. Here, Pak offers a portrayal of everyday neighborhood life in the Korean section of Kyŏngsŏng. The text takes the form of a montage of small-time capitalist exchanges that accompany a lifting of the past (in the form of villagelike relations closely associated with women doing the wash in the Ch'ŏnggye Stream) onto contemporary life in the city. This modernologist text presents us with voices of the washerwomen that are made visible. The disjunctiveness of their location in the modernizing cityscape shows how *Stream Scenes* puts into play a constellation of disjunctive temporalities, a montage of rural and urban. The text narrates the intersection of *hyangt'o* images and the modern or, more precisely, displays *hyangt'o* as a modernism. In this way, *Stream Scenes* rehearses the circulation and display of *hyangt'o* art in colonial and metropolitan exhibition spaces.

As noted in chapter 1, it is entirely possible to think of *Stream Scenes* either as a series of paintings set in verbal motion or as a sequence of stills making up a film. Here, we see how the verbal invoking of the visual is marked by a movement of signifiers capable of setting images themselves in motion, a filmlike montage. *Stream Scenes* is a text-film, moreover, that demonstrates the effects of urban planning, the reworking of the city, and colonial capitalism at the same time as it etches these effects in a visual history. The colonized modernologist third-person narration does not find refuge in a rural communality existing within the decadent city. Instead, the text disrupts the panorama of colonial evolutionary change by its imaging of retrogression (not development) brought on by capitalist exchange and the attempt to make a showcase colonial city. The verbal film (the verbal invoking of a sequence of stills that make up a picture in motion) occurs in slow motion, moving visually, word by image-invoking word. *Hyangt'o*, like a talkie, is given both voice and movement. Following Benjamin's discussion of film and montage, Pak's text calls attention to the material history of the city and the imposition of a "harmonizing panorama," even as we encounter different forms setting everyday life in motion in the city, the co-figuring of *hyangt'o* and the modern.[51]

Ch'oe In-hun's etching of one Kubo (in the 1970s text, a writer and *sirhyangmin*, or refugee from the North) over another reveals the historical, temporal, and visual form of the colonial/postcolonial relation. By naming a text that cannot be cited or read but appears as a title, Ch'oe's work shows how memory of the colonial period is ordered. In its writing over this earlier 1930s writing of the city, Ch'oe's *Kubo* conjures up the unspeakable ruins of the censored colonial literary scene. The return of Kubo in the early 1970s is also the return of Pak T'ae-wŏn as an author and his modernist unpacking of the visuality and temporality of the colonial cityscape in works such as *Stream Scenes*. At the same time, Ch'oe's *Kubo* seeks to make visible the colonial history of Seoul itself. This is a material history manifest in the colonial-period buildings extant in early 1970s Seoul and in the colonial-period emplacement of the grid that "modernized" the city. The return of Kubo to Seoul, then, is a return both to the material history of colonialism that is experienced and looked at daily in early 1970s Seoul but not seen and to Pak T'ae-wŏn's effaced colonial-period attempt to portray this cityscape. We encounter Seoul as Keijō.

Ch'oe's *Kubo* thus presents us with a different inflection of the Benjaminian dialectical image. The double, the simultaneous naming of two flaneurs as one protagonist, sets in motion a disjunctive but shared temporality. The relation between Pak's and Ch'oe's two Kubos becomes its own form of montage. As Benjamin writes, "It is not that the past throws its light on the present, or the present its light on the past, but [the dialectical] image is that wherein the past comes together with the present in a constellation."⁵² The colonial past returns to the present of 1970s Seoul in the form of the flaneuring (post)colonial Kubo, who gazes upon the building formerly housing the Government-General, the building that has become the Capitol of the Republic of Korea. This "return" occurs as the unreconciled image of a contemporary *Kubo* written over but noncoincident with its colonial predecessor: what can be shown as not to be seen or, in the case of a censored literary text, what can be alluded to as not to be acknowledged.

Kubo's flaneuring through contemporary Seoul is an illicit reading of Pak's unseen text, one that makes it visible. As *Kubo* conjures up the excised history and literary production of Pak T'ae-wŏn, a prominent writer in contemporary Pyongyang, it reveals North Korea's association with a past, and a death, that can only be accessed visually via memory. *Kubo* points to the trauma that structures division culture, the production of the North not only as past but as loss, withdrawn from the temporal and linguistic register (neither seen nor heard). The appearance of Kubo in Seoul is thus the manifestation of a writer who is there and not there at the same time, like "North Korea." Through verbal representation, *Kubo* places this history of excision on display.

Kubo writes the Seoul of the early 1970s as the site of a rearticulated colonial modernity. With Japan displaced, the United States reenacts colonialism in Asia in a new form. Kubo offers the following as he observes a movie theater in Seoul: "The areas outside theaters always seem like a foreign country. Billboards advertising Western Movies. Giant pictures of Western actors and actresses. And below them, yellow people [*hwangsaegin*], scurrying about trying to buy tickets. Just as it was in the concessions, a scene out of old-time Shanghai or Hong Kong."⁵³

Kubo proceeds to enter the theater and watch the film—the 1970 U.S. western *Soldier Blue*, starring Candice Bergen, Peter Strauss, and Donald

Pleasance. The film offers a graphic representation of the 1864 Sand Creek Massacre in Colorado, in which an entire Cheyenne village was destroyed by the U.S. Army. Ch'oe's text does something more than to consider, as Kubo does, how the film is recuperated by a white U.S. spectatorship seeking to shore up its moral legitimacy by engaging in a critique of what is no longer threatening, what can now be figured as the wrongs of the past. Later, Kubo thinks of this scene outside the theater and considers that it is here, at this moment, that Koreans become "natives" (*wŏnjumin*). The text unpacks the visual regime of the film, the process in which moviegoers in Seoul identify with the white U.S. imaginary and its ethical dilemma even as they are produced as "yellow people." Here, as Diana Fuss points out in her discussion of Fanon, it "becomes necessary for the colonizer to subject the colonial other to a double command: be like me, don't be like me; be mimetically identical, be totally other."[54] For Ch'oe, this is also the logic of developmentalism, with its attendant racial and civilizational hierarchies. The scene at and in the movie theater portrays a double command of the United States in Cold War East Asia: be white, be yellow. The visual regime revealed at the movie theater extends to the experience of the developmentalist cityscape Kubo encounters throughout the text. The material effects of development, the growth of the city, summons subjects who are offered the *promise* of gazing at themselves as normative, universal.

Art and the Universal/Particular

The relation between art and the imagination as transformative occupies a central place in Ch'oe's works, which have always been closely associated with the genre of *kwannyŏm sosŏl*, or the "novel of ideas." Art as an imaging enables a critique of "ideology." For Ch'oe, "ideology" also involves an imaging, one that spatializes, puts into play opposing territorial sovereignties. The novel of ideas provides a counterspace for an imaging of other forms and loci of association (a "square," for example). At the same time, as in the story of the Ego and its accompanying visual-translation regime, Ch'oe's unpacking of the postcolonial modern takes into account the universal/particular relation and the East/West binary, both of which, as we saw in chapter 1, were central to colonial-period articulations of the subject.

Consider, for example, the dual structure of East and West that informs Chang U-sŏng's 1943 painting "Atelier," in which a modern, Western-clothed

FIGURE 5.1 Chang U-sŏng, *Atelier* (1943).
Source: Copyright Woljeon Museum of Art Icheon.

male artist paints a woman in what is now considered "traditional" dress, in a manner that rehearses the hypericonic framing of *Chunhyang* in *Springtime on the Peninsula*. In this painting about painting, the woman gazes beyond the frame of the metapicture at a magazine she holds in her hands, casting a "look back." Here, this look points to the production of an image and its subsequent circulation in print capitalism. This look back, which is also a look away, combines with that of the painter, who looks away, outside the frame. "Atelier" shows how the relation itself between Western painting (*yanghwa*) and the representation of tradition as oriental (*tongyang*), one that informs the history of twentieth-century Korean cultural production, takes place on the level of metapicture. The new notions of the orient and oriental painting (*tongyanghwa*) always refer to the West and Western painting (*yanghwa*). The colonized observer of this painting is asked to identify at once with the technics of modern, Western-style painting (*yanghwa*) and Chosŏnness, embodied in the woman. But if the painter and the woman to be painted look back/away, outside the metapicture, is it possible that this painting rejects localization, the fixing in place of authenticity within the expanding empire? We see how *hwangminhwa* cultural production is marked by an instability.

Kubo returns to this relation and to a questioning of the local/particular when he considers the unity of East and West while gazing upon a pagoda following his viewing of a Chagall exhibition. The pagoda signals the peace and joy that comes from abandoning desire. Chagall's art points to the peace and joy that occurs in a dream: "These two paths are not as separate and different as they appear at first glance. Kubo thought of the god Janus with his two faces. All people, both Westerners and Asians, share the blood of Janus."[55] Art, the creative, transformative act, leads not to a particularism associated with a national body but a shared, universal bodily communality. Kubo continues:

> This mythological character with two faces is, precisely, the proper form of humans. It is not that Janus is a monstrous deformity; it is the people of today whose bodies are partially paralyzed, who have paralysis of the face.... When humans become Janus again, when everyone is transformed into this mythological figure, the human heart will discover true joy and peace. How can we bring this about? ... Through the reunification of North and South. Kubo had no idea how this last idea had popped into his mind.[56]

This Janus is not hybrid in the sense of a grafting of two separate strands but exists as a primordial, authentic oneness with the appearance of two forms. This mythological subject both privileges the imagination and is the effect of an inversion. It is the effect of East and West coming together, yet it precedes this opposition. It is in this way that the text negotiates the relation between the universal and the particular. The particular is a falling away from the universal as dream, the imaginative faculty of the artist.

This negotiation of universal and particular rejects an East/West opposition that informs both the statist and antistatist ethnonationalisms of the 1950s, 1960s, and early 1970s. "Home" lies not in the ethnonationalized space but in the universality of artistic imagination. Here, as elsewhere in Ch'oe's work, the questioning of post-1945 particularism signals an unspoken return to the attempts in the late 1930s and 1940s to rethink modernity. Lewis Harrington points out that for the philosopher Miki Kiyoshi in the 1930s, the new East Asian culture "is seen not as the mere retention of certain traditions from the past but rather as the creation of a completely new culture that cannot be exclusively Western or Eastern."[57] Why does North/South reunification suddenly pop into Kubo's brain? It is this embodied imagination, the transformative agency of the artist, that Ch'oe casts as a neutral, nonideological site for the overcoming of division (and the modern). Like Miki, Ch'oe rejects both the move to a prelapsarian agrarian communality as unificatory site, a move made by writers in the 1950s and 1960s such as Hwang Sun-wŏn and Yi Ho-ch'ŏl. He also dismisses the emerging emphasis on the *minjung* by writers such as Hwang Sŏg-yŏng in the early 1970s.[58]

Neither does "home" lie in the constitution of an interiorized subject, the Kubo of Pak T'ae-wŏn's 1930s text, nor in the "Ego" of *The Square*. In Ch'oe's text, the imaginative, transformative agency of the artist eventually turns to Buddhism to dismantle the givenness of the "I." The text concludes with Kubo reading his own text, the story he has written of an "I" who dreams of visiting a rural temple site and imagining nonexistent temple buildings. The space is at once utopian, nowhere, nonessentialist, and countermodern, non-national, and atemporal, and, above all, now beyond the universal/particular relation. Class distinctions disappear in this scene of writing: "People come here and realize they are siblings. Kings and beggars acknowledge each other for the first time ... Mountains, streams, grass, trees, birds, animals—all see that they are of the same blood." And later, "People ask what a true self [*chagi*] is and then realize that there is no self. The profundity of this realization is stronger, bigger than the vastness of the world."[59] The text locates a phantasmatic site that rejects the material effects of development (the streets and buildings of the city) and dismisses *chagi*, the term Ch'oe would use to translate "Ego" in his revision of *The Square*.

The text turns to the artistic imagination as enabling an alternative to modernity, a move that counters the emerging leftist nationalism in the South and its accompanying investment of ethnonationalist masculinity in working-class bodies, as well as the coloniality of the West in the form of Myŏng-jun's Ego. Such a move is not without precedent. Takeshi Kimoto shows how the philosopher Kōyama Iwao argues in his *Philosophy of World History* (1942) that an

> absolute nothingness as ultimate universal transcends the world of objective totality.... Absolute nothingness as mediating force thus makes possible the interpenetration of opposites, allowing them to assume their proper place. Kōyama calls this logic "organizational universality" and describes it in terms of the Kegon Buddhist notion of "one-and-yet-all, all-and-yet-one" [*issoku issai, issai soku ichi*].[60]

Needless to say, Ch'oe does not associate a "lack of self" with Japan as universalist site of mediation (the position conferred upon it by Miki Kiyoshi and others).[61] At stake in Ch'oe's works is the attempt to recover a questioning of the modern that allowed for the imagining of some kind of alternative to the Euro-American-centric order, even if it was appropriated by the wartime Japanese state. The questioning begun in the late 1930s and early 1940s was shut down by post-1945 U.S.-led Cold War developmentalism and the South Korean authoritarian regimes located within it. As we saw above, the mid-1960s radio broadcasts of the voice of the Governor-General who remains in Korea represents the overlapping of these pre- and post-1945 statisms.

KOREANS BECAME JAPANESE

As discussed in chapter 3, postcolonial South Korea is marked by an ethnonationalism that removes *nai* from *naisen ittai* or, more precisely, collapses *nai* into *sen*. This excision works on the linguistic register, the post-1945 repression of Japanese, as well as by way of the construction of a post-1945 "Japan" or *Ilbon* that is no longer *nai* or inside. It also involves, as we noted earlier, the reworking in the 1950s by thinkers such as Yi Ŭn-sang of the pan-Asian Greater East Asia Co-Prosperity Sphere in the form of a new kind of *sŏyang/tongyang* (orient/occident) binary. Japan is no longer visible. As we have seen, the invocation of *tongyang*, central to 1950s postcolonial traditionalism, is accompanied by an elision, the continuous slippage between *tongyang* and Han'guk, "oriental spirit" and "Korean spirit."[62]

Ch'oe In-hun's *The Tempest* returns to the late colonial period in an effort to work through the postcolonial statist reiteration of wartime mobilization. An early postcolonial reading of Shakespeare's play, *The Tempest* is the only full-length South Korean novel to place on display the late-colonial-period policy of imperialization and the mobilization of Koreans to fight as soldiers in the Japanese Imperial Army in Southeast Asia. The text traces the history of identifications of its protagonist Otomenakŭ (proper names in the text occur as anagrams: Otomenakŭ read backward is Kanemoto, Kane being one Japanese pronunciation of the sino-Korean character for the surname Kim). Otomenakŭ, a young Korean (Aerokŭ) officer in the Japanese army in Aisenodin (Indonesia), majored in Japanese (Na'payu) classical literature, identifies with Japan, and reveres the emperor.[63] As graduate of the Japanese Military Academy (a personal history that coincides with that of Park Chung Hee) and militarist Japanese imperial subject, Otomenakŭ secures for himself a masculinist position within wartime pan-Asianism. This Naoki Sakai critiques as a monistic, universalist centering of Japan that opposes the West even as it mimes the forms of its modernity.[64]

The Tempest begins with Otomenakŭ's recollection of a Nazi film he saw in colonial Korea. He recalls his pleasure in identifying with the Nazis: their precision and regularity; their citizenlike, modern, voluntarist spirit of service; the "sacred light" that shines from their faces. The narrator tells us that Otomenakŭ feels their bodily movements become his as he steps into the hallway of the former British Government-General. While Otomenakŭ admires the Nazis, he anchors his identity as Japanese. We encounter a visual summoning and an act of spectatorship that resembles the call to mobilization examined earlier in the late colonial film *The Volunteer*.

As we noted in chapter 1, however, *hwangminhwa* did not entail the jettisoning of Koreanness/the local. The local was constitutive of the mobilized, militarized subject in the multiethnic Japanese empire. Unlike the representation of Otomenakŭ in *The Tempest*, the colonized subject residing on the peninsula was never really to "become Japanese" but to become local/imperial. The trajectory of Otomenakŭ in *The Tempest*, then, intersects with the post-1945 forgetting of the importance of the local in favor of a denunciation of the imperial and its association with the "Japanese spirit," the Japanese language, Japanese culture, and the emperor.

Otomenakŭ's becoming Japanese, in fact, occurs as part of the post-1945 discourse of collaboration. *The Tempest* provides the archetypal image of the collaborator precisely to move beyond it. It is only by dispensing with the nationalist/collaborator binary that the text can reopen the late 1930s and early 1940s questioning of the modern shut down by pre-1945 Japanese militarism and the post-1945 incorporation of the Koreas into the Cold War order.

Koreans Were Never Japanese

Collaboration narratives appeared only briefly during the 1945–1948 occupation period, which, as we saw in chapter 2, was a key historical moment in the formation of the postcolonial subject and the framing of what would become the South and North Korean literary and cultural fields. The issue of collaboration was much less discussed following the Korean War, as many of those who had participated actively in the late-colonial-period mobilization efforts were now able to rehabilitate themselves in the name of a strident anticommunism. It was not until the mid-1960s controversy surrounding ROK-Japan normalization that the founding denunciatory text, one that shook up the literary scene, appeared in the form of Im Chong-guk's sensational 1966 *On Pro-Japanese Literature* (*Ch'inil munhangnon*). Im's work consists of a list of collaborators and the excerpts of the pro-Japanese writings of prominent South Korean writers. *Voice of the Governor-General*—which borrows phrases but not names from writings included in Im Chong-guk's collection— counters this denunciatory gesture by rejecting the ethnonationalist, moral condemnation of individual collaboration. Instead, as we saw above, the text moves to uncover the discursive relations between "nation" and "empire."

The Tempest, like *Voice of the Governor-General*, intervenes in the South Korean discourse on collaboration, one we encounter in works by a number of prominent writers. Consider, for example, Ch'ae Man-sik's "The National Sinner" ("Minjok ŭi choein," 1948), Kim Tong-in's "The Traitor" ("Panyŏkcha," 1946), and Yi T'ae-jun's "Liberation: Before and After" ("Haebangjŏnhu," 1946). These texts, by writers associated variously with the right and the left, transform the hybridity of the late colonial local/imperial subject into a site of contestation between the ethnonational and the collaborationist. The task becomes to figure pre-1945 imperialization (*hwangminhwa*) as collaboration.[65]

The immediate post-1945 and mid-1960s discourses on collaboration naturalize the national narrative by isolating specific instances of collaboration as deviating from the preexisting ethnonational subject of history. The figure of the collaborator, however, is produced by way of an inversion. It is the accusation of collaboration that effects the formation of a bounded-off, normative regime of national identity. To confess or to denounce, then, is less to perform oneself or others as collaborationist than to produce the ethnonation that the collaborative act presupposes.

Let us briefly consider the relation among confession, identification, and recantation in late-colonial-period literature. As noted in chapter 2, late 1930s and early 1940s recantations rely on the confessional to negotiate truth. Kim Nam-ch'ŏn's "Management" ("Kyŏngyŏng," 1940) and "Barley" ("Maek," 1941) follow the trajectory of the protagonist O Si-hyŏng, who must, in the end, recant his proletarian affiliation in court. In O's testimony, the texts of Watsuji Tetsurō emerge as the privileged citation enabling a newly discovered pan-Asian identification. O's confession parallels that of his fiancée's mother, a Christian, who must, in the end, tell her daughter of a new-found lover. The text draws a contrast between the legal demands of the court and the moral injunction of the Christian narrative.[66] That the legal and moral registers fail to coincide—the Christian confession occurs away from the gaze of the colonial state—calls the authenticity of the former into question. At the same time, the act of "true" confession remains privileged. O Si-hyŏng's confession in court is discredited precisely because he is a speaking subject transformed into object by the gaze of the legal apparatus. In this way, Kim Nam-ch'ŏn's works dialogize the texts of Watsuji Tetsurō, even as O declares their universal truth.

How to locate August 15, the date marking the formal end of Japanese colonial rule, as history? I asked this question in chapter 2 but would like to return to it in a different way here. An early answer appears in what was by all accounts an immensely popular film, Ch'oe In-gyu's 1946 *Hurrah for Freedom!* (*Chayu manse*). That Ch'oe's work, often considered the inaugural film of what would become South Korean cinema, takes place on August 1945, the eve of liberation, speaks to the need to construct a pre–August 15 trajectory of opposition to Japanese rule within colonial Korea's borders, one that shores up nationalist (and, now, South Korean legitimacy). The underground resistance led by the protagonist Han-jung is made in the name of freedom (*chayu*) and the ethnonation (*minjok*), not in the name of class liberation (proletarian revolution). Han-jung is at once a central figure in the resistance and the romantic lead in a love triangle. Both of his helpmates, Mi-hyang and Hye-ja, are in love with him. Han-jung places patriotism and romantic love on the same register when, finding himself in Mi-hyang's apartment after rescuing his colleague and killing a Japanese policeman, he informs her that "Korea is my lover." This equation of the national and the romantic occurs after he has asked Mi-hyang, "Who are you?" and she has responded "Who do you think I am? I'm Korean [*Han'guk saram*]."[67] The location of national longing on the level of romantic love serves not only to naturalize the former as intimate and modern but, of course, to elide the possibility of "internal" or "domestic" difference. Gen-

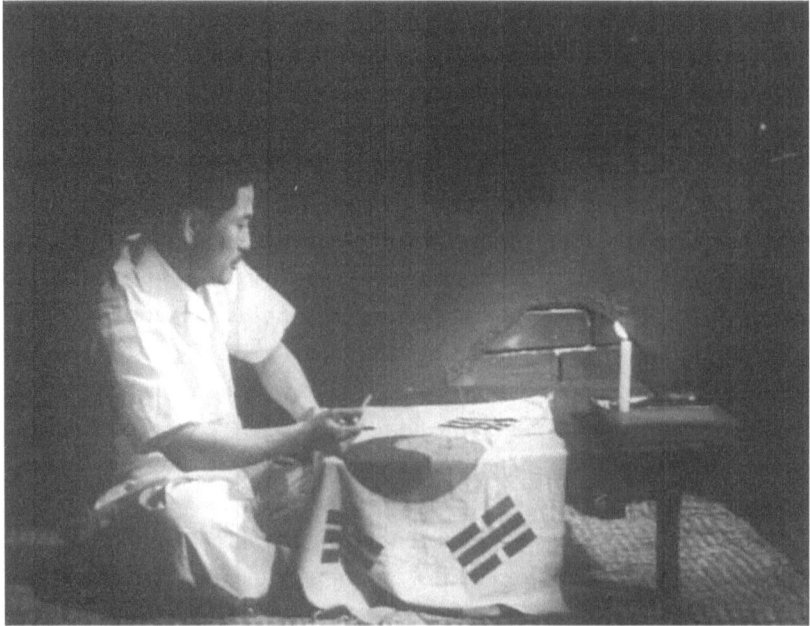

FIGURE 5.2 Empire to nation: transforming the Japanese flag into the Korean flag (*Hurrah for Freedom!*, 1946).

der and class stratifications are covered over in the name of national affect. The altogether self-evident "naturalness" of Mi-hyang's reply obscures its performativity even as it announces the mutability of identity.

Mi-hyang's response is transformative, signaling her disassociation with the imperial and her former lover, Nambu, who works closely with the Japanese. Mi-hyang's move points both to the equation of romance and love of nation (the move away from Nambu is at once a move away from association with Japan) and to the central concern of the film, the new postcolonial discourse of collaboration.[68] Here, we should recall that Korean-Japanese marriage in late-colonial-period texts by writers such as Chŏng In-t'aek enabled the formation of a modern, pan-Asian identity opposing itself to what was considered the backwardness and feudal norms of the older generation. The delinking of Mi-hyang from Nambu (who is racialized in the film text as Japanese) enables a code switching from the pre-1945 local/pan-Asian subject to the ethnonational resistance/collaboration opposition that would structure the writing of colonial-period history in South Korea. At the same time, it is the Christian register in the film, a close-up of the cross, the Christian hospital, that allows not only for a sense of martyrdom to the national cause (the deaths of resistance fighters, including Mi-hyang) but also for a figuring of transgression in the form of collaboration (Mi-hyang's affiliation with Nambu) as sin and recantation as redemptive. Code switching is made explicit in the film when Mi-hyang emphasizes the possibility of redemption: "Doesn't a person have the right to be reborn?"

The film concerns itself with the issue of assimilation and its visual markings. Han-jung tells Mi-hyang that if she is Korean she must help him. Is she truly Korean? For his part, Nambu has become Nabe, Japanese. The extended close-up of his face asks for marks of Japaneseness. Immediate post-1945 code switching entails the elision of the Korean local that made up the imperial subject. It is only at this post-1945 historical juncture that the imperial subject of the late colonial period represents a having "become Japanese," not before. The searching, enlargening look of the close-up in *Hurrah!* signals this moment visually in the form of the suspicion of assimilation. This suspicion will quickly transform itself in South Korea into a decades-long search for another unmarked identity, the communist.

Consider also Kim Tong-in's "The Traitor," a biography of the life of Yi-bae, the thinly disguised story of Yi Kwang-su, who remains to this day the archetypal figure of collaboration in South Korea. The text ends with a moving scene: the image of Yi-bae breaking down in tears in front of the radio at noon on August 15, 1945, as he listens to the emperor announce the surrender of Japan. The image of the traitor. By that point, however, we have learned that Yi-bae's true sympathies were never aligned with those of the emperor (whose own voice is described as choked with tears). Yi-bae's tears are those of the nationalist, tears of joy. Yi-bae's life was never personal nor imperial: Yi-bae "loved the Korean nation like his own body." It was never a question of collaboration but of how best to advance the cause of the Korean people. The young Yi-bae thinks of Japan and declares: "I'll slash you with your own sword. I'll take what I learn from you and make you bow down before me." Later, Yi-bae comes to believe in the inevitability of empire. Still, he works only on behalf of the nation, calling for a gradualist "improvement of culture." It is, Yi-bae considers, better to enjoy the fruits of victory that fall to Korea as a result of its "cooperation" (*hyŏmnyŏk*) with Japan than to exist as a "weak and poor independent state."[69] Class is of no concern to Yi-bae, who prefers the enlightened/unenlightened binary.

Yi-bae's crying in front of the radio on August 15, 1945, performs a national affectivity very much concerned with the moment of the text's production, the immediate post-1945 period. Kim writes against the reemergence of leftist writers and the return to a class-based literature. His task is to construct an essentialist, culturalist transcendence for the nation, one that will legitimate Yi Kwang-su's developmental project as outlining the proper historical trajectory for the postcolonial state. Certainly, we can view the collaborator as a boundary marker, simultaneously inside and outside, ethnonational by birth/blood and betrayer of the ethnonation. Here is where the figure of the collaborator meets that of the North Korean communist. The ritual denunciation of Yi Kwang-su that still occurs in South Korea, moreover, may very well involve a continuing anxiety regarding the culturalist project and the post-1945 assimilation of South Korea into the developmental global order.

Ch'ae Man-sik's "The National Sinner" ("Minjok ŭi choein," 1948) also looks back upon an inner struggle.[70] Kim Nam-ch'ŏn's O Si-hyŏng rejects the late-colonial-period call of the imperial by externalizing the injunction to identify with pan-Asia, locating the injunction outside the self in the court of law. Ch'ae's work tells the story of a narrator who has given speeches at anti-Anglo-American rallies during the war. He has collaborated. The text takes the form of a confession less to the other, asking for forgiveness, than an interiorization, a sifting through of identifications. The question becomes not whether the narrator's activities were collaborationist but whether he truly believed in the empire. The answer is given in a passage where the narrator recalls watching Japanese soldiers march by as a B-29 flew overhead during the war and remembers feeling no animosity toward the plane. Instead, it was the presence of Japanese soldiers in colonial Korea he found threatening. Ch'ae Man-sik's first-person narrator produces ethnonational affect from the turn inward.

Such a separation of the ethnonational from the imperial points to what would take the more general form of a Cold War vigilance, one that entails an internalization of watchfulness while maintaining a concern or care with the "outside." Vigilance involves a looking that takes place both within and without subjects—an in-between look. This regime of vigilance, this in-between look, informs much of South Korean literature, particularly through the early 1990s. Collaboration narratives inaugurate this postcolonial history of vigilance.

Finally, let us consider a trajectory associated with the North, that outlined by Yi T'ae-jun, who would shortly leave the South for the North and leftist literature, in his "Liberation: Before and After." Here we encounter a movement from the premodern Confucian world of the Chosŏn dynasty, represented in the text by Master Kim, a Confucian scholar who has remained "clean" throughout the colonial period by withdrawing to the countryside following his imprisonment for participation in the March First movement in 1919. The text moves to what it calls a "fascist" scene, played out in a convocation of imperialized, Japanese-speaking and Japanese-clothed writers mobilized from different parts of the Greater East Asian Co-Prosperity Sphere. They have gathered to organize the imperial subjects literature movement (*kungmin munhak*). The text then takes us to the occupation period in the South, where the United States military government brings nothing but political repression and the beginnings of crony capitalism, allowing profiteers and Japanese collaborators to flourish.

The third-person narration tells the story of Hyŏn (a stand-in for Yi T'ae-jun), a story less of his refusal to participate in the imperial subjects literature movement, his respect for Master Kim, and his abhorrence of imperialization than of his eventual location of the people, the *inmin*, as the proper subject of a postcolonial Korea. By demonstrating Hyŏn's rejection of imperialization and showing sympathy for Master Kim, Yi's text, like "Dust," discussed in chapter 2, seeks to locate a subject at once revolutionary and ethnonational.

In *The Tempest*, Ch'oe writes against the statist developmentalism of Park Chung Hee as repetition of Yi-bae's call for assimilation as a means to extricate Korea from its "small and weak" position. Ch'oe also dismisses the linkage of the *inmin* to the nation in Yi Ta'e-jun's "Liberation: Before and After" and its later articulation in the form of an emerging leftist nationalism in South Korea in the early 1970s. Unlike *Voice of the Governor-General*, *The Tempest* offers a psychic history of the collaborator. Indeed, at one point the Japanese name of Yi Kwang-su appears in one of the many anagrams.[71] The story of Otomenakŭ in *The Tempest* returns not only to the war in Southeast Asia and colonial-period articulations of the mobilized subject but also to the postcolonial statist history that organizes a national citizenry around the Korea/Japan opposition.

The narrator of *The Tempest* tells us of Otomenakŭ's reflection on "the theory that Nap'ayu and Aerokŭ had originally been one nation [*minjok*] and that their joining together once again would serve as a model for the rest of Asia. Otomenakŭ believed this theory and planned to live his life in accordance with it."[72] *The Tempest* unpacks the structure of identification that both imperialization and ethnonationalization share. Otomenakŭ was not saying one thing (the imperial) while meaning another (the national). He truly believed in *Nissen dōso* (K.: *Ilsŏndongjo*, "Japan and Chosŏn Share a Common Ancestry"). As noted in chapter 1, although this phrase dismisses a racialized colonizer/colonized bifurcation, Japan remains positioned as pan-Asian vanguard. In *The Tempest*, this phrase signals assimilation. Otomenakŭ truly believes that he is Japanese.

Disidentification and the Biopolitics of Seeing

The Tempest follows the dismantling of Otomenakŭ's interpellation as Japan begins to lose the war. The text turns not to the recovery of a suppressed ethnonational subjectivity but to a nonaligned, transformative space in postwar Aisenodin. In the end, Otomenakŭ marries a British (Nibŭrit'a) woman—Nibŭrit'a, in the text, was the former colonizer of Aisenodin—and adopts an Indonesian child, the daughter of the man who emerges as Otemanakŭ's mentor, Karŭnosŭ (Sukarno). But all, the text tells us, perform their identities. As Karŭnosŭ points out, the fact that Otomenakŭ could become Japanese demonstrates he can become Indonesian:

> "Would you like to become Aisenodin?"
> "But I am Aerokŭ."
> "But it wasn't too long ago that you believed yourself to be Na'payu. Now you say you are Aerokŭ. You can also become Aisenodin. In fact,

you could also become Nibŭrit'a. One is physically born only once, but as a person, as a social subject [sahoejŏk chuch'e], one can be reborn any number of times."[73]

Rejecting both the emperor and his own father, Otomenakŭ relocates himself as subject by taking Karŭnosŭ's advice, thus privileging a pan-Asianism that is at once transformative and anticolonial. This is a pan-Asianism that returns to an earlier 1930s emphasis on the creative power of the subject to manufacture identity. Naoki Sakai, for example, points out that for the sociologist Takata Yasuma, "The nation is a gathering of people who actualize who they want to be by the very act of committing themselves to a common destiny. Accordingly, the nation can be understood as a figure of the human being who creates himself; it is a historical or *historial* agent that constitutes itself in its potentiality; *poiesis* is, therefore, an essential element for the nation."[74] The move away from such a creative subject, one necessary for the management of a flexible, multiethnic empire, would only occur after 1945 in Japan.[75] Japan and Korea share this historical trajectory: a move from the potentiality of the pre-1945 pan-Asian universal to the givenness of ethnonational particularism within a different universal, the U.S.-led free world. *The Tempest* seeks to recover *poiesis*.

The extrication of South Korea and Southeast Asia from the Cold War order works only by way of the magical discovery of oil on the island (10 percent of known oil reserves in the world) where Otomenakŭ, his crew, and the Nibŭrit'a prisoners of war have been shipwrecked. At the same time, even as it seeks to construct a performative pan-Asianism, the text relies, at least in part, upon Otomenakŭ's recovery of a now authentic masculinity as a prominent Indonesian leader and father of a pan-Asianized family (a reworking of late-colonial-period forms of intimacy associated with the promotion of Japanese-Korean marriages) as well as upon a climatological figuring of a harmonious, self-sustaining tropical collectivity.

The Indonesia of Karunosŭ becomes a sign of virtues: sexual liberation, autonomy, anticolonialism, and nonacquisitiveness. The contingency of Otomenakŭ's social identifications meets the essentialism of this "neutral" space in Southeast Asia. The appearance of the pastoral, like the irruption of *hyangt'o* images in Pak T'ae-wŏn's modernist texts, provides another example of the ways in which nativist discourse is less a return to the past than a questioning of the present. Here, the pastoral rejects global modernity and national division. The history of white racism is negotiated by creating a utopia that neutralizes global racial hierarchies, and a nonsocialist, noncapitalist space stands apart from the competing modernities playing themselves out on the peninsula in the form of the two Koreas (the text ignores the relation between the value of oil and a continuing industrial capitalism).

The text's representation of a nonaligned communality in Southeast Asia dismantles both Western and Japanese imperialisms. *The Tempest*, in fact, returns not only to the statist imperialization of the late 1930s and early 1940s but to the questioning of capitalist modernity by thinkers such as Miki Kiyoshi and Takata Yasuma in the late 1930s. At stake, as it was in the late 1930s, is the formation of a "cooperativism" or cosmopolitanism that will lead to an alternative modernity. As John Namjun Kim has shown, while Miki's East Asian Cooperative body aims to overcome the atomism of the West by preserving cultural difference and fostering reciprocity, "Japanese culture is occupied by a 'nothingness' that has historically mediated all cultures into which it has come into contact, and thus putatively possesses the most 'excellent' aspects of all."[76] The utopian gesture in Ch'oe's work privilege the act of mediating itself, associated not with Japan but with a transforming and transformative fantasy space, Aisenodin.[77]

This is a questioning that also contests the trajectory of South Korea's statist modernization, its assimilation into the world system. Here, we should recall the "take-off" South Korean industry experienced as a result of its 1965–1973 participation in the war carried out by the United States against Vietnam. The text, then, attempts to perform a counterhistory that dismantles the statist subject. *The Tempest* rejects both what it views as the assimilationism deployed by Japan in its war in Asia and the incorporation of South Korea, at the expense of Vietnam, into a U.S.-led developmental modernity.

The rejection both of colonialism and a reactive, ethnonationalized space does not mean a dismissal of the issue of North/South reunification, one of Ch'oe In-hun's central concerns throughout his work. We learn, at the close of the text, that Korea has achieved reunification, although we do not know what form of political entity has been put into place on the peninsula. It is the production of Aisenodin as neutral space that enables the imagining of an alternative modernity. This represents a turn neither to Shakespeare's Caliban, nor to Prospero, but to Gonzalo's vision of an egalitarian commonwealth of natural abundance, to the 1955 Bandung Conference, and, further back, to the late 1930s questioning of modernity under the Japanese imperium. Performative anagrams, moreover, dispense with the translation regime of the "Ego." Nonalignment extends to the linguistic register, reworking the "neutrality" Ch'oe sought to locate in *The Square*.

Throughout his work, Ch'oe distances himself from proletarian writing, rejected by Yi Myŏng-jun in *The Square* as formulaic, moribund: "There was neither change of color, nor smell in their language."[78] If both the North and an emerging leftist nationalism in 1970s South Korea consider vitality as what is lost to assimilationist capital, *The Tempest* seeks to dispense with the twin and mirroring developmental/proletarian vitalisms structuring division and the competing sovereign claims of rival states. It does this by rearticulating the notion of "life."[79] Biopower becomes geopower, the state of natural abundance that the text locates in Aisenodin. To be sure, this is also pastoral and a recourse to a certain nativism. But it is an attempt to split at once the isomorphism of proper name and place and the equation of "life" and "species" informing a biological modernity. Such an attempt would be one of Ch'oe's last. He would not write another full-length novel for over twenty years. The developmentalist state responds in a different way.

The South Korean state has always sought to legitimize its modernization project in the name of biopower, the ethnonation, and a corporatism that aims to elide domestic class conflict. The evolutionist developmental state calls for a functional differentiation that relies upon the logic Balibar outlines in his discussion of class racism. Balibar locates two identities emerging from the racialization of manual labor, "*body-men*, men whose body is a machine-body, that is fragmented and dominated," and "*men without bodies*," those naturalized as associated with the intellect. Balibar notes that both of these bodies call for the notion of a "superbody" to compensate for fragmentation and absence.[80] If another name for the superbody is the organicist ethnonation, it is the developmental state that privileges itself as life giving, filling the gap between the superbody and the demands of the body-men/men without bodies. In other words, ethnonational, statist developmentalism itself relies upon an organicism, replacing "labor" with the superbody of the nation pressed into life-or-death struggle with other ethnonational subjects on the global capitalist stage. Such a move is not enough, however, to counter the charge of "ideological manipulation," the condemnation of the state's neocollaboration, its status as comprador. As we have seen, this is an accusation that traverses, in different forms, South Korean cultural production from the mid-1940s to the present.

At stake are the ways in which the body, in the form both of labor and ethnonation, are lost in the commodity. In his discussion of commodity fetishism, Derrida writes that "The autonomy lent to commodities corresponds to an anthropomorphic projection. The latter *inspires* the commodities, it breathes the spirit into them, a human spirit, the spirit of a *speech* and the spirit of a *will*."[81] Derrida views Marx's notion of commodity fetishism as an attempt to separate exchange value from use value (a binary Derrida proceeds to dismantle) in order to exorcise the former, figure it as immaterial. As we saw in chapter 2, we can find, on a different register, use value in exchange value. This occurs by way of the projection of an ethnonational body into the commodity form. It is precisely this body that the Cold War developmentalist world system continues to rely upon in the national marking of commodities—for example, "Made in Korea." Here, the site of production elides the laboring body, producing a new formulation, one that continues to organize identities in the present: Nation and Commodity as One Body. It is in this way that the biopolitical takes the form of a specific kind of use value: the commodity becomes a life-giving, proper prosthetic of the ethnonation itself.

South Korean ethnodevelopmentalism is, then, a life-giving, emancipatory narrative seeking to revitalize the ethnonation, to engage in unlimited struggle with all other ethnonationalized capitalist formations, and, particularly through the late 1980s, to exterminate communism (*myŏlgong*). South Korean anticommunism—as well as assimilatory reunification (*hŭp'su t'ongil*)—relies upon this investment of the ethnonational body in the commodity form, a fetishizing not of the commodity as autonomous but of the autonomous national body projected into the commodity. The subject of production is the superbody, the combined forces of body-men and men without bodies. It is given increasing life by its global circulation. Communism (and the North Korean state) must therefore be eliminated, because it is retrograde and disruptive of the life-giving, ethnonationalized commodity form.

The phrase *myŏlgong* reveals the biopolitics (and necropolitics) of the South's sovereign claim over the North, which is included as part of the ethnonational body even as it is othered as communist. The North becomes one form of what Achille Mbembe has called a "death-world," the site of a population to be exterminated and given life at the same time.[82] The division of the peninsula and the developmental South Korean state's claim to sovereignty over it is thus marked by a racialization working on two levels, the assumption of the homogeneous ethnonation (*minjok*)—that which is to be given life—and the figuring of the communist as radical other—that which is to be put to death.

Ch'oe In-hun pays particular attention throughout his work to this disavowal of the North, from unraveling the visible/invisible relation that organizes North/South division in *Kubo* to imagining a reunification of the peninsula that questions the biopolitical order in *The Tempest*. For this reason, Otomenakŭ loses life, his sense of presence, as he begins to unlearn his imperial subjectivity: "He was a ghost; his entire past was lost time."[83] In the end, the disintegration of Otomenakŭ's disciplined, militarized body is accompanied by the attempt to dismantle a biopolitics of seeing. This is a biopolitics that produces and nurtures both a life-giving, mobilizing identification (the identification with masculinized bodies produced by viewing the Nazi film) and the hierarchical racial marking (white, yellow, brown) that Ch'oe links to developmentalist South Korea's location on freedom's frontier.

POSTSCRIPT

THE CULTURAL HISTORY I offer in this book locates literary texts as part and parcel of a visual modernity. While I follow representations of an array of concerns—including the proletarian body, the colonial city, commodity circulation, technology, militarism, national division, developmentalism, race—across media such as literature, art, and film, my focus has been less on thematics as they appear in these different media than on the literary-visual relation itself. The visual inhabits the literary in multilayered ways. As we have seen, literary texts often explicitly incorporate filmic techniques. We also do not have to look far to find references to painting and photography. However, intermediation is always already part of the textuality of a so-called literary work. Intermediation does not first posit separated-out literary and visual cultural forms that are then placed in some kind of relation. The act of reading is itself a visual practice. Interpellation is at once verbal and visual—a summoning that asks for a verbal and visual response. These incorporations and allusions do more than allow us to think about the relations among literature, painting, photography, and film. They are explicit moments in literary texts that open up the ways in which, more generally, words refer to images. Literary works are themselves instances of visual culture; they are verbal-visual texts.

Colonial and postcolonial regimes of surveillance and censorship project different kinds of effacements and silencings. They also occur as gazes at what is to be seen or not seen, written or not written, spoken or not spoken. The colonial or postcolonial verbal-visual text does not simply register the effects of such a power structure. Nor does it represent a repression, a desire to say or show something that is silenced or erased. Rather, in its display of what it can and cannot say or show—in its representation of knowledge and power—the verbal-visual text produces different kinds of position takings that in and of themselves make up what we can call the "political."

I emphasize the relation between pre-1945 colonial modern culture and post-1945 Cold War verbal-visual texts. I do not define this relation in terms of continuity or rupture. If there were shifts, there was also code switching. Nor did a structure of oppression/domination continue in identical form, with one foreign power (the United States) simply taking the place of another (Japan). As we have seen, August 1945 matters, but not as a given. Cultural producers themselves began to debate its meaning almost immediately, and this debate continues into the present. The colonial became not one past but multiple pasts appropriated and remembered, selectively, for different purposes at different historical junctures. The South Korean state has its own views. Although these views have shifted over time, it is fair to say that the binary of oppression/resistance remains central to the figuring of the Japanese colonial period. This binary has rendered the late 1930s and early 1940s largely invisible, since this has been considered a period of radical assimilation and little or no resistance. Also omitted in this binary is any form of anticolonial resistance associated with the left.

Post-1945 South Korean society cannot be understood without considering the organization of colonial-period cultural history. South Korean culture was formed in relation to a selective remembering of the colonial. This remembering extends to the post-1945 reworking of colonial-period cultural movements and discursive formations. We have seen, for example, how the late colonial notion of the orient (*tongyang*) was appropriated in the 1950s even as the pan-Asianism of the late 1930s and early 1940s now became figured as collaborative act. The "colonial modern" is present in post-1945 culture in the form of colonial pasts produced by contemporary historiography and, more importantly, as part of a continuously shifting verbal-visual textuality that traverses temporal divisions. There was no fresh start or blank slate in 1945, only a reorganizing of the cultural field, a reworking of ideas and representations, ways of thinking, writing, and seeing that had emerged in the first half of the twentieth century. As we have seen, this reorganizing took place as part of a transnational Cold War circulation of words and images. It must take into account the 1945 dividing of the Korean peninsula, the 1945–1948 U.S. and Soviet military occupations, and the continuing and global effects of the Korean War. I devoted a chapter of this book to cultural production under U.S. military occupation in an effort to underscore its importance in the formation of South Korean culture.

While not seeking a historical date for the origins of the developmentalist project in South Korea, I do not think we can elide the importance of the pre-1945 colonial industrialization (carried out, of course, in the interests of the Japanese metropole and global capital), its disciplining, its mobilization.[1] South Korea is not the miraculous product (or subject) of the post-1945 era, either one conjured up in the U.S. metropole or one imagined by ethnodevelopmentalists south of the DMZ. Post-1945, South Korea's rise in the global economy has been just that, global, involving, among other things, global-scale wars (particularly the Korean War and the American war in Vietnam but also the two recent wars in Iraq), transnational financial networks, export markets, and the disciplining both of domestic labor and, increasingly, international labor (both within and outside of South Korea's borders).

We see, then, that developmentalist picturing, the serial movement of model to referent, requires another layer of mobilization, the movement of militarized bodies. Staging cannot proceed without a supplemental enforcing linked to a state of continuous war. The current exemplarity of South Korea is an unspoken acknowledgement of the so-called "forgotten war" (the Korean War), largely forgotten in the U.S. on two levels: its hot phase, 1950 to 1953, and its second, mostly cold but occasionally hot phase, which extends into the present, as no peace treaty has ever been signed. This war was from the first ambiguous, inside and outside the law, never declared, not even a war but a "police action." It turns out that the privileged example of global development resides in a continuing state of war that was never a war, a form of the state of exception, what Agamben calls "a zone of indistinction between outside and inside, exception and rule, licit and illicit."[2]

A second layer of forgetting involves a history of deployments and contestations, colonial and postcolonial, made in the name of and against a series of statist mobilizations (carried out under colonial rule, military occupation, a succession of developmentalist regimes). I have traced this cultural history, focusing on the first three decades of the Cold War. Much of this history turns upon the attempt to picture the world otherwise, one that involves an engagement with the relation itself between the verbal and visual as well as with the ways in which the Cold War state orders its subjects via an arrangement of the visible and the invisible. I worked to unpack the visual order enabling the production of the colonial past and the contemporary enforcement of the division system. I showed how the rendering of the North as simultaneously invisible and highly visible as the target-to-be-effaced becomes the lynchpin for the production not only of anticommunist South Korea but for the imagining of a "free Asia." I also noted how the erasure of the left and proletarian culture, one that has taken different forms since the appearance of the proletarian culture movement in the mid-1920s, becomes a constitutive outside in post-1945 South Korea.

I do not offer a teleology leading to the reemergence of the proletarian subject in the form of its *minjung* articulation in the 1970s and especially the 1980s. I do, however, hope that the history of representations I have examined in this book helps to contextualize the cultural production that would follow. In lieu of a conclusion, therefore, I end with one of many images from this period, the prominent artist Lim Ok-sang's "A Questionable Death" ("Ŭimunsa," 1987).

FIGURE P.1 Lim Ok Sang, *A Questionable Death* (1987).
Source: Copyright Lim Ok Sang.

Especially when placed in the context of Lim's other works, "A Questionable Death" can certainly can be seen as enacting a *minjung* hypernationalist masculinism, the embodiment of a primordialist, transhistorical subject, one that reiterates a history of global essentialisms that, articulated in different sets of power relations, have tied people to place, blood to soil, race to class. Here, the male body casts off its clothes and moves spontaneously, of its own accord (presumably toward the North and across division), leaving the brain (the skull) and writing (the book in the lower right hand corner of the painting) behind. The painting offers a visual narrative of reunification that asks not to be spoken but to be understood bodily, spontaneously. The subject is severed, head cut off—a questionable death that we are free to interpret in any way we choose as we negotiate the relation between written title and image. Certainly the questionable death can refer to the refusal of the severed *minjung* subject to die, its movement across an artificial, invisible political border first proposed by the United States, making the national spirit flesh in an undying body. Regardless of any specific intention Lim may have had, the title can also refer generally to a history of student activist deaths, massacres, casualties in war, and other questionable deaths that have been "put aside." I would, though, like to call attention to the ways in which this painting also allows us to consider the temporality of trauma, of "nonreturning," the linking of division not with the ontotheology of a *minjung* subject made incarnate but with the catachresis of the living dead.

We encounter a "nonreturning," a living-dead figure who moves away from the viewer, back turned toward us. Lim's painting thus puts into play a relation between death and life, verbal and visual. The male body looks into the site that has been there and not there at the same time, to be experienced as a visual surface bordering the DMZ, not to be entered into or touched—a constitutive outside produced under the 1945–1948 U.S. military occupation, one that has informed a Cold War way of seeing in South Korea from the mid-1940s to the present. It is the body, headless, that sees in a particular way: the body that looks at "North Korea" without seeing it. The headless body cannot see the invisible border, one that is the product of an imaging associated with the written word, the discarded text in the lower-right-hand corner, and the violence, perhaps, that "ideology" has enacted (the barbed wire covering the book and the site of death recalls the wire used to bind victims during Korean War massacres). The eyes stare from the skull at the viewer of the painting, a look back that questions the ways in which seeing produces meaning, space, the perspectival subjects that continue to naturalize the organization of this space. "A Questionable Death" refers not only to those questionable deaths of the past but to a death that is alive in the form of memories that have been laid to rest but cannot be laid to rest. It is at this point, via this acknowledgment, that memories can become a verbal-visual history that is not of the past but of the present.

NOTES

INTRODUCTION

1. Jacques Rancière, *The Politics of Aesthetics* (London: Continuum, 2006), 13, 45.
2. Friedrich Kittler, *Gramophone, Film, Typewriter*, trans. Geoffrey Winthrop-Young and Michael Wutz (Stanford, Calif.: Stanford University Press, 1999), 70, 73.
3. Rey Chow, *Primitive Passions: Visuality, Sexuality, Ethnography, and Contemporary Chinese Cinema* (New York: Columbia University Press, 1995), 5, 22–23, 180–181.
4. Yi Kwang-su, *Mujŏng* [The heartless] (1917; Seoul: Munhak tongne, 2003). See, for example, 66, 120, 239, and 605. This new, meticulously annotated edition edited by Kim Chul is a valuable resource that recovers the original serialized version of Yi's text. All translations from the Korean are the author's unless otherwise specified.
5. Chow, *Primitive Passions*, 41.
6. W. J. T. Mitchell, *Picture Theory* (Chicago: University of Chicago Press, 1994), 152.
7. Timothy Mitchell, *Questions of Modernity* (Minneapolis: University of Minnesota Press, 2000), 18.
8. Ibid., 19.
9. Kwon Boduerae, *Han'guk kŭndae sosŏl ŭi kiwŏn* [Origins of modern Korean literature] (Seoul: Somyŏng, 2000), 59–63.
10. Nancy Armstrong, *Fiction in the Age of Photography: The Legacy of British Realism* (Cambridge: Harvard University Press, 1999), pp. 8–9.
11. Ibid., 28.
12. Yi Kwang-su, *Mujŏng*, 472. For a translation of Yi's entire novel, see Ann Sung-Hi Lee, *Yi Kwang-su and Modern Korean Literature: Mujŏng* (Ithaca, N.Y.: Cornell East Asia Series, 2005). I follow Ann Lee's translation here.
13. The first Korean nude, Kim Kwan-ho's *Twilight*, was exhibited in Japan in 1916 but censored in colonial Korea. The nude was

seen by thinkers such as Yi Kwang-su, who emerged as a champion of Kim's painting, as liberatory, signaling a break from the feudal past.
14. See Lydia Liu, "The Question of Meaning-Value in the Political Economy of the Sign," in *Tokens of Exchange: The Problem of Translation in Global Circulations*, ed. Lydia Liu (Durham, N.C.: Duke University Press, 1999), 34–37.
15. See Dominick LaCapra, *Writing History, Writing Trauma*, Parallax: Re-visions of Culture and Society (Baltimore, Md.: Johns Hopkins University Press, 2000), 184.
16. Rancière, *The Politics of Aesthetics*, 45.
17. See Pierre Bourdieu, *The Field of Cultural Production* (New York: Columbia University Press, 1993).
18. Paik Nak-chung, "The Idea of Korean National Literature, Then and Now," *positions* 1, no. 3 (1993): 553–580.
19. For the latter, see Namhee Lee, *The Making of Minjung: Democracy and the Politics of Representation in South Korea* (Ithaca, N.Y.: Cornell University Press, 2009).
20. Works that have appeared over the past seven years include Kyung Hyun Kim, *The Remasculinization of Korean Cinema* (Durham, N.C.: Duke University Press, 2004); Nancy Abelmann and Kathleen McHugh, eds., *South Korean Golden Age Melodrama: Gender, Genre, and National Cinema* (Detroit, Mich.: Wayne State University Press, 2005); Suk-Young Kim, *Illusive Utopia: Theater, Film, and Everyday Performance in North Korea* (Ann Arbor: University of Michigan Press, 2010); Jin-kyung Lee, *Service Economies: Militarism, Sex Work, and Migrant Labor in South Korea* (Minneapolis: University of Minnesota Press, 2010); Kelly Y. Jeong, *Crisis of Gender and the Nation in Korean Literature and Cinema: Modernity Arrives Again* (Lanham, Md.: Lexington Books, 2011). There are also a number of scholars working on modern Korean literature and film who have entered the field in recent years. See the bibliography and notes in the following chapters for their dissertations and journal articles.
21. See Lord Halifax, "We Must Defend the Frontier of Freedom," *The Rotarian* (February 1952): 9. U.S. policymakers commonly use the term "freedom's frontier" to refer specifically to South Korea. "Freedom's frontier" remains in wide use to refer both to the DMZ and South Korea as a whole by the U.S. military. "Freedom's frontier" was also used to refer to the border between East and West Germany prior to 1989.

1. Visuality and the Colonial Modern: The Technics of Proletarian Culture, Nativism, Modernism, and Mobilization

1. See Pierre Bourdieu, *The Field of Cultural Production* (New York: Columbia University Press, 1993).
2. No KAPF films are extant; only scripts and stills are available.
3. For a discussion of the link between reenchantment and the aesthetics of Japanese fascism in the Japanese metropole in the 1930s and 1940s, see Alan Tansman, *The Aesthetics of Japanese Fascism* (Berkeley: University of California Press, 2009).

1. VISUALITY AND THE COLONIAL MODERN   213

4. For an analysis of the intertextual relation between 1920s proletarian writing in colonial Korea and prerevolutionary Russian literature, see Heekyoung Cho, "Literary Translation and Appropriation: Korean Intellectuals' Reception of Russian Prose Via Japan, 1900–1927" (Ph.D. diss., University of Chicago, 2007). Samuel Perry details the relation between Korean and Japanese proletarian writing in his "Aesthetics for Justice: Proletarian Writing in Japan and Colonial Korea" (Ph.D. diss., University of Chicago, 2007).
5. For colonial-period realism and KAPF, see Sunyoung Park, "The Colonial Origin of Korean Realism and Its Contemporary Manifestation," *positions: east asia cultures critique* 14, no.1 (Spring 2006): 165–192.
6. See Andre Schmid, *Korea Between Empires, 1895–1919* (New York: Columbia University Press, 2002).
7. See Dipesh Chakrabarty, *Provincializing Europe: Postcolonial Thought and Historical Difference* (Princeton, N.J.: Princeton University Press, 2000).
8. See Michael Robinson, *Cultural Nationalism in Colonial Korea, 1920–1925* (Seattle: University of Washington Press, 1989).
9. KAPF members would shift their positions over the next fifteen years in different ways, particularly as the imperialization policy was implemented in the late 1930s. Pak Yŏng-hŭi would declare famously in the early 1930s that what was lost in KAPF in art was gained in ideology. Kim Ki-jin was subjected to a People's Trial during the North Korean occupation of Seoul in 1950 and would go on to live out the rest of his life in South Korea, becoming president of the PEN Club in the early 1970s.
10. The marking out by the censor renders colonial power at once visible and material, appearing on the page physically to cover print. Certainly censorship calls the visual attention of the text's readership to representation. The mediation of the censor as a first reader confers a certain self-reflexivity upon colonial proletarian texts. The act of the censor calls attention not only to content but also to writing itself, the appearance and disappearance of printed words on the page—the material history of the production of the text. The proletarian literature of the 1920s and 1930s bears relation to 1930s colonial modernism in this material, historical way. Both proletarian texts and, as we will see below, modernist texts by writers such as Pak T'ae-wŏn and Yi Sang involve a self-reflexivity that makes itself manifest by way of a visual act, a seeing of writing and coloniality as material, whether in the form of print or effacement on a circulated page.
11. For this reason, proletarian literature often possesses a self-reflexivity regarding its own means of production, as we see, for example, in texts such as Kim Nam-ch'ŏn's "Factory Newspaper." We should note that the anxiety regarding the "copy" (*mobang*) present in prominent KAPF critics such as Im Hwa can be linked to the advent of mechanical reproduction. Im Hwa's turn to romanticism as a supplement to realism in the mid-1930s demonstrates as much a concern with technics as it does with the question of what he considers a naïve realism. See chapter 2.
12. For the mid-1920s colonial Korean film scene, see Yi Yŏng-il, *Han'guk yŏnghwa chŏnsa* [A comprehensive history of Korean film] (Seoul: Sodo, 2004), 75–102.

13. Yi Sŭng-hŭi notes that 1923 through 1925 was the "heyday" of leftist political cartoons. See her "1920 nyŏndae sinmun manp'yŏng ŭi sahoejuŭi chŏngch'i wa munhwajŏk hyokwa [Socialist politics of newspaper cartoons in the 1920s and their cultural effects]," in Kŭndaejisik ŭrosŏ ŭi sahoejuŭi [Socialism as modern knowledge], ed. Sanhŏhakhoe (Seoul: Kip'ŭn saem, 2008), 80; figure 1.1 appears on p. 84.
14. For Laclau, "Emancipation presupposes the elimination of power, the abolition of the subject/object distinction, and the management—without any opaqueness or mediation—of communitarian affairs by social agents identified with the viewpoint of social totality." Ernesto Laclau, Emancipation(s) (London: Verso, 1996), 1.
15. See Clark Sorensen, "National Identity and the Construction of the Category 'Peasant' in Colonial Korea," in Colonial Modernity in Korea, ed. Gi-Wook Shin and Michael Robinson (Cambridge, Mass.: Harvard University Asia Center, 1999), 288–310.
16. Kim P'al-bong, Kim P'albong munhak chŏnjip [Collected works], ed. Hong Chŏng-sŏn (Seoul: Munhak kwa chisŏngsa, 1988), 1:126. Kim P'al-bong is the penname of Kim Ki-jin.
17. Ibid., 1:128–129.
18. Ibid., 1:129.
19. Ibid., 1:130.
20. Ibid.
21. Ibid., 1:132.
22. Ibid., 1:135–136.
23. Ibid., 1:137.
24. See, for example, Edward W. Soja, Postmodern Geographies: The Reassertion of Space in Critical Social Theory (London: Verso, 1989), 32–33.
25. Im Hwa, Im Hwa munhak yesul chŏnjip [Collected works] (Seoul: Somyŏng, 2009), 4:153.
26. Ibid., 4:146.
27. Kim Ki-jin's 1929 Chŏndoyangyang [A bright future], for example, is omitted from Kim's collected works.
28. Like all other KAPF films, no copy of this film is extant.
29. Yi Chong-myŏng, Yurang [Wandering], in Chosŏn sinario sŏnjip 1 [A selection of Korean scenarios 1], ed. Kim Su-nam (Seoul: Jimmundang, 2003), 1:260.
30. Nearly all full-length novels by major writers such as Yi Kwang-su, Yŏm Sang-sŏp, and Yi Ki-yŏng were serialized in the colonial period.
31. Yi Chong-myŏng, Yurang [Wandering], 282.
32. See Ming-yan Lai's study of nativism for a discussion of the relation between nativism and nationalism as well as the ways in which nativism interrupts the national narrative and points to alternative formations other than capitalism. Ming-yan Lai, Nativism and Modernity: Cultural Contestations in China and Taiwan Under Global Capitalism (Albany, N.Y.: SUNY Press, 2008).
33. Yi Chong-myŏng, Yurang [Wandering], 298.
34. In Origins of Modern Korean Literature, Kwon Bodurae traces the shifting meanings of "art" (misul), noting how in the early 1900s misul was associated with the industrial

1. VISUALITY AND THE COLONIAL MODERN 215

arts (*kongye*) and the precolonial, state-sponsored promotion of commerce and industry (*siksanhŭngŏp*). As Kwon points out, the emergence of *misul* as visual and "fine" art in the 1910s occurs along with the formation of modern literature. Here, Kwon shows how, in addition to the move toward *onmunilch'i* (the correspondence of the spoken and written; J.: *genbunichi*), the location of affect (*chŏng*) and the appreciation of the beautiful (*mi*) within the self produce an interiority. Kwon further notes how the introduction of Western painting brought about the definition of "'*misul*' in the sense of a 'visual art,' and this contained a critique of traditional notions of painting that aimed to portray an unseen spirit. '*Misul*' meant drawing what was actually there, in other words, it was an activity that had reality [*sasil*] as its aim and thus had an ethos that resembled the notion of reality later manifested in literature." Kwon Bodurae, *Han'guk kŭndae sosŏl ŭi kiwŏn* [Origins of modern Korean literature] (Seoul: Somyŏng, 2000), 60. See also 59–63.

35. Karatani Kōjin tells us that "the very concept of the history of Japanese literature, which seems so self-evident today, took place in the midst of our discovery of landscape." For Karatani, the "inversion of a semiotic configuration" in the 1890s associated with the introduction of Western painting allows, among other things, for the perspectival separating out of subject from object. See Karatani Kōjin, *Origins of Modern Japanese Literature* (Durham, N.C.: Duke University Press, 1993), 22.

36. Ch'a Sŭng-gi details the relation between 1920s traditionalism and the contemporary notion of a "national literature" (*kungmin munhak*). As Ch'a points out, 1920s traditionalists such as Ch'oe Nam-sŏn called for a particularism that differentiated genres such as *sijo* from Chinese cultural forms in order to construct a lineage of Chosŏnness that could be recovered in the present. For Ch'a, such a move can only proceed by tacitly acknowledging Western modernity as the new universal. See Ch'a Sŭng-gi's *Pan kŭndaejŏk sangsangnyŏk ŭi imgye tŭl* [Boundaries of the antimodern imagination] (Seoul: P'urŭn yŏksa, 2009), 58, 73.

37. W. J. T. Mitchell notes that "the medium of *writing* deconstructs the possibility of a pure image or pure text, along with the opposition between the "literal" (letters) and the "figurative" (pictures) on which it depends." See W. J. T. Mitchell, *Picture Theory: Essays on Verbal and Visual Representation* (Chicago: University of Chicago Press, 1994), 95. Emphasis in original.

38. For the Japanese metropolitan essentializing of Korean art as exemplified by sorrow and melancholy, see Kim Brandt, *Kingdom of Beauty: Mingei and the Politics of Folk Art in Imperial Japan* (Durham, N.C.: Duke University Press, 2007), 32–33.

39. Sŏ Sŏng-nok, *Han'guk hyŏndae hwoehwa ŭi paljach'wi* [Traces of modern Korean painting] (Seoul: Munye ch'ulp'ansa), 125–127.

40. Rey Chow, *The Protestant Ethnic and the Spirit of Capitalism* (New York: Columbia University Press, 2002).

41. See also Kim Tong-ni's "Portrait of a Shaman" (1936), one of the texts that occupied a central place in the construction of the South Korean canon. Like "Buckwheat," Kim's work serves as an extended caption or commentary upon a *hyangt'o* painting

that is only described, although, of course, portraits of shamans in particular were a popular nativist theme.

42. Yi Hyo-sŏk, "When the Buckwheat Blooms," in *A Ready-Made Life: Early Masters of Modern Korean Fiction*, trans. Kim Chong-un and Bruce Fulton (Honolulu: University of Hawai'i Press, 1999), 138.
43. Visuality is no longer linked, as it was in Yi's earlier proletarian "Tosi wa yuryŏng" [City and Specter], to a coming to consciousness meant to separate out human from animal, the modern from superstition.
44. See Akira Lippit, *Electric Animal: Toward a Rhetoric of Wildlife* (Minneapolis: University of Minnesota Press, 2008).
45. Yi Hyo-sŏk et al., *Hwaryun* [Wheel of fire], in *Chosŏn sinario sŏnjip 2* [A selection of Korean scenarios 2], ed. Kim Su-nam (Seoul: Jimmundang, 2003), 2:292–350.
46. Mary Anne Doane, "The Close-Up: Scale and Detail in the Cinema," *differences* 14 (2005): 5.
47. Kim P'al-bong, *Kim P'albong munhak chŏnjip 1* [Collected works], 112–113.
48. For a discussion of form and Japanese metropolitan modernism, see Seiji Lippit, *Topographies of Japanese Modernism* (New York: Columbia University Press, 2002).
49. See Jonathan Crary, *Suspensions of Perception: Attention, Spectacle, and Modern Culture* (Cambridge, Mass.: The MIT Press, 2001), 60–62, 350.
50. Here, I draw on Crary's analysis of the shift from association to function.
51. See Susan Buck-Morss, *The Dialectics of Seeing: Walter Benjamin and the Arcades Project* (Cambridge, Mass.: The MIT Press, 1991), 67.
52. For an analysis of the everyday, visuality, and urban space in Pak T'ae-wŏn and, more broadly, 1930s modernism, see Janet Poole, "Colonial Interiors: Modernist Fiction of Korea" (Columbia University, Ph.D. diss., 2004).
53. These moments in *Kubo* should also be linked to the importance of punctuation in the text. For an analysis of the jerk or stop, see Crary, *Suspensions of Perception*, 314–315; see also Crary's discussion of aggregation/disaggregation on 184–185.
54. See Friedrich Kittler, *Gramophone, Film, Typewriter*, trans. Geoffrey Winthrop-Young and Michael Wutz (Stanford, Calif.: Stanford University Press, 1999), 141–142. Kittler writes (143) that "Freud attended Londe's filmings of hysteria, but did just the opposite with it. Literally, psychoanalysis means chopping up an internal film, in steps that are as methodical as they are discrete, until all of its images have disappeared. They break into pieces one by one simply because female patients have to translate their visions into depictions or descriptions."
55. The narrator tells us that "Kubo tried to find some sort of meaning from the numbers, but it came to nothing. Moreover, even if the numbers did have some sort of meaning, it certainly wouldn't be a happy one." Pak T'ae-wŏn, *Sosŏlga Kubossi ŭi iril* [A day in the life of Kubo the novelist] (Seoul: Kip'ŭn saem, 1999), 26.
56. For a discussion of language, disease, and desire in Pak T'ae-wŏn's works, see Christopher Hanscom, "A Question of Representation: Korean Modernist Fiction of the 1930s" (Ph.D. diss., UCLA, 2006).

57. See Ming-yan Lai, *Nativism and Modernity* (Albany, N.Y.: SUNY Press, 2008), 37.
58. Discussions of new sensationism (*sin gamgak*) in Korean literary histories center on poets of the early 1930s and the advent of the modernist Group of Nine. It was, however, via art that new sensationist work first appeared in Chosŏn, and this took place as early as 1923. See Sŏ Sŏng-nok, *Han'guk hyŏndae hwoehwa ŭi paljach'wi* [Traces of modern Korean painting], 189. The circulation between metropole and colony of new sensationist painting accompanies the emergence of the nude as a major genre in the mid-1920s. It was not until the 1930s and the work of Kang Kyŏng-ae, however, that new sensationism was appropriated in a proletarian text. If a critic such as Kim Yŏng-jun works to combine anarchism with expressionism to find new ways of producing a proletarian sensory experience in the late 1920s (see chapter 2), it is Kang's linking of new sensationism to proletarian writing in her well-known "Underground Village" (1936) and "Salt" (1934) that best articulates the ways in which bodily sensation goes hand in hand with the coming to awareness of the proletarian subject.
59. A number of former KAPF members played an important part in the production of mobilization films in the late colonial period. Recall that Sŏ Kwang-je co-authored *Wheel of Fire*. An Sŏg-yŏng's screenplay for *The Volunteer*, moreover, is an adaptation of Pak Yŏng-hŭi's original. These films, then, must be located within the constellation of late 1930s recantations.
60. For an analysis of the ways in which a common biopolitical regime structures the racisms informing the wartime Japanese management of colonial Koreans and the internment of Japanese Americans by the U.S. nation-state empire, see Takashi Fujitani, "Right to Kill, Right to Make Live: Koreans as Japanese and Japanese as Koreans in WWII," *Representations* (Summer 2007): 13–39.
61. Jun Uchida points out the anxiety marking the colonial project due to Japan's own late development and the ambiguous position of Japanese settlers in Korea, who were not differentiated from the colonized in the same way that white colonizers were separated out from the colonized in the Euro-American colonial sites. See Jun Uchida, "'Brokers of Empire:' Japanese Settler Colonialism in Korea, 1910–1937" (Ph.D. diss., Harvard University, 2005), 15, 164.
62. See Giorgio Agamben, *The Open: Man and Animal* (Stanford, Calif.: Stanford University Press, 2003), 37.
63. Ibid., 38.
64. For a discussion of militarism and the expendable, see Jin-kyung Lee, *Service Economies: Militarism, Sex Work, and Migrant Labor in South Korea* (Minneapolis: University of Minnesota Press, 2010), 59.
65. In his discussion of the colonial-modern figuring of Silla, Hwang Jongyon points out that calls to mobilize as imperial subjects in the late 1930s and early 1940s were often made in the name of renewing the Silla Hwarang warrior spirit. To become an imperial subject was thus to resuscitate a "forgotten Korean tradition." See Hwang Jongyon, "Silla ŭi palgyŏn," in *Silla ŭi palgyŏn*, ed. Hwang Jongyon (Seoul: Tongguk

University Press, 2008), 50. For the consumption of the colonial local as marking an ambivalent nostalgia in the Japanese metropole, see Nayoung Aimee Kwon, "Translated Encounters and Empire: Colonial Korea and the Literature of Exile" (Ph.D. diss, UCLA, 2007).
66. Laura Mulvey, *Death 24x a Second: Stillness and the Moving Image* (London: Reaktion Books, 2006), 13.
67. Crary demonstrates the shift in Foucault's model of the panopticon: "By the early twentieth century, the attentive subject is part of an *internalization* of disciplinary imperatives in which individuals are made more directly responsible for their own efficient or profitable utilization within various social arrangements." Here is where imperialization meets Taylorism—all occur as part and parcel of a broader, global, modern discourse of responsibilization that we can link to the attentive subject. In other words, the attentiveness accompanying hwangminhwa allows us to consider the relation between the disciplining of imperialization and that of a modern, industrial workforce. See Crary, *Suspensions of Perception*, 73.
68. Yi Yŏng-jae points out that in this tracking shot, the lack of a close-up creates an asymmetry between feeling associated with the face and the objects it looks upon. See *Cheguk Ilbon ŭi Chosŏn yŏnghwa* [The Korean films of imperial Japan] (Seoul: Hyŏnsil munhwa, 2008), 78–79.
69. See Mary Anne Doane, *The Emergence of Cinematic Time: Modernity, Contingency, the Archive* (Cambridge, Mass.: Harvard University Press, 2002), 29.
70. This movement outward is also temporal, a folding of the local into a pan-Asian future that opposes the authenticity of the modern as Western. As Ch'a Sŭng-gi has shown, 1920s traditionalism tends to associate Chosŏnness with the past and thus privileges the modern and the West as universal. Late 1930s traditionalism, however, now provides a site to question modernity itself and suggest the possibility of a different future, one in which the act of recovering the past can be associated with what is to come. In this way, traditionalism, by pointing to the future, becomes associated with the avant-garde. See Ch'a Sŭng-gi, *Pan kŭndaejŏk sangsangnyŏk ŭi imgye tŭl* [Boundaries of the antimodern imagination], 20, 168.
71. See Kittler, *Gramophone, Film, Typewriter*, 124. As Kittler and Paul Virilio have shown, camera and weapon share a scopic regime structured around the target. Virilio, moreover, links the history of cinema to the emergence of modern techniques of war, emphasizing what he calls the dromological, the intersection between militarization and motion. See Paul Virilio, *War and Cinema: The Logistics of Perception* (London: Verso, 2009).
72. In *Military Train*, the homosocial intimacy between Korean friends and the benevolence of the Japanese boss produce affect, which combines with the machine as prosthetic. The machine enables this affect to survive and expand. The machine puts affect into concrete, material motion. This relation between human and machine is a form of hwangminhwa. This is precisely the movement that Kim Yŏng-sŏk's "Trolley Driver" (1946) will seek to disrupt by figuring the colonized subject as

appendage of the machine, rather than machine as proper prosthetic of the people. But as Kittler points out, the "postwar" is really only an intensification of the subordination to the machine and the military technology developed in World War II. *Military Train* can also be read as one among many of the recantation narratives (the director was a former KAPF member).

73. See Mary Anne Doane, *The Emergence of Cinematic Time*, 11. It is for this reason that "the earliest films display ... the fact that chance and contingency are the highly cathected sites not only of pleasure but of anxiety." See also 39.

74. Doane, "The Close-Up," 109.

75. Ibid.

76. Yi Yŏng-jae points out the importance of the production of this film about filmmaking during the reorganization of the colonial film industry. *Springtime on the Peninsula* was the first film to meet the approval of the censors following the promulgation of the Chosŏn Film Law in 1940 and was made in the run-up to the formation of the Chosŏn Film Corporation, which would oversee all film production in the colony under Government-General auspices through the end of colonial rule in 1945. See Yi Yŏng-jae, *Cheguk Ilbon ŭi Chosŏn yŏnghwa* [The Korean films of imperial Japan], 113.

77. Baek Moon Im, "Chŏnjaeng kwa mellodŭrama [War and melodrama]," in *Chŏnjaeng iranŭn munt'ŏk* [On the threshold of war], ed. Hanguk-Taiwan Pigyo munhwa yŏn'guhoe (Seoul: Kŭrinbi, 2010), 277.

78. Baek Moon Im, "Chŏnjaeng kwa mellodŭrama [War and melodrama]," 280.

79. Kim Chul has shown how in the late 1930s "the moment one indentifies as an oriental by securing the 'west' as the other, the colony is elided as a mediating site." See Kim Chul's *"Kungmin" iranŭn noye: Han'guk munhak ŭi kiŏkkwa manggak* [The slave called "citizen": memory and amnesia in Korean literature] (Seoul: Samin, 2005), 96.

80. Alan Tansman, *The Aesthetics of Japanese Fascism*, 15.

81. Ibid., 24.

82. The simultaneous summoning of colonized and metropolitan imperials also involves a translation regime. For a discussion of late-colonial-period translation, see Serk-Bae Suh, "Treacherous Translation: The 1938 Japanese-Language Theatrical Version of the Korean Tale Ch'unhyangjŏn," *positions: east asia cultures critique* 18, no. 1 (Spring 2010): 171–197.

83. Yi Yŏng-jae, *Cheguk Ilbon ŭi Chosŏn yŏnghwa* [The Korean films of imperial Japan], 186–187.

2. Visible and Invisible States: Liberation, Occupation, Division

1. See Kim Yun-sik, *Han'guk sosŏlsa* [History of Korean novels] (Seoul: Yeha, 1994); and Sin Hyŏng-gi, *Haebang chikhu ŭi munhak undong non* [A study of literary movements in the immediate postliberation period] (Seoul: Che 3 munhaksa, 1989).

2. See Bruce Cumings, *The Origins of the Korean War*, vol. 1: *Liberation and the Separation of Regimes, 1945–1947* (Princeton, N.J.: Princeton University Press, 1981), and vol. 2: *The Roaring of the Cataract, 1947–1950* (Princeton, N.J.: Princeton University Press, 1990). For the formation of the North Korean cultural field, see Charles Armstrong, *The North Korean Revolution, 1945–1950* (Ithaca, N.Y.: Cornell University Press, 2004).
3. Yi Sŏn-hŭi, "Ch'ang [Window]," in *Han'guk hyŏndae taep'yo sosŏlsŏn 6* [Representative works of modern Korean literature 6], ed. Im Hyŏng-t'aek et al. (Seoul: Ch'angjak kwa pip'yŏngsa, 1996), 380.
4. See Pierre Bourdieu, *The Field of Cultural Production* (New York: Columbia University Press, 1993).
5. This itself was a rearticulation of the earlier debates in the 1920s, discussed in chapter 1, brought to an end with the elimination of KAPF (Korean Artists Proletariat Federation) in 1935 and the accompanying recanting of a number of prominent KAPF writers and critics. As we saw in chapter 1, the colonial Korean literary field was realigned during the Great East Asian War into a literature in the service of the Greater East Asia Co-Prosperity Sphere *(kungmin munhak)*.
6. For summaries of the formation of leftist and rightist organizations during this period, see Sin Hyŏng-gi, *Haebang chikhu ŭi munhak undong non* [A study of literary movements in the immediate postliberation period] (Seoul: Che 3 munhaksa, 1989), 16–19; Kim Yun-sik, "Haebanghu NamBukhan munhwa undong [North and South Korean postliberation cultural movements]," in *Haebang konggan ŭi munhak undong kwa munhak ŭi hyŏnsil insik* [Literary movements and literary understanding of reality in the liberation period], by Kim Yun-sik et al. (Seoul: Hanul, 1992), 14–22.
7. Chi Ha-ryŏn, *Tojŏng: sosimin* [Journey: Petty bourgeois], in *Han'guk hyŏndae taep'yo sosŏlsŏn 7* [Representative works of modern Korean literature 7], ed. Im Hyŏng-t'aek et al. (Seoul: Ch'angjak kwa pip'yŏngsa, 1996), 220–239.
8. Yi Sŏn-hŭi, "Ch'ang [Window]," 403.
9. Ibid.
10. Ernesto Laclau, *Emancipation(s)* (London: Verso, 1996), 1.
11. See Pak Ch'an-mo, "Kkum kkunŭn maŭl [Village of dreams]," in *Hanguk hyŏndae taep'yo sosŏlsŏn 7* [Representative works of modern Korean literature], ed. Im Hyŏng-t'aek et al. (Seoul: Ch'angjak kwa pip'yŏngsa, 1996), 7:158–181.
12. Yi T'ae-jun, *Soryŏn kihaeng, nongt'o, mŏnji* [Travels in the Soviet Union, farm land, dust] (Seoul: K'ipŭn saem, 2001).
13. The travelogue was also central to the nationalizing of landscape in the colonial period. For an analysis of Yi Kwang-su's travelogues, see Ellie Y. Choi, "Space and National Identity: Yi Kwang-su's Vision of Korea During the Japanese Empire" (Ph.D. diss., Harvard University, 2009).
14. See Akhil Gupta and James Ferguson, "Culture, Power, Place: Ethnography at the End of an Era" and "Beyond 'Culture': Space, Identity, and the Politics of Difference," both in *Culture, Power, Place: Explorations in Critical Anthropology*, ed. Akhil Gupta and James Ferguson (Durham, N.C.: Duke University Press, 1997), 1–29, 33–51.

2. VISIBLE AND INVISIBLE STATES   221

15. Ch'oe Yŏl, *Han'guk hyŏndae misul undongsa* [History of modern Korean art movements] (Seoul: Tolbegae, 1991), 52.
16. Ibid., 57.
17. Jean Baudrillard, *The Mirror of Production* (St. Louis, Mo.: Telos Press, 1975), 18–19.
18. Yi T'ae-jun, *Soryŏn kihaeng, nongt'o, mŏnji* [Travels in the Soviet Union, farm land, dust], 119.
19. For a discussion of the art/work distinction and its breaking down in the nineteenth century, see Jacques Rancière, *The Politics of Aesthetics* (London: Continuum, 2006), 27, 44.
20. Yi T'ae-jun, *Soryŏn kihaeng, nongt'o, mŏnji* [Travels in the Soviet Union, farm land, dust], 385.
21. For Yi's nostalgia and relation to objects, see Ch'a Sŭng-gi, *Pan kŭndaejŏk sangsangnyŏk ŭi imgye tŭl* [Boundaries of the antimodern imagination] (Seoul: P'urŭn yŏksa, 2009), 249.
22. Yi T'ae-jun, *Soryŏn kihaeng, nongt'o, mŏnji* [Travels in the Soviet Union, farm land, dust], 340.
23. Ibid., 373.
24. For both Yŏm Sang-sŏp and Yi T'ae-jun, the antique shop is the site where post-1945 power relations are displayed, the United States replacing Japan as colonial power. For a discussion of pre-1945 Japanese-run antique shops, the production of colonial knowledge, ambivalent Orientalism, and Yanagi Sōetsu's fetishizing of Korean art, see Kim Brandt, "Objects of Desire: Japanese Collectors and Colonial Korea" *positions: east asia cultures critique* 8, no. 3 (Winter 2000).
25. Such a critique of communism as foreign was already available. It had, in fact, enabled the recantations of the late 1930s. Im Hwa's critique of KAPF turned upon the figuring of socialist realism as foreign. See Kim Ye-rim, *1930 nyŏndae huban kŭndae insik ŭi t'ŭl kwa miŭisik* [The modern Korean episteme and aesthetic consciousness in the late 1930s] (Seoul: Somyŏng, 2004), 181.
26. See ibid., 190–212.
27. The lifting of "Buckwheat" out from the 1930s modern and into the South Korean literary canon both elides the context of the *hyangt'o* art scene and the modernism that accompanies it. The post-1945 formation of South Korean literature, by way of its colonial canon, is embedded, then, in a history it does not name. This is a history that involves the relations among *hyangt'o*/proletarian art debates of the 1920s and 1930s, the Chosŏn Art Exhibition, 1920s and 1930s proletarian literature, and the coeval nativist and modernist literature of the 1930s.
28. See Ming-yan Lai, *Nativism and Modernity: Cultural Contestations in China and Taiwan Under Global Capitalism* (Albany, N.Y.: SUNY Press, 2008), 37.
29. Such a refusal complicates notions of sovereignty based on this separation. See Giorgio Agamben, *The Open: Man and Animal* (Stanford, Calif.: Stanford University Press, 2003). The autochthonous, then, refuses the "political" and makes visible the sovereign exception.

30. Here I am thinking not only of Yŏm Sang-sŏp's *haebang konggan* works but also his 1952 *Ch'wiu* [Rain shower], a text portraying the everyday in occupied Seoul during the late summer of 1950.
31. Kwŏn Yŏng-min et al., ed., *Yŏm Sang-sŏp chŏnjip 10* [Collected works of Yŏm Sang-sŏp], vol. 10 (Seoul: Minŭmsa, 1987).
32. Kim Tong-ch'un, *Pundan kwa Han'guk sahoe* [Division and South Korean society] (Seoul: Yŏksa pip'yŏngsa, 1997), 37–121.
33. *Dawn Wind* was interrupted for a week when Yŏm was jailed by U.S. authorities. Yŏm was an editor at a newspaper that opposed holding elections separately in the U.S.-occupied southern half of the peninsula.
34. The text, for example, is not mentioned in Kim Yun-sik's monumental study of Yŏm, a portion of which is devoted to Yŏm's works written during the immediate postliberation period. Neither does *Dawn Wind* appear in the *Yŏm Sang-sŏp chŏnjip* [Collected works of Yŏm Sang-sŏp], ed. Kwŏn Yŏng-min (Seoul: Minŭmsa).
35. Nancy Armstrong, *Desire and Domestic Fiction* (Oxford: Oxford University Press, 1987), 20.
36. For a discussion of the discourse on the new woman, see Ji-Eun Lee, "A New Pedigree: Women and Women's Reading in Korea, 1896–1934" (Ph.D. diss., Harvard University, 2006).
37. Yŏm Sang-sŏp, *Hyop'ung* [Dawn wind] (Seoul: Silch'ŏn munhaksa, 1998), 271–272.
38. See also Yŏm's portrayal of well-intentioned but condescending Japanese settler painters in *Sarang kwa choe* [Love and crime] and *Moran kkot p'ilddae* [When peonies bloom]. Yi Hye-ryŏng locates a patriarchal complicity between Yŏm and the orientalizing/feminizing gaze of these painters. See Yi Hye-ryŏng, *Han'guk sosŏl kwa kolsanghakchŏk t'aja tŭl* [Korean modern novels and the phrenological other] (Seoul: Somyŏng, 2007), 134–141.
39. Yŏm Sang-sŏp, *Hyop'ung* [Dawn wind], 281.
40. Edward Said, *Orientalism* (New York: Vintage, 1979), 18.
41. See ibid., 20–21, for the Orient that cannot speak.
42. We should, of course, consider the ways in which the postcolonial nation-state imposes its own form of coloniality in the name of emancipation, by way of the nationalized identity it tasks itself with enforcing—a move that Derrida calls the "homo-hegemonic." Derrida helps us to understand the ways in which both imperialized and nationalized subjects are formed in the space of "as if"—as if these subjects were giving the law to themselves. The imperialist subject is produced by acting "as if" he/she were giving the law to the colonial other, as if it did not originate from elsewhere. The postcolonial nationalist subject occupies a similar space. This subject acts as if he/she is now giving the law to him/herself, as if he/she were autonomous. In other words, "liberation," insofar as it stakes a claim to autonomy, reinscribes the coloniality it names itself as opposing. For Derrida, it is the assertion of ownership, possession of language as one's own that enables the production of the self as homogeneous; it is this ostensible experience of the self-same that

Derrida considers colonial. The imperial/national binary opposition unravels when we see how both terms claim a common experience of possession, autonomy, sovereignty. Jacques Derrida, *Monolingualism of the Other; or, The Prosthesis of Origin*, trans. Patrick Mensah (Stanford, Calif.: Stanford University Press, 1998), 39–40. We should also note how Derrida problematizes the colonial/imperial binary: "All culture is originarily colonial.... Every culture institutes itself through the unilateral imposition of some 'politics' of language" (39).

43. While Ch'ae was always considered more or less sympathetic to the left in the colonial period, he did not go north in the occupation period. His death in 1950 may have helped in his simultaneous canonization in both North and South Korean literary histories.

44. South Korean literary texts frequently portray changes brought about by land reform in the North and, later, in occupied areas in the South during the Korean War. As one example, Yi Ho-ch'ŏl's "Manjo [High tide]" (1959) offers a memory of life in the pre–land reform North that privileges affective communality over the call to redistribute property. Affect allows for a diminishing of the importance of material possession, sanctioning the existing distribution of property in the colonial ruralscape. One must possess the proper feelings for others. These feelings must then be shared in order to constitute a communal subject. In this way, a distribution of affectivity displaces distribution of property.

45. See Yŏm Sang-sŏp, "Yanggwajagap [The Western cookie box]," in *Isip segi Han'guk sosŏl 2* [Twentieth-century Korean fiction], vol. 2, ed. Ch'oe Wŏn-sik et al. (Seoul: Ch'angjak kwa pip'yŏngsa, 2005), 202–231.

46. Like other anthologies and serialized novels, the *Haebang Munhak sŏnjip* is illustrated. The cover design was done by the well-known painter Kim Hwan-gi.

47. The increasing crackdown on the left by the U.S. occupation caused many leftist writers and critics to go north in 1947 and 1948 (Im Hwa went north in late 1947). Others, including Pak T'ae-wŏn, went north during the Korean War. For a list of these writers, see Kwŏn Yŏng-min, *Haebang chikhu ŭi minjok munhak undong yŏn'gu* [A study of the national literature movement in the immediate postliberation period] (Seoul: Sŏul taehakkyo ch'ulp'anbu, 1996), 28. Kim Chul divides the postliberation history of rightist literary organizations into five periods: (1) "the formative period" (1945–1948), when rightist organizations, aided by the suppression of the left by the U.S. occupation and the unilateral establishment of the Republic of Korea, gradually began to consolidate their position; (2) "the period of settling-in and internal strife" (1949–1954), when writers had no choice but to adhere to a hardline anticommunist position even as they quarreled among themselves over leadership positions within the literary world; (3) "the period of differentiation" (1955–1960), when internal strife led to the formation of rival organizations based not on ideology but on power struggles; (4) "the period of unification and dependence" (1961–1970), when the Park Chung Hee regime created an umbrella literary organization increasingly dependent upon political authority; and (5) the

"1971–present period," when rightist organizations became completely dependent upon the state for their survival. See Kim Chul, "Han'guk posu uik munye chojik ŭi hyŏngsŏng kwa chŏn'gae [The formation and development of Korean rightist literary organizations]," in *Han'guk chŏnhu munhak ŭi hyŏngsŏng kwa chŏn'gae* [The formation and development of postwar literature], by Kim Chae-nam et al. (Seoul: T'aehaksa, 1993), 27–28.

3. Ambivalent Anticommunism: The Politics of Despair and the Erotics of Language

1. See Nancy Abelmann and Kathleen McHugh, eds., *South Korean Golden Age Melodrama: Gender, Genre, And National Cinema* (Detroit, Mich.: Wayne State University Press, 2005).
2. See Yi Yŏng-il, *Hanguk Yŏnghwa chŏnsa* [A comprehensive history of Korean film] (Sodo, 2004), 242.
3. For a discussion of the appropriation of Hollywood filmic technique in the 1950s, see Chung-Kang Kim, "South Korean Golden-Age Comedy Film: Industry, Genre, and Popular Culture (1953–1970)" (Ph.D. diss., University of Illinois, Urbana-Champaign, 2010), 104–117. For the success of Hollywood films in the colonial period, see Brian Yecies, "Systematization of Film Censorship in Colonial Korea: Profiteering from Hollywood's First Golden Age, 1926–1936," *Journal of Korean Studies* 10, no. 1 (Fall 2005): 59–83.
4. His literary career in South Korea was thus important but brief, largely limited to the 1950s.
5. See Dominick LaCapra, *Writing History, Writing Trauma* (Baltimore, Md.: Johns Hopkins Press, 2000), 184.
6. See Achille Mbembe, "Necropolitics," *Public Culture* 15, no. 3 (2003).
7. See Kwŏn Yŏng-min, *Haebang chikhu ŭi minjok munhak undong yŏn'gu* [A study of the national literature movement in the immediate postliberation period] (Seoul: Sŏul taehakkyo ch'ulp'anbu, 1996), 95–100. Kwŏn critiques both of these immediate postliberation articulations of *minjok munhak* as not properly nationalist: the former appropriates the rubric of "national literature" in an effort to disguise its "political ideology" of proletarian internationalism; as for the latter, its emphasis on the "purity of literature" runs the risk of eliding the specific historical circumstances of the nation (131–133).
8. See Sin Hyŏng-gi, *Haebang chikhu ŭi munhak undong non* [A study of literary movements in the immediate postliberation period] (Seoul: Che 3 munhaksa, 1989), 151–155.
9. Naoki Sakai deconstructs the opposition between universalism and particularism in his critique of David Pollack's *The Fracture of Meaning*: "Contrary to what has been advertised by both sides, universalism and particularism reinforce and supplement each other; they are never in real conflict; they need each other and have to seek to form a symmetrical, mutually supporting relationship by every means in order to

avoid a dialogic encounter that would necessarily jeopardize their reputedly secure and harmonized monologic worlds. Universalism and particularism endorse each other's defect in order to conceal their own; they are intimately tied to each other in their complicity. In this respect, a particularism such as nationalism can never be a serious critique of universalism, for it is an accomplice thereof." See Naoki Sakai, *Translation and Subjectivity: On "Japan" and Cultural Nationalism* (Minneapolis: University of Minnesota Press, 1997), 163. For Sakai's discussion of Kyoto School formulations of the particular/universal relation, see 163–170.

10. See Sin Chi-yŏng, "Chŏnsi ch'ejegi [1937–1945] maech'e e sillin chwadamhoe rŭl t'onghae pon, kyŏnggye e taehan kamgak ŭi chaegusŏng [Changes in the concept of border in wartime roundtable discussions published in 1937–1945]," *SAI* 4 (2008): 191–225.
11. *Chayu munhak* [Free literature] (1956:7), 225–235. Hereafter *FL*.
12. In "The Course of the Modern Novel" (1957), Paek Ch'ŏl links the allegorical in Kafka's work to Plato and Kierkegaard and then offers a critique of contemporary writers' representation of the modern: "In other words, Kafka grasps the world and the modern in terms of a certain philosophical idea; his works become allegories because he adheres to this idea as he portrays the world and the modern. In this way, he does not locate his literary world in the direct expression of objects, but as the expression of a single idea. . . . This tendency to grasp the modern in terms of a certain idea can be seen, recently, in the works of our young writers. We see this, for example, in Kim Sŏng-han, Chang Yong-hak, and Son Ch'ang-sŏp. They look at the world in terms of a previously assumed idea and create their works accordingly. For example, the attitude of seeing the space and time of the modern as diseased renders the question of whether or not the writer will become immersed in this world or escape from it a secondary issue" (*FL* 1957:8, 25). While Im Hwa and the left are not mentioned by Paek, recall that the question of "imitation" was most forcefully articulated by Im Hwa in his literary histories and informs the framework of South Korean literary histories up to the present.
13. See Kim Ye-rim, *1930 nyŏndae huban kŭndae insik ŭi t'ŭl kwa miŭisik* [The modern Korean episteme and aesthetic consciousness in the late 1930s] (Seoul: Somyŏng, 2004), 181.
14. Ibid., 230.
15. *Munye* [Literary arts] (1956:2), 114–119. Hereafter *LA*.
16. *Hyŏndae munhak* [Modern literature] (1956:11), 40–48. Hereafter *ML*.
17. Ibid.
18. Ibid., 42.
19. Ibid., 45–46.
20. Ibid., 48.
21. The removal of the left from the South Korean literary scene, of course, meant that discussions of *chuch'e* (a term later dropped in the 1960s as it achieved increasing importance in North Korea) would revolve around tradition, liberal democracy, and existential *anggajyumang/rejisŭtangsŭ*.

22. ML (1958:3), 206–208.
23. The elision took the form of censorship. The works of writers who went north (*wŏlbuk chakka*) were banned in South Korea until 1988.
24. See Stefan Tanaka, *Japan's Orient: Rendering Pasts into History* (Berkeley: University of California Press, 1995).
25. An implied erasure of Japan does exist in some colonial-period imaginings of the relation between Chosŏn and *tongyang*. For a discussion of the Chosŏn/*tongyang* relation in Yi T'ae-jun's colonial-period *Eastern Sentiments*, see Kim Ye-rim, *1930 nyŏndae huban kŭndae insik ŭi t'ŭl kwa miŭisik* [The modern Korean episteme and aesthetic consciousness in the late 1930s], 152.
26. See Andre Schmid, *Korea Between Empires, 1895–1919* (New York: Columbia University Press, 2002).
27. See Michel Foucault, *"Society Must Be Defended": Lectures at the Collège de France, 1975–1976* (New York: Picador, 2003).
28. "The Korean Structure of the Modern," in ML (1956:3), 180–189.
29. See Tomi Suzuki's description of Maruyama Masao's critique of the Japanese I-novel as continuing the premodern, "feudal" tradition of an unmediated self, a tradition that "values only 'immediate reality' and in which 'man's intellectual and spiritual side is neither differentiated nor independent from perceived nature.'" Tomi Suzuki, *Narrating the Self: Fictions of Japanese Modernity* (Stanford, Calif.: Stanford University Press, 1996), 4. The citation is from Maruyama Masao, "From Carnal Literature to Carnal Politics," 251–255. See 3 for Suzuki's view of this notion of the Japanese tradition as a construct, produced by an I-novel metanarrative that emerged in the 1920s.
30. "The Korean Structure of the Modern," 184.
31. Ibid., 188.
32. "The Position of New Writers in Our Literature—Centering on the Modernization of National Literature," in LA (1956:2), 114–119.
33. Ibid., 117.
34. Ibid., 118–119.
35. FL (1957:10–11), 33–34.
36. Culture and Life," in FL (1956:8), 36–44. Yi's investing of national culture with meaning at the expense of *minjung* culture helps us to understand the lineage of calls in the 1970s for *minjung* culture and literature to contest the national narrative sanctioned by the authoritarian state.
37. Ibid., 40.
38. For a discussion of *ilminjuŭi* and An Ho-sang, the first minister of education of the Republic of Korea, see Bruce Cumings, *The Origins of the Korean War*, vol. 2: *The Roaring of the Cataract, 1947–1950* (Princeton, N.J.: Princeton University Press, 1990), 208–214. Sŏ Chung-sŏk's noting of the emphasis the Liberal Party placed on its role as "a party of workers and farmers" allows us to consider the ways in which *ilmin* in the south opposes the *inmin* of the north. See his *Cho Pong-am kwa 1950 nyŏndae: Cho Pong-am ŭi sahoeminjujuŭi wa p'yŏnghwa t'ongillon, sang* [Cho Pong-am and the 1950s:

Cho Pong-am's democratic socialism and theory of peaceful reunification (Seoul: Yŏksa pip'yŏngsa, 1999), 1:322. *Ilminjuŭi*, that is, appropriates the language of socialism even as it attempts to secure the true locus of the nation in the south, opposed to what it views as the duplicitous attempt of "communist imperialism" to equate the nation with *inmin*.
39. FL (1959:4), 290–297.
40. Ibid., 291.
41. Ibid.
42. ML (1956:4), 102–106.
43. Chŏng Hŭi-mo, *1950 nyŏndae Han'guk munhak kwa sŏsasŏng* [1950s Korean literature and narratology] (Seoul: Kip'ŭn saem, 1998), 278.
44. Ibid., 277–278.
45. FL (1958:1), 147–153.
46. Ibid., 153.
47. Taken from the last page of Yŏm Sang-sŏp, *Ch'wiu* [Rainshower] (Seoul: Ŭryu munhwasa, 1952).
48. Kim So-yŏn, "Chŏnhu Han'guk ŭi yŏnghwa tamnon esŏ 'riŏllijŭm' ŭi ŭimi e kwanhayŏ: *P'iagol* ŭi met'abip'yŏng ŭl t'onghan chŏpkŭn [On the meaning of 'realism' in post–Korean War filmic discourse: An approach through the metacritique of *P'iagol*]," in *Maehok kwa hondon ŭi sidae: 50 nyŏndae ŭi Han'guk yŏnghwa* [The age of seduction and chaos: Korean cinema in the 1950s], ed. Kim So-yŏn (Seoul: Sodo, 2003), 48.
49. Ibid., 54.
50. We find a troubling of the South Korean statist narrative in other films as well. For an insightful discussion of global filmic intertextuality and the proximity of South Korean and North Korean political discourse in Sin Sang-ok's films of the early 1960s, see Steven Chung, "Sin Sang-ok and Postwar Korean Mass Culture" (Ph.D. diss., UC Irvine, 2007).
51. Kaja Silverman, *World Spectators* (Stanford, Calif.: Stanford University Press, 2000), 150.
52. Ibid., 157.
53. John Lie, *Han Unbound: The Political Economy of South Korea* (Stanford, Calif.: Stanford University Press, 1998), 36.
54. Ibid., 34.
55. Song Ha-ch'un divides the "new generation" of 1950s writers into two categories: (1) writers such as O Yŏng-su, Kang Sin-jae, and Chŏn Kwang-yong, who emphasize the positive, appealing to tradition and aesthetic sensibility; and (2) writers such as Kim Sŏng-han, Chang Yong-hak, and Son Ch'ang-sŏp, who emphasize the negative, rejecting tradition and contemporaneous reality. Song notes that Son has been considered the "most postwar" of postwar writers. See Song Ha-ch'un, "1950 nyŏndae Han'guk sosŏl ŭi hyŏngsŏng [The formation of 1950s Korean novels]," in *1950 nyŏndae sosŏlga tŭl* [1950s novelists], ed. Song Ha-ch'un and Yi Nam-ho (Seoul: Nanam, 1994), 20. For an attempt to counter the emphasis on the "negative" in Son's work, see Kim Chin-gi's extended discussion of "positive characters" in his *Son*

Ch'ang-sŏp ŭi muŭimi mihak [Son Ch'ang-sŏp's aesthetics of meaninglessness] (Seoul: Pakijŏng, 1999), 152–182.

56. Kim Yun-sik, *Han'guk sosŏlsa* [History of Korean novels] (Seoul: Yeha, 1994), 332.
57. Yi Ki-in, "Kaein ŭi saengjon kwa ingandaun sam e chimnyŏm [Individual existence and the desire for a properly human life]," in *1950 nyŏndae sosŏlga tŭl* [1950s novelists], ed. Song Ha-ch'un and Yi Nam-ho (Seoul: Nanam, 1994), 49.
58. Kwŏn Yŏng-min, *Han'guk hyŏndae munhaksa: 1945–1990* [History of modern Korean literature: 1945–1990] (Seoul: Minŭmsa, 1993), 155. For a discussion of the representation of physical disability in colonial-period literature, see Kyeong-Hee Choi's "Impaired Body as Colonial Trope: Kang Kyŏng-ae's 'Underground Village,'" *Public Culture* 13 (Fall 2001).
59. Yi Chae-sŏn, *Hyŏndae Han'guk sosŏlsa: 1945–1990* [History of modern Korean novels: 1945–1990] (Seoul: Minŭmsa, 1997), 108.
60. Han Su-yŏng, "1950 nyŏndae Han'guk sosŏl yŏn'gu: Namhan p'yŏn [A study of 1950s South Korean novels]," in *1950 nyŏndae NamBukhan munhak* [1950s North and South Korean literature], ed. Han'guk munhak yŏn'guhoe (Seoul: P'yŏngminsa, 1991), 55.
61. For a discussion of Ch'oe Myŏng-ik, see Kim Ye-rim, *1930 nyŏndae huban kŭndae insik ŭi t'ŭl kwa miŭisik* [The modern Korean episteme and aesthetic consciousness in the late 1930s], 91–102.
62. Kim Chong-hun, for example, links Chi-Sang with Mersault of Camus' *The Stranger* and Roquentin of Sartre's *Nausea* insofar as they all suffer from (universal) psychological disorders brought on by modern civilization. See his "Explication and Overcoming of Crisis," *ML* (1956:3), 168–178. Here, the modern is invoked to read the protagonists of Sartre, Camus, and Son as informed by a common psychology.
63. *Ibangin*. See Son Ch'ang-sŏp, *Son Ch'ang-sŏp taep'yojak chŏnjip I* [Representative works of Son Ch'ang-sŏp I] (Seoul: Yemungwan, 1970), 229 for use for use of term as noun and passive verb (*ibanginsi tanghada*). *Ibangin* is the term used to translate Camus' *The Stranger* into Korean.
64. Ibid., 225.
65. For the importance of the Korean War for Cold War behavioralism, the unseen communist, and the new notion of brainwashing, see Catherine Lutz, "Epistemology of the Bunker: The Brainwashed and Other New Subjects of the Permanent War," in *Inventing the Psychological: Toward a Cultural History of Emotional Life in America*, ed. Joel Pfister and Nancy Schmog (New Haven, Conn.: Yale University Press, 1997), 245–267. See especially the concluding section on *The Manchurian Candidate*.
66. For sexuality/anticommunism in the U.S. Cold War context, see Joanne Meyerowitz, "Sex, Gender, and the Cold War Language of Reform," in *Rethinking Cold War Culture*, ed. Peter Kuznick and James Gilbert (Washington, D.C.: Smithsonian Institution Press, 2001), 106–123.
67. Son Ch'ang-sŏp, *Son Ch'ang-sŏp taep'yojak chŏnjip I* [Representative works of Son Ch'ang-sŏp I] (Seoul: Yemungwan, 1970), 376.

68. Slavoj Žižek, *The Sublime Object of Ideology* (London: Verso, 1989), 119.
69. Ibid. Italics in original.
70. Son Ch'ang-sŏp, *Son Ch'ang-sŏp taep'yojak chŏnjip I* [Representative works of Son Ch'ang-sŏp I], 382.
71. Ibid., 380, 383.
72. Ibid., 383.
73. Ibid.
74. See Lynn A. Higgins and Brenda R. Silver, eds., *Rape and Representation* (New York: Columbia University Press, 1991).
75. Ibid., 384. Note the "sociological" terminology used in this sentence: "society" is invoked even as the "individual entity named 'I'" claims he is content to be alone with what is unable to be represented, the "secret."
76. The text represents Son's response to the exhortations of literary critics to move beyond the short story. The dearth of full-length novels was considered by many critics to be a sign of backwardness (*hujinsŏng*) preventing *Han'guk munhak* from emerging as a modern literature, a full-fledged part of world literature. The advertisement for *The Scribblers* in the February 1959 issue of *Sasanggye* makes this clear: "It is altogether regrettable that over fifty years has passed since the beginning of modern literature [*sin munhak*] without the appearance of a single full-length novel worthy of the name." WT (1959:2), 374. The promotion of full-length novels in *Sasanggye*—the journal that dominated intellectual discourse in the 1950s, increasingly viewing itself as a mediator of modernization in all fields (especially liberal democracy)—was very much part of the project of placing South Korea on the level of the "modern."
77. WT (1959:4), 317.
78. Ibid., 319.
79. Ibid., 316.
80. Son Ch'ang-sŏp, *Son Ch'ang-sŏp taep'yojak chŏnjip I* [Representative works of Son Ch'ang-sŏp I], 46.
81. Ibid., 64.
82. Ibid., 65.
83. Ibid., 66.
84. For these instances, see ibid., 77–78, 107, 117. The quotation is from 121.
85. Chŏng Pi-sŏk, "Author's Preface" to *Chayu puin 1* [Madame Freedom] (Seoul: Koryŏwŏn, 1985), 1:8.
86. See Cho Haejoang, "Living with Conflicting Subjectivities: Mother, Motherly Wife, and Sexy Woman in the Transition from Colonial-Modern to Postmodern Korea," in *Under Construction: The Gendering of Modernity, Class, and Consumption in the Republic of Korea*, ed. Laurel Kendall (Honolulu: University of Hawai'i Press, 2001), 165–195.
87. The term *han'gŭl* emerged in the early 1910s. Kang Nae-hui details this shift in "The Ending -da and Linguistic Modernity in Korea," in *Traces: A Multilingual Series of Cultural Theory and Translation* (Hong Kong: Hong Kong University Press, 2004), 3:139–163.

88. Serk-Bae Suh, "Tanil ŏnŏ sahoe rŭl hyanghae [Toward a monolingual society]," Han'guk munhak yŏngu 29) (2005): 185–219.
89. See Schmid, Korea Between Empires, 257–260, for an excellent overview of postliberation language policy.
90. For the relations among libidinal investment, visuality, and language, see Kaja Silverman, World Spectators (Stanford, Calif.: Stanford University Press, 2000), 77–79, 142; and The Threshold of the Visible World (London: Routledge, 1995), 79. Professor Chang libidinally invests hangŭl via a visual regime, here, perhaps, the eroticizing/eroticized look of Sŏn-yŏng.
91. As Kittler has shown, the typewriter transforms writing into communication: "Typescript amounts to the desexualization of writing, sacrificing its metaphysics and turning it into word processing." See Friedrich A. Kittler, Gramophone, Film, Typewriter, trans. Geoffrey Winthrop-Young and Michael Wutz (Stanford, Calif.: Stanford University Press, 1999), 187. See 70–73 for "melody of the heart." For female readership, see 174–175. For the link of body/touch to writing, see 186, 198.
92. Kathleen McHugh points out Sŏn-yŏng's hesitancy in "South Korean Film Melodrama: State, Nation, Woman, and the Transnational Familiar," in South Korea Golden Age Melodrama: Gender, Genre, and National Cinema, ed. Kathleen McHugh and Nancy Abelmann (Detroit, Mich.: Wayne State University Press, 2005), 27.
93. Critique of the postliberation modern girl as sign of decadence was frequent in the 1950s and 1960s. In "Cultural Metamorphosis," for example, Kim Nam-jung describes a contemporary tearoom scene in which women of the leisured class, some with "Hepburn-style" hairdos, "hold court like queens together with American-style gentlemen, creases on their trousers as sharp as knives. Working students, phony students, veterans, peddlers, seniors, beggars walk by casting glances appealing for help, but their entreaties disappear in the jazz music." See FL (1959:7), 257.
94. See Serk-Bae Suh, "Tanil ŏnŏ sahoe rŭl hyanghae [Toward a monolingual society]," 185–219. Yi Yŏng-jae also traces this movement in relation to the construction of a "national cinema" in South Korea. See her analysis of Yi Pyŏng-il's 1956 filmic adaptation of O Yŏng-jin's screenplay "The Happy Event at Elder Maeng's House," the latter written in Japanese and published in the journal Kungmin munhak [Imperial subjects literature] (1943). Yi shows how this translation/adaptation allows for the shift from a figuring of the "peninsula" as "local" under Japanese imperialism to post-1945 ethnonational site. Yi Yŏng-jae, Cheguk ilbon ŭi Chosŏn yŏnghwa [The Korean films of imperial Japan] (Seoul: Hyŏnsil munhwa, 2008), 211.
95. See Jung-en Woo, Race to the Swift: State and Finance in Korean Industrialization (New York: Columbia University Press, 1991).

4. Development as Devolution: Overcoming Communism and the "Land of Excrement" Incident

1. For a discussion of Japan as model minority, see T. Fujitani, "Go for Broke, the Movie: Japanese American Soldiers in U.S. National, Military, and Racial Dis-

4. DEVELOPMENT AS DEVOLUTION

courses," in *Perilous Memories: The Asia-Pacific War(s)*, ed. T. Fujitani, Geoffrey M. White, and Lisa Yoneyama (Durham, N.C.: Duke University Press, 2001), 253.
2. Arturo Escobar, *Encountering Development: The Making and Unmaking of the Third World* (Princeton, N.J.: Princeton University Press, 1995), 22–23.
3. Ibid., 191. Escobar draws on the work of Rey Chow here.
4. Ibid.
5. For colonial-period developmentalism, see Prasenjit Duara, *Sovereignty and Authenticity: Manchukuo and the East Asian Modern* (Lanham, Md.: Rowman and Littlefield, 2003). We should also note that the insertion of Korea into a Western narrative of teleological "progress," the production of the Chosŏn dynasty (1392–1910) as "traditional, the past," had already been put into motion by precolonial Korean enlightenment intellectuals in the late nineteenth and early twentieth centuries. As we have seen, a coauthoring of developmental discourse, a reworking of precolonial enlightenment notions of modernization in the colonial context, occurs via the continuing privileging of progress by writers such as Yi Kwang-su and the Japanese colonial state's location of itself as agent of development.
6. See David Palumbo-Liu, *Asian/American: Historical Crossings of a Racial Frontier* (Stanford, Calif.: Stanford University Press, 1999), particularly the chapter "Written on the Face: Race, Nation, Migrancy, and Sex" (81–115), detailing the connection the cosmetic surgeon D. R. Millard made in mid-1950s South Korea between "'rehabilitating' the state of Korea and Korean bodies" (95). As Palumbo-Liu points out, a racializing narrative of normative whiteness remains central to free-world developmentalism.
7. See Catherine V. Scott, *Gender and Development: Rethinking Modernization and Dependency Theory* (Boulder, Colo.: Lynne Rienner, 1995), 29–33.
8. See Kyung Hyun Kim, *The Remasculinization of Korean Cinema* (Durham, N.C.: Duke University Press, 2004).
9. William J. Lederer and Eugene Burdick, *The Ugly American* (New York: Norton, 1958), 132. See also 197 for "old colonialism."
10. Ibid., 29.
11. The text thus reworks the colonialist appropriation of the figure of rape. See Jenny Sharpe, *Allegories of Empire* (Minneapolis: University of Minnesota Press, 1993).
12. See N. Katherine Hayles, *How We Became Posthuman: Virtual Bodies in Cybernetics, Literature, and Informatics* (Chicago: University of Chicago Press, 1999).
13. Lederer and Burdick, *The Ugly American*: "mainly in the minds of men" (267); "blockage of information" (275).
14. Ibid., 228–231. The notion of developmental transformability in the text also relies, at a key moment, on the immigrant narrative, the turning of a "dark" Lithuanian family into "Tex" (116). This transformability, based on movement (the immigrant narrative), now extends itself beyond its former endpoint, the United States. Motion, not the fixed coordinates of any given space, enables transformation: "Tex" signals a geographical location and a character, both set in motion, now located in Southeast Asia.

15. Etienne Balibar and Immanuel Wallerstein, *Race, Nation, Class: Ambiguous Identities* (London: Verso, 1991), 211.
16. Crary, *Suspensions of Perception: Attention, Spectacle, and Modern Culture*, 74.
17. Bruce Cumings, "Webs with No Spiders, Spiders with No Webs: The Genealogy of the Developmental State," in *The Developmental State*, ed. Meredith Woo-Cumings (Ithaca, N.Y.: Cornell University Press, 1999), 89.
18. For a discussion of Park's ethnic nationalism, see Gi-Wook Shin (with Jim Freda and Gihong Yi), "The Politics of Ethnic Nationalism in Divided Korea," *Nations and Nationalism* 5 (Winter 1999).
19. Giorgio Agamben, *Homo Sacer: Sovereign Power and Bare Life* (Stanford, Calif.: Stanford University Press, 1998), 179.
20. Park Chung Hee, *Kukka wa hyŏngmyŏng kwa na* [The state, the revolution, and I] (Seoul: Hyangmunsa, 1963), 22–23. Hereafter, *SRI*.
21. Slavoj Žižek, *Tarrying with the Negative: Kant, Hegel, and the Critique of Ideology* (Durham, N.C.: Duke University Press, 1993), 210. Italics in original.
22. Ibid. Italics in original.
23. Ibid., 211.
24. Park Chung Hee, *Our Nation's Path: Ideology of Social Reconstruction* (Seoul: Tong-a, 1962), 70.
25. *SRI*, 151.
26. Ibid., 153.
27. Ibid, 130.
28. Paik Nak-chung, "4.19 ŭi yŏksajŏk ŭimi wa hyŏnjaesŏng [The historical and contemporary significance of 4.19]," in *Sawŏl hyŏngmyŏng non* [A study of the April revolution], ed. Kang Man-gil (Seoul: Han'gilsa, 1983), 31. This article was originally published in 1980 following the assassination of Park Chung Hee and prior to Chun Doo Hwan's ascension to power.
29. In an effort to present the views of students who had participated in the April 19 movement, a special issue of *Sasanggye* [World of thought] entitled "Victory of the People" (*minjung ŭi sŭngni*) appeared in June 1960. This issue featured a roundtable discussion that took place on May 3 among high school and college students (the former played a crucial role in the demonstrations) entitled "The Testimony of Angry Lions." Cho Tŏk-haeng, a student at Yonsei University, stated that "of course the leader of the Liberal Party was Dr. Rhee, but doesn't a look at the advisors below him show that the party was made up of officials who didn't have much to do with any sort of political ideology? So the Jap [*waenom*] puppets, those who had passed the civil-service examination during the colonial period, became officials again after liberation, puppets of the Liberal Party. The assertion that democracy was adopted after liberation was a lie; the bureaucratic mindset was what was really there under the surface" (*Sasanggye* [World of thought] 1960:6, 40). Hereafter *WT*. Significant here is the portrayal of the Rhee regime as a continuation of Japanese colonial rule. April 19 enables the expulsion of colonial elements, the achieving of true democ-

racy; it opens the opportunity for a liberation that, Cho implies, August 15 (the August 1945 "liberation") failed to achieve. Cho's remarks point at once to earlier contestations of the meaning of August 15, 1945, that we traced in chapter 2 (contestations largely silenced following the formation of the Republic of Korea on August 15, 1948, and throughout the 1950s), and to the general distrust the younger generation was widely considered to hold for an older generation associated not only, as here, with collaboration but with the failure to repel Japanese imperialism. Critique of the Rhee regime's use of anticommunism to silence its political opponents, moreover, was widespread following April 19. In "Fifteen Years of Socialist Movements—Their History and Character," Sin Sang-ch'o, for example, calls the Rhee regime a "singular combination of McCarthyist methods and palace politics in the style of the Bourbon dynasty" (WT 1960:8, 58).

30. WT 1960:6, 32–33.
31. Kang Man-gil, "4 wŏl hyŏngmyŏng ŭi minjoksajŏk maengnak [The April revolution in the context of national history]," in Sawŏl hyŏngmyŏng non [A study of the April revolution], ed. Kang Man-gil (Seoul: Han'gilsa, 1983), 25.
32. Ibid., 14.
33. Ibid., 17–19.
34. The debate over April 19 as historical event began in its immediate aftermath. While many began to call the event a "revolution," others disagreed. In a June 1960 letter to the *World of Thought* editor entitled "Revolution or Reform?" Kim Yŏng-se, for example, notes that while journalists seem to have reached an agreement to designate April 19 a "revolution," "No one attempts to understand how the April 19 Uprising has come to be named in such a way. To our knowledge, a revolution must bring about change in the political structure, and those who participated in it must assume or take part in political power. But April 19 saw no change in the national polity and has brought about only a partial transformation in terms of the political form of democracy" (WT 1960:6, 31). By contrast, Min Sŏk-hong writes in his essay "Modern History and Liberal Democracy" that "without question this event was a revolution; it was a liberal democratic revolution achieved spontaneously by the Korean people using their own power" (WT 1960:6, 97).
35. In the May 1960s roundtable cited above, Sim Ch'un-sŏp, a student at Tongguk University, offered the following regarding the incomplete nature of April 19: "If we look systematically at the character of April 19, it is a struggle over political sovereignty. We can divide struggles over political sovereignty into two types: the struggle over national sovereign rights and that over democratic rights. April 19 is neither a proletarian nor a bourgeois class struggle but has the character of a struggle for democratic rights.... The democratic struggle does not stop here but will undergo a further stage. If this revolution brought about the so-called Second Republic, it will bring about the Third Republic. In the Third Republic this will manifest itself in a struggle for sovereignty that combines both the struggle for national sovereign rights and democratic rights. What comes first is north and south unification, the

234 4. DEVELOPMENT AS DEVOLUTION

unification of national sovereignty. This could take various forms such as the withdrawal of U.S. troops, free elections, advance upon the north. In any event, I think that the April 19 affair, in the end, is a process directed towards struggle for national sovereignty" (WT 1960:6, 48).

36. SRI, 78–79. Italics appear as bold in original.
37. Scott, *Gender and Development*, 8.
38. The sole appearance of Nam's work in Kim Yun-sik and Chŏng Ho-ung's canon-forming linear chart of Korean literary history occurs because of this event. See Kim Yun-sik and Chŏng Ho-ung, *Han'guk sosŏlsa* [History of Korean novels] (Seoul: Yeha, 1993), 652–655. "Land of Excrement" appears in the works index, but Nam does not appear in the authors index, indicating the importance ascribed to the event rather than the author.
39. Ibid., 401.
40. Im Chin-yŏng, "Kajang kangnyŏkhan usŭm ŭi k'allal [The devastating power of laughter]," in *Punji/Hwanggu ŭi pimyŏng oe* ["Land of excrement," "Scream of a yellow dog," and other stories], *Han'guk sosŏl munhak taegye 43* [Selected works of Korean literature 43], ed. Nam Chŏng-hyŏn and Ch'ŏn Sŭng-se (Seoul: Tonga ch'ulp'ansa, 1995), 557.
41. Nam's continuing association with the representation of South Korea as neocolony, in fact, became clear when his works were republished during the International Monetary Fund crisis of the mid-1990s.
42. For an elaboration of the identification of culture with race in interwar Japan, see Harry Harootunian, *Overcome by Modernity: History, Culture, and Community in Interwar Japan* (Princeton, N.J.: Princeton University Press, 2000), 294. The linkage between race and culture, of course, stretches back at least to the late nineteenth century. For a discussion of the importance of Yi Kwang-su's theories of race and culture in postcolonial South Korea, see Hyung Il Pae, *Constructing "Korean" Origins: A Critical Review of Archaeology, Historiography, and Racial Myth in Korean State-Formation Theories* (Cambridge, Mass.: Harvard University Press, 2000), 258–260.
43. *Chayu munhak* [Free literature] (1956:7), 324–325. Hereafter *FL*.
44. Nam Chŏng-hyŏn, *Kulttuk mit ŭi yusan* [Inheritance under the chimney] (Seoul: Munye ch'ulp'ansa, 1967), 335. Hereafter *IUC*.
45. Ibid., 334.
46. Ibid., 345.
47. For a discussion of "desiring Hollywood," see Chung-Kang Kim, "South Korean Golden-Age Comedy Film: Industry, Genre, and Popular Culture (1953–1970)" (Ph.D. diss., University of Illinois, Urbana-Champaign, 2010), 104–117. Kim offers an important discussion of gender comedies in the late 1960s. See 169–207. See also Hye-seung Cheung, "Toward a Strategic Korean Cinephilia: A Transnational Detournement of Hollywood Melodrama," in *South Korean Golden Age Melodrama: Gender, Genre, And National Cinema*, ed. Nancy Abelmann and Kathleen McHugh (Detroit, Mich.: Wayne State University Press, 2005).
48. The removal of Syngman Rhee from power opened up a space for explicit critique

not only of 1950s political repression but, as we have seen, of the history of national division and the location of the Korean peninsula in the Cold War order. It was in 1960 that those calls for neutrality and nonalignment made in the immediate postliberation period and moved to the margins in the 1950s reappeared. At the same time, even as intellectuals—including those associated with the reemerging socialist political parties—celebrated the possibilities opened up by the fall of the Rhee regime and criticized its repressive anticommunism, they were always careful to distance themselves from communism. Kim Yun-t'ae follows many South Korean literary critics in his emphasis on the importance of the April 19 movement as opening a "new period for literature," one in which writers cast aside despair, anxiety, and existential suffering and confronted the "actual circumstances . . . of national reality." Indeed, the April 19 movement coincided with the coming of age of the "Hangul generation" (the first generation of Koreans to receive an education in vernacular Korean) to highlight the sense of a shift in the literary scene. Kim Yun-t'ae, "4.19 Hyŏngmyŏng kwa minjok hyŏnsil ŭi palgyŏn [The April Revolution and the discovery of national reality]," in *Minjok munhaksa kangjwa* II [Lectures on the history of national literature, vol. 2], ed. Minjok munhaksa yŏn'guso (Seoul: Ch'angjak kwa pip'yŏngsa, 1995), 237.
49. The recovery of Kwan-su's "humanity" occurs at the moment that Sin-ok's transforms from representative of the modern to "*sisihan yŏin* [no account woman]." This refiguring of Sin-ok (who insists upon her right to have extramarital sex) should be seen both in the context of the longer history of representations of the modern girl and new woman in colonial-period texts and as emblematic of the anxiety about the emergence, in the 1950s, of the "promiscuous woman." For example, in "A Twenty-Year History of Ideas," Chŏng T'ae-yong writes that "the Korean War completely altered the sexual ethics of women." Chŏng cites Chŏng Pi-sŏk's popular novel *Madame Freedom* (discussed in chapter 3) as the literary expression of this social alteration, one that led many housewives to become "hedonists," engaging in adulterous sexual liaisons. *Hyŏndae munhak* [Modern literature] (1965:4), 17–18. Hereafter *ML*.
50. *FL* (1961:3), 20–21. Nam revised the text in 1987. In this later version, Sin-ok maintains that the United States provides the ultimate example of strict adherence to the rules of the modern.
51. Dipesh Chakrabarty, *Provincializing Europe: Postcolonial Thought and Historical Difference* (Princeton, N.J.: Princeton University Press, 2000), 30.
52. *FL* (1961:3), 56.
53. *SRI*, 75.
54. See Seungsook Moon, *Militarized Modernity and Gendered Citizenship in South Korea* (Durham, N.C.: Duke University Press, 2005).
55. *WT* (1964:6), 361.
56. See Rey Chow's analysis of ethnicization and the visual regime of the zoo in *The Protestant Ethnic and the Spirit of Capitalism* (New York: Columbia University Press, 2002), 95–100.
57. *WT* (1964:6), 373–374.

58. See Shirley Nelson Garner, Claire Kahane, and Madelon Sprengnether, eds., *The (M)other Tongue: Essays in Feminist Psychoanalytic Interpretation* (Ithaca, N.Y.: Cornell University Press, 1985). See also Marianne Hirsch, *The Mother/Daughter Plot: Narrative, Psychoanalysis, Feminism* (Bloomington: Indiana University Press, 1989), 52. Hirsch, following Naomi Schor, links the figure of mother to otherness in literature—as what both enables literature and must be contained. We should consider the ways in which Yong-dal fathers the symbolic order, narrates events, allegorizes, by representing woman (the object that enables literature and must simultaneously be eliminated). The representation of the murder is the elimination of this ambivalent/threatening space, one that engenders Yong-dal as narrator of the nation.
59. WT (1960:5), 98.
60. WT (1964:6), 374–375.
61. This production of "humanity," like that enabled by the 1906 caging of the African "pygmy" Ota Benga in the monkey house at the Bronx Zoo, is performed by the exhibition itself, the display of the ability to process, enclose, and conduct research on objects.
62. See Palumbo-Liu, *Asian/American*.
63. The text's title is composed of the first four characters of the *Thousand Character Classic*.
64. IUC, 298.
65. Ibid., 299.
66. Nam was released on bail on July 23, 1965. His case was not brought to trial until July 23, 1966.
67. "Land of Excrement" remained censored until the general lifting of press restrictions in 1988.
68. He was found guilty on June 28, 1967, and received a seven-year suspended prison sentence. See "P'ilhwa, Punji sagŏn charyo moŭm [Selected documents from the 'Land of excrement' censorship incident]," in *Punji taep'yo chakp'umsŏn* ["Land of excrement": Selected works] (Seoul: Hangyŏre, 1987), 382.
69. Ibid., 386.
70. Ibid., 408.
71. Ibid., 388.
72. *Time* (March 10, 1967): 41.
73. Jinsoo An has shown how this imaginary plays out in 1960s South Korean action films set in Manchuria. See Jinsoo An, "Popular Reasoning of South Korean Melodramatic Films, 1953–1972" (Ph.D. diss., UCLA, 2005).
74. Tom Engelhardt, *The End of Victory Culture: Cold War America and the Disillusioning of a Generation* (Amherst: University of Massachusetts Press, 1995).
75. Jin-kyung Lee links the text's portrayal of Man-su's impending death to the notion of the "shattering of the jewel" during the Greater East Asia and Pacific War. See *Service Economies: Militarism, Sex Work, and Migrant Labor in South Korea* (Minneapolis: University of Minnesota Press, 2010), 137.

76. Chungmoo Choi also discusses this passage in "Nationalism and Construction of Gender in Korea," in *Dangerous Women: Gender and Korean Nationalism*, ed. Elaine H. Kim and Chungmoo Choi (New York: Routledge, 1998), 9–32.
77. *ML* (1965:3), 81. The yin-yang symbol is located at the center of the Republic of Korea flag.
78. Judith Butler, *Bodies That Matter: On the Discursive Limits of "Sex"* (New York: Routledge, 1993), 125.
79. *ML* (1965:3), 74.
80. *ML* (1965:3), 80.
81. Anne McClintock, *Imperial Leather: Race, Gender, and Sexuality in the Colonial Contest* (New York: Routledge, 1995), 31. McClintock further points out that Britain's emerging national narrative gendered time by figuring women (like the colonized and the working class) as inherently atavistic—the conservative repository of the national archaic. Women were not seen as inhabiting history proper but existing, like colonized peoples, in a perpetually anterior time within the modern nation. White middle-class men, by contrast, were seen to embody the forward-thrusting agency of national progress. Ibid, 359.
82. See Kelly Y. Jeong, *Crisis of Gender and the Nation in Korean Literature and Cinema: Modernity Arrives Again* (Lanham, Md.: Lexington Books, 2011). Jeong's work is the first to take into account both literary and cinematic representations of gender, class, and nationhood from the 1920s to the 1960s.
83. See, for example, Im Chin-yŏng, "Kajang kangnyŏkhan usŭm ŭi k'allal [The devastating power of laughter]."
84. Cited in Richard Slotkin, "Buffalo Bill's 'Wild West' and the Mythologization of the American Empire," in *Cultures of American Imperialism*, ed. Amy Kaplan and Donald E. Pease (Durham, N.C.: Duke University Press, 1993), 165.
85. In a special issue of *Chakka yŏn'gu* [Studies on writers] devoted to Nam Chŏng-hyŏn following September 11, 2001, Im Hŏn-yŏng writes that "Land of Excrement" prefigures what will be the U.S. reaction to the bombing of the World Trade Center. See Im's "Pan oese ŭisik kwa minjok ŭisik: Nam Chŏng-hyŏn ŭi sosŏl segye [Nationalist consciousness and the opposition to foreign powers: Nam Chŏng-hyŏn's literary world]," *Chakka yŏn'gu* 12 (2001): 44–46.
86. Timothy Mitchell, *Questions of Modernity* (Minneapolis: University of Minnesota Press, 2000), 18–19.

5. Return to the Colonial Present: Translation, Collaboration, Pan-Asianism

1. Born in Wŏnsan, in what is now North Korea, in 1936, Ch'oe In-hun belongs to a generation of writers who experienced Japanese colonialism as children and the Korean War as adolescents. These were writers who emerged on the literary scene in the late 1950s and early 1960s, the first generation to have been educated in the

Korean language in middle and high school. Ch'oe came South, alone, during the Korean War and thus, like a number of other prominent writers of the late 1950s and 1960s, is a *sirhyangmin*, or one who has lost his or her home in the North. Like Nam Chŏng-hyŏn, Ch'oe In-hun was formally introduced to the *mundan* in 1959 under the sponsorship of the journal *Free Literature*. His debut work was the short story "The Gray Club," but it was the appearance of his full-length novel *The Square* in late 1960, following the removal of Syngman Rhee from power in April of that year, that granted him a position of immediate prominence in the newly formed postwar South Korean literary world.

2. See Giorgio Agamben, *Homo Sacer: Sovereign Power and Bare Life*, trans. Daniel Heller-Roazen (Stanford, Calif.: Stanford University Press, 1998), 3.

3. In "Modern French Literature" (1956), for example, Yi Hwi-yŏng observes that for Sartre freedom is not to be explained theoretically but must be experienced through action. For Malraux, humans are not composed of the attributes they possess but of what they do. Literature, therefore, must not pursue the essence of what a human is but should delve into the existential issues confronting humans. In other words, literature should not pursue knowledge of human essence but instead the experiential action that realizes human existence. *Chayu munhak* [Free literature] (1956: inaugural issue), 206, 208. Hereafter *FL*. Cho Hong-sik, in "The Recognition of Historical Reality—Current Trends in French Literature" (1959), remarks that the age when literature and action belonged to separate spheres has come to an end. French writers, while maintaining a stance of resistance and struggle, engage in a philosophical examination of the ways in which they can emancipate the self from the condition of despair. They begin with a philosophical inquiry into freedom and the human condition and then move on to assess the historical situation and determine the future course of action. *FL* (1959:1), 296.

4. While the critique of the ROK in *The Square* is very much part of the post–April 19 denunciation of the political repression of the Syngman Rhee regime, we should note that in *Sasanggye* [World of thought] (hereafter *WT*), particularly in the late 1950s, critique of the Rhee regime—made, for the most part, in the name of liberal democracy—became increasingly forceful. In a special issue of *WT* on "Korea and Modernization" (1959: 2), for example, Han T'ae-yŏn, invoking Max Weber, maintains that the particular character of Korean democracy lies in its continuance of an "Asian-style absolutism" (a phrase we find in the preface to *The Square*), one that invests the ruler-patriarch with total power. Continuity between this older form and democracy can be seen in South Korea in the concept of a national father (*kukpu*), the lack of the public/private split (*kongsa ŭi mubunbyŏl*), and the tendency of those in power to interpret democratic ideals in accordance with their own needs. In the end, this has given Korean democracy a top-down rather than a bottom-up character. The lack of the prospect of a peaceful transfer of power, moreover, makes the current situation resemble a dictatorship (19–23). If we think of the square as space of public discourse, the preface of this issue of *WT* figures it as emptied out: the two pages where the preface to the journal should appear are blank, except for the pub-

5. RETURN TO THE COLONIAL PRESENT 239

lisher's name, Chang Chun-ha, on the second page, with the following on the first: "WHAT CAN BE SAID?—After witnessing the violent repression of democratic rights." Min Sŏk-hong offers a not-so-implicit critique of both North and South, writing that it is not only communists who violate freedom but also conservative right-wing extremists: autocratic rulers, absolutists, military dictators (WT 1959:3, 64). The preface to the October 1959 issue of WT takes aim at the contemporaneous political situation in the South, emphasizing the importance of the individual in democratic societies: only when the individual has gained self-awareness can one, in the name of humanity and democracy, courageously oppose and resist the trampling of one's rights by government authorities. If the people (*minjung*) lack the courage to fight the corruption and injustice they see in society, they are not qualified to enjoy democracy. The flower of democracy will never bloom among a people possessing a slave consciousness, one full of cowardice, submission, flattery. Democracy is the possession of the free (*chayuin*). Dictatorship runs rampant in a society characterized by slave consciousness; democracy flourishes in a society characterized by freedom consciousness (WT 1959:10, 18–19).

5. There has been some confusion regarding the date of the original version of *The Square*. The 1968 and 1976 versions of the text list the original as published in the October 1960 issue of *Saebyŏk* [Dawn] (hereafter, *SB*). For clarification of dates and a discussion of different versions, see Han Ki, "*Kwangjang* ŭi wŏnhyŏngsŏng, taehwajŏk yŏksasŏng, kŭrigo hyŏnjaesong [The original form, dialogical historicity, and contemporaneity of *Kwangjang*]," *Chakka segye* [World of writers] (Spring 1990): 81–84. For a discussion of stylistic changes in the different versions, see Kim Hyŏn, "Sarang ŭi chaehwagin—*Kwangjang* kaejak e taehayŏ [A reaffirmation of love—On the different versions of *Kwangjang*]," in Ch'oe In-hun, *Kwangjang/Kuunmong* [The square/The nine-cloud dream] (Seoul: Munhak kwa chisŏngsa, 2000), 313–322. My discussion here is based on the original version, which appeared in the November 1960 issue of *SB*. The text has been translated by Kevin O'Rourke. See Choi In-hoon, *The Square*, trans. K. O'Rourke (Devon: Spindlewood, 1985). Professor O'Rourke does not recall which version of the text he used for his translation. Although his translation appeared in 1985, he translated the text in the mid-1970s, in all likelihood using the 1973 version while consulting the 1976 version (personal communication). It is important to note that the final paragraph of the preface of the original, the only place in the text where April 19 is mentioned, does not appear in the translation. Citations of the text in this chapter follow Professor O'Rourke's excellent translation with minor revisions, particularly when the translation, based as it is on 1970s versions of *The Square*, differs from the text that appeared in the November 1960 issue of *Saebyŏk*. *SB*, 258–259.

6. *SB*, 258. Myŏng-jun's excursus on these political, economic, and cultural squares bears some resemblance to Paklin's impassioned speeches in Turgenev's *Virgin Soil*. See Ivan Turgenev, *Virgin Soil*, trans. Constance Garnet (New York: MacMillan 1951), 155.

7. *SB*, 255.

8. Ibid., 263. The 1989 made-for-TV KBS adaptation of *The Square* elides the detective's reminiscence. Instead, Myŏng-jun is asked by another detective to sympathize with the detective who has beaten him. The beating is justified as a fit of anger arising from the fact that the detective's family was murdered by the "Reds."
9. Ibid., 261.
10. Ibid., 264. Recall that Turgenev's "superfluous man" has a "padlock on my inner self." See "The Diary of a Superfluous Man," in *The Essential Turgenev*, ed. Elizabeth Cheresh Allen (Evanston, Ill.: Northwestern University Press), 112.
11. *SB*, 272.
12. Ibid., 277.
13. Ibid., 279.
14. Ibid.
15. Ibid.
16. Ernesto Laclau, *Emancipation(s)* (London: Verso, 1996), 23. Italics in original.
17. Ibid., 24–25.
18. The sixth and seventh occurrences of "Ego" are transliterated in the 1960 version. All other occurrences are in English: "Ego." In the 1961 and 1968 versions, all occurrences are transliterated. In the 1976 version all occurrences are " 'na' " or "chagi."
19. See Lydia Liu, "The Question of Meaning-Value in the Political Economy of the Sign," in *Tokens of Exchange: The Problem of Translation in Global Circulations*, ed. Lydia Liu (Durham, N.C.: Duke University Press, 1999), 34–37. During his stay in the United States in the early 1970s, Ch'oe embarked upon another translation, replacing all Sino-Korean terms with Korean words. For Ch'oe's discussion of this process, see *Munhak kwa ideollogi: Ch'oe In-hun chŏnjip 12* [Language and ideology: Collected works of Ch'oe In-hun 12] (Seoul: Munhak kwa chisŏngsa, 1994), 361–366. Ch'oe's concern, then, is not only with the condition of hypothetical equivalence vis-à-vis the Western metropole but also with the Sino/Korean relation.
20. Ferdinand de Saussure, *Course in General Linguistics*, trans. Wade Baskin (New York: McGraw-Hill, 1959), 15.
21. Ibid., 66.
22. Ibid., 103.
23. Ibid., 67.
24. Bruce Cumings, "The Origin and Development of the Northeast Asian Political Economy: Industrial Sectors, Product Cycles, and Political Consequences," in *The Political Economy of the New Asian Industrialism*, ed. Frederic C. Deyo (Ithaca, N.Y.: Cornell University Press, 1987), 71.
25. For a discussion of South Korean military involvement in the Vietnam War, see Jin-kyung Lee, *Service Economies: Militarism, Sex Work, and Migrant Labor in South Korea* (Minneapolis: University of Minnesota Press, 2010), 37–77.
26. See Kim Tong-ch'un and Pak T'ae-sun, *1960 nyŏndae ŭi sahoe undong* [Social movements of the 1960s] (Seoul: Kkach'i, 1991), 251–252.

27. Kwŏn Yŏng-min, "Chŏngch'ijŏgin munhak kwa munhak ŭi chŏngch'isŏng [Political literature and the politics of literature]," *Chakka segye* [World of writers] (Spring 1990): 76–77.
28. Ch'oe In-hun, *Ch'ongdok ŭi sori: Ch'oe In-hun chŏnjip 9* [Voice of the Governor-General: Collected works of Ch'oe In-hun 9] (Seoul: Munhak kwa chisŏngsa, 1994), 68–69. Hereafter, VGG.
29. Martin Hart-Landsberg calls the 1967 National Assembly election "possibly the most corrupt election in South Korean history." See his *The Rush to Development: Economic Change and Political Struggle in South Korea* (New York: Monthly Review Press, 1993), 169.
30. VGG I, 88. This follows the listener's hearing various sounds other than the voice of the Governor-General coming in from the dark. Among them is the "groaning sound of a child with a tear gas canister stuck in his eye" (88). This reference to Kim Chu-yŏl, the seventeen-year-old student whose body was found in a bay around Masan on April 11 (the discovery proved to be the catalyst for the April 19 movement), indicates that the listener, in 1967, is thinking very much of the April 19 movement and its ghosts. The Governor-General himself also mentions the April movement on several occasions.
31. M. M. Bakhtin, *The Dialogic Imagination* (Austin: University of Texas Press, 1981), 343.
32. Ibid., 341.
33. Ibid., 345.
34. Ibid., 342.
35. Ibid., 345.
36. Ibid., 348.
37. Ibid., 344.
38. Bakhtin does leave room for the "rare" occasion when a word is "*simultaneously* authoritative and internally persuasive" (ibid., 342). Italics in original.
39. Ibid., 345.
40. Ibid., 343.
41. VGG I, pp. 68–9.
42. Ibid., 69.
43. Ibid., 71.
44. Ibid., 86.
45. Ibid., 72–3.
46. VGG III, pp. 113–4.
47. Ibid., 114.
48. Ibid., 115. See also VGG IV (131) for Japan's uniqueness vis-à-vis other empires.
49. See Friedrich Kittler, *Gramophone, Film, Typewriter*, trans. Geoffrey Winthrop-Young and Michael Wutz (Stanford, Calif.: Stanford University Press, 1999), 99.
50. See ibid., 12, for the "radio specter."
51. Recall Susan Buck-Morss's noting that for Benjamin's dialectical image "the principal construction is that of montage, whereby the image's ideational elements remain unreconciled, rather than fusing into one 'harmonizing perspective.'" See

Susan Buck-Morss, *The Dialectics of Seeing: Walter Benjamin and the Arcades Project* (Cambridge, Mass.: The MIT Press, 1991), 67.
52. Walter Benjamin, *Gesammelte Schriften*, ed. Rolf Tiedmann and Hermann Schweppanhäuser (Frankfurt am Main: Suhrkamp Verlag, 1972), 5:576. Cited in Buck-Morss, *The Dialectics of Seeing*, 291.
53. Ch'oe In-hun, *Sosŏlga Kubossi ŭi iril: Ch'oe In-hun chŏnjip 4* [A day in the life of Kubo the novelist: Collected works of Ch'oe In-hun 4] (Seoul: Munhak kwa chisŏngsa, 1994), 79.
54. Diana Fuss, *Identification Papers* (London: Routledge, 1995), 146.
55. Ch'oe In-hun, *Sosŏlga Kubossi ŭi iril: Ch'oe In-hun chŏnjip 4* [A day in the life of Kubo the novelist: Collected works of Ch'oe In-hun 4] (Seoul: Munhak kwa chisŏngsa, 1994), 164.
56. Ibid., 165.
57. Lewis Harrington, "Miki Kiyoshi and the Shōwa Kenkyōkai: The Failure of World History," *positions: east asia cultures critique* 17, no. 1 (Spring 2009): 63.
58. For a discussion of Hwang Sŏg-yŏng's works and literary representations of the political and ethical in the 1970s, see Youngju Ryu, "The Neighbor and the Politics of Literature in 1970s South Korea: Yi Mungu, Hwang Sŏgyŏng, Cho Sehŭi" (Ph.D. diss., UCLA, 2006).
59. Ch'oe In-hun, *Sosŏlga Kubossi ŭi iril: Ch'oe In-hun chŏnjip 4* [A day in the life of Kubo the novelist: Collected works of Ch'oe In-hun 4], 321–322. Such a gesture resembles one made in the film *P'iagol*, discussed in chapter 3. *P'iagol* contains a remarkable, extended series of shots in a Buddhist temple—a long scene that occurs immediately prior to the partisans attacking the village of Namsan-ni. Here, Taegari, the partisan leader, pauses as he comes face to face with the guardian temple statues. Why such an extended series of shots in the temple? The face-to-face encounter of Taegari and the guardian statues in this borderline space of the temple, one that stands between village and mountains, just as the guardian statues stand in the liminal space between temple and the outside world, results in a breakdown in identification that occurs outside of language. No words are spoken in this temple scene. Most important is the countering of Taegari's look by the guardian statues. It is the eyes, the face of the guardian statues that render Taegari incapable of seeing a reflection of himself, of constituting himself as a subject. It is not only Taegari who is forced to pause, however. The suture of the viewer is with Taegari looking up at the guardian statues. Here, a visual politics of nonalignment emerges, one that refuses to allow the separation out of viewer as anticommunist subject from Taegari as demonized other.
60. Takeshi Kimoto, "Antinomies of Total War," *positions: east asia cultures critique* 17, no. 1 (Spring 2009): 107.
61. See John Namjun Kim, "On the Brink of Universality: German Cosmopolitanism in Japanese Imperialism," *positions: east asia cultures critique* 17, no. 1 (Spring 2009): 89.
62. *FL* (October–November 1957): 33–34. See chapter 4.

5. RETURN TO THE COLONIAL PRESENT   243

63. The scrambled term for Japan is also a play on the Korean term for "bad."
64. Naoki Sakai, *Translation and Subjectivity: On "Japan" and Cultural Nationalism* (Minneapolis: University of Minnesota Press, 1997), 170.
65. For collaboration confessionals, see Kelly Y. Jeong, *Crisis of Gender and the Nation in Korean Literature and Cinema: Modernity Arrives Again* (Lanham, Md.: Lexington Books, 2011).
66. Peter Brooks has pointed out the close relation between religion and law in the act of confession. See his *Troubling Confessions: Speaking Guilt in Law and Literature* (Chicago: University of Chicago Press, 2000).
67. It was in the 1945–1948 period that the shift was made from *Chosŏn* to *Han'guk*, *Chosŏn saram* to *Han'guk saram*.
68. *Hurrah for Freedom!* itself, of course, can be viewed as Ch'oe In-gyu's recantation of his late-colonial-period films such as *Children of the Sun* (*T'aeyang ŭi ai tŭl*, 1944) and *Sons of the Divine Wind* (*Sinp'ung ŭi adŭl tŭl*, 1945).
69. Kim Tong-in, *Kamja* [Potato] (Seoul: Munhak sasangsa), 244–248.
70. Here, we should recall the distinction Leo Ching makes between assimilation (*dōka*) and imperialization (*kōminka*) in his discussion of colonial Taiwan: "In the discourse of *dōka*, the problem of making the colonized into Japanese was perceived . . . as predominantly a project of the colonial government. Under *kōminka* . . . especially through the process of internalizing the strife over identity, becoming Japanese became the sole responsibility of the colonized." Leo Ching, *Becoming "Japanese": Colonial Taiwan and the Politics of Identity Formation* (Berkeley: University of California Press, 2001), 97.
71. I thank Bong Joo Shim for pointing out the Yi Kwang-su anagram.
72. Ch'oe In-hun, *T'aep'ung Ch'oe In-hun chŏnjip 5* [*T'aep'ung*: Collected works of Ch'oe In-hun 5] (Seoul: Munhak kwa chisŏngsa, 1994), 67.
73. Ibid., 360.
74. See Naoki Sakai, "Imperial Nationalism and the Comparative Perspective," *positions: east asia cultures critique* 17, no. 1 (Spring 2009): 188. Emphasis in original.
75. Ibid., 189.
76. See John Namjun Kim, "The Temporality of Empire: The Imperial Cosmopolitanism of Miki Kiyoshi and Tanabe Hajime," in *Pan-Asianism in Modern Japanese History: Colonialism, Regionalism, and Borders*, ed. Sven Saaler and J. Victor Koschmann (New York: Routledge, 2007), 157.
77. Ch'oe, that is, does not follow earlier colonial philosophers such as Sŏ In-sik by invoking a temporality to interrupt the privileging of space in late 1930s wartime thought. For a discussion of Sŏ's critique of Miki, see Ch'a Sŭng-gi, *Pan kŭndaejŏk sangsangnyŏk ŭi imgye tŭl* [Boundaries of the antimodern imagination] (Seoul, P'urŭn yŏksa, 2009), 212.
78. *SB*, 273.
79. Pheng Cheah shows how Marx relies upon an organismic schema: "labor is characterized by the epigenetic motifs of self-formation, growth and development, an organism's assimilation of the external world, and its reproduction as a species."

Pheng Cheah, *Spectral Nationality* (New York: Columbia University Press, 2003), 192–193. Cheah further notes that postcolonial "theories of revolutionary national culture are irrigated by ... vitalist ontology.... These appeals to national culture are emphatically not irrational or mystical. They do not fetishize ancient traditions, but privilege the living culture of workers and peasants in their ongoing struggle to reappropriate what has been alienated from the people by (neo) colonialism" (214). In other words, "the opposition is always between popular vitality and its ideological manipulation" (225).
80. Etienne Balibar and Immanuel Wallerstein, *Race, Nation, Class: Ambiguous Identities* (London: Verso, 1991), 211.
81. Jacques Derrida, *Specters of Marx: The State of the Debt, the Work of Mourning, and the New International* (New York: Routledge, 1994), 157. Italics in original.
82. Achille Mbembe, "Necropolitics," *Public Culture* 15, no. 3 (2003): 40.
83. Ch'oe In-hun, *T'aep'ung Ch'oe In-hun chŏnjip 5* [*T'aep'ung*: Collected works of Ch'oe In-hun 5], 59.

Postscript

1. See Carter Eckert, *Offspring of Emire: The Koch'ang Kims and the Colonial Origins of Korean Capitalism, 1876–1945* (Seattle: University of Washington Press, 1991).
2. See Giorgio Agamben, *The Open: Man and Animal* (Stanford, Calif.: Stanford University Press, 2003).

SELECTED BIBLIOGRAPHY

Sources in Korean

All entries published in Seoul. Preferred personal romanization of authors is used when available.

Baek, Moon Im. "Chŏnjaeng kwa mellodŭrama [War and melodrama]." In *Chŏnjaeng iranŭn muntŏk* [On the threshold of war], ed. Hanguk-Taiwan Pigyo munhwa yŏn'guhoe. Kŭrinbi, 2010.

Ch'a Sŭng-gi. *Pan kŭndaejŏk sangsangnyŏk ŭi imgye tŭl* [Boundaries of the antimodern imagination]. P'urŭn yŏksa, 2009.

Chayu munhak [Free literature]. 1956–1963. Hanguk chayu munhakcha hyŏphoe.

Chi Ha-ryŏn. "Tojŏng: sosimin [Journey: Petty bourgeois]." In *Han'guk hyŏndae taep'yo sosŏlsŏn* [Representative works of modern Korean literature], ed. Im Hyŏng-t'aek et al. Vol. 7. Ch'angjak kwa pip'yŏngsa, 1996.

Cho Nam-hyŏn. *Han'guk hyŏndae sosŏl ŭi haebu* [Anatomy of modern Korean novels]. Munye ch'ulp'ansa, 1993.

Ch'oe In-hun. *Ch'oe In-hun chŏnjip* [Collected works of Ch'oe In-hun]. 12 vols. Munhak kwa chisŏngsa, 1991–94.

——. *Kwangjang* [The square]. Chŏnghyangsa, 1961.

——. *Kwangjang* [The square]. Minŭmsa, 1973.

——. *Kwangjang/Kuunmong: Ch'oe In-hun chŏnjip 1* [The square/Nine cloud dream: Collected works of Ch'oe In-hun 1]. Munhak kwa chisŏngsa, 1976, repr. 1989.

Chŏn Ki-ch'ŏl. "Haebanghu silchonjuŭi munhak ŭi suyong yangsang kwa Han'guk munhak pip'yŏng ŭi mosaek [An exploration of Korean literary criticism and the reception of existential literature in the postliberation period]." In *Han'guk ŭi chŏnhu munhak* [Postwar Korean literature], ed. Han'guk hyŏndae munhak yŏn'guhoe. T'aehaksa, 1991.

Chŏng Ho-ung. "T'arhyang, kŭ ch'ulbal ŭi sosŏlchŏk ŭimi—Yi Ho-ch'ŏl ŭi *Sosimin* non [The fictional significance of leaving the countryside as a point of departure—on Lee Ho-Chul's *Sosi-*

min]." In *1960 nyŏndae munhak yŏn'gu* [Studies of 1960s literature], ed. Munhaksa wa pip'yŏng yŏn'guhoe. Yeha, 1993.

Chŏng Hŭi-mo. *1950 nyŏndae Han'guk munhak kwa sŏsasŏng* [1950s Korean literature and narratology]. Kip'ŭn saem, 1998.

Chŏng Kyu-ung. *Kŭl tongne esŏ saenggin il: 60 nyŏndae iyagi* [Happenings in the writers' neighborhood: Stories from the 1960s literary world]. Munhak segyesa, 1999.

Han Ki. "Kwangjang ŭi wŏnhyŏngsŏng, taehwajŏk yŏksasŏng, kŭrigo hyŏnjaesŏng [The original form, dialogical historicity, and contemporaneity of *Kwangjang*]." *Chakka segye* [World of writers] (Spring 1990): 81–98.

Han Su-yŏng. "1950 nyŏndae Han'guk sosŏl yŏn'gu: Namhan p'yŏn [A study of 1950s South Korean novels]." In *1950 nyŏndae NamBukhan munhak* [1950s North and South Korean literature], ed. Han'guk munhak yŏn'guhoe. P'yŏngminsa, 1991.

Hwang Jongyon. "Silla ŭi palgyŏn [The discovery of Shilla]." In *Shilla ŭi palgyŏn* [The discovery of Silla], ed. Hwang Jongyon, 13–52. Tongguk taehakkyo ch'ulp'anbu, 2008.

Hyŏndae munhak [Modern literature]. 1955–1965. Hyŏndae munhak.

Im Chin-yŏng. "Kajang kangnyŏkhan usŭm ŭi k'allal [The devastating power of laughter]." In *Punji/Hwanggu ŭi pimyŏng oe* [Land of excrement/Scream of a yellow dog, and other stories], 547–571. Han'guk sosŏl munhak taegye [Selected works of Korean literature] 43. Tonga ch'ulp'ansa, 1995.

Im Chong-guk. *Ch'inil munhak non* [On pro-Japanese literature]. 8th ed. P'yŏnghwa ch'ulp'ansa, 1993.

Im Hwa. *Im Hwa munhak yesul chŏnjip* [Collected works]. Somyŏng, 2009.

Im Kyŏng-sun. "Hyŏlsŏ ŭi segye wa yongmang ŭi chwajŏl [The world of 'Written in blood' and the frustration of desire]." In *1950 nyŏndae munhak ihae* [Understanding 1950s literature], ed. Cho Kŏn-sang. Sŏnggyungwan taehakkyo, 1996.

Im Tae-sik. "1950 nyŏndae Miguk ŭi kyoyuk wŏnjo wa ch'inmi ellit'ŭ ŭi hyŏngsŏng [U.S. educational aid and the formation of a pro-American elite in the 1950s]." In *1950 nyŏndae NamBukhan ŭi sŏnt'aek kwa kulchŏl* [1950s North and South Korea: Choices and refractions], ed. Yŏksa munje yŏn'guso. Yŏksa pip'yŏngsa, 1988.

Kang Man-gil et al. *Sawŏl hyŏngmyŏng non* [A study of the April revolution]. Han'gilsa, 1983.

Kim Chin-gi. *Son Ch'ang-sŏp ŭi muŭimi mihak* [Son Ch'ang-sŏp's aesthetics of meaninglessness]. Pakijŏng, 1999.

Kim Chul. *"Kungmin" iranŭn noye: Han'guk munhak ŭi kiŏk kwa manggak* [The slave called "citizen": Memory and amnesia in Korean literature]. Samin, 2005.

Kim Chae-nam, et al. *Han'guk chŏnhu munhak ŭi hyŏngsŏng kwa chŏn'gae* [The formation and development of post–Korean War literature]. T'aehaksa, 1993.

———. *"Kungmin" iranŭn noye: Han'guk munhak ŭi kiŏk kwa manggak* [The slave called "citizen": Memory and amnesia in Korean literature]. Samin, 2005.

Kim Hyŏn. "Sarang ŭi chaehwagin—*Kwangjang* kaejak e taehayŏ [A reaffirmation of love—On the different versions of *Kwangjang*]." In *Kwangjang/Kuunmong* [The square/The nine-cloud dream], by Ch'oe In-hun. Munhak kwa chisŏngsa, 2000.

Kim P'al-bong. *Kim P'albong munhak chŏnjip* [Collected works]. Vol. 1. Ed. Hong Chŏng-sŏn. Munhakkwa chisŏngsa, 1988.

Kim So-yŏn, ed. *Maehok kwa hondon ŭi sidae: 1950 nyŏndae ŭi Han'guk yŏnghwa* [The age of seduction and chaos: Korean cinema in the 1950s]. Sodo, 2003.

Kim Su-nam, ed. *Chosŏn sinario sŏnjip 1* [A selection of Korean scenarios]. Jimmundang, 2003.

Kim Sŭng-hwan. "Yi Ho-ch'ŏl lon" [On Lee Ho-Chul]. *Chakka yŏn'gu* [Studies of writers] (September 2000): 10–30.

Kim Tong-ch'un and Pak T'ae-sun. *1960 nyŏndae ŭi sahoe undong* [Social movements of the 1960s]. Kkach'i, 1991.

Kim Tong-sik and Kim Pyŏng-ik. "4.19 sedae ŭi munhak i kŏrŏon kil" [The path traveled by the literature of the 4.19 generation]. In *Chakka yŏn'gu* [Studies of writers] (September 2000): 157–211.

Kim Uk-tong. *"Kwangjang" ŭl ingnŭn ilgop kaji pangbŏp* [Seven ways to read The square]. Munhak kwa chisŏngsa, 1996.

Kim Wŏn-gil. *Yi Ho-chŏl sosŏl ŭi pyŏnmo kwajŏng yŏn'gu* [A study of the process of transformation in Lee Ho-Chul's novels]. Sŏul taehakkyo taehagwŏn hyŏndae munhak yŏn'guhoe, 1998.

Kim Ye-rim. *1930 nyŏndae huban kŭndae insik ŭi t'ŭl kwa miŭisik* [The modern Korean episteme and aesthetic consciousness in the late 1930s]. Somyŏng ch'ulp'an, 2004.

Kim Yong-hwa. *Pundan sanghwang kwa munhak* [Literature and the condition of national division]. Seoul: Kukhak charyowŏn, 1992.

Kim Yun-sik. *Han'guk sosŏlsa* [History of Korean novels]. Yeha, 1994.

———. "Haebanghu NamBukhan munhwa undong [North and South Korean postliberation cultural movements]." In *Haebang konggan ŭi munhak undong kwa munhak ŭi hyŏnsil insik* [Literary movements and literary understanding of reality in the liberation period], by Kim Yun-sik et al. Hanul, 1992.

Kim Yunsik and Kim Hyŏn. *Han'guk munhaksa* [A literary history of Korea]. Minŭmsa, 1973.

Kim Yun-t'ae. "4.19 Hyŏngmyŏng kwa minjok hyŏnsil ŭi palgyŏn [The April revolution and the discovery of national reality]." In *Minjok munhaksa kangjwa II* [Lectures on the history of national literature II], ed. Minjok munhaksa yŏn'guso. Ch'angjak kwa pip'yŏngsa, 1995.

Kwon Bodurae. *Han'guk kŭndae sosŏl ŭi kiwŏn* [Origins of modern Korean literature]. Somyŏng, 2000.

Kwŏn Yŏng-min. *Haebang chikhu ŭi minjok munhak undong yŏn'gu* [A study of the national literature movement in the immediate postliberation period]. Sŏul taehakkyo ch'ulp'anbu, 1996.

———. *Han'guk hyŏndae munhaksa: 1945–1990* [History of modern Korean literature: 1945–1990]. Minŭmsa, 1993.

———. "Chŏngch'ijŏgin munhak kwa munhak ŭi chŏngch'isŏng" [Political literature and the politics of literature]. *Chakka segye* [World of writers] (Spring 1990): 73–80.

Lee Ho-Chul. *Yi Ho-chŏl munhak sŏnjip* [Selected works]. 7 Vols. Kukhak charyowŏn, 2001.
Munye [Literary arts]. 1953–1960. Munyesa.
Nam Chŏng-hyŏn. *Kulttuk mit ŭi yusan* [Inheritance under the chimney]. Munye ch'ulp'ansa, 1967.
——. *Punji taep'yo chakp'umsŏn* ["Land of excrement": Selected works]. Hangyŏre, 1987.
O Yŏn-ho. *Nogŭn-ri kŭhu* [After Nogŭn-ri]. Mal, 1999.
Ŏm Hae-yŏng. *Han'guk chŏnhu sedae sosŏl yŏn'gu* [A study of the novels of the post–Korean War generation]. Kukhak charyowŏn, 1994.
Paik Nak-chung. *Minjok munhak kwa segye munhak I* [National literature and world literature I]. Ch'angjak kwa pip'yŏngsa, 1978.
Pak Ch'an-mo. "Kkum kkunŭn maŭl [Village of dreams]." In *Han'guk hyŏndae taep'yo sosŏlsŏn* [Representative works of modern Korean literature], ed. Im Hyŏng-t'aek, vol. 7. Ch'angjak kwa pip'yŏngsa, 1996.
Pak Chŏng-hŭi [Park Chung Hee]. *Uri minjok ŭi nagal kil: sahoe chaegŏn ŭi inyŏm* [Our nation's path: Ideology of social reconstruction]. Tonga ch'ulp'ansa, 1962.
——. *Kukka wa hyŏngmyŏng kwa na* [The state, the revolution, and I]. Hyangmunsa, 1963.
Pak Myŏng-gyu and Kim Yŏng-bŏm. "Munhwa pyŏndong [Cultural transformations]." In *Han'guk hyŏndaesa wa sahoe pyŏndong* [Modern Korean history and social transformations], ed. Han'guk sahoesahak. Munhak kwa chisŏngsa, 1997.
Pak Myŏng-nim. "1950 nyŏndae Han'guk ŭi minjujuŭi wa kwŏnwijuŭi [Korean democracy and authoritarianism in the 1950s]." In *1950 nyŏndae nambukhan ŭi sŏnt'aek kwa kulchŏl* [1950s North and South Korea: Choices and refractions], ed. Yŏksa Munje yŏn'guso. Yŏksa pip'yŏngsa, 1988.
Saebyŏk [Dawn]. November 1960. Saebyŏksa.
Sasanggye [World of thought]. 1953–1963. Sasanggyesa.
Sedae [Generation]. July 1964–August 1965. Sedaesa.
Sin Ch'ae-ho. "Nanggaek ŭi sinnyŏn manp'il [Random New Year's jottings]." In *Sin Ch'ae-ho yŏksa nonsŏl chip* [Selected historical essays of Sin Ch'ae-ho], ed. Chŏng Hae-ryŏm. Hyŏndae sirhaksa, 1995.
Sin Chi-yŏng. "Chŏnsi ch'ejegi [1937–1945] maech'e e sillin chwadamhoe rŭl t'onghae pon, kyŏnggye e taehan kamgak ŭi chaegusŏng [Changes in the concept of border in wartime roundtable discussions published in 1937–1945]." *SAI* 4 (2008): 191–225.
Sin Hyŏng-gi. *Haebang chikhu ŭi munhak undong non* [A study of literary movements in the immediate postliberation period]. Che 3 munhaksa, 1989.
Sin Kyŏng-dŭk. *Han'guk chŏnhu sosŏl yŏn'gu* [A study of post–Korean War novels]. Ilchisa, 1988.
Sŏ Chun-sŏp. "Chŏngjidoen segye ŭi sosŏl—Son Ch'ang-sŏp non [Novels of a static world—A study of Son Ch'ang-sŏp]." In *Han'guk chŏnhu munhak ŭi hyŏngsŏng kwa chŏn'gae* [The formation and development of post–Korean War literature], by Kim Chae-nam et al. T'aehaksa, 1993.

Sŏ Chung-sŏk. *Cho Pong-am kwa 1950 nyŏndae: Cho Pong-am ŭi sahoeminjujuŭi wa p'yŏnghwa t'ongillon* [Cho Pong-am and the 1950s: Cho Pong-am's democratic socialism and theory of peaceful reunification]. Vol. 1. Yŏksa pip'yŏngsa, 1999.

Sŏ Sŏng-nok. *Han'guk hyŏndae hoehwa ŭi paljach'wi* [Traces of modern Korean painting]. Munye ch'ulp'ansa, 1993.

Son Ch'ang-sŏp. *Son Ch'ang-sŏp taep'yojak chŏnjip* [Representative works of Son Ch'ang-sŏp]. 5 vols. Yemungwan, 1970.

——. "Amach'uŏ chakka ŭi pyŏn [In defense of an amateur writer]." In *Hyŏndae Han'guk munhak chŏnjip* [Collected works of modern Korean literature]. Vol. 3. Sin'gu munhwasa, 1968.

Song Ha-ch'un. "1950 nyŏndae Han'guk sosŏl ŭi hyŏngsŏng [The formation of 1950s Korean novels]." In *1950 nyŏndae sosŏlga tŭl* [1950s novelists], ed. Song Ha-ch'un and Yi Nam-ho. Nanam, 1994.

Suh, Serk-Bae. "Tanil ŏnŏ sahoe rŭl hyanghae [Toward a monolingual society]." In *Han'guk munhak yŏn'gu* [Korean literary studies] 29. Tongguk University Institute for Korean Literary Studies, 2005.

Yi Chae-sŏn. *Hyŏndae Han'guk sosŏlsa: 1945–1990* [History of modern Korean novels: 1945–1990]. Minŭmsa, 1997.

Yi Chong-myŏng. *Yurang* [Wandering]. In *Chosŏn sinario sŏnjip* [A selection of Korean scenarios], ed Kim Su-nam, vol. 1. Jimmundang, 2003.

Yi Hye-ryŏng. *Han'guk sosŏl kwa kolsanghakchŏk t'aja tŭl* [Korean modern novels and the phrenological other]. Somyŏng, 2007.

Yi Hyo-sŏk et al. *Hwaryun* [Wheel of fire]. In *Chosŏn sinario sŏnjip* [A selection of Korean scenarios], ed. Kim Su-nam, vol. 2. Jimmundang, 2003.

Yi Ki-in. "Kaein ŭi saengjon kwa ingandaun sam e chimnyŏm [Individual existence and the desire for a properly human life]." In *1950 nyŏndae sosŏlga tŭl* [1950s novelists], ed. Song Ha-ch'un and Yi Nam-ho. Nanam, 1994.

Yi Kwang-su. *Mujŏng* [The heartless]. 1917. Munhak tongne, 2003.

Yi Sŭng-hŭi, "1920 nyŏndae sinmun manp'yŏng ŭi sahoejuŭi chŏngch'i wa munhwajŏk hyokwa [Socialist politics of newspaper cartoons in the 1920s and their cultural effects]." In *Kŭndae chisik ŭrosŏ ŭi sahoejuŭi* [Socialism as modern knowledge], ed. Sanhŏ hakhoe. Kip'ŭn saem, 2008

Yi T'ae-jun. *Soryŏn kihaeng, nongt'o, mŏnji* [Travels in the Soviet Union, farm land, dust]. K'ipŭn saem, 2001.

Yi Ŭn-ja. *1950 nyŏndae chisigin sosŏl yŏn'gu* [A study of 1950s Korean intellectual novels]. T'aehaksa, 1995.

Yi Yŏng-il. *Han'guk Yŏnghwa chŏnsa* [A comprehensive history of Korean film]. Sodo, 2004.

Yi Yŏng-jae. *Cheguk Ilbon ŭi Chosŏn yŏnghwa* [The Korean films of imperial Japan]. Hyŏnsil munhwa, 2008.

Yŏm Sang-sŏp. *Hyop'ung* [Dawn wind]. Silch'ŏn munhaksa, 1998.

———. "Yanggwajagap [The Western cookie box]." In *Isip segi Han'guk sosŏl* [Twentieth-century Korean fiction], ed. Ch'oe Wŏn-sik et al., 2:202–231. Ch'angjak kwa pip'yŏngsa, 2005.

Sources in English

Abelmann, Nancy. *Echoes of the Past, Echoes of Dissent: A South Korean Social Movement.* Berkeley: University of California Press, 1995.

Abelmann, Nancy, and Kathleen McHugh, eds. *South Korean Golden Age Melodrama: Gender, Genre, and National Cinema.* Detroit, Mich.: Wayne State University Press, 2005.

Agamben, Giorgio. *Homo Sacer: Sovereign Power and Bare Life.* Trans. Daniel Heller-Roazen. Stanford, Calif.: Stanford University Press, 1998.

———. *The Open: Man and Animal.* Stanford, Calif.: Stanford University Press, 2003.

An, Jinsoo. "Popular Reasoning of South Korean Melodramatic Films (1953–1972)." Ph.D. diss., University of California–Los Angeles, 2005.

Anderson, Benedict. *Imagined Communities: Reflections of the Origin and Spread of Nationalism.* Rev. ed. London: Verso, 1993.

Armstrong, Charles. "The Myth of North Korea." Chicago Occasional Papers on Korea 6. Ed. Bruce Cumings. Chicago: Center for East Asian Studies, 1991.

———. *The North Korean Revolution, 1945–1950.* Ithaca, N.Y.: Cornell University Press, 2004.

Armstrong, Nancy. *Desire and Domestic Fiction.* Oxford: Oxford University Press, 1987.

———. *Fiction in the Age of Photography: The Legacy of British Realism.* Cambridge, Mass.: Harvard University Press, 1999.

Bakhtin, Mikhail. *The Dialogic Imagination.* Trans. Caryl Emerson and Michael Holquist. Ed. Michael Holquist. Austin: University of Texas Press, 1981.

———. *Rabelais and His World.* Trans. Helene Iswolsky. Bloomington: Indiana University Press, 1984.

Balibar, Etienne, and Immanuel Wallerstein. *Race, Nation, Class: Ambiguous Identities.* London: Verso, 1991.

Baudrillard, Jean. *The Mirror of Production.* St. Louis: Telos Press, 1975.

Bourdaghs, Michael. "The Disease of Nationalism, the Empire of Hygiene." *positions* 6, no. 3 (Winter 1998): 637–673.

Bourdieu, Pierre. *The Field of Cultural Production.* New York: Columbia University Press, 1993.

Brandt, Kim. *Kingdom of Beauty: Mingei and the Politics of Folk Art in Imperial Japan.* Durham, N.C.: Duke University Press, 2007.

Brooks, Peter. *Troubling Confessions: Speaking Guilt in Law and Literature.* Chicago: University of Chicago Press, 2000.

Buck-Morss, Susan. *The Dialectics of Seeing: Walter Benjamin and the Arcades Project.* Cambridge, Mass.: The MIT Press, 1991.

Butler, Judith. *Bodies That Matter: On the Discursive Limits of "Sex."* New York: Routledge, 1993.
Chakrabarty, Dipesh. *Provincializing Europe: Postcolonial Thought and Historical Difference.* Princeton, N.J.: Princeton University Press, 2007.
Chatterjee, Partha. *Nationalist Thought and the Colonial World: A Derivative Discourse.* Minneapolis: University of Minnesota Press, 1986.
Cheah, Pheng. *Spectral Nationality.* New York: Columbia University Press, 2003.
Ching, Leo. *Becoming "Japanese": Colonial Taiwan and the Politics of Identity Formation.* Berkeley: University of California Press, 2001.
Cho Haejoang. "Living with Conflicting Subjectivities: Mother, Motherly Wife, and Sexy Woman in the Transition from Colonial-Modern to Postmodern Korea." In *Under Construction: The Gendering of Modernity, Class, and Consumption in the Republic of Korea*, ed. Laurel Kendall. Honolulu: University of Hawai'i Press, 2001.
Cho, Heekyoung. "Literary Translation and Appropriation: Korean Intellectuals' Reception of Russian Prose Via Japan, 1900–1927." Ph.D. diss., University of Chicago, 2007.
Choi, Ellie Y. "Space and National Identity: Yi Kwang-su's Vision of Korea During the Japanese Empire." Ph.D. diss., Harvard University, 2009.
Choi, In-hoon. *The Square.* Trans. Kevin O'Rourke. Devon: Spindlewood, 1985.
Choi, Jang Jip. "Political Cleavages in South Korea." State and Society in Contemporary Korea. Ed. Hagen Koo. Ithaca, N.Y.: Cornell University Press, 1993.
Choi, Kyeung-Hee. "Another Layer of the Pro-Japanese Literature: Ch'oe Chunghui's 'The Wild Chrysanthemum.'" *Hyŏndae munhak ŭi yŏn'gu* [Studies on modern literature] (February 2000): 191–227.
———. "Impaired Body as Colonial Trope: Kang Kyŏng'ae's 'Underground Village.'" *Public Culture* 13 (Fall 2001): 431–458.
Chow, Rey. *The Age of the World Target: Self-Referentiality in War, Theory, and Comparative Work.* Durham, N.C.: Duke University Press, 2006.
———. "Introduction: Chineseness as a Theoretical Problem." In *Modern Chinese Literary and Cultural Studies in the Age of Theory: Reimagining a Field*, ed. Rey Chow. Durham, N.C.: Duke University Press, 2000.
———. *Primitive Passions: Visuality, Sexuality, Ethnography, and Contemporary Chinese Cinema.* New York: Columbia University Press, 1995.
———. *The Protestant Ethnic and the Spirit of Capitalism.* New York: Columbia University Press, 2002.
Chung, Hye-seung. "Toward a Strategic Korean Cinephilia: A Transnational Detournement of Hollywood Melodrama." In *South Korean Golden Age Melodrama: Gender, Genre, and National Cinema*, ed. Nancy Abelmann and Kathleen McHugh. Detroit, Mich.: Wayne State University Press, 2005.
Chung, Steven. "Sin Sang-ok and Postwar Korean Mass Culture." Ph.D. diss., University of California–Irvine, 2007.

Clifford, James, and George Marcuse, eds. *Writing Culture: The Poetics and Politics of Ethnography*. Berkeley: University of California Press, 1986.
Crary, Jonathan. *Suspensions of Perception: Attention, Spectacle, and Modern Culture*. Cambridge, Mass.: The MIT Press, 2001.
Cumings, Bruce. "The Legacy of Japanese Colonialism in Korea." In *The Japanese Colonial Empire, 1895–1945*, ed. Ramon H. Myers and Mark R. Peattie. Princeton, N.J.: Princeton University Press, 1984.
——. "The Origin and Development of the Northeast Asian Political Economy: Industrial Sectors, Product Cycles, and Political Consequences." In *The Political Economy of the New Asian Industrialism*, ed. Frederic C. Deyo. Ithaca, N.Y.: Cornell University Press, 1987.
——. *The Origins of the Korean War*. Vol. 1: *Liberation and the Separation of Regimes, 1945–1947*. Princeton, N.J.: Princeton University Press, 1981.
——. *The Origins of the Korean War*. Vol. 2: *The Roaring of the Cataract, 1947–1950*. Princeton, N.J.: Princeton University Press, 1990.
——. "Webs with No Spiders, Spiders with No Webs: The Genealogy of the Developmental State." In *The Developmental State*, ed. Meredith Woo-Cumings. Ithaca, N.Y.: Cornell University Press, 1999.
Derrida, Jacques. *Monolingualism of the Other; or, The Prosthesis of Origin*. Trans. Patrick Mensah. Stanford, Calif.: Stanford University Press, 1998.
——. *Of Grammatology*. Corrected ed. Baltimore, Md.: The Johns Hopkins University Press, 1998.
——. *On Touching—Jean-Luc Nancy*. Stanford, Calif.: Stanford University Press, 2005.
——. *Positions*. Chicago: University of Chicago Press, 1981.
——. *Specters of Marx: The State of the Debt, the Work of Mourning, and the New International*. New York: Routledge, 1994.
Doane, Mary Anne. *The Emergence of Cinematic Time: Modernity, Contingency, the Archive*. Cambridge, Mass.: Harvard University Press, 2002.
——. "The Close-Up: Scale and Detail in the Cinema." *differences* 14, no. 5 (2005).
Duara, Prasenjit. *Sovereignty and Authenticity: Manchukuo and the East Asian Modern*. Lanham, Md.: Rowman and Littlefield, 2003.
Duncan, John. "Proto-nationalism in Premodern Korea." In *Perspectives on Korea*, ed. Sang-oak Lee and Duk-soo Park. Sydney: Wild Peony, 1998.
Eckert, Carter J. *Offspring of Empire: The Koch'ang Kims and the Colonial Origins of Korean Capitalism, 1876–1945*. Seattle: University of Washington Press, 1991.
Em, Henry. "'Overcoming' Korea's Division: Narrative Strategies in Recent South Korean Historiography." *positions* 1, no. 2 (Fall 1993): 450–485.
Engelhardt, Tom. *The End of Victory Culture: Cold War America and the Disillusioning of a Generation*. Amherst: University of Massachusetts Press, 1995.
Escobar, Arturo. *Encountering Development: The Making and Unmaking of the Third World*. Princeton, N.J.: Princeton University Press, 1995.

Foucault, Michel. *Discipline and Punish.* Trans. Alan Sheridan. New York: Vintage Books, 1979.
———. *The History of Sexuality.* Vol. 1: *An Introduction.* Trans. Robert Hurley. London: Allen Lane, 1979.
———. *"Society Must Be Defended": Lectures at the Collège de France, 1975–1976.* New York: Picador, 2003.
Fujitani, Takashi. "Go for Broke, the Movie: Japanese American Soldiers in U.S. National, Military, and Racial Discourses." In *Perilous Memories: The Asia-Pacific War(s),* ed. T. Fujitani, Geoffrey M. White, and Lisa Yoneyama. Durham, N.C.: Duke University Press, 2001.
———. "Right to Kill, Right to Make Live: Koreans as Japanese and Japanese as Koreans in WWII." *Representations* (Summer 2007): 13–39.
Fulton Bruce. "*Kijich'on* Fiction." In *Nationalism and the Construction of Korean Identity,* ed. Hyung Il Pai and Timothy R. Tangherlini, 13–32. Los Angeles: University of California Center for Korean Studies, 1998.
Fuss, Diana. *Identification Papers.* London: Routledge, 1995.
Gallop, Jane. *The Daughter's Seduction: Feminism and Psychoanalysis.* Ithaca, N.Y.: Cornell University Press, 1982.
———. *Reading Lacan.* Ithaca, N.Y.: Cornell University Press, 1985.
Garner, Shirley Nelson, Claire Kahane, and Madelon Sprengnether, eds. *The (M)other Tongue: Essays in Feminist Psychoanalytic Interpretation.* Ithaca, N.Y.: Cornell University Press, 1985.
Gupta, Akhil, and James Ferguson. "Culture, Power, Place: Ethnography at the End of an Era." In *Culture, Power, Place: Explorations in Critical Anthropology,* ed. Akhil Gupta and James Ferguson. Durham, N.C.: Duke University Press, 1997.
Habermas, Jurgen. *The Structural Transformation of the Public Sphere: An Inquiry Into a Category of Bourgeois Society.* Trans. Thomas Burger with the assistance of Frederick Lawrence. Cambridge, Mass.: The MIT Press, 1989.
Hanscom, Christopher. "A Question of Representation: Korean Modernist Fiction of the 1930s." Ph.D. diss., University of California–Los Angeles, 2006.
Harootunian, Harry. *Overcome by Modernity: History, Culture, and Community in Interwar Japan.* Princeton, N.J.: Princeton University Press, 2000.
Harrington, Lewis. "Miki Kiyoshi and the Shōwa Kenkyōkai: The Failure of World History." *positions: east asia cultures critique* 17, no. 1 (Spring 2009): 43–72.
Hart-Landsberg, Martin. *The Rush to Development: Economic Change and Political Struggle in South Korea.* New York: Monthly Review Press, 1993.
Hayles, N. Katherine. *How We Became Posthuman: Virtual Bodies in Cybernetics, Literature, and Informatics.* Chicago: University of Chicago Press, 1999.
Higgins, Lynn A., and Brenda R. Silver, eds. *Rape and Representation.* New York: Columbia University Press, 1991.
Hirsch, Marianne. *The Mother/Daughter Plot: Narrative, Psychoanalysis, Feminism.* Bloomington: Indiana University Press, 1989.

Jameson, Fredric. "Third-World Literature in the Era of Multinational Capital." *Social Text* 15 (Fall 1986): 65–88.

Janelli, Roger, with Dawnhee Yim. *Making Capitalism: The Social and Cultural Construction of a South Korean Conglomerate*. Stanford, Calif.: Stanford University Press, 1993.

Jeong, Kelly Y. *Crisis of Gender and the Nation in Korean Literature and Cinema: Modernity Arrives Again*. Lanham, Md.: Lexington, 2011.

Kang, Nae-hui, "The Ending -da and Linguistic Modernity in Korea." In *Traces: A Multilingual Series of Cultural Theory and Translation*, vol. 3. Hong Kong: Hong Kong University Press, 2004.

Kendall, Laurel, ed. *Under Construction: The Gendering of Modernity, Class, and Consumption in the Republic of Korea*. Honolulu: University of Hawai'i Press, 2001.

Kim, Chong-un, and Bruce Fulton eds. *A Ready-Made Life: Early Masters of Modern Korean Fiction*. Honolulu: University of Hawai'i Press, 1999.

Kim, Chung-Kang. "South Korean Golden-Age Comedy Film: Industry, Genre, and Popular Culture (1953–1970)." Ph.D. diss., University of Illinois, Urbana-Champaign, 2010.

Kim, Eun Mee. *Big Business, Strong State: Collusion and Conflict in South Korean Development, 1960–1990*. Albany: State University of New York Press, 1997.

Kim, John Namjun. "The Temporality of Empire: The Imperial Cosmopolitanism of Miki Kiyoshi and Tanabe Hajime." In *Pan-Asianism in Modern Japanese History: Colonialism, Regionalism, and Borders*, ed. Sven Saaler and J. Victor Koschmann, 151–167. New York: Routledge, 2007.

———. "On the Brink of Universality: German Cosmopolitanism in Japanese Imperialism." *positions: east asia cultures critique* 17, no. 1 (Spring 2009): 73–95.

Kim, Kyung Hyun. *The Remasculinization of Korean Cinema*. Durham, N.C.: Duke University Press, 2004.

Kim, Suk-Young. *Illusive Utopia: Theater, Film, and Everyday Performance in North Korea*. Ann Arbor: University of Michigan Press, 2010.

Kimoto, Takeshi. "Antinomies of Total War." *positions: east asia cultures critique* 17, no. 1 (Spring 2009): 97–125.

King, Ross. "Western Missionaries and the Origins of Korean Language Modernization." *Journal of International and Area Studies* 11, no. 3: 7–38.

Kittler, Friedrich A. *Gramophone, Film, Typewriter*. Trans. Geoffrey Winthrop-Young and Michael Wutz. Stanford, Calif.: Stanford University Press, 1999.

Kōjin, Karatani. *Origins of Modern Japanese Literature*. Ed. Brett de Bary. Durham, N.C.: Duke University Press, 1993.

Kwon, Nayoung Aimee. "Translated Encounters and Empire: Colonial Korea and the Literature of Exile." Ph.D. diss., University of California–Los Angeles, 2007.

LaCapra, Dominick. *History and Criticism*. Ithaca, N.Y.: Cornell University Press, 1985.

———. *A Preface to Sartre*. Ithaca, N.Y.: Cornell University Press, 1978.

———. *Rethinking Intellectual History: Texts, Contexts, Language*. Ithaca, N.Y.: Cornell University Press, 1983.

———. *Writing History, Writing Trauma*. Parallax: Re-visions of Culture and Society. Baltimore, Md.: Johns Hopkins University Press, 2000.
Laclau, Ernesto. *Emancipation(s)*. London: Verso, 1996.
Lai, Ming-yan. *Nativism and Modernity: Cultural Contestations in China and Taiwan Under Global Capitalism*. Albany, N.Y.: SUNY Press, 2008.
Lederer, William J., and Eugene Burdick. *The Ugly American*. New York: Norton, 1958.
Lee, Ann Sung-Hi. *Yi Kwang-su and Modern Korean Literature: Mujŏng*. Ithaca, N.Y.: Cornell East Asia Series, 2005.
Lee, Ji-Eun. "A New Pedigree: Women and Women's Reading in Korea, 1896–1934." Ph.D. diss., Harvard University, 2006.
Lee, Jin-kyung. *Service Economies: Militarism, Sex Work, and Migrant Labor in South Korea*. Minneapolis: University of Minnesota Press, 2010.
Lee, Namhee. *The Making of Minjung: Democracy and the Politics of Representation in South Korea*. Ithaca, N.Y.: Cornell University Press, 2009.
Lie, John. *Han Unbound: The Political Economy of South Korea*. Stanford, Calif.: Stanford University Press, 1998.
Lippit, Akira. *Electric Animal: Toward a Rhetoric of Wildlife*. Minneapolis: University of Minnesota Press, 2008.
Lippit, Seiji. *Topographies of Japanese Modernism*. New York: Columbia University Press, 2002.
Liu, Lydia. "The Question of Meaning-Value in the Political Economy of the Sign." In *Tokens of Exchange: The Problem of Translation in Global Circulations*, ed. Lydia Liu. Durham, N.C.: Duke University Press, 1999.
———. *Translingual Practice: Literature, National Culture, and Translated Modernity-China, 1900–1937*. Stanford, Calif.: Stanford University Press, 1995.
Lowe, Lisa, and David Lloyd, eds. *The Politics of Culture in the Shadow of Capital*. Durham, N.C.: Duke University Press, 1997.
Lutz, Catherine. "Epistemology of the Bunker: The Brainwashed and Other New Subjects of the Permanent War." In *Inventing the Psychological: Toward a Cultural History of Emotional Life in America*, ed. Joel Pfister and Nancy Schmog. New Haven, Conn.: Yale University Press, 1997.
Mbembe, Achille. "Necropolitics." *Public Culture* 15, no. 3 (2003).
McClintock, Anne. *Imperial Leather: Race, Gender and Sexuality in the Colonial Contest*. New York: Routledge, 1995.
McHugh, Kathleen. "South Korean Film Melodrama: State, Nation, Woman, and the Transnational Familiar." In *South Korea Golden Age Melodrama: Gender, Genre, and National Cinema*, ed. Kathleen McHugh and Nancy Abelmann. Detroit, Mich.: Wayne State University Press, 2005.
Meyerowitz, Joanne. "Sex, Gender, and the Cold War Language of Reform." In *Rethinking Cold War Culture*, ed. Peter Kuznick and James Gilbert. Washington, D.C.: Smithsonian Institution Press, 2001.

Mitchell, Timothy. *Questions of Modernity.* Minneapolis: University of Minnesota Press, 2000.
Mitchell, W. J. T. *Iconology: Image, Text, Ideology.* Chicago: University of Chicago Press, 1987.
———. *Picture Theory: Essays on Verbal and Visual Representation.* Chicago: University of Chicago Press, 1994.
Moon, Katharine H. S. "Prostitute Bodies and Gendered States in U.S.-Korea Relations." In *Dangerous Women: Gender and Korean Nationalism*, ed. Elaine H. Kim and Chungmoo Choi. New York: Routledge, 1998.
———. *Sex Among Allies.* New York: Columbia University Press, 2007.
Moon, Seungsook. *Militarized Modernity and Gendered Citizenship in South Korea.* Durham, N.C.: Duke University Press, 2005.
Mulvey, Laura. *Death 24x a Second: Stillness and the Moving Image.* London: Reaktion, 2006.
Pae, Hyung Il. *Constructing "Korean" Origins: A Critical Review of Archaeology, Historiography, and Racial Myth in Korean State-Formation Theories.* Cambridge, Mass.: Harvard University Press, 2000.
Paik, Nak-chung. "The Idea of a Korean National Literature, Then and Now." *positions* 1, no. 3 (Winter 1993): 553–580.
Palumbo-Liu, David. *Asian/American: Historical Crossings of a Racial Frontier.* Stanford, Calif.: Stanford University Press, 1999.
Park, Chung Hee. *Our Nation's Path: Ideology of Social Reconstruction.* Seoul: Tong-a, 1962.
Park, Hyun Ok. *Two Dreams in One Bed: Empire, Social Life, and the Origins of the North Korean Revolution in Manchuria.* Durham, N.C.: Duke University Press, 2005.
Park, Sunyoung. "The Colonial Origin of Korean Realism and Its Contemporary Manifestation." *positions: east asia cultures critique* 14, no. 1 (2006): 165–192.
Perry, Samuel. "Aesthetics for Justice: Proletarian Writing in Japan and Colonial Korea." Ph.D. diss., University of Chicago, 2007.
Pincus, Leslie. *Authenticating Culture in Imperial Japan: Kuki Shuzo and the Rise of National Aesthetics.* Berkeley: University of California Press, 1996.
Poole, Janet. "Colonial Interiors: Modernist Fiction of Korea." Ph.D. diss., Columbia University, 2004.
Poole, Janet, trans. *Eastern Sentiments.* New York: Columbia University Press, 2009.
Radhakrishnan, R. "Nationalism, Gender, and the Narrative of Identity." In *Nationalisms and Sexualities*, ed. Andrew Parker, Mary Russo, Doris Sommer, and Patricia Yeager. New York: Routledge, 1992.
Rancière, Jacques. *The Politics of Aesthetics.* London: Continuum, 2006.
Robinson, Michael. *Cultural Nationalism in Colonial Korea, 1920–1925.* Seattle: University of Washington Press, 1989.
Rousseau, Jean-Jacques. *The Social Contract and Discourses.* New York: Dutton, 1973.
Ryu, Youngju. "The Neighbor and the Politics of Literature in 1970s' South Korea: Yi Mungu, Hwang Sŏgyŏng, Cho Sehŭi." Ph.D. diss., University of California–Los Angeles, 2006.

Said, Edward. *Orientalism*. New York: Vintage, 1979.
Sakai, Naoki. "Imperial Nationalism and the Comparative Perspective." *positions: east asia cultures critique* 17, no. 1 (Spring 2009): 159–205.
———. *Translation and Subjectivity: On "Japan" and Cultural Nationalism*. Minneapolis: University of Minnesota Press, 1997.
Sartre, Jean-Paul. *Nausea*. Trans. Lloyd Alexander. New York: New Directions, 1964.
———. *"What Is Literature?" and Other Essays*. Cambridge, Mass.: Harvard University Press, 1988.
Schmid, Andre. *Korea Between Empires, 1895–1919*. New York: Columbia University Press, 2002.
Scott, Catherine V. *Gender and Development: Rethinking Modernization and Dependency Theory*. Boulder, Colo.: Lynne Rienner, 1995.
Sharpe, Jenny. *Allegories of Empire*. Minneapolis: University of Minnesota Press, 1993.
Shin, Gi-Wook. "Agrarianism: A Critique of Colonial Modernity in Korea." *Comparative Studies in Society and History* (October 1999): 784–804.
———. "Nation, History, and Politics." In *Nationalism and the Construction of Korean Identity*, ed. Hyung Il Pai and Timothy R. Tangherlini. Berkeley: Institute of East Asian Studies, 1998.
———. *Peasant Protest and Social Change in Colonial Korea*. Seattle: University of Washington Press, 1996.
Shin, Gi-Wook, James Freda, and Gihong Yi. "The Politics of Ethnic Nationalism in Divided Korea." *Nations and Nationalism* 5 (Winter 1999): 465–484.
Silverberg, Miriam. "Remembering Pearl Harbor, Forgetting Charlie Chaplin, and the Case of the Disappearing Western Woman: A Picture Story." *positions* 1, no. 1 (Spring 1993): 24–76.
Silverman, Kaja. *The Threshold of the Visible World*. London: Routledge, 1995.
———. *World Spectators*. Stanford, Calif.: Stanford University Press, 2000.
Slotkin, Richard. "Buffalo Bill's 'Wild West' and the Mythologization of the American Empire." In *Cultures of American Imperialism*, ed. Amy Kaplan and Donald E. Pease. Durham, N.C.: Duke University Press, 1993.
Soja, Edward W. *Postmodern Geographies: The Reassertion of Space in Critical Social Theory*. London: Verso, 1989.
Sorensen, Clark. "National Identity and the Construction of the Category 'Peasant' in Colonial Korea." In *Colonial Modernity in Korea*, ed. Gi-Wook Shin and Michael Robinson. Cambridge, Mass.: Harvard University Asia Center, 1999.
Spivak, Gayatri. *The Postcolonial Critic: Interviews, Strategies, Dialogues*. New York: Routledge, 1990.
Suh, Serk-Bae. "Treacherous Translation: The 1938 Japanese-Language Theatrical Version of the Korean Tale Ch'unhyangjŏn." *positions: east asia cultures critique* 18, no. 1 (2010): 171–197.
Suzuki, Tomi. *Narrating the Self: Fictions of Japanese Modernity*. Stanford, Calif.: Stanford University Press, 1996.

Tanaka, Stefan. *Japan's Orient: Rendering Pasts into History.* Berkeley: University of California Press, 1993.

Tansman, Alan. *The Aesthetics of Japanese Fascism.* Berkeley: University of California Press, 2009.

Time Magazine. "Hope in the Hermit Kingdom." *Time* (March 10, 1967).

Uchida, Jun. "'Brokers of Empire:' Japanese Settler Colonialism in Korea, 1910–1937." Ph.D. diss., Harvard University, 2005.

Virilio, Paul. *War and Cinema: The Logistics of Perception.* London: Verso, 2009.

Weber, Samuel. *Targets of Opportunity: On the Militarization of Thinking.* New York: Fordham University Press, 2005.

Wells, Kenneth M., ed. *South Korea's Minjung Movement: The Culture and Politics of Dissidence.* Honolulu: University of Hawaii Press, 1995.

Williams, Raymond. *The Country and the City.* Oxford: Oxford University Press, 1973.

Woo, Jung-en. *Race to the Swift: State and Finance in Korean Industrialization.* New York: Columbia University Press, 1991.

Yecies, Brian. "Systematization of Film Censorship in Colonial Korea: Profiteering from Hollywood's First Golden Age, 1926–1936." *Journal of Korean Studies* 10, no. 1 (Fall 2005): 59–83.

Yi Hyo-sŏk. "When the Buckwheat Blooms." In *A Ready-Made Life: Early Masters of Modern Korean Fiction,* trans. Kim Chong-un and Bruce Fulton. Honolulu: University of Hawai'i Press, 1999.

Žižek, Slavoj. *The Sublime Object of Ideology.* London: Verso, 1989.

FILMOGRAPHY

An Sŏk-yŏng. *The Volunteer* [Chiwŏnbyŏng]. 1940.
Ch'oe In-gyu. *Hurrah for Freedom!* [Chayu manse]. 1946.
Englund, George. *The Ugly American.* 1963.
Han Hyŏng-mo. *Female Executive* [Yŏsajang]. 1959.
Han Hyŏng-mo. *Hand of Fate* [Unmyŏng ŭi son]. 1954.
Han Hyŏng-mo. *Madame Freedom* [Chayu puin]. 1954.
Hitchcock, Alfred. *Rear Window.* 1954.
Kim Ki-dŏk. *Yongary, Monster from the Deep* [Taegwoesu yonggari]. 1967.
Pak Ki-ch'ae. *The Straits of Chosŏn.* 1943.
Sŏ Kwang-je. *Military Train* [Kunyongyŏlch'a]. 1938.
Yi Kang-ch'ŏn. *P'iagol.* 1955.
Yi Pyŏng-il. *Springtime on the Peninsula* [Pando ŭi pom]. 1941.

INDEX

action (*haengdong*), 141
Agamben, Giorgio, 51, 136–37, 166, 207
aid, U.S., 86–90
anarchism, 23, 73, 217n58
An Hoe-nam, 72
An Ho-sang, 104, 226n38
An Sŏg-yŏng, 39, 217n59. *See also* Volunteer, The; Wheel of Fire
An Sŏk-chu, 24
anticolonial resistance, 13, 117–19
antique shops, 85, 221n24
antistatism, 104–6, 153
April 19 movement, 138, 232n29, 233n34, 233n35, 234n48, 241n30
"Arirang," 162
Armstrong, Nancy, 5–6, 7, 82–83
art, 214n34; aesthetic socialism and labor for sake of, 71–77; fetishizing of, 221n24; with sorrow and melancholy, 215n38; transvisual with nativist, 34–38; two categories of, 35; universal/particular with, 186–90. *See also hyangt'o*
art, modern (*misul*), 34; *The Heartless* and influence of, 6
art critics, 36
artists, proletarian, reemergence of, 9

assimilation (*dōka*), 243n70
Atelier, 187
August 15, 1945 (Kim Nam-ch'ŏn), 68–69, 87

Back from the U.S.S.R. (Gide), 76
Baek Moon Im, 58
Bakhtin, M. M., 177–78, 241n38
Balibar, Etienne, 133, 201
Balzac, Honoré de, 99
Bank of Chosŏn, 24
bans, 19, 145; on KAPF, 12, 62, 66; on North Korean writers, 12, 62, 64, 68. *See also* censorship
Barbusse, Henri, 27
Baudrillard, Jean, 74, 161
Benjamin, Walter, 45, 52, 241n51
body, 52–54; development of nation, state and, 147–53; energy, 78; Korea and Japan as one, 49–52; male, 209; unruly signifier of dancing, 119–28; woman with fragmented, 48
borders: crossing with "Land of Excrement" incident, 153–64; drawing of, 1–3
brainwashing, 228n65
Brando, Marlon, 132, *134*
Brooks, Peter, 243n65

Buck-Morss, Susan, 241n51
Burdick, Eugene, 132, 133
Butler, Judith, 157

Camus, Albert, 114, 228n62
capitalist urban space, 48–49
cartoons, 24, 26
"Cave Dwellers" (Kim Tong-ni), 77, 89
censorship: as first reader, 213n10; of KAPF, 24, 27; of "Land of Excrement," 236n67; of North Korean culture by South Korea, 19, 24; South Korea's culture influenced by, 19–20; *Springtime on the Peninsula* with, 219n76
Ch'ae Man-sik, 11, 223n43; with Cold War order, 86. See also "National Sinner, The"; "Once Upon a Rice Paddy"; *Peace Under Heaven*
Chakrabarty, Dipesh, 146
Chang, Key Young, 155
Ch'angbi Press, 89
Chang Chun-ha, 238n4
Chang U-sŏng, 187
Chang Yong-hak, 225n12, 227n55
Ch'a Sŭng-gi, 17, 215n36, 218n70
Ching, Leo, 243n70
Cho Chi-hun, 67
Ch'oe Il-su, 99
Ch'oe In-gyu, 59
Ch'oe In-hun, 14–15; history of, 237n1; with translation, 240n19. See also "Gray Club, The"; *Square, The*; *Tempest, The*; *Voice of the Governor-General*
Ch'oe Nam-sŏn, 215n36
Cho Myŏng-hŭi, 39
Chŏng Pi-sok, 13, 94. See also *Madame Freedom*
Chŏng Pong-nae, 104–5
chŏngsin (spirit), 51
Chŏn Kwang-yong, 227n55
Chosŏn Art Exhibition (*Sŏnjŏn*), 21, 24, 27, 36–37, 221n27

Chosŏn Federation of Cultural Organizations, 66
Chŏson Film Law, 219n76
Chosŏnness, 36, 39, 218n70
Chosŏn Proletarian Literature Alliance (CPLA), 66
Cho Tŏk-haeng, 232n29
Chow, Rey, 4, 36
Cho Yŏn-hyŏn, 67
chuché, 225n21
Chun Doo Hwan, 232n28
Chunhyang (film), 57
cinema, Godard's definition of, 52
Clarté movement, 27
close ups, 218n68; imperial, 56–60; in *Wheel of Fire*, 40
coercive mimeticism, 36
Cold War, 60, 206, 228n65; colonial/postcolonial and order in early, 8–12; developmentalism in, 81–86; traditionalism in South Korea, 101–4; U.S. aid and economy of, 86–90; visual order on display, 114–17
collaboration: confessionals, 10; return to translation with Pan-Asianism and, 165–203
coloniality, 1, 11, 15, 222n42
colonial modern: with literary and visual culture, 3–8; with *The Square*, 14–16; with visuality, 19–60; world-as-picture and influence on, 4–5
colonial other (*sŏn*), 51–52
colonial/postcolonial: double with, 175–79; double with *Kubo*, 182–86; with early Cold War order, 8–12
colonial present, 14–17
communication, development as know-how and, 131–35
communism: anti-, 91–128; eradicate, 3; overcoming, 129–64. See also "Land of Excrement"
confessionals, 10, 243n65

consciousness: creative, 103; move from feeling to, 28–29, 33; stream of, 44; visuality with, 216n43

"Content and Expression" (Kim Ki-jin), 42

coup d'état, 14, 136, 140, 141, 172. *See also* Park Chung Hee

Course in General Linguistics (Saussure), 48, 173

CPLA. *See* Chosŏn Proletarian Literature Alliance

Crary, Jonathan, 44, 135, 216n50, 218n67

creative consciousness, 103

critics: art, 36; on dearth of full-length novels, 229n76; KAPF, 213n11, 221n25

"Cultural Metamorphosis" (Kim Nam-jung), 230n93

culture: colonial modern with literary and visual, 3–8; disavowals with shifts in, 1–2; of mobilization, 49–52; nativism, modernism and mobilization with proletarian, 19–60; race and link to, 234n42. *See also* wartime mobilization culture

culture, North Korea, censorship by South Korea of, 19, 24

culture, proletarian, 1; nativism, modernism and mobilization with, 19–60

culture, South Korea, censorship's influence on, 19–20, 24

Cumings, Bruce, 136

dancing body, unruly signifier of, 119–28

Dante, 99

Darwin, Charles, 45

Dawn Wind (Yŏm Sang-sŏp), 68, 222n33; ethnonation under occupation in, 81–86

Day in Fall, A, 37

Day in the Life of Kubo the Novelist, A (Pak T'ae-wŏn): colonial/postcolonial double of, 182–86; comma use in, 45–46, 216n53; gaze in, 47; as *hyangt'o* stills in motion in colonial urban space, 8; illustrations by Yi Sang, 46, 47, 48, 49; mapping of space in, 44; modernism in, 41–46; numbers in, 216n55

debates: film and novel with literature, 26–34; form/content relation, 20; popular culture, 20; popular literature, 26–29, 33–34; proletarian art, 20

Debord, Guy, 135

demilitarized zone. *See* DMZ

Derrida, Jacques, 202, 222n42

Descendants of Cain (Hwang Sun-wŏn), 76, 86

despair, politics of, 110–14

development: border crossing with, 153–64; as communication and know-how, 131–35; as devolution, 141–47; with nonalignment in 1950s and 1960s, 12–14; as revolution, 135–41; of state, nation, body, 147–53

devolution, development as, 141–47

dialectical realism, 28–29

disavowals, 1–2, 203

disidentification, with biopolitics of seeing, 198–203

displacement, of Koreans, 12–13, 21, 24, 91

distribution of the sensible, 2, 10, 40

divided literature, 11, 63

division: of Korean peninsula, 9–10; occupation and liberation with, 60–90

DMZ (demilitarized zone), 59, 91, 92, 95, 102, 160, 207, 212n21

Doane, Mary Anne, 56, 219n73

dromological, 218n71

"Dust" (Yi T'ae-jun), 72, 74–76, 85

Early Winter, 35

economic emancipation, 130

economy, U.S. aid and Cold war, 86–90

education, 24, 83, 143, 150, 234n48

ego, 240n18; *The Square* and, 167–75
ekphrastic hope, 4–5, 118–19
elections, 180, 241n29
Eliot, T. S., 98
emancipation, 68, 139; coloniality with, 222n42; economic, 130; Laclau on, 214n14; of texts in 1988, 62
empire, 175–79
Engelhardt, Tom, 155
English language, 87–88
Englund, George, 14, 132
"Enlightenment of the Dominant Class" (Kim Ki-jin), 27
"eradicate communism" slogan (*myŏlgong*), 3
erasure: of culture with censorship's influence, 3, 19–20; of Japan, 226n25
Escobar, Arturo, 129–30, 150
eternal, race as, 179–82
ethnonation (*minjok*), 23, 142; Koreans became Japan, 190–92; under occupation, 81–86; Park Chung Hee with, 14–15
existentialism, 104–6, 106
expressionism, 217n58

"Factory Newspaper" (Kim Nam-ch'ŏn), 213n11
fascism, 58, 197, 212n3
feelings: communal subject with shared, 223n44; to consciousness, 28–29, 33
Female Executive (film), 158–59; "We young people should fight until we hang our flag on top of Mt. Paektu," 159
feminizing gaze, 222n38
fiction, Victorian, 5–6
Fig (Yŏm Sang-sŏp), 82
filmic adaptation, 119–28
film noir, 95
film-novels (*yŏnghwa sosŏl*): first appearance of, 29–30; KAPF and, 24, 31–32; romantic, 29; verbal/visual relationship in, 8; Yi Chong-myŏng on, 31

films: within film, 50, 57; Hollywood techniques, 224n3; KAPF, 27, 212n2, 214n28; as novels, 26–34; reading film-novels akin to watching, 31; silent, 31–32. *See also* film-novels; *specific films*
"Fire" (An Hoe-nam), 72
form/content relation: debate, 20; importance of, 42–43
Foucault, Michel, 95, 218n67
fragmentation, 48
freedom's frontier, 212n21
Free Literature, 90, 237n1
French literature, modern, 238n3
Freud, Sigmund, 216n54

Gauguin, Paul, 37–38
gaze: feminizing, 222n38; mechanical device as, 4; self, 4, 47
ghosts, 203, 241n30. *See also* hauntings, postcolonial
Gide, Andre, 76
"Globalization of the Clarté Movement" (Kim Ki-jin), 27
Godard, Jean-Luc, 52
Goethe, Johann Wolfgang von, 99
Government-General, as censorship apparatus, 24, 27, 175–76
"Gray Club, The" (Ch'oe In-hun), 237n1
Greater East Asia Co-Prosperity Sphere (*kungmin munhak*), 60, 77, 191, 220n5
Greene, Graham, 132
Group of Nine (*kuinhoe*), 31, 41–42, 65, 217n58

Haebang Munhak sŏnjip, 223n46
Halifax (Lord), 17
Hand of Fate, The (film), 95, 96, 97, 120
Han'guk munhak (South Korean literature), 9; early colonial-period history linked to, 11
han'gŭl, 122, 229n87
Han Hyŏng-mo, 95

Hart-Landsberg, Martin, 241n29
hauntings, postcolonial, 175–79
HCCL. *See* Headquarters for the Construction of Chosŏn Literature
Headquarters for the Construction of Chosŏn Literature (HCCL), 66
Heartless, The (Mujŏng) (Yi Kwang-su), 3; modern art and influence on, 6; motion pictures and influence on, 6; newspaper serialization of, 27; technologized visuality in, 4, 6
Heidegger, Martin, 4–5, 56
Hirsch, Marianne, 236n58
historical rupture, 11
history, world. *See* world history
"History of the Storm" (An Hoe-nam), 72
Hitchcock, Alfred, 115
Hollywood, 161; desiring, 234n47; film techniques, 224n3
home: soil's link to, 34–38, 49; as timeless, 49
Homeless Angels (Ch'oe In-gyu), 59
homo economicus, 74
homo-hegemonic, 222n42
homosocial intimacy, 218n72
humanity, 235n49, 236n61
humans, machines and relationship to, 218n72
Hurrah for Freedom! (film), 243n67; Korean flag transformed from Japanese flag, *194*
hwaldongsajin moyangŭro (like a motion picture), self gaze as, 4
Hwang Jongyon, 17, 217n65
Hwang Sun-wŏn, 65, 76, 77, 78, 86
hyangt'o (nativist art), 215n41; art critics on, 36; in *Kubo*, 8; modernism with, 41–46, 221n27; space and link to, 34–38; in *Stream Scenes*, 21; as transvisual, 34–38
Hyangt'o Association, 34
hyangt'o (nativist) painting, 8

hypericonicity, 37, 38, 50
hypothetical equivalence, 6–7
hysteria, 216n54

"Idea of a National Literature, The" (Paik Nak-chung), 16
ideology (*sasang*), 77
illustrations: picturing streams and Yi Sang's, 46–49; text's link to, 32; as visual intertitles, 31–32; Yi Sang's coins, *47*
ilminjuŭi, 104, 226n38
ilsŏndongjo (Japan and Chosŏn share a common ancestry), 50
Im Chin-yŏng, 141
Im Chong-guk, 192
Im Hwa, 8, 16, 19, 73, 98, 213n11; on film-novels, 30; form dismissed by, 42; KAPF criticized by, 221n25; Kim Ki-jin as adversary of, 26, 29; on question of imitation, 225n12
imitation, 225n12
immortal, kokutai as, 179–82
imperialism, 217n65; close up of, 56–60; Japan and Korea as one body under, 49–52; time, 47; visuality and kinetics of, 52–56
imperialization (*hwangminhwa*), 49, 218n67, 243n70
imperial subjects literature (*kungmin munhak*), 24, 48
I-novel, 127, 226n29
inside (*nae*), 51–52, 80
invisibility: with North Korea, 77–81; state's visibility and, 60–90

James, William, 44
Japan: erasure of, 226n25; fascism in, 58, 212n3; with Korea as one body, 49–52; treaty with South Korea, 175; United States as colonial power replacing, 221n24

Japanese, 87; Koreans as never, 192–98; Koreans became, 190–92
Japanese Americans, internment of, 217n60
Jeong, Kelly Y., 237n82
Joyce, James, 44

Kabo Peasants' War, 139
Kafka, Franz, 225n12
Kang, Kyŏng-ae. *See* "Salt"; "Underground Village"
Kang Man-gil, 138–39, 140
Kang Nae-hui, 229n87
Kang Sin-jae, 227n55
KAPF. *See* Korea Artists Proletarian Federation
Karatani Kōjin, 34, 215n35
Kawabata, Yasunari, 176
KBS-TV, 240n8
Kelly, Grace, 115
Kierkegaard, Søren, 225n12
Kim, John Namjun, 200
Kim Chong-hun, 228n62
Kim Chul, 17, 211n4, 219n79, 223n47
Kim Chu-yŏl, 241n30
Kim Hwan-gi, 223n46
Kim Il Sung, 176
Kim Ki-dŏk, 161
Kim Ki-jin, 8, 24, 213n9; on form's importance, 42–43; as Im Hwa's adversary, 26, 29; with popular literature debate, 26–29, 33–34; *taejung* people defined by, 28. *See also* "Content and Expression"; "Englightenment of the Dominant Class"; "Globalization of the Clarté Movement"; "On Popular Novels"; "Promenade Sentimental"
Kim Kwan-ho, 211n13
Kim Kyŏng-t'ak, 149
Kim Nam-ch'ŏn, 68–69, 87, 213n11. *See also August 15, 1945*; "Factory Newspaper"
Kim Nam-jung, 230n93

Kim Pok-chin, 19, 73
Kim Sŏng-han, 225n12, 227n55
Kim Tong-ni, 65, 67, 77, 127, 215n41. *See also* "Cave Dwellers"
Kim U-jong, 117–18
Kim Yang-su, 100
Kim Ye-rim, 17, 77
Kim Yŏng-jun, 19, 217n58
Kim Yŏng-sŏk. *See* "Trolley Driver"
Kim Yun-sik, 61, 111, 222n34
Kim Yu-yŏng, 31, 39, 41; with Group of Nine, 42. *See also Wheel of Fire*
Kittler, Friedrich, 3, 46, 216n54, 218n71; on postwar, 218n72; on typewriter, 230n91
know-how, 131–35
kokutai, 179–82
Korea: division of, 9–10; with Japan as one body, 49–52. *See also* North Korea; South Korea
Korea Artists Proletarian Federation (KAPF), 213n9; ban lifted on, 12, 62, 66; censorship of, 24; as center of emerging cultural sphere in 1920s, 20; critics of, 213n11, 221n25; disbanding of, 49, 220n5; films, 27, 212n2, 214n28; Im Hwa's critique of, 221n25; Korea Artista Proleta Federatio and, 19, 121; as leftist, 22, 24–25; members evacuated to north, 19; modernism's close relation to, 42; with popular literature debate, 26–34; social reality of *minjung* influenced by, 7; verbal/visual relationship in works by, 8, 24–26; writers, 26. *See also* film-novels (*yŏnghwa sosŏl*)
Koreans: became Japanese, 190–92; displacement of, 12–13; as never Japanese, 192–98
Korean War, 13, 90, 92, 228n65
Kubo. *See Day in the Life of Kubo the Novelist, A*
kungmin chŏngsin ch'ongdongwŏn (total spiritual mobilization of the people), 51

Kwon Boduerae, 5, 34, 214n34
Kwŏn Yŏng-min, 61, 224n7
Kyŏngsŏng Station, 24

labor, for art's sake, 71–77
LaCapra, Dominick, 94
Laclau, Ernesto, 26, 171, 214n14
"Land of Excrement" (Nam Chŏng-hyŏn), 141, 234n38; with 9/11, 237n85; border crossing with, 153–64; censorship of, 236n67; state, nation and body in, 147–49
land reform, 223n44
landscape: nationalizing of, 220n13; sexuality and becoming, 39
language: ekphrastic hope with, 4; English, 87–88; filmic adaptation and erotics of, 119–28; Japanese, 87; as medium for literature, 42; national, 94, 120; our, 122; of power from Japanese to English, 87
Lederer, William, 132, 133
Lee, Ann Sung-Hi, 211n12
Lee, Jin-kyung, 236n75
leftists, 22, 24–25, 220n6; removal from South Korean literary scene, 225n21. *See also* Korea Artists Proletarian Federation
Lerner, David, 130
"Letter to Father" (Nam Chŏng-hyŏn), 156; state, nation and body in, 147–53
Liberal Party, 226n38, 232n29
liberation (*haebang*), 12, 60–90
"Liberation: Before and After" (Yi T'ae-jun), 89
liberation space (*haebangkonggan*), 65, 74–75; of 1945 through 1948, 9–11; proletarian subject in history and, 65–71
Lie, John, 110
Lim Ok-sang, *208*, 209
literacy, 27–28, 29

Literary Arts, 90
literary culture, 3–8
literary journals, 90
literary nativism: nativist art and relationship with, 21; painterly text with, 38–41; *Wheel of Fire* and, 39–41; with "When the Buckwheat Blooms," 8, 38–39
literature: divided, 11, 63; film and novel with popular debate of, 26–34; imperial subjects, 24, 48; language as medium for, 42; modern French, 238n3; mothers linked to otherness in, 236n58; motion pictures and influence on, 6–7; national literature as South Korean, 94–101; pure, 61, 77; realism and photography's influence on, 5–6, 7; South Korean, 9, 11; verbal/visual relationship's influence on, 2–3, 24–26
Liu, Lydia, 6–7, 37
Love and Crime (Yŏm Sang-sŏp), 45

machines, 49; anthropological, 51; humans and relationship to, 218n72
Madame Freedom (*Chayu puin*) (Chŏng Pi-sok), 13, 94, 119–28
Madame Freedom (film), 158–59; body as unruly signifier in, 119–28; mambo scene, *123*; Professor Change teaches Korean grammar in, *125*
male body, 209
"Manjo" ("High Tide") (Yi Ho-ch'ŏl), 223n44
mapping: of space in *Kubo*, 44; of space in *Wandering*, 32–33, 34
March First independence movement, 20, 22–23, 39
Maruyama Masao, 102, 226n29
Marxism, 29, 74, 202, 243n79
May 1960s roundtable, 232n29, 233n35
Mbembe, Achille, 202
McClintock, Anne, 158, 237n81
melancholy, 58, 215n38

metapicture, 37
Miki, Kiyoshi, 200
militarization, 218n71
Military Train (Sŏo Kwang-je): homosocial intimacy in, 218n72; motion in, 54–56; wartime mobilization culture in, 8, 22, 50
Millard, D. R., 231n6
Ming-yan Lai, 49, 78, 214n32
minjung. *See* people
Min Sŏk-hong, 233n34
Mitchell, Timothy, 160–61; on endless set-up of realities, 7; on world-as-picture with colonial modern, 4–5
Mitchell, W. J. T.: on ekphrastic hope, 4; on metapicture and hypericonic, 37; on writing, 215n37
mobilization (*ch'ongdongwŏn*): culture of, 49–52; proletarian culture, nativism and modernism with, 19–60
modern art. *See* art, modern
modernism, 1; fragmentation and, 48; with *hyangt'o*, 41–46, 221n27; KAPF's close relation to, 42; proletarian culture, nativism and mobilization with, 19–60; as urban forms of painting/writing, 8, 21; U.S. with, 235n50. *See also* art, modern
Modern Literature, 90
mothers, with otherness, 115, 236n58
motion: dromological with militarization and, 218n71; with imperial subject, 49–52; language of power with, 87; in *Military Train*, 54–56; space with, 34–38; in *Springtime on the Peninsula*, 55; transformability based on, 231n14
motion pictures: *The Heartless* and influence of, 6; literature and influence of, 6–7
mountains and streams (*sansu*), 34
movements: April 19, 138, 232n29, 233n34, 233n35, 234n48, 241n30; Clarté, 27; March First independence, 20, 22–23,

39; National Literature, 16; People's, 16; proletkult, 7; in *The Volunteer*, 52–54
Mulvey, Laura, 52

naesŏn ilch'e (Japan and Korea as One Body), 50–51
Na Hye-sŏk, 35
naisen ittai. *See naesŏn ilch'e*
"Naktong River" (Cho Myŏng-hŭi), 39
Nam Chŏng-hyŏn, 14, 141, 234n41; trial of, 154–55, 236n66, 236n68. *See also* "Land of Excrement"; "Letter to Father"
NAPF, 22
narrative, 117–19
nation: development of state, body and, 147–53; interstices of empire and, 175–79
National Assembly, 241n29
nationalism, 214n32
nationalizing, of landscape, 220n13
national language (*kugŏ*), 94, 120
"National Literature as Agrarian Literature" (Paek Ch'ŏl), 98
National Literature Movement (*minjok munhak undong*), 16
National Security Law, 113, 153
"National Sinner, The" (Ch'ae Man-sik), 67
nativism, 1, 214n32; proletarian culture, modernism and mobilization with, 19–60; as urban forms of painting/writing, 8, 21. *See also* literary nativism
nativist art. *See hyangt'o*
nativist paintings, 34–38
nature, 39
Nausea (Sartre), 105, 228n62
Nazis, 99
necrophilia, 106–7
neocology, 234n41
new sensationism (*sin gamgak*), 217n58
newspaper novels, 27. *See also Heartless, The*
Nine Cloud Dream, 28

INDEX 267

nissen dōso. See *ilsŏndongjo*
nonalignment: development in 1950s and 1960s with, 12–14; with necrophilia, 106–7
North Korea: division of south from, 9–10; KAPF cultural producers evacuated to, 19, 223n47; rendered invisible, 77–81; South Korea's censorship of culture from, 19, 24; writers, 12, 19
novels: critics on dearth of full-length, 229n76; films as, 26–34; I-, 127, 226n29; Korea's first modern, 3; newspaper, 27; popular, 28; serializations of full-length, 214n30. See also film-novels; *specific titles*
nudes, 211n13
numbers, 216n55

occupation: Cold War developmentalism and ethnonation under, 81–86; liberation and division with, 60–90
"Once Upon a Rice Paddy" (Ch'ae Man-sik), 86, 89
One-People Principel, 127
"On Popular Novels" (Kim Ki-jin), 28
On Pro-Japanese Literature (Im Chong-guk), 192
Orientalism, 221n24
oriental painting (*tongyanghwa*), 34, 35
Origins of Modern Korean Literature (Kwŏn Podŭrae), 214n34
O'Rourke, Kevin, 239n5
otherness, 51–52, 115, 236n58
Our Nation's Path (Park Chung Hee), 14, 136
O Yŏng-su, 78, 227n55, 230n94

Paek Ch'ŏl, 98–99, 118, 225n12
painterly text: literary nativism with, 38–41; in *Wheel of Fire*, 39–41; in "When the Buckwheat Blooms," 38–39
painters: Japanese settler, 222n38; nativist art as transvisual and, 34–38. See also *specific painters*

painting: modernism and nativism as urban forms of writing and, 8, 21; about painting, 37. See also nativist paintings; oriental painting; Western painting
Pak Ch'an-mo, 11, 71. See also "Village of Dreams"
Pak Nak-chung, 16
Pak T'ae-wŏn, 8, 19, 21, 182–86, 213n10, 223n47; comma use by, 45–46, 216n53; modernism and *hyangt'o* in works of, 41–46. See also *Day in the Life of Kubo the Novelist, A*; *Stream Scenes*
Pak Yŏng-hŭi, 42, 126, 213n9, 217n59
Palumbo-Liu, David, 231n6
Pan-Asianism: reinventing, 101–4; return to translation, collaboration and, 165–203
panopticon, model of, 218n67
Park Chung Hee, 14–15, 128, 131, 136, 137–38, 141, 223n47, 232n28
Parsons, Talcott, 130
particular. See universal/particular
particularism, 224n9
"Parting and Meeting" (Yŏm Sang-sŏp), 80, 85
Peace Under Heaven (Ch'ae Man-sik), 86
PEN Club, 213n9
"peninsula, the" (*pando*), 50
people (*minjung*), 7, 23; awakening and education of, 24; farmers as, 33
people (*taejung*), 7, 23, 25, 28
People's Movement (*minjung undong*), 16
Perry, Samuel, 213n4
Pheng Cheah, 243n79
photography: literature influenced by realism and, 5–6, 7. See also motion pictures
P'iagol (film), 126; Ae-ran returns from mountains, *108*; extended shots of temples in, 242n59
Plato, 225n12
plot: development, 28; *Wandering*, 32–34

politics: of despair, 110–14; of disidentification and seeing, 198–203
popular culture, 20
popularization (*taejunghwa*), 27
popular novels (*taejung sosŏl*), 28
"Portrait of a Shaman" (Kim Tong-ni), 215n41
"Position of the Stairs" (Son Ch'ang-sŏp), 114
postcolonial. *See* colonial/postcolonial
posters, 24
postwar, 218n72
Primitive Passions (Chow), 4
projection, as temporal, 4
proletarian arts (*p'uro yesul*), 20, 22
proletarian culture. *See* culture, proletarian
proletarian subject: imaging of, 22–26; liberation space and return of, 65–71; visuality with, 22–26
proletarian texts. *See* texts, proletarian
proletkult movement, 7
"Promenade Sentimental" (Kim Kijin), 27
punctuation. *See* commas, use of
pure literature (*sunsu munhak*), 61, 77

Questionable Death, A, 208, 210

race: culture's link to, 234n42; as eternal and kokutai as immortal, 179–82
Rancière, Jacques, 2
Rank, Otto, 46
rape, 157–58, 231n11
readers: censorship as first, 213n10; of film-novels, 31, 41
reading: film-novels akin to watching films, 31; new way of, 8, 24, 45, 69; visual act of, 32, 47, 53, 205
realism, 34; dialectical, 28–29; literature influenced by photography and, 5–6; *minjung* and social, 7
reality (*hyŏnsil*), 24, 26, 33
Rear Window (film), 115

resistance (*rejisŭt'angsŭ*), 13, 117–19, 141
"Reunion" (Yŏm Sang-sŏp), 80, 85
revolution, development as, 135–41
Rhee, Syngman, 102, 110, 127, 138, 145, 172, 177, 234n48, 238n1
rightists, 220n6, 223n47
ROK-Japan Normalization Treaty, 175
romantic film-novels (*yŏnae yŏnghwa sosŏl*), 29
Rostow, W. W., 14, 130, 131, 135
roundtable. *See* May 1960s roundtable
Russian Revolution, 22

Saebyŏk, 239n5
Sakai, Naoki, 224n9
"Salt" (Kang, Kyŏng-ae), 217n58
Sartre, Jean-Paul, 105, 228n62, 238n3
Sasanggye, 117, 229n76
Saussure, Ferdinand de, 48, 172–73, 174
Schor, Naomi, 236n58
Scott, Catherine, 130, 140–41
screenplays (*sinario*), 30, 217n59
Scribblers, The (Son Ch'ang-sŏp), 117–19, 229n76
seeing, disidentification and biopolitics of, 198–203
Selected Stories of Liberation Literature, 89
self gaze, 4, 47
serializations, 161, 223n46; of full-length novels, 214n30. *See also Heartless, The*; *Madame Freedom*; *Wandering*; *Wheel of Fire*
settler painters, 222n38
sexuality: with Chosŏnness, 39; narrative of anticolonial resistance with, 13, 117–19; women with, 82–83, 115–16
sex workers, 143
Shakespeare, William, 99, 191
Shim Hun, 23
Shin Hyŏng-gi, 61
Shinto Shrine, 45
silent films, 31–32
Silla, 217n65
Sim Ch'un-sŏp, 233n35

Sin Sangok, 227n50
Sin Tong-han, 142
sirhyangmin, 237n1
sisihan yŏin (no account woman), 235n49
social engagement (*anggajyumang*), 141
socialism, aesthetic, 71–77
soil: home's link to, 34–38, 49; as timeless, 49
"Solitary Confinement" (Pak Yŏng-hŭi), 126
Son Ch'ang-sŏp, 13, 225n12, 227n55; history of, 93–94; with narrative of anticolonial resistance, 117–19. *See also* "Position of the Stairs"; *Scribblers, The*
Song Ha-ch'un, 227n55
Sŏo Kwang-je, 39. *See also Military Train*; *Wheel of Fire*
sorrow, 215n38
South Korea (*Han'guk*): censorship of North Korean culture by, 19, 24; Cold War traditionalism in, 101–4; critique of, 238n4; division of north from, 9–10; literature of, 9, 11; national literature as literature of, 94–101; as neocolony, 234n41; treaty with Japan, 175; triple disavowals with culture shifts in, 1–2
space, 243n77; capitalist urban, 48–49; *hyangto*'s link to seeing, 34–38; *Kubo* and mapping of, 44; motion's link to seeing, 34–38; *Wandering* and remapping of, 32–33, 34. *See also* liberation space
spectral form (*hwanyŏng*), 33
Springtime on the Peninsula (film), 57; censors' approval of, 219n76; motion in, 55, 56; wartime mobilization culture in, 8, 22, 50
Square, The (Ch'oe In-hun): colonial modernity with, 14–16; critique of South Korea, 238n4; and ego, 167–75; KBS-TV's adaptation of, 240n8
Stages of Economic Growth, The: A Non-Communist Manifesto (Rostow), 14, 131, 135

state: development of nation, body and, 147–53; visible and invisible, 60–90
State, the Revolution, and I, The (Park Chung Hee), 14, 136
Stewart, James, 115
Stewart, Susan, 56
storybooks (*iyagi ch'aek*), 28
Straits of Chosŏn, The (film), 58
Stranger, The (Camus), 114, 228n62
stream of consciousness, 44
streams: Yi Sang's illustrations and picturing, 46–49. *See also* mountains and streams
Stream Scenes (Pak T'ae-wŏn), 8, 21
students, 232n29, 233n35
subject: as cinematic with visuality and imperialism, 52–56; Korea as imperial, 49–52. *See also* proletarian subject
Suh, Serk-Bae, 121
superfluous man, 240n10
Suzuki, Tomi, 226n29
Syngman Rhee, 16

taejung. *See* people; popular novels
taejung fiction, 29, 33
Takata, Yasuma, 200
Tale of Ch'unhyang, 28
talking cure, 46
Tansman, Alan, 58
Taylorism, 218n67
technologized visuality, 4, 6
Tempest, The (Ch'oe In-hun), 15–16, 191, 198
Tempest, The (Shakespeare), 191
texts: emancipation in 1988, 62; illustration's link to, 32; proletarian, 24. *See also* painterly text
Thirty-eighth parallel, 92. *See also* DMZ
"Thirty-Eighth Parallel" (Yŏm Sang-sŏp), 79–80, 85
Three Generations (Yŏm Sang-sŏp), 82
time: imperial, 47; with soil and home, 49; women in anterior, 237n81

Tokyo School of Art, 36
Tong-in Literary Prize, 145
tongpo (same womb), 149–50
tongyanghwa. *See* oriental painting
traditionalism, 101–4
transformability, 231n14
translation, 239n5; Ch'oe In-hun with, 240n19; Pan-Asianism, collaboration and return to, 165–203; regime, 7, 219n82
transvisual, 34–38
travelogues, 72–73, 79, 220n13. *See also* "Dust"; "Thirty-Eighth Parallel"; *Travels in the Soviet Union*
Travels in the Soviet Union (Yi T'ae-jun), 72–73
triple alliance, 110
"Trolley Driver" (Kim Yŏng-sŏk), 218n72
Turgenev, Ivan, 99, 240n8
Twlight, 211n13
typewriters, 230n91

Uchida, Jun, 217n61
Ugly American, The (film), 14, 151; development as communication in, 131–35; Sarkhan superimposed over American suburb in, *134*
"Underground Village" (Kang, Kyŏng-ae), 217n58
United States: Cold War and aid from, 86–90; as colonial power, 221n24, 223n47; with modernism, 235n50; reaction to 9/11, 237n85
United States Military Government in Korea (USAMGIK), 62, 64, 86, 130
universalism, 224n9
universal/particular, art with, 186–90
uri mal (our language), 122
USAMGIK. *See* United States Military Government in Korea

verbal/visual relationship, 12, 17; in colonial period and influence on literature, 2–3, 24–26; in *The Heartless*, 4, 6; in KAPF works, 8, 24–26; in *Kubo*, 46–49
Victorian fiction, 5–6
"Village of Dreams" (Pak Ch'an-mo), 71
Virilio, Paul, 218n71
visual culture, 3–8
visuality: act of reading with, 32, 47, 53, 205; with Cold War on display, 114–17; colonial modern and, 19–60; with consciousness, 216n43; with film and novel, 26–34; *The Heartless* and technologized, 4, 6; imperial as close-up with, 56–60; Japan and Korea as one body with, 49–52; kinetics of imperialization with, 52–56; with *Kubo*, 41–46; with nativist art as transvisual, 34–38; painterly text with, 38–41; proletarian subject with, 22–26; with Yi Sang's illustrations, 46–49
Voice of the Governor-General (Ch'oe In-hun), 15, 165, 175–80, 190, 192
Volunteer, The (An Sŏg-yŏng), 52–54, 57, 217n59; wartime mobilization culture in, 8, 22, 50

Wandering (*Yurang*) (Yi Chong-myŏng): installment of, with illustration, *30*; as KAPF film-novel, 31–32; plot, 32–34; serialization of, *30*, 34; space remapped in, 32–33, 34
wartime mobilization culture, 1, 21; in *Military Train*, 8, 22, 50; in *Springtime on the Peninsula*, 8, 22, 50; in *The Volunteer*, 8, 22, 50
Weber, Max, 238n4
Western painting (*yanghwa*), 34, 214n34; as modern and self aware, 35
"Western Cookie Box, The" (Yŏm Sang-sŏp), 86–89
Wheel of Fire (*Hwaryun*) (films), 217n59; close ups in, 40; co-authors of, 39; installment, with still, *40*; painterly text in, 39–41

INDEX

"When the Buckwheat Blooms" (Yi Hyo-sŏk): as hypericonic, 38; literary nativism and, 8, 38–39; painterly text in, 38–39; in South Korean literary canon, 221n27
White Bull (Yi Chung-sŏp), 79
"Wide Plain" (Son Ch'ang-sŏp), 117
"Window" (Yi Sŏn-hŭi), 63, 69–70, 89
women: in anterior time within modern nation, 237n81; critique of postliberation modern, 230n93; with fragmented body, 48; new, 222n36; with otherness and mothers, 115, 236n58; rape of, 157–58; sexuality with, 82–83, 115–16; sex workers, 143
workers (*nodongja*): Liberal Party with, 226n38; with literacy, 27–28, 29
workers of the world (*manguk nodongja*), 41
world-as-picture, 4–5
world history, 29, 33
World of Thought (*Sasanggye*), 135, 233n34; year of publication in English, 13–14
writers: censorship of, 24; five periods of rightists literary organizations, 223n47; hand severed from writing, 48; with mental activity as content, 42–43; modernist, 8, 19; North Korean, 12, 19, 62, 64, 68, 223n47; reemergence of proletarian, 9; two categories of, 227n55. *See also specific writers*
writers, KAPF, reality reflected in works of, 26
writing: Mitchell, W. J. T., on, 215n37; modernism and nativism as urban forms of painting and, 8, 21; writer's hand severed from, 48

Yanagi Sōetsu, 221n24
yanghwa. See Western painting
Yi Chong-myŏng, 8, 41; with Group of Nine, 42; on readership and spectatorship with film-novels, 31 (*See also Wandering*)
Yi Chung-sŏp, 79. *See also White Bull*
Yi Ho-ch'ŏl, 78, 223n44
Yi Hwi-ynŏg, 238n3
Yi Hyo-sŏk: with Group of Nine, 42; with painterly text, 38–39. *See also Wheel of Fire*; "When the Buckwheat Blooms"
Yi In-sŏng: *A Day in Fall*, 36, 37; on Gaugin's work, 37–38
Yi Kang-ch'ŏn, 126
Yi K'wae-dae, 19
Yi Kwang-su, 3–4, 23, 24, 27; as Kim Kwan-ho's supporter, 211n13. *See also Heartless, The*
Yi Pyŏng-il, 50. *See also Springtime on the Peninsula*
Yi Sang, 8, 21, 43, 213n10; illustrations of, 46–49; *Kubo* illustrations, 47, 48
Yi Sang-bŏm: *Early Winter*, 35; with transvisual nativist art, 34–35
Yi Sŏn-hŭi, 11, 63
Yi Sŭng-hŭi, 214n13
Yi T'ae-jun, 11, 19; on antique shop's importance, 221n24; labor for art's sake and aesthetic socialism of, 71–77. *See also* "Dust"; "Liberation: Before and After"; *Travels in the Soviet Union*
Yi ŭn-sang, 142, 191
Yi Yŏng-jae, 59, 219n76; on close ups, 218n68
Yŏm Sang-sŏp, 11, 23, 79; on antique shop's importance, 221n24. *See also Dawn Wind*; *Love and Crime*
Yongary, Monster from the Deep (film), 161; Republic of Korea National Space Research Center in, 162
yŏnghwa sosŏl, with popular literature debate, 26–34
yŏnjak sosŏl (series of interconnected stories published separately), 175
Yu Chong-ho, 118

Žižek, Slavoj, 115, 137
zoologist, 150, 236n61

GPSR Authorized Representative: Easy Access System Europe, Mustamäe tee
50, 10621 Tallinn, Estonia, gpsr.requests@easproject.com

www.ingramcontent.com/pod-product-compliance
Lightning Source LLC
Chambersburg PA
CBHW020301010526
44108CB00037B/279